The Armed Forces of Asia

Series editors: **Professor Desmond Ball**, Strategic and Defence Studies Centre, Australian National University; **Air Marshal Ray Funnell** (Retired), Principal of the Australian College of Defence and Strategic Studies

The Armed Forces of Asia series presents single-country studies of the nations in the arc from Pakistan in the west to the Russian Far East in the north. Each title provides a succinct survey encompassing each service of the armed forces including territorial and paramilitary formations. It assesses the role of the armed forces with regard to national defense and security policy, and their social, political and economic functions, and analyzes their defensive and offensive capabilities and the ambitions of sectors within the armed forces establishments.

THE ARMED FORCES OF ASIA SERIES

Forthcoming titles

Australia	David Horner
Burma	Andrew Selth
China	You Ji
India	Vijai K. Nair and K.K. Hazari
Japan	Akio Watanabe and Naoko Sajima
Malaysia	Joon-Num Mak and Russ Swinnerton
North Korea	Joseph Bermudez Jr
Pakistan	Pervaiz Iqbal Cheema
Papua New Guinea	Ron May
Philippines	Carolina G. Hernandez and Gina Pattugalan
Russia in Asia	Greg Austin
Singapore	Tim Huxley
South Korea	Taeho Kim
Taiwan	Andrew N. D. Yang
Thailand	Noel Adams
Vietnam	Carlyle A. Thayer

THE ARMED FORCES OF THE USA IN THE ASIA–PACIFIC REGION

STANLEY B. WEEKS
CHARLES A. MECONIS

I.B.Tauris *Publishers*
LONDON • NEW YORK

Published in 1999 by I.B.Tauris & Co Ltd
Victoria House, Bloomsbury Square, London WC1B 4DZ
175 Fifth Avenue, New York NY 10010

In the United States and Canada distributed by St. Martin's Press
175 Fifth Avenue, New York NY 10010

Copyright © Stanley B. Weeks & Charles A. Meconis 1999

All rights reserved. Except for brief quotations in a review, this book, or part thereof, may not be reproduced, stored in or introduced into a retrieval system, or transmitted, in any form or by any means, electronic, mechanical, photocopying, recording or otherwise, without the prior written permission of the publisher.

ISBN 1 86064 498 8 hardback
ISBN 1 86064 488 0 paperback

A full CIP record for this book is available from the British Library
A full CIP record for this book is available from the Library of Congress

Library of Congress catalog card: available

Manufactured in Singapore

Foreword

The United States of America is the world's only 'superpower'. Since the collapse of the Soviet Union and the end of the Cold War, only the US has maintained a balanced strategic nuclear capability, including modern versions of intercontinental ballistic missiles (ICBMs), submarine-launched ballistic missiles (SLBMs), and long-range strategic bombers, as well as comprehensive and sophisticated global command, control, communications and intelligence (C^3I) systems.

And only the US possesses the ability to engage in major conventional conflicts anywhere around the globe. Few other countries are able to deploy and sustain substantial military forces much beyond their own region, even in coalition operations. In fact, a fundamental basis of US defense planning since 1991 has been the requirement to fight and win two simultaneous major regional conflicts (MRCs), now called major theater wars (MTWs). It is generally assumed that one of these theaters is likely to be in Asia.

However, since the end of the Cold War, one of the principal security concerns throughout much of the Asia–Pacific region, shared by policy-makers and independent analysts alike, has been about the integrity of the US presence in and commitment to the region. Some Asians believe that an American withdrawal is inevitable, or, at least, that the US will lose its ability to balance the growing capabilities of the major regional countries (i.e. Japan and China). The apprehensions about the future US commitment have contributed to the pervasive strategic uncertainty throughout the region, as well as to larger defense build-ups in some countries.

In fact, the US will remain deeply involved in the region. The financial and economic dimension of this has been expressed by the massive American aid and loans to the countries hardest hit by the economic crisis which befell the region in 1997–98. There are also critically important geostrategic bases to the US involvement. The Pacific coast (counting Alaska) is America's widest flank; and there are important American interests to protect in the region itself.

Hence, the Asia–Pacific region was hardly affected by the cuts in US defense capabilities in the early 1990s. These fell much more than proportionally on the Army and on European deployments, and less on the Navy and on the Pacific theater. The number of aircraft carriers has fallen from fourteen to twelve, but there are still six in the Pacific (although it had been expected in the early 1990s that there would be a reduction of one and possibly two in the Pacific). By the mid-1990s, the Pacific Air Forces (PACAF) were the largest of any theater. There are still nearly 100 000 US troops forward deployed in the region.

With regard to strategic nuclear forces, eight (out of eighteen) Trident ballistic missile submarines, each with 24 Trident C–4 SLBMs (each with eight warheads), are currently based at Bangor, Washington, and operate in the northern Pacific. It is planned that in 2003, seven (of a total fleet of fourteen) Trident submarines, equipped with the highly accurate D–5 SLBM, and carrying as many as 1344 warheads, will be based at Bangor.

This book provides a comprehensive and authoritative account of the US armed forces in the Pacific. The authors have brought different backgrounds to this endeavour. Dr Stanley Weeks served in the US Navy for twenty years, and had destroyer command at sea and substantial experience in the Pacific. Dr Charles Meconis has been a proponent of naval arms control and maritime confidence and security building measures (CSBMs) since the 1970s. Their book should dispel any doubts about the scale and potency of the US forces in the Pacific. It is a contribution to transparency, and alleviation of uncertainty, thus enhancing confidence and security in the region, for which they deserve many thanks.

Desmond Ball
Strategic and Defence Studies Centre
Australian National University
Canberra

Contents

Tables, figures and maps	viii
Glossary of acronyms	ix
Preface	xvii
Metric conversion table	xx
Introduction	1
1 A brief history of the US military presence	6
2 US interests and strategic policy	30
3 National command and control and US Pacific Command	65
4 US base infrastructure in the Asia–Pacific region	82
5 US nuclear forces	99
6 US Navy and US Marine Corps	122
7 US Air Force and US Space Command	157
8 US Army and US Special Operations Command	184
9 The future of US armed forces	212
10 Conclusion	235
Appendix	252
Notes	256
Bibliography	275
Index	293

Tables, figures and maps

TABLES

2.1	EASI II (1992): planned phased US East Asia troop reductions	35
2.2	Force options for major regional conflicts (MRCs)	40
2.3	US force structure 1999 in the *Bottom-Up Review*	41
5.1	US and Soviet/Russian strategic nuclear forces, July 1997	100
6.1	Changes in US naval force structure	133
7.1	Increasing precision/effectiveness of US Air Force weapons	178
8.1	Weapons density by type of US Army division	192

FIGURES AND MAPS

3.1	Office of the Secretary of Defense	68
3.2	Department of Defense	70
3.3	Unified Combatant Commands	71
3.4	Joint Chiefs of Staff	72
3.5	Command relationships in USPACOM	77
3.6	PACOM area of responsibility	78
4.1	USPACOM forces and stations	83
4.2	Deployment of US forces in Japan outside Okinawa	89
4.3	US bases on Okinawa	93
4.4	US bases in the Republic of Korea	95
6.1	Organization of the Department of the Navy	123
6.2	Organization of the Operating Forces of the US Navy	125
6.3	Organization of the US Pacific Fleet	136

Glossary of acronyms

AAAV	Advanced Amphibious Assault Vehicle
AB	Air Base
ABIS	Advanced Battlespace Information System
ABL	Airborne Laser
ABM	Anti-Ballistic Missile
ABS	Automated Battlefield System
AC	Active Component
ACTD	Advanced Concept Technology Demonstration
AEF	Air Expeditionary Forces
AFB	Air Force Base
AFR	Air Force Reserve
AFSCN	Air Force Satellite Control Network
AIM	Air Intercept Missile
AIS	Automated Information System
AIT	Automatic Identification Technology
ALCM	Air-Launched Cruise Missile
AMRAAM	Advanced Medium-Range Air-to-Air Missile
ANG	Air National Guard
APC	Armored Personnel Carrier
AOR	Area of Responsibility
APAM	Antipersonnel/Antimateriel
ARF	ASEAN Regional Forum
ARG	Amphibious Ready Group
ARL	Airborne Reconnaissance Low
ARNG	Army National Guard
ASCM	Antiship Cruise Missile
ASEAN	Association of Southeast Asian Nations
ASW	Antisubmarine Warfare
ATACMS	Army Tactical Missile System
ATCC	Antiterrorism Coordinating Committee

AWACS	Airborne Warning and Control System
BAT	Brilliant Anti-armor Submunition
BM/C3	Battle Management/Command, Control and Communications
BMD	Ballistic Missile Defense
BMDO	Ballistic Missile Defense Organization
BPI	Boost Phase Intercept
BRAC	Base Realignment and Closure
BUR	Bottom-Up Review
BURU	Bottom-Up Review Update
BW	Biological Weapon
BWC	Biological Weapons Convention
C^2	Command and Control
C^2W	Command and Control Warfare
C^3	Command, Control and Communications
C^3I	Command, Control, Communications and Intelligence
C^4I	Command, Control, Communications, Computers and Intelligence
C^4ISR	Command, Control, Communications, Computers, Intelligence, Surveillance and Reconnaissance
CA	Civil Affairs
CALCM	Conventional Air-Launched Cruise Missile
CAW	Carrier Air Wing
CB	Chemical and Biological
CBIRF	Chemical/Biological Incident Response Force
CBT	Combating Terrorism
CD	Counterdrug
CDL	Common Data Link
CEC	Cooperative Engagement Capability
CG	Guided Missile Cruiser, conventional propulsion
CGN	Guided Missile Cruiser, nuclear propulsion
CIA	Central Intelligence Agency
CINC	Commander in Chief
CINCPAC	Commander in Chief, US Pacific Command
CIWS	Close-In Weapon System
CJCS	Chairman of the Joint Chiefs of Staff
CLF	Combat Logistics Force
CMA	C^4ISR Mission Assessment
CMD	Cruise Missile Defense
CMTC	Combat Maneuver Training Center
COE	Common Operating Environment

CONUS	Continental United States
CORM	Commission on Roles and Missions of the Armed Forces
COTS	Commercial Off-the-Shelf
CP	Counter-proliferation
CRAF	Civil Reserve Air Fleet
CS	Combat Support
CSAR	Combat Search and Rescue
CSBM	Confidence and Security Building Measure
CTBT	Comprehensive Test Ban Treaty
CTR	Cooperative Threat Reduction
CV	Large-deck aircraft carrier, conventional propulsion
CVBG	Carrier Battle Group
CVN	Large-deck aircraft carrier, nuclear propulsion
CW	Chemical Weapon
CWC	Chemical Weapons Convention
DA	Direct Action
DARO	Defense Airborne Reconnaissance Office
DARPA	Defense Advanced Research Projects Agency
DCI	Director of Central Intelligence
DIA	Defense Intelligence Agency
DII	Defense Information Infrastructure
DIVARTY	Division Artillery
DLA	Defense Logistics Agency
DMA	Defense Mapping Agency
DOD	Department of Defense
DPRK	Democratic People's Republic of Korea (North Korea)
DSCS	Defense Satellite Communications System
DSMOA	Department of Defense/State Memorandum of Agreement
DSWA	Defense Special Weapons Agency
EAM	Emergency Action Message
EELV	Evolved Expendable Launch Vehicle
EFOG-M	Enhanced Fiber Optic Guided Missile
EHF	Extremely High Frequency
EIPC	Enhanced International Peacekeeping Capabilities
ELINT	Electronic Intelligence
ELV	Expendable Launch Vehicle
ESSM	Evolved Sea Sparrow Missile
EUSC	Effective US Control

FMFPAC	Fleet Marine Force Pacific
FMS	Foreign Military Sales
FMTV	Family of Medium Tactical Vehicles
FPDA	Five Powers Defence Agreement
FWE	Fighter Wing Equivalent
GAM	GPS-Aided Munition
GAO	General Accounting Office
GBI	Ground-Based Interceptor
GCC	Gulf Cooperation Council
GCCS	Global Command and Control System
GCSS	Global Combat Support System
GDP	Gross Domestic Product
GEO	Geosynchronous Orbit
GPS	Global Positioning System
HAE	High Altitude Endurance
HDBTDC	Hard and Deeply Buried Target Defeat Capability
HEO	Highly Elliptical Orbit
HQDA	Headquarters, Department of the Army
HUMINT	Human Intelligence
ICBM	Intercontinental Ballistic Missile
IMET	International Military Education and Training
INF	Intermediate Range Nuclear Forces
INS	Inertial Navigation System
IOC	Initial Operational Capability
IRR	Individual Ready Reserve
IRST	Infrared Search and Track
ISR	Intelligence, Surveillance and Reconnaissance
IW	Information Warfare
IWS	Information Warfare Squadron
JAGDF	Japanese Ground Self-Defense Force
JASDF	Japanese Air Self-Defense Force
JASSM	Joint Air-to-Surface Standoff Missile
JAST	Joint Advanced Strike Technology
JCS	Joint Chiefs of Staff
JDAM	Joint Direct Attack Munition
JMSDF	Japanese Maritime Self-Defense Force
JROC	Joint Requirements Oversight Council
JRTC	Joint Readiness Training Center
JSF	Joint Strike Fighter
JSIMS	Joint Simulation System
JSOTF	Joint Special Operations Task Force
JSOW	Joint Standoff Weapon

JSTARS	Joint Surveillance Target Attack Radar System
JTF	Joint Task Force
JTIDS	Joint Tactical Information Distribution System
JWARS	Joint Warfare System
JWCA	Joint Warfighting Capabilities Assessment
JWCO	Joint Warfighting Capability Objective
LAMPS	Light Airborne Multipurpose System
LEO	Low Earth Orbit
LHA/D	Amphibious Assault Ships
LMSR	Large Medium-Speed Roll-On/Roll-Off
LOS	Law of the Sea
LPD	Landing Platform Dock Amphibious Ship
LPH	Landing Platform Helicopter Amphibious Ship
MACOM	Major Command
MAE	Medium-Altitude Endurance
MAGTF	Marine Air-Ground Task Force
MAP	Military Assistance Program
MARDIV	Marine Division
MARFORPAC	Marine Forces Pacific
MARFORRES	Marine Forces Reserve
MBT	Main Battle Tank
MCAS	Marine Corps Air Station
MCS	Mine Countermeasures Ship
MCTFS	Marine Corps Total Force System
MEADS	Medium Extended Air Defense System
MEB	Marine Expeditionary Brigade
MEF	Marine Expeditionary Force
MEU	Marine Expeditionary Unit
MEU/SOC	Marine Expeditionary Unit (Special Operations Capable)
MILES	Multiple Integrated Laser Engagement System
MILSATCOM	Military Satellite Communications
MIRV	Multiple, Independently-Targeted Reentry Vehicle
MOB	Mobile Offshore Bases
MLRS	Multiple-Launch Rocket System
MOOTW	Military Operations Other Than War
MOUT	Military Operations in Urban Terrain
MPA	Maritime Patrol Aircraft
MPF	Maritime Prepositioning Force
MSC	Military Sealift Command
MSI	Multispectral Imagery
MTC	Military Transport Command
MTCR	Missile Technology and Control Regime

MTI	Moving-Target Indicator
NAS	Naval Air Station
NATO	North Atlantic Treaty Organization
NBC	Nuclear, Biological and Chemical
NCA	National Command Authorities
NDP	National Defense Panel
NEO	Noncombatant Evacuation Operations
NIMA	National Imagery and Mapping Agency
nm	Nautical Mile
NMD	National Missile Defense
NMS	National Military Strategy of the United States
NORAD	North American Aerospace Defense Command
NPT	Nuclear Non-Proliferation Treaty
NRO	National Reconnaissance Office
NSA/CSS	National Security Agency/Central Security Service
NSNF	Non-Strategic Nuclear Forces
NSW	Naval Special Warfare
NSB	Naval Submarine Base
NTC	National Training Center
NUDET	Nuclear Detonation
O&M	Operation and Maintenance
OMFTS	Operational Maneuver from the Sea
PAC	Patriot Advanced Capability
PACAF	Pacific Air Forces, US
PACFLT	Pacific Fleet, US
PAL	Permissive Action Link
PFP	Partnership for Peace
PLA	People's Liberation Army
PLA-N	People's Liberation Army-Navy
PMAI	Primary Mission Aircraft Inventory
PRC	People's Republic of China
PSYOP	Psychological Operations
PTR	Proliferation: Threat and Response
QDR	Quadrennial Defense Review
R&D	Research and Development
RAM	Rolling Airframe Missile
RIMPAC	Bi-annual Rim of the Pacific naval exercise
RLV	Reusable Launch Vehicle
RMA	Revolution in Military Affairs
ROK	Republic of Korea (South Korea)
RO/RO	Roll-On/Roll-Off Ship
ROV	Remotely Operated Vehicle

RRF	Ready Reserve Force
SADARM	Sense and Destroy Armor
SATCOM	Satellite Communication
SBIRS	Space-Based Infrared System
SBL	Space-Based Laser
SDV	SEAL Delivery Vehicle
SEAL	Sea, Air, Land
SF	Special Forces
SFW	Sensor Fused Weapon
SIGINT	Signals Intelligence
SITES	Standard Installation Topic Exchange Service
SLAM	Standoff Land Attack Missile
SLAM-ER	Standoff Land Attack Missile Expanded Response
SLBM	Submarine-Launched Ballistic Missile
SLCM	Sea-Launched Cruise Missile
SLEP	Service Life Extension
SOA	Special Operations Aviation
SOC	Special Operations Command
SOF	Special Operations Force
SPACECOM	Space Command, US
SSBN	Ballistic Missile Submarine
SSC	Smaller-scale Contingency Operations
SSN	Attack Submarine
START	Strategic Arms Reduction Treaty
STRATCOM	Strategic Command, US
TAI	Total Aircraft Inventory
TAMD	Theater Air and Missile Defense
TBM	Theater Ballistic Missile
TBMD	Theater Ballistic Missile Defense
THAAD	Theater High Altitude Area Defense
TLAM	Tomahawk Land Attack Missile
TMD	Theater Missile Defense
TUAV	Tactical UAV
UAV	Unmanned Aerial Vehicle
UHF	Ultra High Frequency
USACOM	United States Atlantic Command
USAF	United States Air Force
USAR	United States Army Reserve
USARJ	United States Army Japan
USARPAC	United States Army Pacific
USASOC	United States Army Special Operations Command
USEUCOM	United States European Command

USFJ	United States Forces Japan
USFK	United States Forces Korea
USN	United States Navy
USPACOM	United States Pacific Command
USSOCOM	United States Special Operations Command
UUV	Unmanned Undersea Vehicle
UW	Unconventional Warfare
V/STOL	Vertical/Short Takeoff and Landing
WAM	Wide Area Munition
WCMD	Wind-Corrected Munitions Dispenser
WESTPAC	Western Pacific
WMD	Weapons of Mass Destruction
WPNS	Western Pacific Naval Symposium

Preface

This book describes the structure and roles of the Armed Forces of the United States in the Asia–Pacific region, within the overall context of official US national security interests, strategy and policy as they relate to the region. By law and custom, the all-volunteer Armed Forces of the United States play no role in internal security or politics, and only an indirect one in economics, so our discussion of those areas is very limited. Although we offer our own estimates of the capabilities and limitations of US forces and include outside criticism of those forces where appropriate, we have tried to provide primarily a factual source of information, with only the minimum of critical analysis.

Following a brief history of the US military presence in the Asia–Pacific region, we offer an overview of US national interests, strategy and policy as they relate to the region. We then outline the national command and control chain leading to the US armed forces in the region, and the base infrastructure that supports those forces. After a brief survey of US nuclear forces in the regional context, we devote a chapter each to consideration of naval forces (US Navy and Marine Corps), air and space forces (US Air Force and Space Command) and ground forces (US Army and Special Operations Command) for the region. Because many US forces have global mobility, we include relevant information about US forces outside the region. We then offer our view of the future of the US armed forces in the Asia–Pacific region. We conclude with a chapter which briefly summarizes our findings and can thus be read as a kind of 'executive summary'.

We are indebted to the Armed Forces of Asia series editors, Professor Desmond Ball and Air Marshal Ray Funnell (Ret'd), for their trust in selecting us to write this book and their positive assistance and encouragement throughout. We are also appreciative of the staff of Allen & Unwin, especially Ann Crabb, who have supported us at every step and whose efforts were essential to preparing the manuscript for publication. Professor Michael Wallace reviewed Chapter 5 for us. Barbara Sherman provided invaluable assistance with the index.

With regard to sources, we have made every effort to base our work on official, non-classified US sources. By law, and within its tradition of free speech, the United States makes public a great deal of official information on its armed forces. However, this is in no sense an official publication, and as authors we bear sole responsibility for the views and information provided in this book.

We are grateful to the Public Information offices of the White House, the Secretary of Defense, the Joint Chiefs of Staff, the US Pacific Command, the Office of Naval Intelligence and especially Marine Forces Pacific for providing us with printed documentation. The Institute of National Strategic Studies at the National Defense University and the Bethesda office of the National Imagery and Mapping Agency were also important sources of printed information.

In addition, we have made extensive use of the enormous amount of official information on the US armed forces now available 'online' by computer via the Internet's World Wide Web (WWW). We could not begin to list all the official, non-classified 'websites' we have utilized, much less their individual URL addresses, which seem to change every few months anyway. Readers should know that the best way to *begin* exploring official US armed forces Internet websites is by accessing the Pentagon's 'homepage' at the following address (as of March 1998), spelled exactly as indicated here (i.e. defenSe with an 's', not defenCe with a 'c'):

http://www.defenselink.mil/

While most of the information available on these websites is identical in substance to traditional printed documents, page numbering and illustrations sometimes differ. Therefore, those sources are listed in the Bibliography as being an 'online version'.

With regard to language, the US military makes such an extensive use of acronyms (e.g. DOD for Department of Defense) that some critics argue that there is a dialect called 'Pentagonese'. Although we have made an effort to reduce this phenomenon, it is not possible to eliminate the practice. We have listed important acronyms within the text enclosed in parentheses the first time they appear and have provided readers with a select 'Glossary of acronyms' to help in this regard.

We both owe our wives and children a deep debt of gratitude for their patience with us throughout a two-year project that proved more difficult and took more time than we anticipated.

Finally, it is our hope that this book will contribute to a better understanding of the nature and importance of the Armed Forces of the United States in the Asia–Pacific region, and do justice to the dedication of those American men and women who have served there honorably in the past and continue to do so today.

Moclips, Washington, on the Pacific coast
March 1998

Metric conversion table

Quantity	Imperial Unit	Metric Unit	Imperial to Metric Units	Metric to Imperial Units
Length	inch (in)	millimetre (mm) or centimetre (cm)	1 in = 25.4 mm	1 cm = 0.394 in
	foot (ft)	centimetre (cm) or metre (m)	1 ft = 30.5 cm	1 m = 3.28 ft
	yard (yd)	metre (m)	1 yd = 0.914 m	1 m = 1.09 yd
	mile	kilometre (km)	1 mile = 1.61 km	1 km = 0.621 mile
Mass	ounce (oz)	gram (g)	1 oz = 28.3 g	1 g = 0.0353 oz
	pound (lb)	gram (g) or kilogram (kg)	1 lb = 454 g	1 kg = 2.20 lb
	ton	tonne (t)	1 ton = 1.02 tonne	1 tonne = 0.984 ton
Area	square yard (yd^2)	square metre (m^2)	1 yd^2 = 0.836 m^2	1 m^2 = 1.20 yd^2
	acre (ac)	hectare (ha)	1 ac = 0.405 ha	1 ha = 2.47 ac
	square mile (sq. mile)	square kilometre (km^2)	1 sq. mile = 2.59 km^2	1 km^2 = 0.386 sq. mile

Introduction

Some may question the inclusion of the US armed forces in a series devoted to 'the armed forces of Asia'. After all, technically, little US territory is located in Asia proper. However, both history and current reality warrant the inclusion of US forces in this series.

As the first chapter of this book briefly recalls, substantial US military forces have been present in the Asia–Pacific region for a hundred years, through four wars and countless smaller contingencies. Today, about 100 000 American soldiers, sailors, Marines and air personnel are 'forward deployed' in the Western Pacific, including over 36 000 on the Asian mainland in Korea—at the request and, with the obvious exception of forces on the high seas, with the permission of Asian host nations. Moreover, as the world's sole remaining 'superpower', only the US currently possesses a military force with a truly 'global' reach, which means that even US units based thousands of miles away from the Asia–Pacific region can be deployed there in a matter of hours in some cases, and weeks at most. Whether these facts are viewed with approval or concern, they remain facts.

This book aims to show how the Armed Forces of the United States, which are collectively organized in the Department of Defense (DOD), play—and will continue to play—a major role in the security framework of the Asia–Pacific region. It examines how these all-volunteer forces are structured, organized, equipped, based and staffed and the challenges they face in an era of economic constraints, rapid technological change and uncertain threats. In all cases, only publicly available, non-classified sources have been utilized in the preparation of this book. However, given the very high degree of 'transparency' the US government maintains about its military forces, and the freedom of the press guaranteed by US law, too *much* information has proven to be a greater challenge than too little. Readers should be aware that, although this is by no means an 'official' publication, every effort has been made to utilize authoritative, official sources. Going beyond official sources, an effort has been made to give an honest appraisal of the capabilities and *limitations* of US military forces, realizing that the conclusions reached may be disputed by some.

The book's second chapter locates US military forces in the broader context of US 'national security', including economic and political interests and strategic policy, with an emphasis on the Asia–Pacific region. There have been many excellent recent publications on this topic[1] and this work is meant to complement them by providing non-specialists with a thorough survey of American armed forces and military strategy as they apply to the Asia–Pacific region.

At this juncture the US Department of Defense continues to make the enormous adjustment called for by the end of the Cold War. This adjustment has included a major 'drawdown' in forces that is still continuing, and a fundamental re-examination of US defense strategy and force structure. This was most recently embodied in the 1997 *Quadrennial Defense Review*, but was also laid out in such seminal documents as the Joint Chiefs of Staff 1996 publication *Joint Vision 2010*, which emphasized the importance of all US military services operating together—that is, 'jointly'. While the findings of these studies are included throughout this book, their main tenets are summarized in Chapter 3. Of course, particular attention is paid to the strategy and organization of the US Pacific Command (USPACOM), headquartered in Hawaii.

The United States was founded by people who had suffered from authoritarian rule often imposed by military forces. Consequently, as the third chapter makes clear, under the US Constitution the armed forces must play no role in domestic politics, and only a very limited role in domestic security. Thus, national command and control is firmly in the hands of civilian leadership. This is a matter of utmost importance with regard to nuclear forces, but it extends throughout the Department of Defense.

This is not to say that the military has no impact on US domestic politics or economics. Since the US Congress makes the final decisions on government spending, the Department of Defense must justify its funding requests to the Congress. The debate over the defense budget is an annual exercise in American politics. In light of the fact that as of 1994 the US share of *world* military spending was 34 per cent, this is a serious matter.[2]

It is also interesting to note that many—but not all—recent US Presidents have served in the military. For example, Presidents Kennedy, Johnson, Nixon, Carter and Bush were officers in the US Navy, with all but Carter serving in the Pacific theater in World War II. Since the President is also the Commander-in-Chief of the US armed forces, a military background, or the lack of one, sometimes plays a role in domestic presidential politics. But these are matters beyond the scope of this work.

The central point is that the Armed Forces of the United States are subservient to civilian command and control. They offer advice, but follow orders.

Chapter 4 directly addresses an issue of great interest throughout the region, namely the military base infrastructure of US forces in the Asia-Pacific region. Of course, the US maintains or has access to military bases across the globe, although their number has diminished sharply over the last twenty years. The great mobility of US forces, especially air and sea forces, means that virtually *any* US military base could play a role in deploying forces to the Asia-Pacific region. For reasons of space, the description here is limited to those bases located within the area of responsibility of the US Pacific Command, plus those bases located on the Pacific coast of the continental United States which are most likely to play a significant role in augmenting or supporting US forces deployed in the region. Although the future of these facilities is touched on in this chapter, it is discussed more fully in Chapter 9 on the overall future of US Asia-Pacific forces.

With the end of the Cold War, the likelihood of global nuclear war has greatly declined. In a recent statement, the senior director for US defense policy at the National Security Council declared that 'nuclear weapons now play a smaller role in our nuclear security strategy than at any point during the nuclear era'.[3] Nevertheless, as of July 1997 the US continued to deploy nearly 8000 nuclear warheads, all of them capable of reaching or being delivered to the Asia-Pacific region.[4] For that reason Chapter 5 presents a thorough review of US nuclear strategy, targeting, forces and command and control, as well as an update on the status of major arms control efforts. The new command formed in 1992 to oversee all US nuclear forces, the US Strategic Command (USSTRATCOM), is described in detail. Particular emphasis is given to the deterrence role of nuclear weapons vis-á-vis the

Asia–Pacific's two other nuclear powers, Russia and China. The troubling issue of the proliferation of nuclear weapons—and the possible role of the US military in preventing and/or countering it—is dealt with in Chapter 9.

Chapter 6 covers the strategic vision, organization, force structure, capabilities and limitations of the US Navy and its partner sea service, the US Marine Corps, with an emphasis on those forces forward deployed in the Western Pacific. Although Navy-Marine Corps strategic and operational concepts are fully described in this review, a great deal of emphasis is placed on describing weapons technology. This is so for two reasons: (1) the current US lead in weapons technology has had an effect on every aspect of US military forces, especially following the 1991 Gulf War; and (2) among the traditional services, the US Navy, because of its operating environment, has always had a particular interest in technology. This information may not seem important to those readers already familiar with the capabilities of modern US weaponry, but it is justified by the importance of the potential development which some have called a 'Revolution in Military Affairs' (RMA).

The same approach is taken with Chapter 7's coverage of the US Air Force, for even more obvious reasons. The US Air Force's 'Global Reach' is both a fact and a strategic concept. Within that context, the US Air Force, while declining dramatically in size, continues to devote great resources to fielding cutting-edge technologies such as 'stealth' aircraft and 'smart' munitions. Beyond those developments, the Air Force has declared space to be the new 'high ground' and therefore a considerable portion of the chapter is devoted to the organization and forces of the US Space Command (USSPACECOM). The increasing reliance of all US military forces on satellite technology is reviewed in this chapter.

Although in popular perception the US Army is often seen to have a secondary role in the Asia–Pacific region, as of 1998 over 20 000 US Army soldiers were on the ground on the Asian mainland in South Korea, helping to maintain the uneasy peace there. Chapter 8 places heavy emphasis on those forces, while reviewing the changes occurring in US Army force structure, strategic vision and weapons technology. Although the likelihood of US Army forces becoming involved in another lengthy major Asian land conflict outside Korea is low, the US Army is continuing to improve the technology and mobility of its 'Light' infantry divisions for possible use in lesser contingencies in the region, if called upon.

Indeed, the increase in the number of 'Military Operations Other Than War' (MOOTW) has increased the importance of US Special Operations Forces (SOF) from all military services. Consequently, Chapter 8 includes a description of the organization, force structure and operations of the US Special Operations Command (USSOCOM), within the limits of publicly available information.

In Chapter 9 an effort is made to assay the future of US armed forces in the region. No claim to special insight or sources is made therein. Still, some basic trends can be discerned and, within limits, extrapolated. Substantial US forces will remain in the region for the foreseeable future, but their size, capabilities and base infrastructure are likely to change in ways discussed. The controversial issue of the future of US bases on Okinawa is examined, as is the possible future of US forces in South Korea. The ongoing debate—and results to date—about the deeper impact of the 'Revolution in Military Affairs' is described. Particular emphasis is paid to the issue of how the United States intends to address so-called 'asymmetric threats', that is, means by which a future adversary may seek to avoid, undermine or circumvent the current US lead in 'conventional' military capability. US efforts toward developing a Theater Ballistic Missile Defence (TBMD), for example, are reviewed in this chapter. So is the topic of possible US responses to the disturbing spread of terrorism and weapons of mass destruction (WMD).

The final chapter offers a summary of the conclusions reached throughout the book, set in the wider context of Asia–Pacific regional security.

1
A brief history of the US military presence

At the end of the 20th century the armed forces of the United States will have completed more than a hundred years of significant presence in the Asia–Pacific region. The approximately 100 000 American military personnel 'forward deployed' in the Western Pacific are not a large force in terms of numbers. Nevertheless, the superiority of their weaponry and their training, together with the rapidly deployable additional forces located in the continental United States, make them the most powerful military force in the region. This has been the case for over 50 years.

How powerful are these forces today, and how long will this state of affairs last? Before attempting to answer these critical questions, it is important to briefly review the long and often costly history of the presence of US military forces in the region. Emphasis will be placed on those historical factors which continue to have a significant impact on today's developments.

FROM FIRST CONTACT TO THE 1853–54 MISSION OF COMMODORE PERRY

From the moment of its birth as an independent nation, the United States was heavily engaged in overseas trade. In the 1790s the US merchant marine was the second largest in the world. Even though the young nation's boundaries did not yet extend to the Pacific, in that decade as many as 30 US merchant vessels per year visited Chinese ports.[1]

In 1800 the US Navy warship *Essex* conducted a cruise to the Western Pacific. In 1821 the US Navy established a 'station' for a squadron of ships in the Eastern Pacific. In 1835 the establishment of the US Navy's 'East India Station' in the Western Pacific initiated a more or less continuous US 'forward presence' in the Asia–Pacific region in the form of a small squadron of sailing ships.[2] By 1855 the Secretary of the Navy defined the squadron's mission in these terms:

> The primary objects of the Government . . . in maintaining a Naval Force in the East India and China Seas are the protection of our valuable trade with China and the isles of India, and our whale fisheries . . . to protect the persons or property of American citizens by persuasive yet firm measures . . . to enlarge the opportunities of commercial intercourse and to increase the efficiency of our Navy by affording active service to the Officers and crews of vessels ordered to that station.[3]

The annexation of California and Oregon in 1848 following the war with Mexico finally extended the geographic boundaries of the United States to the Pacific, and San Francisco became an important port for trade with the Orient. Next, the mission of US Navy Commodore Matthew Perry to Japan in 1853–54 had lasting significance.

When Perry's five steamships—the first ever seen in the region—entered a hostile Tokyo Bay unannounced on 8 July 1853, the subsequent events marked a turning point in a critical bilateral relationship that endures to this day.

Perry was the first US government representative who thought of what was then called 'the Far East' in terms of its strategic significance to his country. By a combination of implied force and skilful diplomacy, he succeeded in 'opening' a resistant Japan to western trade and diplomatic contact. His goal was to ensure US dominance of the San Francisco–Tokyo–Shanghai trade routes. In addition to negotiating a treaty of peace, friendship and trade with Japan on 31 March 1854, Perry also established a coaling and recreation base on Okinawa for $10 a month, and another base at Keelung on Formosa, which he claimed as an American protectorate.[4] In less than a year Perry had established effective US strategic dominance in the Western Pacific.

FROM THE CIVIL WAR TO THE WAR WITH SPAIN, 1861–1898

America's interest in the Asia–Pacific region, and its ability to play a major role there, declined dramatically due to the terrible civil war that ravaged the nation from 1861 to 1865. In particular the torn-apart US merchant marine fell victim to the war at sea, and in some measure never recovered. With fewer US flagships to protect, through much of this period the American high-seas fleet declined in numbers and even in technology as sailing ships proved less costly to operate and did not require coaling stations.[5]

On the other hand, US Pacific territory expanded substantially in 1867 with the purchase of Alaska and the Aleutian Islands, and the annexation of the island of Midway, resulting in the establishment, for a time, of a North Pacific naval squadron. In 1876 Japan forced Korea to open some ports to trade, and western powers also soon entered that country. In 1882 US Navy Commodore Robert W. Shufeldt established trade relations with Korea in a manner similar to Perry.[6] But the early era of US dominance in the Western Pacific was over, as Japan, Russia and the major European imperial powers expanded their influence in the region.

It can be said that the impetus of commercial rivalry with these powers led to the rebirth, particularly in the US Navy, of serious American strategic thought about the Asia–Pacific region's importance. The most influential outcome was the publication in 1890 of Admiral Alfred Thayer Mahan's classic work *The Influence of Seapower upon History 1660–1783*. Mahan argued that a strong navy, naval bases in Latin America and Asia, and a revitalized US merchant marine were essential if the United States was to become a major world power. His views were appreciated by future US President Theodore Roosevelt. But they were not widely shared at first by either the US government or the American people.[7]

THE WARS WITH SPAIN AND IN THE PHILIPPINES, 1898–1902

In early 1898 only a small squadron of second-rate US naval vessels patrolled the Western Pacific, and there were no American ground troops there. This minimal military presence matched the lack of commitment to the region at that time. Less than 10 per cent of the United States' trade crossed the Pacific, and that consisted almost entirely of imports from China, Japan and Korea. Although some in the US Navy worried about the growing strength of Japan's navy, and the *New York Times* occasionally published an editorial expressing worries about European powers carving up China into exclusive spheres of influence, neither the American people nor their leaders were very interested.[8]

When Americans paid any attention at all to foreign policy matters, it was the nearby Caribbean, not the Western Pacific, that received the bulk of that attention. An insurrection in the Spanish colony of Cuba came to be seen as a concern to American security interests. The US battleship *Maine* was dispatched to protect American citizens there and mysteriously blew up and sank in February 1898. The United States concluded that Spain was responsible and declared war on that country in April 1898.

Ironically, the first battle of that war took place in the Pacific. The Philippines were also a Spanish colony and a Spanish fleet consisting of ten ships was deployed near Manila. For the sole purpose of preventing the transfer of this enemy force from the Pacific to the Caribbean, the United States dispatched its Asiatic Squadron of six ships under Admiral George Dewey to attack the Spanish. On 1 May 1898 Dewey destroyed the entire Spanish fleet in Manila Bay without the loss of a single American life, and then blockaded Manila and waited for American troops to arrive.

On 13 August 1898 the first US ground troops to set foot for an extended period in the Western Pacific occupied Manila—much to the dismay of the Filipino independence movement which had been active since 1896 and had seized control of much of the archipelago. In the treaty of Paris signed on 10 December 1898, Spain granted Cuba independence, and ceded Puerto Rico, Guam and the Philippines to the United States. The year 1898 also saw the annexation of Hawaii and Wake Island by the United States.[9]

It might be said that the commitment of US armed forces to the Philippines in 1898 set a pattern that was to be repeated several times in the Asia–Pacific region in the following century. What was originally thought to be an involvement that would not prove lengthy, costly or unpopular turned out to be exactly the opposite.

A bloody armed clash between Emilio Aguinaldo's Filipino independence fighters and US troops took place on 4 February 1899. This inflamed anti-imperialist sentiment in the United States to such an extent that the Senate ratified the Paris peace treaty on 6 February 1899 by only one vote. The proposed 5000-man US force in the Philippines soon grew, until by the end of 1899 it numbered over 50 000 troops in the field.

By November 1899 US forces under General E. S. Otis had defeated Aguinaldo's army in conventional battles across the central Luzon plain, and it seemed that total victory was at hand.

Instead the Filipinos retreated to the jungle and initiated highly effective guerrilla warfare. Hoping to influence the American presidential election in 1900, the guerrillas resisted fiercely and caused heavy US casualties. However, the defeat of the anti-war candidate William Jennings Bryan and the re-election of President McKinley led to a renewed—and sometimes brutal—US military effort that also included good works as part of an increasingly effective policy of 'pacification' of the countryside.

Demoralized by McKinley's re-election, without any source of outside help, and crippled by internal divisions, the Filipino independence fighters could not win. Many came over to the American side. Finally, in July of 1902 the US Secretary of War declared an official end to the conflict, although some guerrilla activity continued for several more months.[10] In the end the victory was decisive, but it had taken four years, involved four times more US troops than served in the war with Spain—and resulted in more battle deaths.

In a similar fashion, the dispatch of a small China Relief Expedition of US sailors, soldiers and Marines in 1900 to defend the American legation in Beijing during the so-called Boxer rebellion eventually led to the deployment of 6300 men there. A year later there were still 200 US troops there and as late as 1902 the US Asiatic Squadron was the largest in the US Navy.[11]

THE DECLINE OF US COMMITMENT, 1907–1938

The commitment of significant US forces in the Philippines and China from 1898 to 1902 did have lasting consequences, but it did not lead immediately to a major commitment to the region. Among the major consequences were the continuing, albeit small, US military presence in the Philippines and China, the annexation of a portion of Panama in 1903 and the subsequent construction of the Panama Canal in 1914. In 1907 the US Navy established a Pacific Fleet, although all US battleships were stationed in the Atlantic, and in 1910 the Asiatic Squadron was upgraded to become the Asiatic Fleet.[12]

Worried by the Anglo-Japanese alliance of 1905, President Roosevelt sent all sixteen US battleships in 'The Great White Fleet' around the world in 1907–08 primarily to impress Japan. He then negotiated agreements with Japan that in effect recognized that country's dominance over Korea, Manchuria and Formosa in exchange for a non-aggression pledge by Japan regarding the Philippines and Hawaii.[13]

However, four factors soon contributed to the lack of a major US military commitment to the Asia–Pacific region as the twentieth century began to unfold. First, although US economic interests in the region continued to grow, Europe remained preeminent as an American trade partner, accounting for about six out of every ten US dollars earned in foreign commerce.

Second, there was no real, or at least widely perceived, threat to an American presence in East Asia—nor, for that matter, was there any single US military body responsible for threat assessment. A host of newly created bodies including the Navy's General Board, the Army's General Staff and even the Joint Board of the Army and Navy failed to produce either a coherent strategic vision or effective 'joint' war plans.

Third, no bureaucratic commitments to East Asia emerged either in the State Department or the military, even the Navy. For example, in 1907 the Navy acquiesced to the Army's demand that the main Pacific base should be located at Pearl Harbor, not Subic Bay in the Philippines.

The fourth and final factor preventing a major commitment to the Asia–Pacific region was the rapid decline of interest among the American public once most US troops had left the Philippines and the rebellion had quietened down.[14]

So enduring were these four factors that they shaped the declining American presence for 30 years. The Great War drew US attention almost entirely to Europe, although in 1914 the Joint Army-Navy Board did produce the first draft of 'Plan ORANGE' for a possible war with Japan. This plan called for US forces in the Philippines to hold out for over 60 days until the US Navy could send the fleet from the Atlantic, defeat the Japanese Navy in a sea battle and rescue the Philippines.[15]

In 1914 Japan, as an ally of England, had declared war on Germany. Consequently, Japan captured and then in 1919 received control of German possessions in the Asia–Pacific region, including the Shandong Peninsula and Tsingtao in China and the Caroline, Marshall and Mariana island groups (except Guam). Japan soon began fortifying these new holdings.

In the 1921 Washington Arms Limitation conference, the United States, Great Britain and Japan concluded an agreement which had lasting impact on Pacific strategy. That agreement included a ratio of 5:5:3 for the major warships of those three countries, major reductions in naval tonnage, and a ban on further development of bases and fortifications in the Pacific, including the Philippines. The results of that agreement remain a matter of controversy among proponents and opponents of the role of arms control in national security.[16] Its immediate impact was to hasten the decline of an American presence in the Pacific.

Since the US intervention during the Boxer rebellion, that presence had included a company and eventually a battalion of US Marines at the legation in Peking. A regiment of US Army troops was stationed in Tientsin, China, beginning in 1912. Beginning in 1927 two regiments of US Marines were sent to Shanghai and Tientsin 'to protect American citizens and their property' in the war-torn nation. The terms 'China Marine' and 'China duty' had a special meaning in the US military of that era.[17]

However, in 1931 President Herbert Hoover declined to become directly involved over Japan's invasion of Manchuria. In 1934 President Franklin D. Roosevelt granted commonwealth status to the Philippines and promised independence. Even the outbreak of war between Japan and China in 1937 led—at first—to a further decline in the American presence. In early 1938 the US Army left Tientsin and all but one regiment of US Marines in Shanghai were withdrawn from mainland China. The Fourth Marine Regiment finally left Shanghai for the Philippines in November 1941, only to be surrendered on Corregidor in May 1942. The Asiatic Fleet was reduced to a bare minimum. But by late 1938 the tide had begun to turn.

THE PACIFIC WAR, 1938–1945

American commitment to the region began to grow again in 1938 as China became a symbol of American-sponsored resistance to Japanese aggression, as advocated by several prominent non-governmental pro-China groups in the United States. At their urging, the US provided over $251 million to Chiang Kai-shek's government.[18]

In May 1940 Germany's stunning defeat of France and the Low Countries created a power vacuum in their colonies in Southeast Asia and created the perception in the United States that there was a growing strategic threat which linked events in Europe and East Asia. When Japan joined Nazi Germany and fascist Italy in the Axis alliance in September 1940, it became clear that the strategic link between Europe, Asia and the security of the United States was inextricable.[19]

Consequently, economic sanctions were imposed upon Japan, and America began to rebuild its military strength. The US Navy, which had always felt a strong commitment to the Asia–Pacific region, grew in total size from a low of 335 ships, including 15 battleships, in 1937 to a fleet of 790 ships in 1941. In particular, the Navy had come to realize the growing importance of airpower in modern warfare. It had begun experimenting with ship-based aircraft in the 1920s, and began constructing aircraft carriers. By late 1941 it possessed seven, up from only three in 1937.[20]

Battleships were still seen as the supreme capital ship, however. In April 1940 nine battleships were moved from the US west coast to Pearl Harbor as a deterrent to Japanese aggression, despite strong misgivings by fleet commander Admiral James O. Richardson. On 1 December 1941 the combined US Pacific and Asiatic fleets consisted of those nine battleships, three aircraft carriers, 24 cruisers, 80 destroyers and 55 submarines. The Imperial Japanese Navy outnumbered them in every category, especially in aircraft carriers, of which they possessed ten.[21] The carrier was about to become the queen of battle in the Pacific.

The devastating surprise attack on Pearl Harbor by aircraft from six Japanese carriers on the morning of 7 December 1941 was a major turning point in the history of the 20th century. Out of the shock and outrage caused by the attack and the subsequent Japanese attack on the Philippines grew an American military commitment to the Asia–Pacific region that was *fundamentally different from that of 1898–1902*, in at least five ways.

First, unlike the US involvement in the Philippines, after Pearl Harbor *there was no politically significant question about the legitimacy of the US commitment*. The American people were united to an extent not seen before—or since. 'Remember Pearl Harbor' remains to this day a powerful slogan in the United States about the dangers of isolationism and military unpreparedness.

Second, *the size and duration of the US military commitment to the Pacific theater of World War II dwarfed previous efforts* by an order of magnitude. It is far beyond the scope of this chapter to chronicle or even summarize the Pacific War that began on 7 December 1941 and ended with complete American victory on 2 September 1945.[22] Instead, a few key facts will serve to illustrate the point.

Approximately two million Americans served in the military for the full duration in the Pacific and China–Burma–India theaters during World War II. Approximately 90 000 Americans died there from all causes.[23]

The US Army, including its Air Corps, played an important role, but the brunt of the fighting in the Pacific theater was borne by the US Navy and its sister service, the Marine Corps—which was almost exclusively committed there. In 1940 the US Navy consisted of 13 162 officers and 744 824 enlisted personnel. At war's end, on 31 August 1945, the Navy had grown to 316 675 officers and nearly 3 million enlisted personnel. In 1940 the US Marine Corps consisted of 1819 officers and 26 545 enlisted personnel. On 31 August 1945 the Corps possessed 36 851 officers and 427 017 enlisted personnel.[24]

From 1941 to 1945 the US Navy had grown from 790 ships to 6800, from 17 battleships to 23, and, most significantly, from seven large fleet aircraft carriers to 28, and a total carrier force (including smaller escort carriers) of 105. This force was the largest navy the world had ever seen, and probably ever will.[25]

Finally, in 1941 the US Army's Air Corps in the Pacific consisted of a handful of B–17 Flying Fortress bombers and P–39 and P–40 fighters at Pearl Harbor and Clark Field in the Philippines. By the end of the war, the XXIst Bomber Command, based in the Marianas, deployed over 400 huge B–29 'Superfortresses', supported by an equal number of P–47 and P–51 fighters. This force laid waste to Japan itself. B–29s dropped the atomic bombs on Hiroshima and Nagasaki that played a major role in ending the war, thus ushering in a new era in military history.[26]

The third factor that made the World War II American military commitment qualitatively different from any previous engagement was *the unprecedented level of public attention given to the Asia–Pacific region in the United States*. Despite the official policy of defeating Nazi Germany first, historian Roger Dingman notes that 'in three out of four years of combat, the volume of *New York Times* reportage on the war [in the Pacific theater] exceeded that for any of the European fronts. By 1944 it surpassed that for all of them put together, and in 1945 nearly six out of every ten *Times* articles focused on its East Asian phase'.[27] Pacific commanders such as Douglas MacArthur, Admiral 'Bull' Halsey and Admiral Chester Nimitz became household names back in the United States.

Finally, *World War II in the Pacific stirred passions in America to a depth and in a direction far different from any previous engagement in the region*. This was in part due to the fact that race—on both sides—characterized the emotional tenor of the Pacific war to a much greater extent than America's conflict with Germany.[28] Despite the 'Germany first' policy, in February 1943,

53 per cent of those polled in the United States considered Japan to be the major enemy. Most significantly, by 1944 nearly 70 per cent of Americans believed that the United States should keep 'forever' the islands west of Hawaii for which its soldiers, sailors and marines were dying in ever larger numbers. Furthermore, by 1945 Americans felt that they 'had to maintain strength sufficient to deal single-handedly with any future threat to the peace in the Pacific and East Asia'.[29]

Faced with these passions and changing attitudes, long before the fighting ended President Franklin D. Roosevelt gave his blessing to intensive postwar planning both within and outside of government. This planning laid the groundwork for the basic structure of the American military presence in the Asia–Pacific region that endures to the present.

Outside of the government, the planning effort engaged academics, business leaders and journalists in such prominent organizations as the Council on Foreign Relations and the Foreign Policy Association. In addition to postwar planning, education of the American public about East Asian issues was a major objective of these groups.

Within the government, for the first time a substantial bureaucratic structure devoted to the Asia–Pacific region was created in both the civilian and military spheres. On the military side, by late 1944 the Far East Subcommittee of the State-War-Navy Coordinating Committee (SWNCC) had become the single most important official postwar planning agency dealing with the Pacific theater.[30]

The central military planning issue was obvious: assuming an Allied victory, which by the second half of 1943 seemed certain, the number and location of postwar US military bases in the Asia–Pacific region had to be determined. As early as 1942 President Roosevelt had asked the Joint Chiefs of Staff to begin studying the issue on a global level, in the context of forming an 'International Police Force'.[31] On 8 November 1943 the Joint Strategic Survey Committee of the Joint Chiefs of Staff completed the study, JCS Memorandum 570/2, which has been called 'the Base Bible'.[32]

The study's primary concern was the military security of the United States. One fact stood out: given the reach of modern air and seapower, the oceans were no longer an impenetrable security barrier. Army Chief of Staff General George Marshall put it succinctly: 'It no longer appears practical to continue what we once conceived as hemispheric defense as a satisfactory basis for our security. We are now concerned with the peace of the entire world'.[33] World War II had definitively ended the era of isolationism in the United States. The groundwork for what is now called US 'Forward Deployment' had been laid.

Although they were paramount, military considerations were not the only factor shaping the base plan. America's 'Open Door' free trade economic expansion plan already had a global reach. The establishment and protection of postwar commercial air and shipping routes to the Far East were also key factors, especially among those members of Congress whose states had strong maritime trade interests.[34]

The 'Base Bible' envisioned bases in the Philippines and Micronesia where the United States would have 'exclusive military rights' and bases in the southwest Pacific, Indochina, eastern China, Korea and Japan, where the United States would have 'participating rights' as one of the 'Great Powers enforcing peace'.[35] As the war in the Pacific neared its bloody end, it became clear that the United States would insist on exclusive military rights over any territory occupied by American military forces (and, in particular, resist Soviet participation in the occupation of Japan). The Joint Chiefs of Staff declared, 'In many cases, possession will be nine points of the law and present United States occupancy or control of any required base or facility should not be relinquished so long as negotiations for its future use . . . are pending or in process'.[36]

After American forces had suffered horrendous casualties in the battle of Okinawa in the Spring of 1945, President Harry Truman, who had assumed office following the death of Franklin D. Roosevelt, was faced with a difficult decision on how to end the war. Some US Navy and Army Air Corps leaders believed that further conventional bombing and a naval blockade would cause Japan to surrender. Most military planners believed an extremely costly invasion of the Japanese homeland would be necessary. There was a third, top-secret option: the newly developed atomic bomb.

President Truman's decision to drop the atomic bomb on the Japanese cities of Hiroshima and Nagasaki in August 1945 constituted the final shattering chapter of the Pacific war. Estimates vary, but at least 100 000 Japanese were killed in the two attacks. Japan surrendered on 14 August 1945, five days after the second bomb. The decision to use atomic weapons remains controversial, and the 50th anniversary of the end of World War II revived the debate.[37] There is no debate about the fact that a new era of world history had begun.

The advent of the atomic bomb served to increase the importance of establishing forward bases. The Joint Chiefs stated that:

> The importance of adequate bases, particularly in advanced areas, is enhanced by the advent of the new weapons in that defensively they keep the enemy at a distance, and offensively they project our operations, with new weapons or otherwise, nearer the enemy. The necessity for wide dispersion of naval forces in port as well as at sea will tend to increase the number and extent of anchorage areas required in our system of bases.[38]

By the end of World War II, the main characteristics of the enduring US military presence in the region had thus been established. First, the United States would not return to isolationism. Citing both military and economic rationales, it would maintain military bases throughout the Asia–Pacific region for years to come. Second, the geography of the region, combined with the new supremacy of airpower, meant that naval forces centered around aircraft carriers, together with air forces based in the region, would form the backbone of the US military presence. Finally, nuclear weapons would play a major role in that presence.

THE BEGINNING OF THE COLD WAR, 1946–1950

The end of World War II led to a drastic reduction in the size of active duty US military forces as a war-weary public demanded, 'Bring the boys back home!' For example, by 1950 the US Navy had declined from a 6800-ship fleet with 23 battleships and 28 large carriers to a 630-ship navy with one battleship and eleven aircraft carriers.[39]

However, despite this huge drawdown, the United States' commitment to the Asia–Pacific region endured and even grew. True, the American military forces remaining in the region shrank greatly in size, but they retained great striking power and occupied a series of bases in Japan and across the Pacific. For example, 21 per cent of the US Army was in Japan.[40] The establishment in 1947 of the new Pacific Command in Hawaii ensured the maintenance of an effective command structure (see Chapter 3).

The breakdown of the wartime alliance and the outbreak of the Cold War between the West and the Soviet Union by 1947 solidified this commitment. It was further strengthened by the fall of China to Mao Zedong's communists in 1949. Late in 1949 the US Chief of Naval Operations ordered an additional aircraft carrier and more anti-submarine forces to the Pacific Fleet in response to the new threat.[41]

In terms of the US economic interest, although actual trade was still very low due to postwar turmoil, American investment in the Asia–Pacific region grew immensely. From 1945 to 1950 Washington poured $4.1 billion in aid to the East Asian region, with a focus on Japan. As a result, US–Japan trade began to grow rapidly, causing many experts to believe that the basis for a reliable economic relationship had been formed, and that similar results could be obtained throughout the region.[42]

The growing political importance of the Asia–Pacific region was based on the persistent US perception of three possible threats: (1) a re-emergence of Japanese militarism; (2) the Far Eastern forces of the Soviet Union, now an enemy; (3) the new threat of a People's Republic of China, seen as a firm Soviet ally. In response, the United States adopted a policy of disarming and democratizing Japan on the one hand, and 'containing' communism on the other. In December 1948 the newly established National Security Council defined American objectives in East Asia in terms of reducing Sino-Soviet power and influence in the region.[43]

Strong advocates for the preservation of a US commitment to the Asia–Pacific region emerged in the military, with General Douglas MacArthur, commander of US occupation forces and the US Far East Command in Japan, being by far the most influential. The US Navy had always been heavily interested in the Pacific and succeeded in arguing the importance of Japanese bases.

Strong support also came from the newly formed US Air Force following its birth in the reorganization of the entire US military structure in 1947. By far the largest component of the new Air Force was its Strategic Air Command, which was in many ways a direct descendant of the Pacific War experience of the B–29 campaign against Japan. As General Jimmy Doolittle put it, 'The Navy had the transport to make the invasion of Japan possible. The ground forces had the power to make it successful; and the B–29 made it unnecessary'.[44]

A great debate arose in the late 1940s between the Navy and the Air Force about their respective roles in projecting power and a continuing presence in the Asia–Pacific region, pitting the aircraft carrier against the strategic bomber. In large measure that debate has continued to the present time.[45] But there was no debate about maintaining a strong US military commitment in the region.

THE KOREAN WAR AND ITS AFTERMATH, 1950-1962

Although committed to containing communism in East Asia, by 1948 virtually all US troops had left the mainland after completing the disarmament and removal of Japanese troops. In Southeast Asia, the United States supported France's re-entry into Indochina and provided the French with massive financial aid (but no troops or direct military support) in its battle against the Vietminh forces.

In Northeast Asia, all US troops had left China before the communists completed their victory there. Only 400 US military advisors of a force that had numbered 50 000 troops remained behind in the southern half of the Korean peninsula as that country became bitterly divided along the 38th parallel into separate communist and pro-Western occupation zones and, subsequently, states.[46]

The Joint Chiefs of Staff had concluded that if 'the present diplomatic ideological warfare [in Korea] should become armed warfare, Korea could offer little or no assistance in the maintenance of our national security' and thus 'the United States has little strategic interest in maintaining present troops and bases in Korea'.[47] Following their lead, in a controversial January 1950 speech before the National Press Club, US Secretary of State Dean Acheson declared that America's Far East defense perimeter

> runs along the Aleutians to Japan and then goes to the Ryukus [Okinawa] and from the Ryukus to the Philippine islands . . . So far as the military security of the other areas in the Pacific is concerned, it must be clear that no person can guarantee these areas against military attack . . . Should such an attack occur . . . the initial reliance must be upon the people attacked.[48]

On 25 June 1950 the communist forces of the Democratic People's Republic of Korea, with massive Soviet aid and support, launched a full-scale attack against the Republic of Korea in the south. South Korea's army was lightly equipped, largely because the United States was worried that Syngman Rhee's government might, if better equipped militarily, attack the North.[49]

President Truman immediately began to send American troops to Korea and also ordered the US Seventh Fleet to protect Formosa. On 27 June the United Nations Security Council, with the

Soviet Union absent, voted unanimously to support the US action.[50] The North Koreans nearly succeeded in overrunning all of the south before significant American strength could be deployed in a successful defence of the Pusan perimeter at the southern end of the peninsula.

In a bold stroke, American forces under General Douglas MacArthur then conducted a surprise amphibious assault on 15 September 1950 at Inchon on Korea's west coast and routed the North Koreans. In early October US and ROK forces crossed the 38th parallel into the North, intent on complete victory. By 25 October the 165 000 ground troops under MacArthur's command were approaching the Yalu river, confident that they would be 'home by Christmas'.

The intervention of tens of thousands of Chinese soldiers on the side of North Korea at the end of October 1950 came as a complete surprise and a severe shock to the United Nations Command, as did the appearance of Soviet-built MiG–15 jets based in China. Moving under cover of darkness and smoke from deliberately set crop fires, this army of 300 000 'volunteers' of the Chinese People's Liberation Army first put a halt to and then reversed the advance of UN forces by the end of November. *Newsweek* magazine called it 'America's worst military licking since Pearl Harbor'.[51]

By January 1951 the Chinese had driven UN forces south of the 38th parallel and taken Seoul. UN forces drove them back in February, but General MacArthur became openly critical of President Truman's refusal to widen the war by direct attacks on China, claiming on 20 March 1951 that 'There is no substitute for victory'. On 10 April President Truman, with the unanimous support of the Joint Chiefs of Staff, relieved MacArthur of command in one of the most serious civilian–military disputes in US history.[52]

By November 1951 the Korean War had turned into a brutal stalemate reminiscent of World War I along a line not very different from its starting point at the 38th parallel a year and a half before. Another year and a half of bloody stalemate finally ended with a cease-fire signed by the United States, China and North Korea (but not South Korea, which objected to its terms) on 27 July 1953 after nearly a year of highly contentious negotiations at Panmunjon. Prisoners were exchanged and a Demilitarized Zone was established between the North and the South, but no peace agreement was achieved. That remains the case to this day.

By the time the Armistice was signed, there were more than 225 000 US troops in Korea. During the war the US suffered 142 000 casualties, with nearly 34 000 killed.[53] There had been no total victory, but North Korea's attempt to reunify Korea by force had been defeated, albeit at a high price.

Coming on the heels of the post–World War II demobilization, the Korean War had a enormous impact on the size of the US military. From 1950 to 1952 US military spending increased nearly fourfold from $13 billion to $50 billion. At the same time the size of the armed forces doubled to almost three million, Navy ships increased from 630 to 1120, and Air Force wings rose from 48 to 108.[54] The draft would continue for another twenty years after the Korean War ended, facilitating the maintenance of a large standing military force.

The Korean War had emphasized both the importance and limitations of airpower in a war against a numerically superior enemy with few 'strategic' targets. The importance of aircraft carriers in a situation where land-based airfields were not available and rapid intervention was needed had been highlighted. The introduction of combat jets on both sides ushered in a new era of aerial warfare.

Nuclear weapons were not used by the United States in Korea, although their employment was seriously considered. There were three factors precluding their use.

First, North Korea's ally the Soviet Union had achieved a nuclear capability in 1949. In that light, American Allies and the American public reacted negatively when President Truman, in an offhand remark, referred to using nuclear weapons in Korea at a November 1950 press conference. Later, at a 20 May 1953 meeting of the National Security Council, President Eisenhower cited the fear of Soviet intervention as the main reason for refraining from the use of nuclear weapons.[55]

Second, in March 1951 a study conducted for the US Far East Command by Johns Hopkins University noted that a nuclear attack on the North Korean capital of Pyongyang—the only suitable 'strategic' target—would result in heavy civilian casualties.

Third, that same study concluded that US forces lacked the capability to effectively and safely target dispersed and mobile Chinese troops in close proximity to UN forces.[56]

Similar factors have continued to affect US political and military leaders with regard to the use of nuclear weapons. Since the Korean War, China's acquisition of nuclear weapons in 1964 and North Korea's possible recent development of them have added new dimensions to this issue in the Asia–Pacific region.

The Korean War was also seen to demonstrate the importance of the actual presence of forward deployed American forces to deter attack on threatened areas. At the time of writing, approximately 36 000 US military personnel remain stationed in South Korea.

Moreover, US bases in Japan proved essential to the war effort. That fact played a role in the concluding of both the US–Japan Peace Treaty and concomitant US–Japan Security Treaty in 1951. These agreements allowed the United States to maintain bases in Japan after the end of the formal US occupation of its former enemy. At the time of writing, approximately 44 000 US military personnel are stationed in Japan.

Finally, during and immediately after the Korean War, the United States established bilateral mutual defense treaties with South Korea (1954) and the Philippines (1952), and three collective defense treaties: (1) ANZUS with Australia and New Zealand (1952); (2) the Pacific Charter with the United Kingdom, Thailand, Philippines, Pakistan, New Zealand, France and Australia (1954); (3) the Southeast Asia Collective Defence Treaty (Manila Pact or SEATO) with the United Kingdom, France, Australia, New Zealand, Philippines and Thailand (1955).[57]

In May 1954 the People's Republic of China asserted sovereignty over several small offshore islands occupied by the nationalist forces of Chiang Kai-shek, who had retreated to Taiwan after Mao's triumph on the mainland in 1949. The US Navy sent five carriers to the Seventh Fleet to patrol the Taiwan straits in response to the crisis. In August 1958 mainland Chinese forces began shelling the islands of Quemoy and Matsu and the United States dispatched nuclear-capable Air Force bombers and Navy carrier-based bombers to Taiwan in response.[58] Tensions between mainland China and Taiwan persist, and as recently as March 1996 two US aircraft carriers were sent in response to provocative moves by the People's Republic of China.[59]

THE VIETNAM WAR, 1965–1975

Following the French defeat by the Vietminh in Indochina in 1954, the United States became a signatory to the Geneva Accords, ending the French phase of that conflict. America's subsequent involvement would lead to the longest war in the nation's history.

From the signing of the Geneva Accords on 21 July 1954 through to 1960, only a few hundred American military advisers of the US Military Assistance Advisory Group were stationed in what eventually became South Vietnam to assist that state's fledgling army in what was perceived as a part of the Cold War against communism. They did not succeed in helping to create an effective Army of the Republic of Vietnam.[60]

In the spring of 1961 President John F. Kennedy secretly sent an additional 500 military advisers to South Vietnam, breaching the Geneva Accord on the US side. In October 1961 South Vietnam requested the introduction of US combat troops. The United States declined, but did send more advisers, beginning a buildup process that would result in a force of 2646 in January 1962, and 16 732 by October 1963.[61]

The situation continued to deteriorate. In February 1964 the US began a series of covert operations against North Vietnam and communist forces in Laos known as Operation Plan 34A. In August 1964 two US Navy destroyers engaged in an intelligence-gathering aspect of those operations, code-named the De Soto patrols, were believed attacked by North Vietnamese torpedo boats in the Gulf of Tonkin. US carrier-based bombers retaliated. On 7 August the US Congress, having been told that North Vietnam had made 'unprovoked' attacks on US naval vessels in international waters, overwhelmingly approved a resolution granting President Lyndon Johnson authority to 'take all necessary measures to prevent further aggression'. This so-called 'Gulf of Tonkin Resolution' would later become a focus of debate in the United States over the authority of the US President to commit forces to a war in Vietnam.[62]

The situation in South Vietnam worsened in 1965 as insurgents of the National Liberation Front, called the Vietcong by US forces, inflicted defeats on the South Vietnamese Army. Following a February attack on a US military advisers' compound at Pleiku, the United States initiated a bombing campaign against North Vietnam code-named 'Rolling Thunder'. On 8 March 1965, 3500 US Marines landed in South Vietnam to defend the airfield at Da Nang. Within three weeks their mission was changed to offensive operations.

By mid-July 1965 President Johnson approved the request of the US Military Assistance Command, Vietnam (MACV) commander, Army General William Westmoreland, for nearly 200 000 troops.[63] For the third time in less than 25 years, the United States was involved in a major war in the Asia–Pacific region.

By the beginning of 1968 there were nearly half a million US troops in South Vietnam, many engaged in 'search and destroy' operations against Vietcong guerrillas and increasing numbers of North Vietnamese Army regulars who infiltrated via the Ho Chi Minh trail in Laos and Cambodia. US forces launched many successful operations, but often US and South Vietnamese forces did not hold the ground they had cleared of the enemy. Meanwhile, MACV headquarters in Saigon and the Pentagon issued optimistic progress reports, but the American press and, eventually, the American public became increasingly skeptical as tactical success was not followed by strategic progress toward ending the war.

Then on 31 January 1968, the Lunar New Year (Tet) holiday in Vietnam, the Vietcong launched a nationwide assault against urban centers. They penetrated the US embassy in the capital city of Saigon and captured a major portion of the provincial (and old imperial) capital of Hue. American and South Vietnamese forces employed their vastly superior firepower to deadly effect and within three weeks the Vietcong had been repulsed with enormous casualties. Casualties on the American side were much lighter, but still serious.

By purely military standards, the Tet Offensive was a major defeat for the communists. But the war in Vietnam had never been a classic military conflict. It had become a test of political endurance, and on that score the Tet Offensive served to shock and dismay both the American public and their leaders. When news then leaked out that US commander General Westmoreland had requested 206 000 more troops at the end of February 1968, the public reaction was negative. President Johnson refused to further increase US forces in Vietnam and emphasized the need to begin negotiations with North Vietnam for an end to the war.[64] Shortly thereafter President Johnson decided not to run for re-election as anti-war sentiment continued to mount in the United States.

President Richard Nixon was elected in 1968, having promised to end the war. He began steadily withdrawing US troops and trying to strengthen the South Vietnamese armed forces in a process called 'Vietnamization'. But when American and South Vietnamese troops entered Cambodia in May of 1970 to disrupt Vietcong and North Vietnamese sanctuaries there, another wave of anti-war protest occurred in the United States.

By early 1972 there were only 140 000 American troops left in South Vietnam. American land- and sea-based airpower helped to stem a major North Vietnamese military offensive in the late spring of 1972 (even mining Haiphong harbor in May), but the communists held on to considerable territory. Finally, after Nixon sent B–52 bombers to hit targets in the North Vietnamese capital of Hanoi in December 1972, the United States, over strong objections from South Vietnam, signed a cease-fire agreement with North Vietnam on 27 January 1973. By 29 March 1973 the last American troops had left Vietnam (and the last known US prisoners of war were released by Hanoi) after eight years of active combat and nearly twenty years of presence. Two years later a North Vietnamese military offensive overwhelmed the demoralized South Vietnamese forces (which had been cut off by the US Congress from further direct US military assistance) and at last succeeded in reunifying the country by force.[65]

Nearly 57 000 Americans died in the Vietnam War.[66] Although more than twenty years have passed, it is in some ways too soon to render any definitive accounting of that war's impact on the United States. Still, what has become known as 'the Vietnam syndrome' continues to play a major role in American national security strategy. Deeply scarred by the Vietnam experience, American leaders have generally concluded that, in the future, American forces should be committed to serious combat only under certain circumstances.

First, there must be a national consensus that clear and vital American interests are at stake. In retrospect, it appeared to many that the original US involvement in Vietnam was a mistake engineered in secrecy.

Second, the United States should help defend only allies who are stable nations willing and able to help defend themselves. Many felt that South Vietnam did not ever meet those criteria.

Third, any commitment of US troops should have a clear and declared goal and timeline. This was a reaction to the fact that, despite tactical successes in Vietnam, the strategic 'light at the end of the tunnel' was seen as ill-defined and receding into the future.

Fourth, US casualties should be kept to a minimum by the application of overwhelming force employing all means necessary.

In sum, this current policy is termed 'fight and win'.[67]

The large-scale employment of helicopters in direct combat first occurred during the Vietnam War. Once again, as in Korea, both the utility and limitations of strike airpower were manifested. The tonnage of bombs dropped by US forces was triple that of all of World War II.[68] 'Smart' bombs, guided missiles, satellite imagery, night-vision devices and remotely-monitored sensors were all employed by the end of that conflict.[69]

FROM VIETNAM TO THE END OF THE COLD WAR, 1976–1991

The withdrawal of the US from Indochina by 1975 led some in the United States and in the Asia–Pacific region to conclude that the United States no longer intended a serious military commitment and presence in the Western Pacific. Earlier, President Nixon's so-called 'Guam Doctrine' statement of 25 July 1969 had signaled a US policy of avoiding large overseas commitments of US military forces in favor of assistance to the national forces of friends and allies.[70] That had initially raised concerns regarding the depth of US commitment to regional presence, despite the US rapprochement with mainland China in 1971. Regional concerns were further strengthened when President Jimmy Carter in 1977 briefly advocated withdrawal of US ground forces from South Korea.

However, the Soviet invasion of Afghanistan in 1979 and the subsequent election of President Ronald Reagan in 1980 ushered in a new—and final—era of the Cold War that put an end, for the decade of the 1980s, to perceptions of American withdrawal from the Asia–Pacific region.

Although Europe was the primary focus of the renewed tension between the United States and the Soviet Union, by the 1980s Japan's booming economy and increasingly capable 'self-defense' forces had made it an increasingly important American ally, as was the increasingly strong South Korea. Seen in this context, the Soviet threat to the Far Eastern forces of the United States and its allies grew in significance in the new administration's estimate.[71]

A buildup of intercontinental nuclear weapons and warfighting plans was a major characteristic of this final phase of the Cold War, with concomitant efforts at nuclear arms control. Fears concerning the actual use of nuclear weapons in a global conflict grew and sparked considerable anti-nuclear sentiment in the West, including US allies in Japan, Australia and especially New Zealand.[72]

But the strategic nuclear buildup and debate had relatively little direct impact on the Asia–Pacific region, despite the fact that both the United States and the USSR enlarged and enhanced their ballistic missile nuclear submarine fleets based on each side's Pacific coasts.

However, by 1982 US strategists had concluded that a major war with the Soviet Union, presumably following an invasion of western Europe by the Red army, might well remain conventional in nature, or limited to a relatively small nuclear exchange. Planning for such a war again centered on the air–land battle that might engulf the central European theater. The Korean peninsula presented a similar scenario, albeit one of relatively secondary importance in the global scheme of total war with the Soviet Union.

The naval aspect of that war plan began to be formulated in 1982 and a declassified summary was eventually publicly revealed in January 1986 under the title 'The Maritime Strategy'.[73] That strategy

> envisioned a global war which would be at the initiative of the Soviet Union. The strategy called for naval forces to *indirectly influence* events on the Central [European] Front by establishing and *defending the fleet's battlespace* in sea areas on the Soviet flanks, thereby threatening the Soviet homeland, and containing the Soviet fleet which otherwise would threaten our sea lines of communications.[74]

As the Maritime Strategy was fleshed out in congressional testimony, it envisioned potential 'horizontal escalation' against the Soviet Pacific 'flank' in the Far East.[75] In order to 'defend the fleet's battlespace', the threat of early naval air and missile attacks against Soviet land bases in the Far East was emphasized in order to stop Soviet strike aircraft and ships before they could launch attacks against the US fleet or the cargo ships bringing supplies and reinforcements to Japan and South Korea.

However, the Soviet Union's large submarine force posed perhaps the greatest threat to US naval forces and shipping reinforcements. In order to 'contain' or pin down these submarines (and other Soviet naval forces) US nuclear attack submarines (SSNs) would reportedly also have the capability to be in position to conduct early attacks on Soviet ballistic missile submarines (SSBNs) in their so-called 'bastions' near the Russian Pacific coast. In theory, this would force the Soviets to principally use their other naval assets (especially SSNs) to guard their SSBNs rather than interdict naval forces and shipping on the trans-oceanic routes to the United States. This potential mission was called 'strategic anti-submarine warfare' and was officially described as a top-priority mission of the US Navy, despite doubts about its feasibility expressed by some analysts.[76]

The US Navy's Maritime Strategy reflected a broader renaissance in US military and naval strategic thinking, force structure and morale following the post-Vietnam Carter era low point. By 1980 the US Navy had declined to 470 ships. But by the end of 1982 the US Navy had already successfully argued that a force structure centered around at least fifteen deployable aircraft carrier battle groups, four battleship battle groups and 100 nuclear attack submarines was essential to carry out the new strategy. A strategic rationale and force structure plan was thus in place to achieve the declared goal of a '600 ship' Navy.[77]

As the US Navy grew, the US Pacific Command and its Commander, US Pacific Fleet, began to train for and test the Maritime Strategy in a series of large-scale exercises, predominantly in the North Pacific, beginning in 1982. These exercises featured multiple carrier battle groups and signaled US offensive strike capabilities against Soviet Far East forces.[78]

In September 1983 Soviet interceptors shot down a civilian airliner, Korean Airlines Flight 007, which had somehow strayed into Soviet airspace over the Kamchatka peninsula and then Sakhalin Island, killing all 269 aboard. This precipitated a major crisis in US–Soviet relations,[79] and along with concerns over the offensive capabilities being signaled by US forces in the North Pacific, led to calls for arms control in the region which grew stronger in the mid-to-late 1980s.[80]

By 1985 New Zealand was denying US nuclear-powered or nuclear-armed warships entry for port visits. This in turn led to US abrogation of security ties to New Zealand under the ANZUS Treaty, a condition that persists in 1998.

By 1988 the US Pacific Command had essentially put in place the Asia–Pacific component of the Maritime Strategy and the US Navy reached a top strength of over 590 ships—just as the threat it was designed to counter collapsed with a suddenness that surprised even the most seasoned analysts.

The fall of the Berlin Wall in 1989 symbolized the end of the Cold War. What began as a modest program of reform in the Soviet Union under then-President Gorbachev soon gained an irresistible momentum that ultimately led to the loss to the Soviets of eastern Europe, and ultimately the downfall of Gorbachev and the breakup of the Soviet Union in December 1991.

The impact of these events on US military strategy and force structure was swiftly felt. Already, President Bush's 2 August 1990 speech 'In Defense of Defense' had publicly outlined a 'new national security strategy' which recognized the end of the Cold War and focused on 'regional threats'. Iraq's invasion of Kuwait on that very same day at once overshadowed the speech and validated its central theme.

The Joint Chiefs of Staff issued their 1991 Joint Military Net Assessment in March of that year. It outlined five possible scenarios of future post–Cold War conventional conflict. In escalating order of significance, they were: (1) a relatively low-level counter-insurgency or counter-narcotics contingency; (2) a 'lesser' regional contingency such as Panama or the Philippines; (3) a 'major' regional contingency [MRC] in either Korea or Southwest Asia; (4) two simultaneous major regional contingencies (Korea and Southwest Asia); and (5) an invasion of Poland and Lithuania by Russia and Belarus.

Despite the buildup for Operations Desert Shield and Desert Storm, by the spring of 1991 spokespeople for the Bush administration had outlined a 25 per cent reduction in US defense spending based on these new geopolitical realities. The New 'Base Force' envisioned reduced the size of all the armed services by approximately the same amount.[81] A new era had begun.

SUMMARY

Over their first 150 years of presence in the Asia–Pacific region, the Armed Forces of the United States of America had engaged in four 'hot' wars, 45 years of the Cold War, and countless smaller engagements on land, sea and in the air, from the Aleutians to the jungles of New Guinea. Over 180 000 members of the American armed forces had died in those efforts. This legacy of commitment would not end with the Cold War.

However, in light of the enormous changes in the geopolitical situation in 1992 the United States began to seriously re-evaluate its interests, its strategy—and thereby its military presence—in the Asia–Pacific region. The next chapter examines those interests, and the evolving strategy designed to defend them.

2
US interests and strategic policy

The Armed Forces of the United States are present today in the Asia–Pacific region in order to implement a military strategy that flows from a national security strategy designed to protect American interests and those of her allies. The size, location and missions of those forces reflect that objective. Before examining the make-up and missions of US forces in the region, it is therefore necessary to describe those interests and strategies as laid out in official statements and amplified in authoritative commentary.

TRANSITION TO A POST–COLD WAR WORLDVIEW, 1990–1992

The fall of the Berlin Wall in 1989 marked an irreversible beginning of the end of the Cold War which had dominated US national security strategy for 40 years. In short order the American people and many of their representatives in Congress came to expect an economic benefit, called a 'peace dividend', from the reduced military spending presumably made possible by the reduced threat.

At the end of 1989 the US Congress required the Department of Defense to report on 'specific ways our Asian allies can increase their participation in regional stability and how we can reduce and restructure our military presence in East Asia'. In April of 1990 the Department of Defense responded with a report informally known as the 'East Asia Strategic Initiative' or 'EASI'. The report acknowledged three developments that lay behind its genesis: (1) the declining threat of the Soviet Union; (2) rising nationalist sentiment in the Asia–Pacific region leading to a resentment over the presence of US forces; and (3) domestic considerations, including both a public perception of the diminished Soviet threat and fiscal pressures centering around the growing US budget deficit.[1]

At the time the US Pacific Command consisted of 362 000 personnel, of whom 135 000 were forward deployed, with 50 000 in Japan, 44 000 in South Korea, 14 800 in the Philippines and 25 800 afloat.[2] Many in Congress felt that so large a force was no longer necessary and wanted a new rationale for retaining forces forward deployed in the region.

In response, the 1990 'EASI' still cited two Cold War military threats as the primary rationale for the US military presence. The USSR, although 'not as serious a menace', was still 'the major threat' with 'capabilities [that] still appear to far exceed those needed for defense'. North Korea posed a more immediate threat while 'maintaining a favorable military balance' over the South with the help of the Soviet Union.[3]

The Pentagon did realize that further changes were likely, but concluded that:

> our regional interests in Asia will remain similar to those we have pursued in the past: protecting the United States from attack; supporting our global deterrence policy; preserving our political and economic access; maintaining the balance of power to prevent the rise of any regional hegemony; strengthening the Western orientation of the Asian nations; fostering the growth of democracy and human rights; deterring nuclear proliferation; and ensuring freedom of navigation.[4]

Although this list of basic US interests would be reordered and enlarged, it remains intact in current US policy.

The EASI then began to expand on one of the US 'interests': 'maintaining regional stability'. In addition to its concern over the development of a destabilizing 'power vacuum' in the region, the Pentagon declared that it was not 'merely motivated by altruism' in its regional forward presence. Instead, it stated that:

> we must play this role because our military presence sets the stage for our economic involvement in this region. With a total two-way transPacific trade exceeding 300 billion dollars annually, 50 per cent more than our transAtlantic trade, it is in our own best interest to help preserve peace and stability.[5]

The frank and almost bluntly self-interested outlook in these passages is an indication that this first post–Cold War document was primarily intended for domestic consumption, particularly congressional critics of US overseas involvement.

Having briefly outlined continuing US interests and a three-pronged strategy, the report then asserted the continuing validity of the three principal instruments of that policy: (1) forward-deployed forces; (2) overseas bases; and (3) bilateral security arrangements. Some 'fine tuning' would be required, but nothing more.[6]

With regard to forward-deployed forces, the 'fine tuning' would consist of 'measured reductions of ground and some air forces in Korea, Japan and the Philippines'. A three-phase plan was unveiled.

Phase I, over 1–3 years, would see US forward-deployed forces reduced by about 15 000 personnel, including 7000 from Korea, 5000–6000 from Japan, including Okinawa, and possibly 2000 from the Philippines. Phase II, 3–5 years in the future, would entail 'proportionally greater reductions in combat forces . . . undertaken incrementally'. Phase III, 5–10 years out, would further reduce forces, but then 'stabilize at a somewhat lower level as circumstances permit'. Beyond Phase I no specific figures were offered.[7]

Concerning US bases in the region, the EASI reported that during Phase I in Japan 'excess facilities' would be returned to the government of Japan, particularly on Okinawa which had a large concentration—and where local opposition was becoming increasingly evident. Otherwise, in Japan's main islands the major US airbases at Yokota, Misawa, Atsugi and Iwakuni, the small Army facilities (like Camp Zama) and homeports for US Navy ships at Yokosuka and Sasebo would be retained.

In response to growing nationalist pressures for US forces to leave Clark airbase and Subic/Cubi Point naval base in the Philippines, EASI declared that these bases were a 'cornerstone of our regional basing structure and military presence' whose continued existence clearly served both US and Philippine interests despite the end of the Cold War. The report then admitted that worst-case scenario prudence had already produced a study of basing alternatives which concluded that they did exist, although they would be expensive, time consuming to develop, and *operationally less effective*.[8]

The report clearly stated that 'in the area of cost sharing, we expect increasing assistance from our allies', primarily Japan and South Korea, without decreeing specific criteria as to what constitutes a 'fair share'.

The EASI concluded by reiterating the US commitment to traditional bilateral security arrangements (the so-called 'hub and spokes' concept), while acknowledging the importance of the US relationship to friends and allies in the Association of Southeast Asian Nations (ASEAN). The report downplayed the role of 'multilateral consultations on security concerns' on the grounds that East Asian nations were generally reluctant to enter into them, that Japan's Constitution forbade their participation in collective defense, and that multilateral efforts were simply not needed due to the success of the US bilateral approach.

Arms control agreements and even confidence-building measures were described as 'not applicable' to the Asia–Pacific region, with the possible exception of the Korean peninsula, due to their unique European origins, the likelihood that they would include naval forces—which the United States regarded as non-negotiable—and the suspicious Soviet origin of most proposals.[9]

The ink had barely dried on the first EASI report before much of it was overtaken by events. All three of the factors that had led to its drafting continued to increase in importance.

First, the decline of the Soviet Union continued to accelerate, culminating in an attempted coup in August 1991 and the subsequent breakup of the USSR in December. In the meantime Iraq invaded Kuwait for purely regional reasons and the United States was suddenly called upon to fight a war it hadn't foreseen.

Second, Mother Nature and rising nationalist sentiment in the Philippines put an end to nearly 100 years of US military presence there. First, Mt Pinatubo erupted in June 1991, forcing the evacuation of Clark airbase, which was then relinquished to the Philippines in November of that year. Although the US and Philippine negotiators then reached a scaled-down agreement for continued US use of the Subic/Cubi Point naval base, in December 1991 the Philippine Senate voted to require US forces to leave the Subic/Cubi naval base by the end of 1992.[10]

Finally, the US economy worsened, putting additional fiscal pressure on the defense budget.

In response, the Bush administration continued to adjust US strategy to these new realities. Beginning with a speech by the President on 2 August 1990, later formalized in the August 1991 release of a revised *National Security Strategy of the United States* and then culminating in the January 1992 publication of *The National Military Strategy of the United States*, a new strategy and force structure were announced.[11]

This new strategy, sometimes called 'the regional defense strategy' or 'the regionally focused defense strategy', recognized that the former Soviet Union now posed only a potential long-term threat. 'Regional' adversaries like Iraq and North Korea were seen as the more probable short- to medium-term threats.

The new strategy included a plan for a new 'Base Force' which reduced US forces—and the defense budget—by roughly 25 per cent across the board. The Army would decline from 18 active and 10 ready reserve divisions to 12 active and 6 ready reserve divisions. The Navy would be reduced from a 545-ship fleet with 14 deployable aircraft carriers to 452 ships with 12 deployable carriers. The Air Force would go down from 36 active and reserve fighter wings to 26. Similar cuts affected the strategic forces.[12]

In the Pacific, the US forward-deployed presence would consist of the one carrier battle group homeported in Yokosuka, Japan, one amphibious ready group with its ships homeported in Sasebo, Japan, and one Marine Expeditionary Force (less a regiment stationed in Hawaii) based in Okinawa, 'less than a [Army] division' in Korea, and '2 to 3 fighter wing equivalents' in Korea and Japan. These forces would be backed up by Crisis Response forces based in the Continental US [CONUS], Hawaii and Alaska, consisting of '1+division, 1 fighter wing, and 5 carrier battlegroups'.[13]

In March 1992 General Colin Powell, then Chairman of the Joint Chiefs of Staff, testified to Congress that:

> If forward presence is reduced beyond projected levels, there is an increasing risk of reduced influence, the loss of infrastructure in critical regions, and the perception by friends, allies and potential adversaries that the United States is withdrawing from global participation.[14]

Reaction to these announcements was mixed. On the one hand, advocates of a post–Cold War 'peace dividend' strongly felt that the reductions were too small. On the other hand, some US friends and allies in the Asia–Pacific region were alarmed by the reductions and the lack of detail about the future of US forces in the region.

Responding again to a congressional mandate, in April 1992 the Department of Defense released another report updating US strategy for the Asian Pacific Rim, inevitably called 'EASI II'. EASI II differed from its predecessor in several important ways.

First, it acknowledged immediately that the new national security strategy outlined above 'marked the end of our Cold War global containment strategy' and that 'the world has changed in fundamental ways and continues to do so, in sometimes unpredictable ways, and often at blinding speed'. The 'residual power projection capability of Russian naval and air forces' was said to

Table 2.1 EASI II (1992): planned phased US East Asia troop reductions

Country and service	1990 starting strength	Phase I reductions 1990–92	Philippines withdrawal	1993 strength	Phase II reductions 1992–95	1995 strength (approx.)
JAPAN	50 000	4773		45 227	700	44 527
Army personnel	2 000	22		1 978		1 978
Navy, shore	7 000	502		6 498		6 498
Marines	25 000	3 489		21 511		21 511
Air Force	16 000	560		15 440	700	14 740
Joint billets		200				
KOREA	44 000	6 987		37 413	6 500[a]	30 913[a]
Army personnel	32 000	5 000		27 000		27 000
Navy, shore	400			400		400
Marines	500			500		500
Air Force	11 500	1 987		9 513		9 513
PHILIPPINES	14 800	3 490	11 310			
Army personnel	200		200	relocated		
Navy, shore	5 000	672	4 328	elsewhere		
Marines	900		900	in region:		
Air Force	8 700	2 818	5 882	1 000		1 000[b]
TOTAL	109 200	15 250	11 310	83 640	7 900	76 440
	25 800[c]			25 800[c]		25 800[c]
	135 000			109 440		102 240

Notes: [a] Korean troop reductions deferred in light of North Korean threat. [b] Estimated relocations to Japan, Korea and Singapore; does NOT include Guam. [c] 'Afloat or otherwise deployed'.

Source: *A Strategic Framework for the Asian Pacific Rim: Report to Congress 1992*, US Department of Defense, p. 22.

remain a 'major concern', but the entire document devoted only one paragraph to Russia.[15]

Second, the report provided a detailed accounting of reductions to date of US forces forward deployed in the Asia–Pacific region, and a timetable and figures for future reductions, as shown in Table 2.1.

EASI II indicated that, between 1990 and the end of 1992, 15 250 US personnel were to have been voluntarily withdrawn from the region, including the originally planned 3500 from the Philippines, plus the remaining 8310 US forces from the Philippines as a result of the Philippines Senate's rejection of the new Subic/Cubi Point bases agreement. This meant a total US regional force reduction of some 27 000 personnel, which amounted to about a 20 per cent reduction from the 1990 force of 135 000.

The further Phase II reductions, however, were minimal to begin with—only an additional 7200—and the planned reductions to US forces in South Korea were suspended for the time being, in view of the increasing concern over North Korea's military threat and nuclear weapons program. The bottom line was that at the end of Phase III over 102 000 US troops would remain in the region, counting the 25 800 afloat with the Seventh Fleet.[16]

Third, EASI II emphasized new threats and pointed out new potential hot spots in the region. North Korea's recently revealed quest for a nuclear weapons capability was deemed 'the most urgent threat to security in Northeast Asia', amplified by its possession of Scud ballistic missiles of the type that Iraq had used against US forces with deadly effect in the Gulf War. In response to this threat, the United States announced in November 1991 that it would not move forward with the planned Phase II reductions of US forces in South Korea.

The People's Republic of China was listed as a potential source of regional instability due to its impending leadership transition, the modernization of its military forces, its policies regarding nuclear and missile proliferation, and its uncertain relationship with Taiwan. The document also mentioned the Spratly Islands in the South China Sea as a potential flashpoint due to the PRC's February 1992 claim to sovereignty over them in the face of several competing claims in the region.[17]

In the main, however, EASI II reiterated the interests and strategy outlined in EASI I. There were some additions, such as the incorporation of ballistic missiles in the anti-proliferation agenda, and the inclusion of 'reducing drug trafficking' in the list of US security interests. In terms of military missions, there was a greater emphasis on defending lines of communications (LOCs) throughout the Pacific.[18]

The 1992 report ended with the following statement:

> We reaffirm the conclusions of the 1990 report that:
> our engagement in the Asia–Pacific region is critical to the security and stability of the region;
> our forward-deployed presence is the very foundation of stability in [the] region and allows the United States to play its unique role as regional balancer and honest broker;
> stability in the Asia–Pacific region serves the vital national interest in the United States and the interests of our allies;
> accordingly, the United States can and must play a role in securing the future of this vast, complex, and dynamic region.[19]

It would remain to be seen whether, in the absence of so clear and present a perceived threat as the Soviet 'evil empire' and in the presence of increasing economic concerns, the United States would continue to stay this course.

This became apparent when, after twelve years of Republican Presidents in the White House, President Bush was defeated by 46-year-old former Arkansas Governor Bill Clinton in November 1992. The economy had apparently been the deciding factor in the campaign. But in any event, a completely new administration and national security team entered the scene. Clinton was the first US President born after the end of World War II, and the first to begin office after the end of the Cold War. Change was inevitable.

ENTER THE CLINTON ADMINISTRATION

Upon taking office in January 1993, the new administration inherited the national security strategy, national military strategy and projected Base Force structure developed in the final two years under President Bush. Although foreign and defense policy had very much taken a back seat to domestic economic concerns during the election campaign, as a candidate Clinton had indicated his agreement with those who thought further changes were necessary in accord with still-changing geopolitical realities, especially in light of continuing economic concerns. It became clear soon after Clinton took office that US national security policy would undergo a review once the new administration had established itself.

It is important to have a basic understanding of the *process* whereby national security policy is determined in the United States. Foreign and military policy are determined in the end by elected civilians. In the representative form of democracy embodied in the US Constitution and amplified in subsequent legislation, there is a mandated 'invitation to struggle' between the executive branch (the President and National Security Council, the Department of Defense, the Department of State and the intelligence community) and the legislative branch (both houses of Congress, including their staffs). In recent times the domestic political environment (the public, the media and interest groups) has also gained a role in shaping that policy.

In general, foreign and military policy is formulated and implemented by the executive branch, with the President as Commander in Chief of US military forces, advised by civilian leaders such as the Secretary of Defense, and military leaders such as the Joint Chiefs of Staff (see Chapter 3).

Congress plays several critical roles in the process, however.

First, final decisions on government spending are made by the Congress, that is, Congress controls 'the purse strings'. Second, the US Senate must confirm any formal foreign treaty by a two-thirds majority. Third, the Senate must confirm the appointment of major executive branch officials such as the Secretary of Defense.

Finally, public opinion plays an important role in an era of mass-media exposure to international issues, and heightened public concern over a wide variety of foreign and defense policy issues, from economic impacts to potential US military casualties to human rights.

It took the Clinton administration more than two years to fully complete its foreign and defense policy review process and produce its first full reformulation of America's foreign and military policy in general and its Asia–Pacific policy in particular.

THE *BOTTOM-UP REVIEW*, 1993

President Clinton's first Secretary of Defense was former member of Congress and House Armed Services Committee chairman Les Aspin, a defense intellectual who had been a frequent critic of US defense spending. In early 1993, at the President's request, he initiated a comprehensive review of the nation's defense strategy and force structure. In the introduction to that document he wrote:

> I felt that a department-wide review needed to be conducted 'from the bottom up' because of the dramatic changes that have occurred in the world as a result of the end of the Cold War and the dissolution of the Soviet Union. These changes in the international security environment have fundamentally altered America's security needs. Thus, the underlying premise of the Bottom-Up Review was that we needed to reassess all of our defense concepts, plans, and programs from the ground up.[20]

The *Bottom-Up Review* (BUR) made virtually no mention of the potential Russian or other 'Resurgent/Emergent Global Threat' described in the previous administration's documents. However, it confirmed the basic 'regional' emphasis of the Bush national security and military strategies. It also employed the same two 'most likely' major regional conflict (MRC) scenarios: another Iraqi invasion of Kuwait, and an invasion of South Korea by the North. The worsening civil war in Croatia and Bosnia was also listed as a potential threat.[21]

The report, however, went further in its analysis of the potential dangers posed by regional aggressors:

> Regional aggressors represent a danger that must be deterred and, if necessary, defeated by the military capability of the United States and its allies. Moreover, if we were to be drawn into a war in response to the armed aggression of one hostile nation, another could well be tempted to attack its neighbors—especially if it were convinced the United States and its allies did not possess the requisite military capability or will to oppose it.[22]

The *Bottom-Up Review* then arrived at this crucial conclusion: 'Therefore it is prudent for the United States to *maintain sufficient military power to be able to win two major regional conflicts that occur nearly simultaneously*'.[23]

A second rationale for the 'win two simultaneous major regional conflicts' strategy was offered:

> . . . fielding forces sufficient to win two wars nearly simultaneously provides a hedge against the possibility that a future adversary—or coalition of future adversaries—might one day confront us with a larger-than-expected threat.[24]

A major regional aggressor was defined as a power that could field military forces in the following ranges:

- 400 000–750 000 total personnel under arms
- 2000–4000 tanks
- 3000–5000 armored fighting vehicles
- 2000–3000 artillery pieces
- 500–1000 combat aircraft
- 100–200 naval vessels, primarily patrol craft armed with surface-to-surface missiles, and up to 50 submarines
- 100–1000 Scud-class ballistic missiles, some possibly with nuclear, chemical or biological warheads.[25]

The question that remained to be answered was the size and make-up of the US force structure necessary to carry out the 'win two MRCs' strategy.

The *Bottom-Up Review* considered four force options for major regional conflicts. *Option 1*, 'Win one MRC', required the fewest resources, but would leave the United States vulnerable to a second aggressor and would require a major reduction in US world influence.

Option 2, 'Win one MRC with hold in second', would provide more forces, but require inadequate US forces facing a second

Table 2.2 Force options for major regional conflicts (MRCs)

Strategy	Win one MRC	Win one MRC with hold in second	Win two nearly simultaneous MRCs	Win two nearly simultaneous MRCs plus conduct smaller operations
Army	• 8 active divisions • 6 reserve division equivalents	• 10 active divisions • 6 reserve division equivalents	• 10 active divisions • 15 reserve enhanced readiness brigades	• 12 active divisions • 8 reserve enhanced equivalents
Navy	• 8 carrier battle groups	• 10 carrier battle groups	• 11 carrier battle groups • 1 reserve carrier	• 12 carrier battle groups
Marine Corps	• 5 active brigades • 1 reserve division	• 5 active brigades • 1 reserve division	• 5 active brigades • 1 reserve division	• 5 active brigades • 1 reserve division
Air Force	• 10 active fighter wings • 6 reserve fighter wings	• 13 active fighter wings • 7 reserve fighter wings	• 13 active fighter wings • 7 reserve fighter wings	• 14 active fighter wings • 10 reserve fighter wings

Source: *Report on the Bottom-Up Review*, Office of the Secretary of Defense, 1993, p. 30.

regional aggressor to hold out until rescued by the victorious forces employed in a first major regional conflict.

Option 3, 'Win two nearly simultaneous MRCs', would provide enough additional forces to accomplish the stated goal, but with nothing left over for other lesser contingencies such as peacekeeping operations.

Option 4, 'Win two nearly simultaneous MRCs plus conduct smaller operations' provided forces that looked very much like the Base Force called for by the Bush strategy, but 'to maintain forces of this size would require significant additional resources, thereby eliminating any "peace dividend" the American people are expecting as a result of the end of the Cold War'.[26]

The *Bottom-Up Review* chose Option 3, perhaps because it offered the best of both worlds, allowing some further reductions in force structure and economic savings on the one hand, while offering a thoroughly post–Cold War rationale for maintaining a still large force on the other. The announced 1999 force structure goal, including strategic nuclear forces, is contained in Table 2.3.

Compared with the Bush Base Force, the *Bottom-Up Review* force called for significant further reductions in all three armed

Table 2.3 US force structure 1999 in the *Bottom-Up Review*

Service	Active forces	Reserve forces
Army	10 divisions	5+ divisions
Navy	11 aircraft carriers	1 aircraft carrier
	45–55 attack submarines	(reserve/training)
	346 ships	
Air Force	13 fighter wings	7 fighter wings
	up to 184 bombers	
	(B–52H, B–1, B–2)	
Marine Corps	3 Marine Expeditionary Forces	42 000 personnel
	174 000 personnel	
Strategic Nuclear Forces (by 2003)	18 ballistic missile submarines	
	up to 94 B–52H bombers	
	20 B–2 bombers	
	500 Minuteman III ICBMs (single warhead)	

Source: Report on the Bottom-Up Review, Office of the Secretary of Defense, 1993, p. 28.

forces. The Army would go from 12 active and 8 reserve divisions to 10 and 5+. The Air Force was slated to go from 26 to 20 active and reserve fighter wings, and the Navy faced a reduction from 452 ships to 343.

From the standpoint of the US forward presence in the Asia–Pacific region, however, the *Bottom-Up Review* mostly held the line. 'Close to 100 000' troops were to be retained in Northeast Asia, a total very near the 1993 figure of 103 000 contained in EASI II. The freeze on further troop reductions in Korea announced by the Bush administration in November of 1990 would be maintained, although 'plans call for the eventual withdrawal of one of our two Army brigades from South Korea'. A Marine Expeditionary Force, Amphibious Ready Group, carrier battle group homeport and one and a half Air Force fighter wings would remain in Japan.

The Seventh Fleet would remain active in the Western Pacific, despite the loss of the Philippines bases. Although the US Pacific fleet would decline from a Cold War peak of 259 ships to 197—a drop of 24 per cent—by mid-1995, a higher proportion of the fleet would be deployed in Asian waters, thus maintaining something close to previous levels of presence.[27] Indeed, a major aspect of the *Bottom-Up Review* was the explicit recognition that forward presence requirements might necessitate additional force structure beyond that required to execute two MRCs, particularly in the case of naval forces (especially aircraft carrier battle groups and amphibious ready groups).[28]

In the final estimate, the *Bottom-Up Review* 'developed a strategic framework for defense reductions' and projected $91 billion in savings during fiscal years 1995–99.[29] That was both its strength and its weakness. It mollified some advocates for reduced defense spending, but left others demanding more. The military was satisfied with the 'Win two MRCs' strategy, but (mostly privately) was convinced that funding was inadequate to maintain the projected force structure.

Perhaps the most serious criticism was that this report should have *followed* upon the development of a new national security strategy and military strategy, not preceded them. Stung by this critique, the Clinton administration slowly set about formulating those strategies.

THE 1994 NATIONAL SECURITY STRATEGY AND 1995 ASIA–PACIFIC STRATEGY

US strategic planners have traditionally considered three basic elements in formulating national policy: *goals*, *threats* and *resources*. In July 1994 the Clinton administration followed this tradition in releasing its first comprehensive policy statement, entitled *A National Security Strategy of Engagement and Enlargement*. This was in belated response to a recent congressional requirement for an annual National Security Strategy from the President. The sprawling 50-page document began by enumerating three 'pillars' or *goals* of American national security strategy: (1) *security*, defined in the classic military sense of maintaining a defense capability strong enough to sustain American commitments; (2) *economics*, described as bolstering America's economic revitalization, dependent on the growth and integration of the global economy; and (3) *democracy*, which meant enlarging the community of democracies and free markets throughout the world.[30]

The February 1995 publication of President Clinton's *National Security Strategy of Enlargement and Engagement* was an update in virtually identical form that reiterated the three basic goals outlined above.

Concerning *threats*, in the absence of a global threat as once presented by the Soviet Union, the new strategy enumerated three: (1) *regional states*, such as North Korea, Iran and Iraq, with interests opposed to those of the United States and its allies; (2) the *proliferation* of weapons of mass destruction and ballistic missiles; and (3) *'transnational phenomena'*, including terrorism, narcotics trafficking, refugee flows, and 'an emerging class of environmental and natural resources issues'.[31]

If one were to attempt to describe these diverse threats in a single phrase, that phrase might be 'the threat of regional instability'.

With regard to the third central planning factor, *resources*, the new strategy was very explicit:

> These basic objectives will guide the allocation of our *scarce* national security resources. Because deficit reduction is also central to the long-term health and competitiveness of the American economy, we have made it . . . a major priority. Under the Clinton economic plan, the deficit will be reduced over 700 billion dollars by Fiscal Year 1998.[32]

The 1995 statement made it very clear that the resources issue was a central—and perhaps predominant—factor in formulating strategy and policy.

Concerning US defense strategy and force structure, the 1995 national security strategy reaffirmed the conclusions reached by the 1993 *Bottom-Up Review*. 'Win two nearly simultaneous major regional contingencies' remained the strategy. With regard to force structure the strategy declared that:

> The President has set forth a defense budget for Fiscal Years 1996–2001 that funds the force structure recommended by the [Bottom-Up] Review, and he repeatedly stressed that he will draw the line against further cuts that would undermine that force structure or erode US military readiness.[33]

An overseas presence of US military forces was strongly supported, but the definition of 'presence' was expanded to include permanently stationed forces and prepositioned equipment, deployments and combined exercises, port calls and other force visits, as well as military-to-military contacts.[34]

With regard to the Asia–Pacific region, the 1995 national security strategy seemed to indicate that US *economic* interests had replaced Cold War military security interests in order of importance. 'Our economic relations,' it declared, 'depend vitally on our ties with the Asia Pacific region, which is the world's fastest-growing economic region.' Indeed, in November 1993 President Clinton had convened in Seattle the first-ever summit of the leaders of the economies that constituted the recently formed multilateral Asia–Pacific Economic Cooperation forum (APEC). In the economic realm, the era of US bilateralism was over.[35] At that APEC summit, President Clinton revealed the outline for his vision of a 'New Pacific Community' marked by prosperity, freedom and peace.[36]

In applying the national security strategy to distinct regions, the 1995 US National Security Strategy adopted an 'integrated' approach which attempted to link American security, economic goals and political goals. In fact, with respect to the Asia–Pacific region, the 1995 statement asserted that 'nowhere are the strands of our three-pronged strategy more intertwined, nor is the need for continued US engagement more evident'.[37]

Security was still described as the 'first' pillar of the New Pacific Community. Tensions on the Korean peninsula remained the greatest concern. The 100 000 forward-deployed US force was described as the foundation for America's security role in the region. US concerns over the proliferation of weapons of mass destruction and their delivery vehicles was highlighted. Agreements with North Korea to stop its development of nuclear weapons, and with China to limit its sale of ballistic missiles, were indicated to be an important part of the US security strategy for the region.

In a major departure from the Bush-era Asia–Pacific strategy, the 1995 Clinton strategy, while reaffirming existing bilateral security agreements, avowed its support for new *multilateral* regional exchanges. This included the ASEAN Regional Forum (ARF) annual meeting of foreign ministers on security issues, which had been initiated by ASEAN in 1994. Multilateral security meetings were described as enhancing regional security through dialog and transparency. In rhetoric at least, the era of an exclusively bilateral US security approach was over—although it was recognized that multilateral exchanges were only a complement to, not a substitute for, US bilateral security ties in the region.[38]

If security was called the 'first' pillar, however, economics seemed to be an increasingly important pillar of the US strategy. The usual statistics were cited. 'A prosperous and open Asia Pacific' was said to be 'the key to the economic health of the United States'.

A prosperous and open Asia–Pacific meant one where Japanese trade markets were opened up to help make US goods more competitive and thus reduce the US trade deficit with Japan. Economic considerations also played a key role in the US decision in early 1995 to 'delink' China's Most Favored Nation (MFN) trade status with the United States from that country's poor record on human rights. The even larger consideration was the stated goal of remaining 'engaged' with China, rather than trying to isolate or contain that huge nation.

In the political realm, the Asia–Pacific region presented the United States with a serious challenge because of the many non-democratic governments there, including the still-communist states of China, Vietnam and North Korea, as well as other authoritarian states such as Burma (Myanmar). The United States declared its support for democratic reform in the region. It rejected the accusation that human rights, especially civil and political rights, were somehow relative or different in the Asian context, and that the United States and Europe were engaging in 'Western cultural imperialism' in trying to defend them.[39]

Simultaneous with the White House release of the *National Security Strategy* document in February 1995, the US Department of Defense released the first in a series of regional reviews consistent with that strategy. It is significant that the first in the series was the *United States Security Strategy for the East Asia–Pacific Region*.

This new Asia–Pacific strategy reiterated the remarkably consistent 'permanent' American interests in the region: peace and security; commercial access to the region; freedom of navigation; and the prevention of the rise of any hegemonic power or coalition.[40]

The Security Strategy briefly reviewed the continuing US commitment to its five 'inviolable' bilateral security relationships with Japan, South Korea, Australia, the Philippines and Thailand. It then proceeded to elaborate on the significance of Asia's new economic success for American interests.

First, the US economy has become increasingly dependent on *trade*. For example, as a share of the US Gross Domestic Product (GDP), merchandise exports have more than doubled in the last two decades from 5.5 per cent to 11.6 per cent. Asia accounts for much of the growth in this sector. As of 1995 American two-way trade with Asia accounted for more than 36 per cent of total American world trade. People in Asian countries import more American goods than do people in European countries, on a per capita basis. US exports to the Asia–Pacific region are approaching one-third of worldwide US merchandise exports.

Second, because of its national debt and budget deficits, the US economy has become increasingly dependent on *access to foreign capital*. Here too Asia's importance has risen dramatically. Since 1980 the percentage of global bank reserves in the seven leading East Asian economies has risen from 17 per cent to nearly 40 per cent. Together, Japan, the People's Republic of China, Taiwan, Hong Kong and Singapore have foreign reserves totaling 270 billion dollars.[41]

Despite the 1997–98 East Asian financial crisis, the overall economic importance of the Asia–Pacific region to US prosperity will probably continue to grow. In 1992 the Gross National Product of the Asia–Pacific region accounted for 25 per cent of the Gross World Product. Assuming the financial crisis abates, the region will produce approximately one-third of the Gross World Product (on a purchasing power parity basis) by 2001.[42]

These factors in themselves make it clear that the stability and resulting continuing prosperity of the Asia–Pacific region 'is a matter of vital national interest affecting the well-being of all Americans'.[43] It then becomes incumbent upon the United States to play a central, visible, stabilizing role in the region.

The Security Strategy applies the national strategy of 'engagement' to the diverse and rapidly changing Asia–Pacific region. The United States will attempt to modernize and strengthen its existing alliances and friendships.

The US relationship with *Japan* is 'fundamental to both our Pacific security objectives and our global strategic objectives. Our security alliance with Japan is the linchpin of United States security policy in Asia'.[44] But the Security Strategy also acknowledges that if public support for the security alliance is to be maintained over the long term, then progress must be made in addressing the two nations' differences over economic issues, especially trade.

The US security relationship with the *Republic of Korea* is termed 'central to the stability of the Korean Peninsula and Northeast Asia' and 'a vital component in our national objective of supporting and promoting democracy'. The United States reaffirms its commitment to deterrence of North Korea, as well as efforts to reach a peaceful solution.

The US–*Australia* alliance 'makes a major contribution to regional stability' by facilitating US military activities in the region and by contributing to peacekeeping, nonproliferation, and multilateral dialog and negotiation efforts.

It is interesting to note that the 1995 Security Strategy discusses the US bilateral security relationships with the *Philippines* and *Thailand* only in the context of their membership in *ASEAN*. ASEAN is seen as having become an 'increasingly influential regional actor', which is said to be 'an important positive development'. According to this Asia–Pacific Security Strategy, the United States and ASEAN share an interest in 'precluding Southeast Asia from becoming an area of strategic competition among regional powers'. The United States seeks to broaden its network of access and pre-positioning arrangements in Southeast Asia.

In 1986 the United States suspended its security obligations to its long-time ally *New Zealand* under the ANZUS Treaty because of a conflict between that country's anti-nuclear legislation and the US policy of neither confirming nor denying the presence of nuclear weapons aboard specific ships, as well as New Zealand restrictions on nuclear-powered warship visits (see Chapter 5). Under President Clinton that suspension has been softened by the resumption of high-level foreign and security officials visits, but not reversed, even though New Zealand's global contributions to peacekeeping and humanitarian missions are acknowledged as 'admirable' in the Security Strategy.

The Security Strategy also emphasizes that the United States has defense responsibility for those *Pacific Islands* which are US territories (Guam, American Samoa and the Commonwealth of the Northern Marianas) or have signed Compacts of Free Association (the Republic of the Marshall Islands, the Republic of Palau and the Federated States of Micronesia). The presence there of shipping lanes and economic interests such as access to fishing grounds also affects US security.[45]

In a marked change from its views before the December 1991 collapse of the Soviet Union, the United States in the 1995 Security Strategy signaled its constructive participation in, and support for, *multilateral regional security dialogs*. During his Seoul visit in 1993, President Clinton listed multilateral dialogs as one of the 'overlapping plates of armor' which make up US security policy in the region and indicated, 'I see [multilateral dialogs] as a way to supplement our alliances and forward military presence, not to supplant them. These dialogs can ensure that the end of the Cold War does not provide an opening for regional rivalries, chaos and arms races.'

The United States supported the establishment in 1993 of the ASEAN Regional Forum (ARF), which is described as 'Asia's first broadly based consultative body concerned with security issues'. In addition to ASEAN members (Brunei, Indonesia, Laos, Malaysia, Myanmar, Philippines, Singapore, Thailand and Vietnam), the ARF includes the United States, Australia, Canada, China, the European Union, India, Japan, the Republic of Korea, Laos, New

Zealand, Papua New Guinea and Russia. According to the 1995 Report, the United States believes that:

> the ARF can play a useful role in conveying governments' intentions, easing tensions, constraining arms races and cultivating habits of consultation and cooperation on security issues. We envision that the ARF will develop over time into an effective region-wide forum for enhancing preventive diplomacy and developing confidence-building measures.

At present there is still no comparable multilateral body in the Northeast Asia sub-region. The United States has supported a series of unofficial dialogs on Northeast Asian security and believes that a separate sub-regional security dialog for Northeast Asia is needed, although to date North Korea has resisted participation.[46]

In the Asia–Pacific region, the US national policy of 'engagement' means reaching beyond its traditional allies and friends to include engagement with China, Russia, Vietnam and even North Korea.

The 1995 Security Strategy declared that 'it is . . . essential for peace, stability and economic growth in the Asia–Pacific region that the People's Republic of *China* is stable and continues to develop friendly relations with its neighbors'. This is true because China's economic, military and political strength are growing.

Although China's per capita GNP is still relatively low, it has one of the largest and fastest growing economies in the world. In 1996 Chinese imports to the United States grew by 17 per cent to a record $39.5 billion, second only to Japan.[47] China is a nuclear weapons state and, according to its own published figures, has doubled its defense spending over the past five years while American, Japanese and Russian defense spending has declined. On the political front, China is a permanent member of the UN Security Council. It has normalized relations with Indonesia, Singapore, Vietnam and the Republic of Korea. China is actively participating in the ASEAN Regional Forum.

For all of these reasons, the United States under President Clinton has put economic engagement with China as its top priority, despite serious misgivings about China's human rights policies. The United States has also attempted to enhance its military dialog with China, in the hope of better understanding China's plans, capabilities and intentions.[48]

The death of Deng Xiaoping on 19 February 1997 marked the end of a critical transitional era in Chinese history. The United

States will remain greatly concerned about and engaged with China as it enters a new era of leadership.

Once the source of the greatest security threat in the Asia–Pacific region, *Russia* is now seen by the United States as a partner in international peace efforts, particularly in connection with Cambodia, North Korea and China. This is true despite Russia's continuing economic and military decline in the Far East.

Twenty years after a bitter war, the United States and *Vietnam* have restored full diplomatic relations. While the United States remains concerned about a full accounting for its personnel Missing in Action in that war and Vietnam's current human rights policies, now that Vietnam is a full ASEAN member (since 1996) economic engagement is seen as the main road towards improving relations with the United States.[49]

After explicating US interests in the region, the 1995 Asia–Pacific Security Strategy reviewed the major longstanding regional security issues to be addressed, given the primary US objective of deterring aggression and preventing the rise of a hegemonic regional power.

North Korea remains a source of unpredictability and potential danger. The combination of North Korea's military strength, uncertain intentions, and potential internal instability due to the death of Kim Il Sung and the dramatic decline of the economy have kept the situation on the Korean peninsula volatile, despite the end of the Cold War.

The situation in *Cambodia* is still not settled even though two decades of war have ended. In addition to serious reconstruction and development challenges, Cambodia is still faced with a continuing, if diminished, Khmer Rouge insurgency, as well as structural weaknesses in its young democracy.

The 1995 Strategy then listed an issue that appears new to many in the US, but is well-known in the region itself: *territorial disputes*. For nearly 45 years, *land*-based territorial disputes such as those between North and South Korea, and between Russia and China, have dominated Western perceptions of Asia–Pacific security issues. Also, disputes between China and India still linger. Now, however, the growing importance of the ocean to Asia's economies has raised the significance of *maritime* territorial disputes, particularly under the regime of the United Nations Convention on the Law of the Sea (UNCLOS), which took effect in 1994 and extended certain jurisdictions to the 200 nautical mile Exclusive Economic Zone (EEZ) and, for Indonesia and the Philippines, to Archipelagic waters.

The most publicized dispute has been among the six claimants (China, Taiwan, Vietnam, the Philippines, Malaysia and Brunei) to all or parts of the *Spratly Islands in the South China Sea*. This dispute is less about the tiny islands themselves than about control over the potentially oil-rich waters that lie around them. The islands also sit astride some of the world's most important shipping lanes. Consequently, the United States has refused to take sides regarding claims to sovereignty, but has stated that 'our strategic interest in maintaining the lines of communication linking Southeast Asia, Northeast Asia and the Indian Ocean make it essential that we resist any maritime claims beyond those permitted by the Law of the Sea Convention'.[50] On 10 May 1995, following a series of incidents involving Chinese and Philippine forces in the Spratlys, the US State Department issued an official policy statement that declared that:

> The United States strongly opposes the use or threat of force to resolve competing claims and urges all claimants to exercise restraint and to avoid destabilizing actions . . . unhindered navigation by all ships and aircraft in the South China Sea is essential for the peace and prosperity of the entire Asia Pacific region, including the United States.[51]

The 1995 Security Strategy only described one other territorial dispute, that between *Russia and Japan* over the four southern Kurile islands, which Japan regards as its *Northern Territories*. However, it included a detailed map indicating the large number of serious disputes currently in existence.

The continuing sovereignty dispute between China and *Taiwan* is included in the Security Strategy's list of serious regional issues. US arms sales to Taiwan are said to serve the end of peace in the Taiwan Strait. Tensions during the March 1996 elections on Taiwan served as a reminder of the continuing salience of this regional dispute.[52]

Combating the spread and use of weapons of mass destruction and ballistic missiles capable of delivering them is the second major US security objective in the Asia–Pacific region, according to the 1995 Security Strategy. The US strategy seeks both to stem the proliferation of such weapons and to develop an effective military capability to deal with these threats.

With regard to nuclear weapons, the United States intends to maintain 'robust strategic nuclear forces' for the purpose of deterrence, and to dissuade regional non-nuclear states from developing such a capability. US anti-proliferation efforts include support of the Nonproliferation (NPT) and Comprehensive Test Ban (CTB) Treaties, and a strengthening of the Nuclear Suppliers Group and the International Atomic Energy Agency (IAEA), along with efforts to control, constrain and reduce the accumulation of fissile materials. The implementation of existing strategic nuclear arms control agreements is also a key element of US policy (see Chapter 4).

Within the region, the most urgent aspect of this issue is North Korea's nuclear weapons development program. On 21 October 1994 the United States and the Democratic People's Republic of Korea (DPRK) signed an Agreed Framework as a first step towards halting and ultimately dismantling North Korea's nuclear weapons program.

The still-controversial agreement calls for North Korea to (1) immediately halt operations of all elements of its graphite-moderated nuclear reactor program under a monitored freeze; (2) comply with its full NPT safeguard obligations; (3) over time dismantle its existing nuclear reactor and additional reactor complexes under construction, its reprocessing plant and other related facilities; and (4) forgo any spent fuel rod reprocessing. In return the DPRK will receive (at the end of ten years) two light-water reactors to generate electricity with far less risk of plutonium diversion. North Korea will also receive heavy fuel oil shipments in the interim to compensate for the shutdown of the existing reactors. In one of the most contentious aspects of the agreement, financing for these reactors will come largely from South Korea, as well as Japan, through an international Korea Energy Development Organization (KEDO) headed by US officials.

According to the 1995 Security Strategy, the Agreed Framework accomplishes four key US objectives: (1) it is a first step towards sustaining overall peace and stability in Northeast Asia; (2) it ensures that the DPRK will not acquire plutonium now contained in spent reactor fuel rods; (3) it brings the DPRK nuclear activity freeze under IAEA supervision, and brings the DPRK into full compliance with its NPT obligations; and (4) the Agreed Framework will result in the dismantling of nuclear facilities that lend themselves to destabilizing proliferation activity.[53] There remains considerable controversy about the adequacy of this framework, and the DPRK's compliance with it (see Chapter 9).

Concerning chemical and biological weapons, the United States is supporting the ratification and entry-in-force on 29 April 1997 of the Chemical Weapons Convention (CWC) in addition to new measures to increase the transparency of, and compliance with, the Biological Weapons Convention (BWC).

The issue of combating ballistic missile proliferation hit home during the 1991 Gulf War when Iraqi Scuds caused serious US military casualties in Saudi Arabia, and inflicted serious civilian casualties in Israel. To stem missile proliferation, the United States urges all countries to adhere to the Missile Technology Control Regime (MTCR) guidelines and is seeking to broaden membership in that regime. In particular, the United States and the People's Republic of China signed a joint statement on 4 October 1994 reaffirming China's original commitment to observe the MTCR restrictions and adding an agreement to ban all exports of ground-to-ground MTCR-class missiles.

At the same time, the United States is developing regional Theater Missile Defense (TMD) systems to play a key role in its strategy. Such a system is said to be 'essential to counter long range ballistic missile delivery systems in the inventory of many East Asian nations'.[54]

The 1995 *United States Security Strategy for the East Asia–Pacific Region* concludes with a brief discussion of the United States' force structure in Asia 'for the rest of the century'.

The *rationale* stated for a continued US forward presence in Asia expands on the earlier EASI statements.

> [US] forward deployed forces in the Pacific ensure a rapid and flexible worldwide crisis response capability; discourage the emergence of a regional hegemony; enhance our ability to influence a wide spectrum of important issues in the region; enable significant economy of force by reducing the number of United States forces required to meet national security objectives; overcome the handicaps of time and distance presented by the vast Pacific Ocean; and demonstrate to our friends, allies and potential enemies alike a tangible indication of the United States' interest in the security of the entire region.[55]

Two elements of the 1995 rationale stand out. First, given the end of the Cold War, the lead role cited for US Asia–Pacific forces is participation in a *worldwide* crisis response capability. This became apparent during the 1991 Gulf War in three ways: (1) US forces deployed in the Asia–Pacific region maintained deterrence there, allowing forces from Hawaii, California and elsewhere to deploy in the Middle East; (2) US bases and allied bases in the region facilitated the transit of some personnel, ships and aircraft to the Middle East; and (3) US Asia–Pacific allies provided combat troops (Australia), naval forces, and financial and other resource assistance (Japan and South Korea).

Second, the Security Strategy notes that US forward-deployed Asia–Pacific forces actually *reduce* the number of overall US forces required to meet national security objectives. In an increasingly budget-constrained environment, this is an important claim. The 1995 Security Strategy highlights that this is true because of the cost-sharing program with its Asia–Pacific allies (primarily Japan), making it 'actually less expensive to the American taxpayer to maintain our forces forward deployed than in the United States'.[56]

The 1995 Security Strategy then reiterates the oft-stated US commitment to maintaining a *forward-deployed force structure* that 'requires approximately 100 000 personnel'. The major elements of this force are also unchanged: (1) in South Korea, a US Army division with support elements, plus a US Air Force combat wing, with earlier planned further reductions indefinitely halted, pending developments in North Korea; and (2) in Japan, a Marine Expeditionary Force, an aircraft carrier battle group, an amphibious ready group and another Air Force combat wing. Afloat, the US Seventh Fleet remains on station in the Western Pacific.[57]

Following the withdrawal of US forces from the Philippines, the 1995 Strategy highlights the growing value of 'access' to a variety of national bases and maintenance facilities in Southeast Asia. Formal *access agreements*, such as that with Singapore, enable rotational US force deployments to the region. Informal/occasional arrangements facilitate exercises and training, ship and aircraft transits, visits and maintenance.

Myriad other forms of military engagement characterize the US presence in the region, ranging from joint exercises to conferences. The US-sponsored International Military Education and Training program (IMET) is said to be 'an essential element of our regional strategy'.[58]

The 1995 *United States Security Strategy for the Asia–Pacific Region* ends with the following statement: 'There can be no doubt that the United States will remain a Pacific power in the Twenty-first Century'.[59] As to how the overall global military power of the United States will be employed in the coming years, the US Joint Chiefs of Staff National Military Strategy of February 1995 is revealing.

THE 1995 *NATIONAL MILITARY STRATEGY OF THE UNITED STATES*

The 1995 US National Military Strategy was derived from the President's National Security Strategy and the defense framework outlined in the *Bottom-Up Review*. In his preface, the Chairman of the Joint Chiefs, General Shalikashvili, stated:

> The fundamental purpose of the Armed Forces must remain to fight and win our nation's wars whenever and wherever called upon . . . The challenge of the new strategic era is to selectively use the vast and unique capabilities of the Armed Forces [of the US] to advance national interests in peacetime while maintaining readiness to fight and win when called upon.[60]

US *national military objectives* are said to be twofold: (1) to promote stability, through regional cooperation and constructive interaction, and (2) to thwart aggression, through credible deterrence and robust warfighting capabilities.

According to the 1995 National Military Strategy, regional instability in military, economic and political terms can escalate into a global conflict that directly threatens US interests. Stability, on the other hand, establishes conditions under which democracy and free-market economies can take hold and expand, and therefore long-term stability is advantageous to the United States.

The most serious measure of US engagement is its commitment to protect its extended interests and its allies. This commitment is intended to prevent conflict if possible, but to defeat aggression if necessary. It is interesting to note that the 1995 National Military Strategy lists the Persian Gulf and Northeast Asia as two regions where a threat clearly exists.[61] This Strategy confirms the 'win two nearly simultaneous major regional conflicts' requirement laid out in the 1993 *Bottom-Up Review*.

Two fundamental and complementary *strategic concepts* are said to lie at the heart of the US National Military Strategy: (1) overseas presence; and (2) power projection.

The United States has global interests. Because it is girded on the east and west by the Atlantic and Pacific oceans, some 'overseas' military presence is necessary to defend those interests, according to the 1995 Strategy. US overseas presence forces promote stability and prevent conflict by having the capability of rapidly responding to a wide range of threats throughout the world, and by providing a visible proof of a US commitment to defend its interests and allies worldwide. In addition, a US overseas presence 'helps to keep important infrastructure available and ready. Permanently stationed forces maintain support and basing that are vital for receiving reinforcement . . . in time of crisis and conflict'.

The National Military Strategy notes that in recent years the size of the US overseas presence has decreased, even 'dramatically' in Europe, although to a lesser degree in the Asia–Pacific region.

For that reason, the United States must 'increase' its capability to project forces abroad from US territory. This in turn 'depends on four strategic mobility enhancements: increased airlift capability, additional pre-positioning of heavy equipment afloat and ashore, increased surge capacity of our sealift, and improved readiness of the Ready Reserve Force'. The most critical tasks of power projection capability are deterrence, conflict prevention and warfighting.[62]

The three *components of the US National Military Strategy* are enumerated as: (1) peacetime engagement; (2) deterrence and conflict prevention; and (3) fight and win.

'*Peacetime engagement*' describes a broad range of non-combat activities undertaken by tens of thousands of US armed forces personnel worldwide on any given day. These activities include, but are not limited to, military-to-military contacts, nation assistance to combat lawlessness, subversion and insurgency, security assistance to furnish allies and friends with the means to defend themselves from aggression, humanitarian and disaster relief operations, counterdrug and counterterrorism operations, and traditional 'peacekeeping' operations.

The second component of the US National Military Strategy is '*deterrence and conflict prevention*'. It envisions 'vigorous efforts' in the following tasks: nuclear deterrence, participating in regional alliances, crisis response, arms control and confidence-building measures, non-combatant evacuation operations, sanctions enforcement and peace enforcement.[63]

Despite the end of the Cold War, the 1995 Strategy declares that 'the highest priority of our military strategy is to deter a nuclear attack against our Nation and allies'. In 1994 the US Department of Defense had conducted a comprehensive *Nuclear Posture Review* to determine the nuclear systems needed to achieve this objective for the foreseeable future. It concluded that, although further reductions under the Strategic Arms Reduction Treaties (START) were desirable, the United States still needed to maintain a survivable 'triad' of strategic nuclear delivery systems. 'Deployable nonstrategic nuclear weapons' were also described as 'still needed' in the mix 'to provide deterrent coverage over our allies, and because extended deterrence . . . is a decisive factor in our nonproliferation efforts'.[64]

US regional defense strategies, according to the 1995 Strategy Statement, are built on the foundation of strong and effective regional alliances. Those alliances must be both preserved and adapted to new challenges.

It is noted that five of the seven US mutual defense treaties are with partners in the Asia–Pacific region, 'helping to underpin the stability of an area that is home to the world's fastest growing economies'. ASEAN, with its Regional Forum (ARF), is prominently mentioned as a group with which the United States 'will remain engaged'.

The bilateral security relationship with Japan 'remains fundamental to US security'. The defense of South Korea 'will remain a key element of US strategy in this region'. In addition to the US forces permanently based in those two countries, vigorous military exercise programs represent 'an unambiguous demonstration' of US commitment to the region.[65]

With regard to crisis response, the United States will 'respond initially to crises using our forces stationed and deployed overseas', but will employ power projection forces from the United States if necessary, as has occurred in the Persian Gulf region since the 1991 war ended.[66]

Efforts to achieve arms control and to implement confidence-building measures are said to limit and reduce the number and type of weapons that can threaten US forces, reduce regional arms buildups that can raise tensions and risks, and foster openness and transparency in military affairs. For those reasons US military forces will continue to be directly involved in such efforts, according to the 1995 National Military Strategy.

It should be noted that the Asia–Pacific region does not have nearly as extensive a history of formal arms control treaties and confidence-building measures as Europe. Moreover, because of the maritime nature of the Asia–Pacific region and US opposition to 'naval arms control' which would focus constraints on the United States' most flexible regional military capabilities, the United States had been reluctant to emphasize arms control in the Asia–Pacific region, especially during the Cold War. More recently, the United States has become more receptive to the possibility of regional confidence-building measures, both on the Korean peninsula and, at least in terms of greater cooperation, at sea (see Chapter 9).

'Noncombatant Evacuation' refers to the US government's commitment to protecting the lives and safety of its citizens abroad. When necessary, US armed forces 'will use all appropriate means to extract American citizens promptly and safely'.

Enforcement of economic sanctions and participation in peace enforcement operations resulting from national policy decisions and UN Security Council resolutions round out the non-combat aspects of the employment of US armed forces. Early post–Cold War experience (particularly in Somalia) has led the United States to set very strict guidelines concerning such operations. They require the United States to:

- Commit sufficient forces to achieve clearly defined objectives.
- Plan to achieve those objectives decisively.
- Reassess, and adjust, as necessary, the size, composition and disposition of their forces to achieve their objectives.

Moreover, the 1995 National Military Strategy emphasizes the critical importance of command and control arrangements when it declares that 'the greater the US military contribution and the greater the likelihood of combat, the more inclined we will be to lead the operation. The President, however, will never relinquish command authority over US forces'.[67]

The third and final component of the US National Military Strategy is titled *'fight and win'*. This capability is the foremost responsibility and prime consideration governing all US military activities.

The use of American military forces in combat is to follow a clear set of principles. First, the defining of *clear military objectives* and the *application of decisive force* will characterize any application of force by the United States, according to the Strategy. This principle stems in part from the US experience in the Vietnam War.

Second, while forward-deployed American forces will assist regional allies in rapidly halting an invasion and forming the basis for a subsequent buildup, the United States anticipates that for the most part in wartime, *power projection of major air, land and sea forces from the US and other overseas areas* will either augment those forward deployed forces, or establish a US presence in their absence. Such an effort requires detailed deliberate plans for reinforcement, building on the experience gained in Operation Desert Storm during the Persian Gulf War.

Third, US armed forces will *'fight combined and fight joint'*. At a tactical level, the United States will maintain a unilateral capability to wage decisive campaigns, as it did in Grenada in 1983 and in Panama in 1989, for example. However, the 1995 Strategy statement acknowledges that 'our Armed Forces will most often fight in concert with regional allies and friends, as coalitions can decisively increase combat power and lead to a more rapid and favorable outcome to the conflict'. This type of military engagement with allies or friendly nations in coalition is termed *'combined* operations'.[68]

Whether American troops are operating as part of such an international coalition or unilaterally, 'modern warfare requires US forces to fight as a *joint* team'. In other words, the unique—and complementary—capabilities of each of the US military services, land, sea and air, will be brought to bear at the right times and places, under a unified command. Joint warfighting requires the balanced contribution of *all* the armed services.

For reasons of organization and focus the individual services are covered in separate chapters later in this book, but this joint warfighting principle is now central to the US National Military Strategy. The Strategy also highlights the increasingly important role that space capabilities play in conducting joint warfare, especially in facilitating effective command and control.

Fourth, special emphasis is also given to the 'remarkable leverage' that is now attainable from high technology reconnaissance, intelligence gathering and analysis, and high-speed data processing and transmission. These systems enable US forces to *'win the Information War'* and thereby 'dominate' the battlefield. Here too the US experience in Operation Desert Storm is cited as a source for developing new doctrine, training and control programs.[69]

The fifth principle entails *'countering weapons of mass destruction'*. The 1995 National Military Strategy points out that in the event that weapons of mass destruction were employed against American and allied forces, the United States would employ its own conventional and, if needed, nuclear capability to 'dominate any escalation of conflict'. In addition, defensive measures against such weapons are being maintained and strengthened.

It is interesting to observe that the *'two major regional contingency focus'* is listed as the sixth principle in the 1995 National Military Strategy—rather different from the prominent place it occupied in other earlier documents. As the Joint Chiefs describe it, this principle means that should a second major contingency arise while a decisive victory is still being ensured in a first conflict,

> we will be enhancing the readiness of other assets to handle a challenge elsewhere. Some high-leverage capabilities could be used in one major regional contingency and then reallocated and redeployed to another as conditions permit. Other capabilities essential to fighting and winning the first conflict will remain in the theater where they are committed.[70]

'Force generation' is the seventh principle. The United States will quickly generate combat power in wartime by: (1) recalling, reorganizing, retraining and redeploying active forces engaged overseas in lower priority missions (e.g. peacekeeping/peace enforcement); (2) turning over activities not involving critical US interests to the United Nations or other responsible regional security organizations; and (3) mobilizing and committing reserve forces to combat and combat support missions 'early in any major regional contingency'.

Finally, in order to *'win the peace'*, the United States will begin planning for post-conflict operations prior to and continuing throughout any conflict. This will enable US forces to meet numerous demands to attend to the needs of the indigenous population in a conflict zone, and then transfer those functions to non-military organizations while being redeployed following a war.[71]

In its description of *US Military Capabilities*, the 1995 National Military Strategy endorsed the *force posture and size* called for by the 1993 *Bottom-Up Review*. It went on to enumerate five *fundamental force building foundations*.

First and foremost of these foundations are *high-quality people* to make up the US armed forces, as again demonstrated by the experience of Operation Desert Storm. 'In a smaller force with diverse requirements,' the statement declares, 'quality people provide the fundamental edge over any adversary'.

Second, given the unpredictability of regional crises and the speed with which they can escalate, US forces must maintain a high degree and wide range of *readiness*. 'They must be ready to fight today.' Whereas in the past traditional measures of readiness were defined in service-specific terms, today the United States is strengthening joint and combined doctrine, measures of joint readiness, and joint training and exercises.

The third foundation consists of the *enhancements* of the US armed forces that are being implemented according to the 1995 National Military Strategy, including an upgrading of: (1) strategic mobility (airlift, sealift and prepositioning); (2) battlefield surveillance; (3) communications architecture; and (4) firepower.[72]

Modernization is the fourth foundation, and the one that is held to 'preserve the essential combat edge that US forces now possess'. Through a program called 'recapitalization' the US armed forces are consciously retiring certain weapons systems and platforms, and closing unnecessary bases in the United States, in order to afford the procurement of more capable and modern equipment. This is clearly an attempt to come to terms with 'a more constrained budget' compared with the Cold War era.

The fifth and final foundation is *balance*. According to the 1995 National Military Strategy, 'despite its smaller size [US] Armed Forces must retain an appropriate mix of forces and capabilities to provide versatility and a hedge against the unknown'. Balance is necessary in several categories: (1) combat and capable support forces; (2) active duty and Reserve capabilities; and (3) force structure and infrastructure (bases).[73]

In its conclusion, the 1995 National Military Strategy of the United States described itself as continuing 'the evolution from the strategies developed during the Cold War'. This strategy of 'flexible and selective global engagement'—and the force structure necessary to implement it—was seen as appropriate to protecting the nation's security worldwide, including the increasingly important Asia–Pacific region.

THE 1997 *QUADRENNIAL DEFENSE REVIEW*

By late 1996, following President Clinton's re-election, it had become apparent that continuing changes in both the international environment and in domestic US politics, especially fiscal realities, were leading to yet another stage in the post–Cold War evolution of US security and military strategy and the armed forces meant to implement them. On 12 December 1996, in response to a mandate of Congress earlier that year, the US Department of Defense announced that it had begun a new large-scale review of long-term strategies and forces. Coming four years after the *Bottom-Up Review*, this new study is called the *Quadrennial Defense Review* (QDR). The QDR was released in May 1997, along with *A National Security Strategy for a New Century* from the White House.

The 1997 *National Security Strategy for a New Century* outlined three threats to US interests: (1) Regional or State-centered Threats; (2) Transnational Threats (such as terrorism); and (3) Threats from Weapons of Mass Destruction. It then proposed a threefold 'integrated approach' to defeating these threats: (1) *Shaping the International Environment* in ways favorable to US interests and global security; (2) *Responding to the Full Spectrum of Crises* that may arise; and (3) *Preparing Now for an Uncertain Future*. The third and last element opened up the overarching question of the longer-term future of US National Security.[74]

The QDR assesses *every* aspect of US armed forces—within the context of the 1997 *National Security Strategy*, and within the context of a US fiscally-constrained defense budget that apparently will not exceed about $250 billion per year (plus inflation) for the foreseeable future.

The QDR follows the lead of the 1997 *National Security Strategy* by describing in broad terms a corollary Defense Strategy of 'Shaping, Responding, and Preparing for the Future'. In the main, the QDR's Defense Strategy reiterates the main tenets of US defense strategy since 1995 as outlined above. However, it does include some new emphases and terminology that are important to understanding the direction of that strategy.

With regard to the 'high end' of military involvement, the QDR replaces the term 'major regional conflict' (MRC) with 'major theater war' (MTW), while insisting that the United States must retain the 'core capability . . . to deter and defeat large-scale, cross-border aggression in two distant theaters in overlapping time frames, preferably in concert with regional allies'. Concerning the conduct of major theater warfare, the QDR notes that 'in the face of overwhelming US conventional dominance' potential future adversaries are likely to resort to 'asymmetric means' of warfare including, but not limited to, NBC (nuclear, biological, chemical) weapons, information warfare and terrorism, and that 'US forces must plan and prepare to fight and win major theater wars under such conditions'.[75]

As a result of recent experience and intelligence projections, the QDR puts new emphasis on the response of US military forces to 'smaller-scale contingency (SSC) operations' which are defined as 'joint military operations beyond peacetime engagement activities but short of major theater warfare' including 'show-of force operations, interventions, limited strikes, noncombatant evacuation operations, no-fly zone enforcement, peace enforcement, maritime sanctions enforcement, counterterrorism operations, peacekeeping, humanitarian assistance, and disaster relief'.⁷⁶ The QDR notes that the demand for US participation in SSCs is expected to remain high over the next 15 to 20 years, and that careful management will be necessary to prevent excess stress on US forces.

In addressing the force structure required to implement US defense strategy, the QDR reiterates the US commitment to 'maintaining a substantial overseas presence posture' without offering any details. However, the document puts more emphasis on US global power projection capabilities 'to shape, deter, and respond even when we have no permanent presence or a limited infrastructure in a region'.⁷⁷ In terms of actual force size, the QDR outlined further modest reductions, including:

- The US Army would be reduced by some 15 000 active duty personnel, but retain ten active, combat-ready divisions. The Army's Reserve component would be reduced by some 45 000 personnel.
- The US Navy would reduce the number of surface combatants from 128 to 116, but retain 12 carrier battle groups and 12 amphibious ready groups.
- The US Air Force would shift one active component fighter wing to the Reserve component, and reduce its personnel by approximately 27 000.
- In overall terms the total active duty end strength of US military forces would be reduced to 1 360 000 (down 36 per cent from 1989), with 835 000 in the Reserve forces (down 29 per cent from 1989). Civilian personnel would decline to 640 000 (down 42 per cent from 1989).⁷⁸

Further details on the QDR force structure decisions are discussed in the individual service chapters.

By far the most significant—and controversial—contribution of the QDR is its estimate of how to address the issue of 'Preparing Now for an Uncertain Future'. The QDR states that the task of 'transforming' the US Department of Defense for the future has 'four main parts':

- Pursue a focused modernization effort in order to replace aging systems and incorporate cutting-edge technologies into the force to ensure continued US military superiority over time;
- Continue to exploit the 'Revolution in Military Affairs' (RMA) in order to improve the US military's ability to perform near-term missions and meet future challenges;

- Exploit the 'Revolution in Business Affairs' (RBA) to radically re-engineer DOD infrastructure and support activities;
- Insure or hedge against unlikely but significant future threats (so-called 'wild cards') in order to manage risk in a resource-constrained environment.[79]

The QDR was not to be the final word. On 6 February 1997 Secretary of Defense William S. Cohen announced the appointment of a National Defense Panel (NDP) of experts to review and make recommendations on the QDR by 15 December 1997, including an independent assessment of a variety of possible force structures for the US armed forces through the year 2010 and beyond.[80] In its initial assessment of the QDR's strategy section on 20 May 1997, the NDP praised the Review's 'much richer view of the challenges facing DOD in asymmetric warfare and Smaller Scale Contingencies', but went on to state that in the QDR 'there is insufficient connectivity between strategy on the one hand, and force structure, operational concepts, and procurement decisions on the other'—an important shortcoming in an era characterized by 'an even greater array of challenges than we faced in the past' and 'even fewer resources than were available four years ago'.[81]

In its final report in December 1997, the NDP elaborated its criticisms of the QDR—and in large measure the Department of Defense rejected them at least in the short term, leaving open the question of how deep and how rapid the 'transformation' of US defense forces will be. This critical question runs through the entire discussion of US defense strategy, policy and forces on the verge of the 21st century. The Joint Chiefs of Staff 'conceptual template' for joint operations and warfighting in the future is discussed in the next chapter on command and control. The broader topic of the mid- and long-term future of the US armed forces, especially in the Asia–Pacific region, is the subject of Chapter 9.

Finally, in September 1997 the Joint Chiefs of Staff released a new version of the National Military Strategy of the United States (NMS) reflecting the new National Security Strategy and the QDR's Defense Strategy. Subtitled 'Shape, Respond, Prepare Now: A Military Strategy for a New Era', the 1997 NMS declared two *ends* or US National Military Objectives: (1) promote stability; and (2) defeat adversaries. The document is careful to point out that promoting stability 'does not imply a resistance to change; rather it underscores a desire for peaceful change'. Concerning adversaries, the 1997 NMS, taking its lead from the QDR, puts new emphasis on 'asymmetric challenges' which include 'unconventional or inexpensive approaches that circumvent our strengths, exploit our vulnerabilities, or confront us in ways we cannot match in kind'.[82]

In terms of *ways* to implement the strategy, the 1997 NMS lists four 'strategic concepts':

- *Strategic agility*, the timely concentration, employment, and sustainment of US military power anywhere at our own initiative, at a speed which our adversaries cannot match;
- *Overseas presence*, the visible posture of US forces and infrastructure strategically positioned forward in or near key regions;
- *Power projection*, the ability to rapidly and effectively deploy and sustain US forces in and from multiple dispersed locations;
- *Decisive force*, the commitment of sufficient military power to overwhelm all armed resistance in order to establish new military conditions and achieve political objectives.[83]

Concerning the *means* to implement these strategic concepts, the 1997 NMS simply repeats the force structure called for by the QDR, as briefly outlined above and presented in more detail in later chapters.

With regard to 'preparing for the future', the 1997 NMS calls for a 'balanced evolution' of US armed forces, with the rationale that the fundamental challenge facing the United States is 'to shape and respond in the current and near-term security environment, while we concurrently prepare for the future'.[84] Whether such a 'balanced evolution' is feasible and even desirable lies at the heart of the ongoing debate over the future development of US defense strategy and force structure.

3

National command and control and US Pacific Command

The tradition of civilian control of military forces—and of non-involvement of the military in civilian government—is a deep and abiding one in the history of the United States of America. This tradition is embodied in the numerous governmental organizations and agencies responsible for the planning and execution of military operations. This chapter briefly reviews their history, organizational structure and command relationships, with emphasis on US forces in the Asia–Pacific region.

NATIONAL COMMAND AUTHORITIES

The system of 'checks and balances' spelled out in the United States Constitution divided governmental power into three branches: the executive, legislative and judicial. With regard to command and control of military forces, Article One on the legislative branch of government states in Section Seven that Congress has the right:

> To declare War, grant Letters of Marque and Reprisal, and make Rules concerning captures on Land and Water;
> To raise and support Armies, but no Appropriation of Money to that Use shall be for a longer term than two Years;
> To provide and maintain a Navy;
> To make Rules for the Government and Regulation of the land and Naval forces . . .[1]

In that same document, Article Two on the executive branch states, in Section Two, that: 'The President shall be Commander in Chief of the Army and Navy of the United States, and of the Militia of the several States, when called into actual Service of the United States . . .'[2]

During the more than two centuries of United States history, the changing nature of war in the modern age has resulted in the consolidation and expansion of the powers of the President as Commander in Chief of the US armed forces, and a relative decline in the powers of Congress with regard to influence over military operations. The stated need for rapid, decisive and often secret action on the part of US armed forces has been the main argument in favor of this development. Thus, for example, the US Congress has not 'declared war' since the beginning of official US participation on the side of the Allies in World War II in December of 1941, although US armed forces have been engaged in three major conflicts—two of them in the Asia–Pacific region—since then.

Following the bitter experience of the war in Vietnam, the US Congress attempted to reassert some of its role with the passage in 1973 of the War Powers Resolution, over President Richard Nixon's veto. That Resolution attempts to require the President to report fully to Congress upon the introduction of US troops into foreign hostilities, to specify a maximum time limitation on the involvement in hostilities in the absence of affirmative congressional action, and to provide a means for Congress to require an end to hostilities in advance of the time set.[3]

However, to date all US Presidents operating under the Resolution have considered it to be an unconstitutional infringement on presidential powers, and even when fulfilling its reporting requirements they have denied the legal necessity to do so.[4] Thus, for example, upon Iraq's invasion of Kuwait in 1990 President Bush did not at first seek US congressional authorization for the use of US troops. Instead, he sought a United Nations Security Council Resolution authorizing the use of force by member nations. Although President Bush did at the last minute seek and receive congressional approval for the counterattack on Iraqi forces, he denied the legal need to do so.[5]

In other words, although the US Congress retains control over the appropriation of funds to support the US armed forces, the actual command and control of US armed forces has resided and continues to reside in the 'National Command Authorities' (NCA). That term is used to signify constitutional authority to direct the US armed forces in their execution of military action. Specifically, NCA refers to the President of the United States and, since the passage of the National Security Act of 1947, the civilian Secretary of Defense, together with their duly deputized alternates or successors.

The US Constitution and its 20th and 25th Amendments, along with the Presidential Succession Act of 1886 and subsequent additions, contain the following order of succession in the event of the death or incapacitation of the President:

Vice-President
Speaker of the House
President *pro tempore* of the Senate
Secretary of State
Secretary of the Treasury
Secretary of Defense
Attorney-General
Secretary of the Interior
Secretary of Agriculture
Secretary of Commerce
Secretary of Labor
Secretary of Health and Human Services
Secretary of Housing and Urban Development
Secretary of Transportation
Secretary of Energy
Secretary of Education
Secretary of Veterans' Affairs

This lengthy succession chain attempts to ensure that the Commander in Chief of US Armed Forces, the acting President, will be a civilian even under the worst-case scenario of nuclear war or some equivalent disaster.

Following World War II, the entire US military establishment was reorganized. The monumental National Security Act of 1947 named the Secretary of Defense as the President's principal assistant in all matters relating to the Department of Defense. By law, both inter-theater movement of troops and execution of military action must be directed by the President and the Secretary of Defense or their duly authorized alternates or successors. No one else in the chain of command has the authority to take such action.[6]

The National Security Act of 1947 also established the National Security Council (NSC) as an advisory body to consider national security issues that require Presidential decision. The President calls the meetings. The NSC has four statutory members: the President, Vice-President, Secretary of State and Secretary of Defense. The military Chairman of the Joint Chiefs of Staff and the Director of the Central Intelligence Agency (CIA) serve

Figure 3.1 Office of the Secretary of Defense

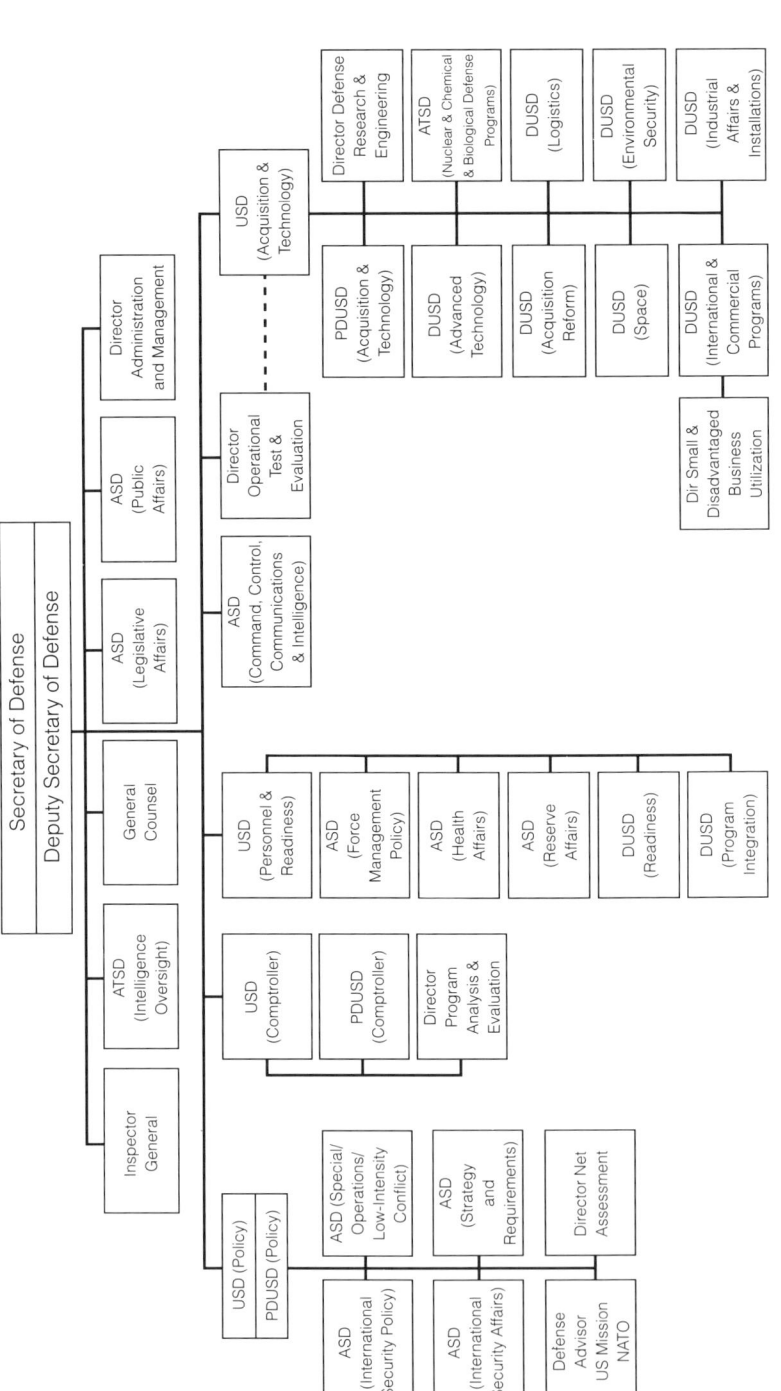

Source: Department of Defense

as statutory advisers to the NSC. The appointed Assistant to the President for National Security Affairs and staff assist the NSC.

Significant changes in the national chain of command and control occurred in 1986, when the US Congress passed the Goldwater-Nichols Department of Defense Reorganization Act. This Act clarified the command line to US combatant commanders and further refined civilian control of the military. The Act states that the operational chain of command runs from the President to the Secretary of Defense and then directly to the combatant commanders.[7]

The Secretary of Defense is a civilian appointed by the President, subject to the approval of the US Senate. As the second person in the legal chain of command, the Secretary of Defense is the principal defense policy adviser to the President and is responsible for the formulation of general defense policy and policy related to all matters of direct concern to the US national military establishment, the Department of Defense (DOD). The Secretary of Defense has nearly full authority, direction and control of the entire department, with the help of the many staff organizations included in the Office of the Secretary of Defense (OSD), as illustrated in the organization chart in Figure 3.1.

This is an enormous responsibility, given the size and complexity of the Department of Defense, with its major service departments, other defense agencies and field activities. The DOD organizational chart in Figure 3.2 gives some idea of the scope of the responsibility.

THE COMBATANT COMMANDS

The legal chain of command of the US armed forces extends from the President to the Secretary of Defense, and then directly to the Commanders-in-Chief (CINCs) of US 'Unified Combatant Commands'. As first described by statute in the 1947 National Security Act and later updated by Goldwater-Nichols, Unified Combatant Commands are composed of forces from two or more armed services, have a broad and continuing mission, and are normally, but not entirely, organized on a geographic basis. Their number is not fixed by law or regulation and may vary from time to time.

As of 1998 the US Unified Combatant Commands and their headquarters are as follows:
- US Pacific Command, Honolulu, Hawaii
- US European Command, Stuttgart-Vaihingen, Germany

Figure 3.2 Department of Defense

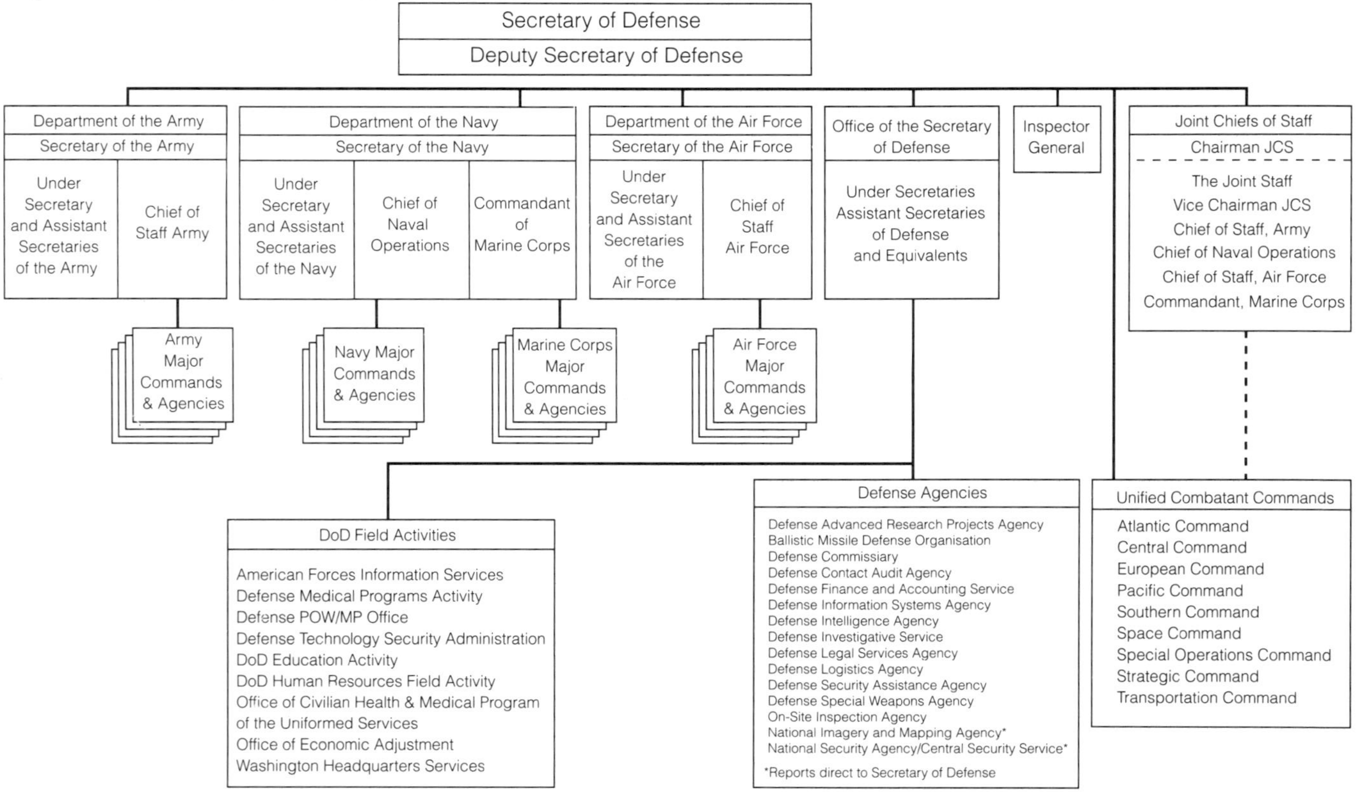

Secretary of Defense
Deputy Secretary of Defense

Department of the Army
- Secretary of the Army
- Under Secretary and Assistant Secretaries of the Army
- Chief of Staff Army
- Army Major Commands & Agencies

Department of the Navy
- Secretary of the Navy
- Under Secretary and Assistant Secretaries of the Navy
- Chief of Naval Operations
- Commandant of Marine Corps
- Navy Major Commands & Agencies
- Marine Corps Major Commands & Agencies

Department of the Air Force
- Secretary of the Air Force
- Under Secretary and Assistant Secretaries of the Air Force
- Chief of Staff Air Force
- Air Force Major Commands & Agencies

Office of the Secretary of Defense
- Under Secretaries Assistant Secretaries of Defense and Equivalents

Inspector General

Joint Chiefs of Staff
- Chairman JCS
- The Joint Staff
- Vice Chairman JCS
- Chief of Staff, Army
- Chief of Naval Operations
- Chief of Staff, Air Force
- Commandant, Marine Corps

Unified Combatant Commands
- Atlantic Command
- Central Command
- European Command
- Pacific Command
- Southern Command
- Space Command
- Special Operations Command
- Strategic Command
- Transportation Command

DoD Field Activities
- American Forces Information Services
- Defense Medical Programs Activity
- Defense POW/MP Office
- Defense Technology Security Administration
- DoD Education Activity
- DoD Human Resources Field Activity
- Office of Civilian Health & Medical Program of the Uniformed Services
- Office of Economic Adjustment
- Washington Headquarters Services

Defense Agencies
- Defense Advanced Research Projects Agency
- Ballistic Missile Defense Organisation
- Defense Commissary
- Defense Contact Audit Agency
- Defense Finance and Accounting Service
- Defense Information Systems Agency
- Defense Intelligence Agency
- Defense Investigative Service
- Defense Legal Services Agency
- Defense Logistics Agency
- Defense Security Assistance Agency
- Defense Special Weapons Agency
- On-Site Inspection Agency
- National Imagery and Mapping Agency*
- National Security Agency/Central Security Service*

*Reports direct to Secretary of Defense

Source: Department of Defense

Figure 3.3 Unified Combatant Commands

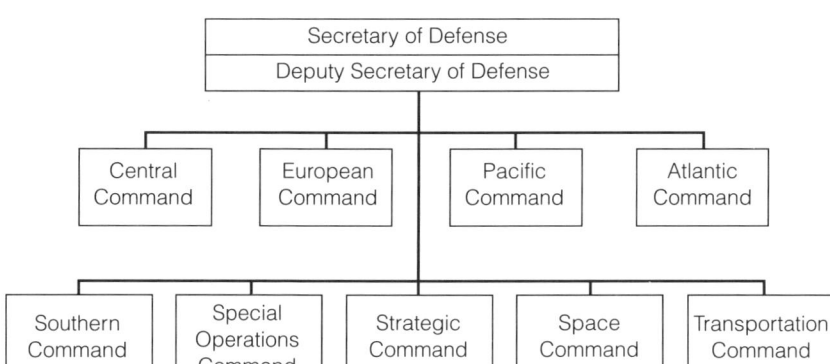

Source: Department of Defense

- US Atlantic Command, Norfolk, Virginia
- US Southern Command, Miami, Florida
- US Central Command, MacDill Air Force Base, Florida
- US Space Command, Peterson Air Force Base, Colorado
- US Special Operations Command, MacDill Air Force Base, Florida
- US Transportation Command, Scott Air Force Base, Illinois
- US Strategic Command, Offutt Air Force Base, Nebraska.[8]

The legal operational chain of command of the US armed forces is displayed in Figure 3.3.

THE ROLE OF THE JOINT CHIEFS OF STAFF

As currently constituted, the Joint Chiefs of Staff (JCS) of the US armed forces consist of the Chairman, the Vice-Chairman, the Chief of Staff of the Army, the Chief of Naval Operations, the Chief of Staff of the Air Force and the Commandant of the Marine Corps, assisted by a Joint Staff of over 200 officers from all the services (see Figure 3.4).

Under the Goldwater-Nichols DOD Reorganization Act of 1986, the Joint Chiefs of Staff have no executive authority to command combatant forces. However, the Act permits the President to direct that communications with Combatant Commanders pass through the Chairman of the Joint Chiefs of Staff (CJCS), and by current Presidential directive that is the case. Thus the

Figure 3.4 Joint Chiefs of Staff

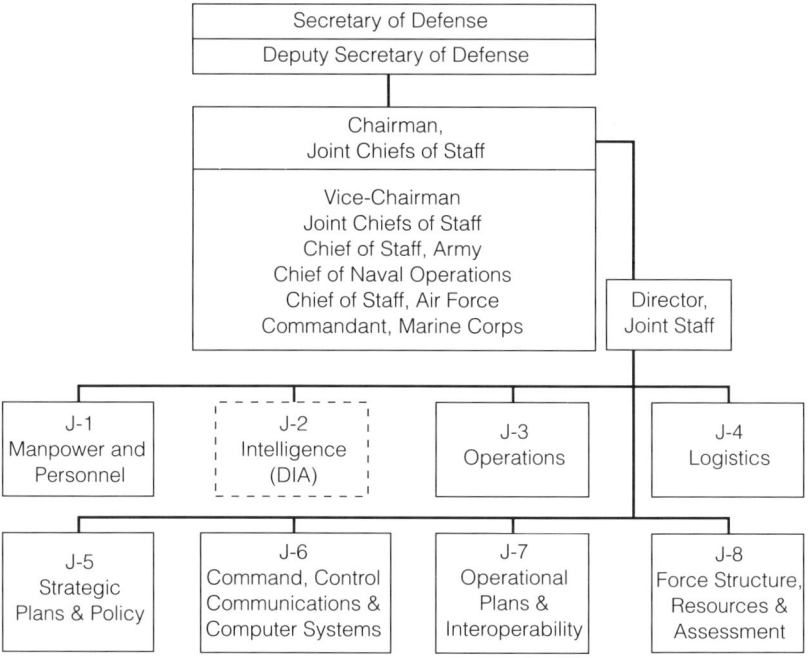

Source: Department of Defense

CJCS is in the communications chain, but not in operational command.[9]

In addition, the Goldwater-Nichols Act identifies the Chairman of the Joint Chiefs of Staff as the senior ranking member of the armed forces. As such, the CJCS is the principal military adviser to the President, the Secretary of Defense and the National Security Council. The CJCS is appointed by the President, and must be confirmed by the Senate. By law, all members of the Joint Chiefs of Staff are official military advisers and they may respond to a request, or voluntarily submit, through the Chairman, advice or opinions to the National Command Authorities.[10] In that capacity, in 1996 the Chairman and the Joint Chiefs produced a document entitled *Joint Vision 2010*.

JOINT VISION 2010

Joint Vision 2010 is described as 'an operationally based template for the evolution of the Armed Forces for a challenging and uncertain future' which is meant to become 'a benchmark for Service and Unified Command visions'.[11] The document focuses on the US armed forces 'achieving dominance across the range of military operations through the application of new operational concepts'.[12]

Joint Vision 2010 goes on to develop four central operational concepts: dominant maneuver, precision engagement, full dimensional protection and focused logistics.

'Dominant maneuver' is defined as 'the multidimensional application of information, engagement, and mobility capabilities to position and employ widely dispersed joint air, land, sea and space forces to accomplish the assigned operational task'. This will require 'forces that are adept at conducting sustained and synchronized operations from dispersed locations'.[13]

'Precision engagement' consists of 'a system of systems that enables our forces to locate the objective or target, provide responsive command and control, generate the desired effect, assess our level of success, and retain the flexibility to reengage with precision when required'.[14] As articulated by the then Vice-Chairman of the Joint Chiefs, Admiral William A. Owens, this 'system of systems' will consist of 'a system of intelligence, targeting systems, battle-damage-assessment systems, and stand-off weapons that can destroy targets quickly and precisely without exposing our forces to danger'. The effectiveness of such a system would rest on the capacity of the US armed forces to develop 'omniscience and synergistic integration'.[15]

According to the Joint Chiefs, 'the primary prerequisite for full-dimensional protection will be control of the battlespace to ensure our forces can maintain freedom of action during deployment, maneuver and engagement, while providing multi-layered defenses for our forces and facilities at all levels'. This protection will be 'pro-active', not merely reactive, and will depend on information superiority. Both active and passive measures will be combined 'to provide a more seamless joint architecture for force protection, which will leverage the contributions of individual Services, systems, and echelons'.[16]

'Focused logistics' is described as 'the fusion of information, logistics, and transportation technologies to provide rapid crisis response, to track and shift assets even while enroute, and to deliver tailored logistics packages and sustainment directly at the strategic, operational, and tactical level of operations'.[17] Here, too, new information technologies are central to improved capabilities.

This vision, if properly implemented, will, according to the

Joint Chiefs, enable the US armed forces 'to dominate the full range of military operations from humanitarian assistance, through peace operations, and up to the highest intensity conflict'—in other words, to achieve 'full spectrum dominance'.[18]

As important as these operational concepts and their ultimate goal are, the Joint Chiefs recognized that in an environment of declining or flat defense budgets, smaller forces and fewer forces stationed overseas, the US armed forces will need to 'wring every ounce of capability from every available source'—and that can only be accomplished through a more seamless integration of individual service capabilities. They state that '[t]o achieve this integration while conducting military operations we must be *fully joint*: institutionally, organizationally, intellectually, and technically'.[19] Simply put, 'jointness' is now an *imperative* in the overarching vision of the future of the US armed forces. This fact must not be lost sight of when individual US services, commands or forces are, for reasons of organization, described in separate chapters in the remainder of this book. *Joint Vision 2010* goes on to say that 'jointness' is not enough. US armed forces must 'find the most effective methods for integrating and improving interoperability with allied and coalition partners'.[20]

US PACIFIC COMMAND

In the operational chain of command, all US armed forces stationed in the Asia–Pacific theater are assigned to the US Pacific Command (USPACOM), the Unified Combatant Command for the region.

In 1997 USPACOM celebrated its 50th anniversary as America's first unified command, an outgrowth of the Pacific Ocean Area and Southwest Pacific Area command structure used during World War II. In 1957 the responsibilities of the former Far East Command were added to USPACOM, along with some responsibilities of the Alaskan Command. In 1972 USPACOM's Area of Responsibility (AOR) was expanded to include military forces and elements in the Indian Ocean, Southern Asia and the Arctic. The AOR was further expanded in 1976 to the east coast of Africa. Yet another enlargement of the USPACOM area took place in 1983, when the People's Republic of China, the Democratic People's Republic of Korea, the Mongolian People's Republic and the Democratic Republic of Madagascar were included. Finally, in 1989 the Alaskan Command was re-established as a subordinate unified command of USPACOM. USPACOM's AOR was only slightly reduced in 1989 and 1996 by the transfer of the Gulfs of Oman and Aden and the Seychelles islands and adjacent waters to the US Central Command (USCENTCOM).[21]

Today, from USPACOM headquarters at Camp H. M. Smith in Hawaii, the Commander in Chief, US Pacific Command (USCINCPAC), has responsibility for the largest geographical area of any of the US Unified Commands. This area equals about 50 per cent of the earth's surface—more than 250 million square kilometers—including 44 countries, ten US territories and twenty territories and possessions of other countries, containing over 60 per cent of the world's population. USPACOM's area of responsibility extends from the west coast of the United States mainland to the east coast of Africa, from the Arctic to the Antarctic, and includes the states of Alaska and Hawaii.[22]

As of July 1998 the USPACOM total force consisted of some 300 000 military personnel from the Army, Navy, Air Force and Marines, (about 20 per cent of all active-duty US military forces). This force consists of service components, subordinate Unified Commands, and standing Joint Task Forces (JTF).

The *service components* are as follows:

- US Army Pacific (USARPAC)
- US Pacific Fleet (PACFLT), including Marine Force Pacific (MARFORPAC)
- US Pacific Air Forces (PACAF).

The *subordinate unified commands* consist of forces from all the services:

- US Forces Japan (USFJ), headquartered at Yokota Air Base Japan, conducts the activities of the 44 000 US Air Force, Navy, Marine Corps and Army personnel stationed at 97 locations in Japan.
- US Forces Korea (USFK), headquartered in Seoul, Republic of Korea, conducts the activities of 37 000 US Army, Air Force and Navy personnel in more than 120 locations in South Korea. The Commander of US Forces in Korea also serves as Commander in Chief of the United Nations Command (CINCUNC) and of the ROK/US Combined Forces Command (CFC).
- Special Operations Command Pacific (SOCPAC) exercises operational control over Army, Navy and Air Force Special

Operations Forces (SOF) assigned to USCINCPAC (see Chapter 8).
- Alaskan Command (ALCOM), headquartered at Elmendorf Air Force Base outside Anchorage, is responsible for the unified defense of Alaska's land and territorial waters, including the Aleutian Islands, and consists of nearly 18 000 Army, Navy and Air Force personnel.

Standing joint task forces include the following:

- Joint Interagency Task Force West (JIATF-WEST), headquartered on Coast Guard Island, Alameda, California, supports national counterdrug initiatives in USPACOM.
- Joint Task Force—Full Accounting (JTF-FA), headquartered at Camp H. M. Smith, Hawaii, conducts field operations to achieve the fullest possible accounting for Americans still unaccounted for in Southeast Asia as a result of the Vietnam War.
- Other contingency Joint Task Forces are included as necessary, such as Joint Task Force 510, which is USCINCPAC's crisis response, rapid deployment Joint Task Force.

In addition, designated representatives, known by the acronym (CINCPACREP), report directly to USCINCPAC for the following areas as of 1997:

- Australia/Nauru
- Guam/Commonwealth of the Northern Mariana Islands/Federated States of Micronesia/Republic of Palau
- Republic of the Marshall Islands (RMI)
- Singapore
- Fiji/French Polynesia/New Caledonia/Tonga/Tuvalu/Wallis and Futuna
- Thailand
- New Zealand/Cook Islands/Niue/Tokelau/Western Samoa
- Sri Lanka/Maldives.[23]

In the operational chain of command, USCINCPAC reports directly to the Secretary of Defense and the President of the United States. Administratively, CINCPAC reports through the Chairman of the Joint Chiefs of Staff, as explained above. The Command relationships in the US Pacific Command extend from the USCINCPAC to the Commanders (COM or CDR), Commanders-in-Chief (CINC), or Commanding Generals (CG) of the above named elements, and are illustrated in Figure 3.5.

Figure 3.5 Command relationships in USPACOM

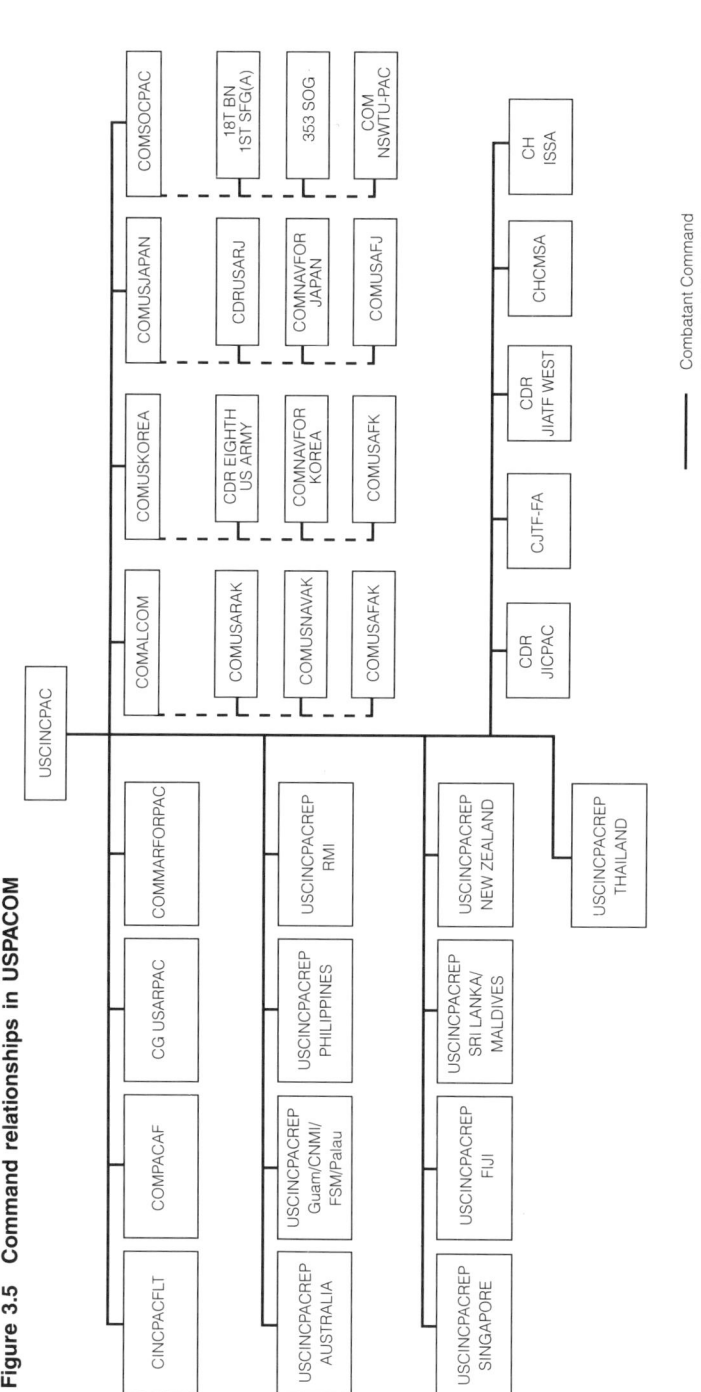

Source: USPACOM Digest, 1996

Figure 3.6 PACOM area of responsibility

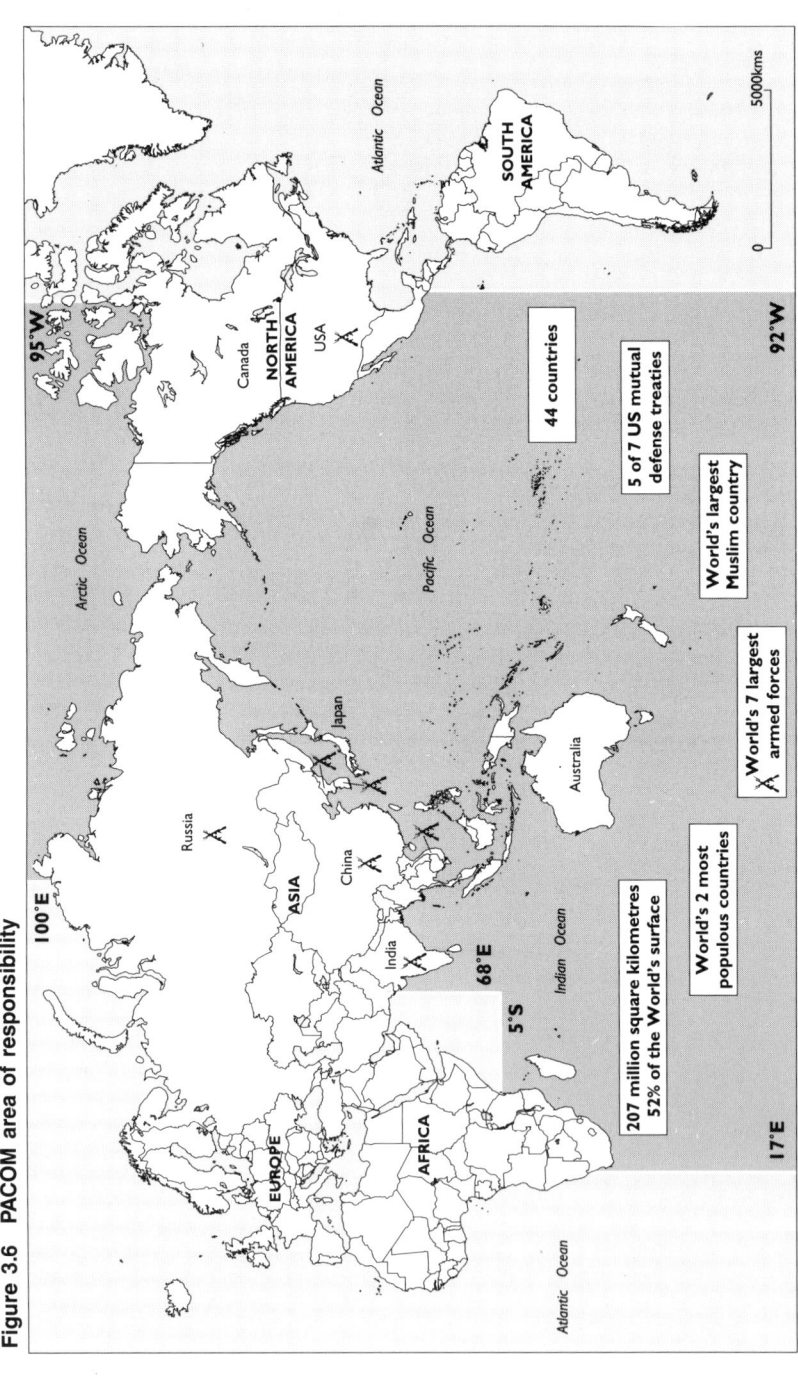

Source: US Marine Forces Pacific

The forces of US Pacific Command are spread throughout the Command's Area of Responsibility (AOR), as indicated in Figure 3.6. The Base Infrastructure of USPACOM is the subject of Chapter 4. The individual services in the Asia–Pacific region are covered in detail in chapters 6 to 8.

THE GLOBAL COMMAND AND CONTROL SYSTEM (GCCS)

It is one thing to outline command and control relationships on paper. It is quite another to actually have the ability to communicate intelligence information and to control and command far-flung military units—and to do so rapidly, accurately and securely. Since the late 1960s the equipment used by the US armed forces to ensure this Command, Control, Communications and Intelligence (C^3I) capability has been referred to as the Worldwide Military Command and Control System (WWMCCS).

At this time, the US military is in the process of greatly improving its already superior capability in this arena by fielding a new system named, more simply, the Global Command and Control System (GCCS). The role of computers, while central in WWMCCS, has been so greatly increased that the acronym C^3I has been modified to C^4I for Command, Control, Communications, *Computers* and Intelligence.

The Global Command and Control System is 'an automated information system designed to support deliberate and crisis planning with the use of an integrated set of analytic tools and flexible data transfer capabilities'.[24] In time the GCCS will become 'the single C^4I system to support the warfighter from foxhole to command post'.[25]

In the past, command and control systems typically grew weaker and less effective the greater the distance from headquarters. Today, however, the strategic vision for US forces as articulated by the Joint Chiefs of Staff and outlined above calls for 'full spectrum dominance' in all types of military operations, and at *all levels*, from the strategic to the tactical.

This vision calls for full 'warfighter support' and that means the implementation of a Command, Control, Communications, Computers and Intelligence system for the warfighter (C^4IFTW) that will provide the warrior 'a fused, real-time true picture of the battlespace and the ability to order, respond, and coordinate vertically and horizontally to prosecute the mission in that battlespace'.[26]

Given the commitment to the cooperation among individual services known as 'jointness' that is central to *Joint Vision 2010*, US commanders now require a single integrated or 'fused' view of the joint battlespace. That, in turn, means that the GCCS must provide a core functionality that establishes a *common* command and control standard for all the individual US military services. (This has not always been the case in the past, as the 1983 Grenada operations and some aspects of the 1991 Gulf War revealed.) The goal is to implement a new Defense Information Infrastructure Common Operating Environment (DII COE).[27]

The implementation of GCCS began in 1995 and continues today in phases. It is important to understand that the GCCS is much more than a 'replacement' for its predecessor WWMCCS. In terms of capabilities, the WWMCCS provided to 35 key US military headquarters:

- news
- the global status of resources and training
- sensitive reconnaissance scheduling
- deliberate planning
- crisis action planning and execution.

The current version (2.1) of the GCCS provides the following *additional* capabilities to *over 500* locations, including USCINCPAC, US Pacific Air Forces, US Pacific Fleet, US Army Pacific, and US forces in Korea at Taegu and Yongsan:

- a common operational picture
- intelligence support
- a capability to read joint air strike commands known as air tasking orders, thus correcting a major deficiency encountered during the Gulf War (see Chapter 7).

Future versions of the GCCS will reportedly provide:

- a secret web for electronic mail, home pages, etc.
- an ability to correct the initial operating capability deficiencies of new weapons systems
- versions to be shared with US allies
- enhancements of the common operational picture
- intelligence imagery support/database
- theater ballistic missile defense warnings
- battlefield planning and execution.[28]

In terms of computer hardware and software, the WWMCCS was based on a mainframe computer, connected to only 35 sites, capable of 6.8 million instructions per second (MIPS) (dual processor) with 45 Megabytes of random access memory (RAM), 32 Gigabytes of storage and 2.1 Gigabytes in executable code, and costing $5500 a month to maintain. The GCCS is a Client/Server system connected to an increasing total of over 500 sites. Its 6 Processor main Server is capable of 600 million instructions per second, has 1 Gigabyte of RAM and 15 Gigabytes in executable code. The main server maintenance cost reportedly amounts to about $500 a month and the individual work stations each cost $80 or less a month to maintain.[29]

In summary, although the GCCS is *not* the theoretical 'system of systems' described above by Admiral Owens, it is 'the DOD's *integrated* C⁴I system, supporting all aspects of C⁴I from deployment planning to battlefield execution'. Unlike its predecessor, the GCCS is reportedly 'scaleable' from the National Command Authorities through the Combatant Commanders in Chief, the CINC Service components, Commanders of Joint Task Forces and their components and, ultimately, all the way down to the 'foxhole'.[30]

No other armed forces in the world operate such a rapid, secure and powerful global C⁴I system. This system enables US commanders to exercise an unprecedented level of effective command and control, even over the vast distances which characterize the Asia–Pacific theater.

4

US base infrastructure in the Asia–Pacific region

In the course of World War II and the subsequent 45 years of the Cold War, the United States established a vast network of military bases at home and overseas (see Chapter 1). In the Asia–Pacific region, that network stretched from the west coast of the continental United States to the Asian mainland. As the end of the 20th century approaches, a broad spectrum of geo-political, economic and military factors has led to a steady reduction in that global network from a total of 115 major overseas air and sea bases in 1956 to 27 in 1997.[1] Still, the United States at the time of writing maintains a significant base infrastructure in the Asia–Pacific region. This chapter briefly reviews that infrastructure. The discussion is limited to major or particularly significant bases on the west coast of the US mainland, Hawaii, and in the Western Pacific region that provide forces and training to the US Pacific Command, as shown in the map in Figure 4.1. Details about the units stationed at these bases can be found in the following chapters devoted to individual branches of the US armed forces.

BASES IN THE CONTINENTAL US, ALASKA AND HAWAII

The United States has an extensive sovereign presence in the Eastern Pacific—a geographic fact that ensures a permanent military infrastructure. In the far north, *Alaska*, with its far-flung Aleutian archipelago, was the site of combat during World War II and frequent confrontational incidents during the Cold War. Although the end of the Cold War has led to significant base closings, a number of major bases remain active. They consist of:

- Eielson Air Force base, located in the interior of Alaska, about

Figure 4.1 USPACOM forces and stations

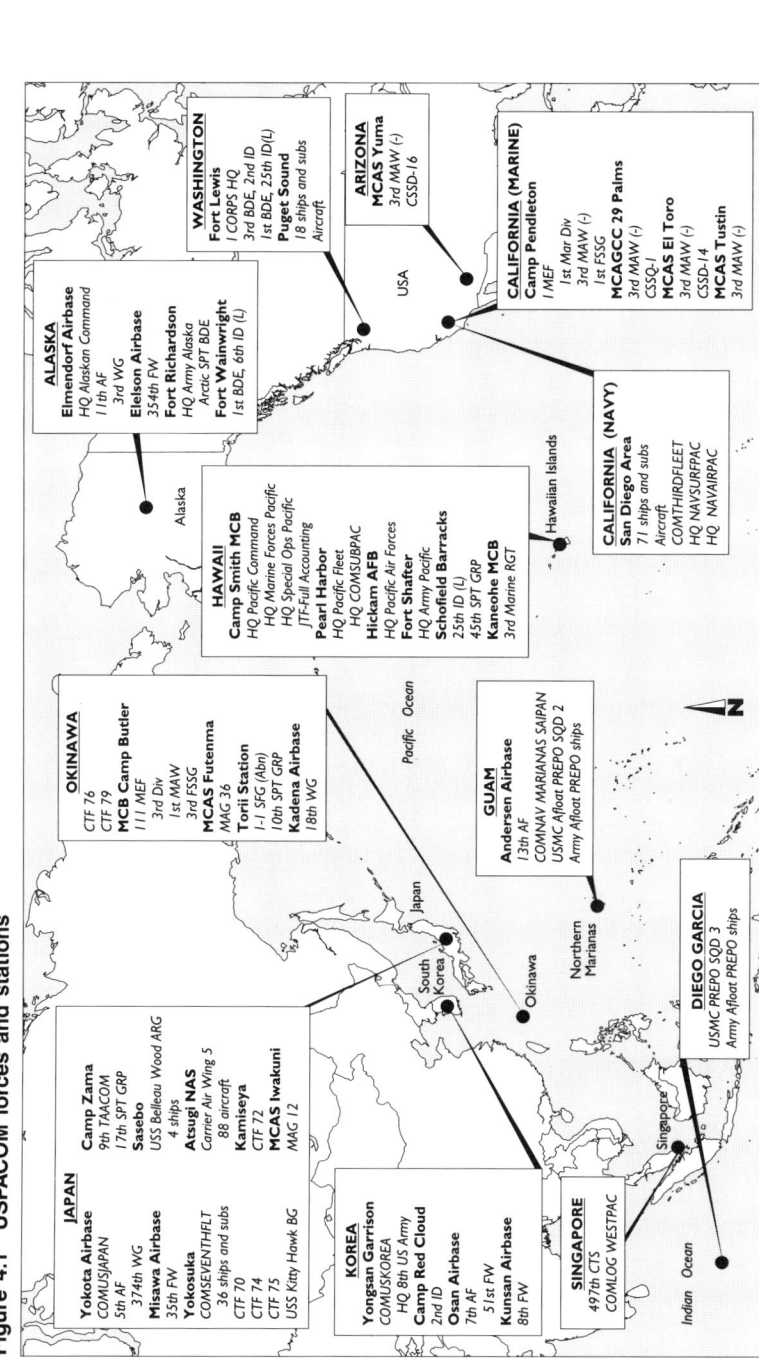

Source: USPACOM Digest, 1996

46 kilometers from the city of Fairbanks. Approximately 2700 active-duty Air Force personnel are stationed there. The major current host unit is the Pacific Air Force's (PACAF) 354th Fighter Wing, equipped with F–16 and A–10 fighter jets, flying off the base's 4400-meter runway. An Air National Guard Air Refueling Group is also stationed there. In addition to its basic mission of providing close air support and interdiction, the Wing also supports one of the largest and most realistic training exercises in PACAF, COPE THUNDER, which takes place over three large practice ranges—the Yukon, Oklahoma and Blair Lake ranges. Together they constitute PACAF's largest air-to-ground bombing range complex.[2]

- Fort Wainwright, also located near Fairbanks in Alaska's interior. Approximately 4100 active-duty Army personnel are stationed there. The major command is the First Brigade of the 6th Light Infantry Division, capable of being rapidly deployed in the Pacific theater and worldwide.
- Elmendorf Air Force Base, located next to the city of Anchorage on Alaska's Pacific coast. Approximately 7000 active-duty Air Force personnel are stationed there. The host unit is the 3rd Air Wing, the largest and principal unit in PACAF's 11th Air Force. The unit's main missions are providing air defense and air superiority in Alaska, as well as supporting PACAF during any contingencies in the Pacific Command Area of Responsibility. The units main weapons are the F–15 fighter and E–3 AWACS aircraft, flying off a 3000-meter runway.

While many areas of the mainland United States have experienced the closure of military bases following the end of the Cold War, the Pacific Northwest *state of Washington* has seen its military role increase in size and importance. Among its major bases are:

- Naval Air Station (NAS) Whidbey Island, located on Puget Sound, Washington State's 'inland sea', 80 kilometers north of the city of Seattle. Approximately 8100 active-duty US Navy personnel are stationed there. The Commander Electronic Combat Wing US Pacific Fleet is the Commander of all EA–6B *Prowler* Fleet squadrons based there. Patrol Wing Ten also operates the P–3 aircraft from NAS Whidbey.
- Naval Station Everett, also located on Puget Sound, 40 kilometers north of Seattle. Encompassing some 47 hectares of land and the surrounding 70 hectares of water, Naval Station Everett is the homeport of a seven-ship Carrier Battle Group.

Approximately 5900 active-duty naval personnel are stationed there. Everett is one of the US Navy's newest 'state-of-the-art' bases, having become officially operational in April 1994.
- Naval Submarine Base (NSB) Bangor, located on the Kitsap peninsula, in Puget Sound, 40 kilometers west of Seattle. Approximately 8700 Navy, Marine Corps and civilian personnel work at the 2800-hectare base. NSB Bangor is the homeport of all eight *Ohio* class Trident ballistic missile submarines, the Trident Training Facility, and Strategic Weapons Facility Pacific, a likely nuclear weapons storage site (see Chapter 5).
- Puget Sound Naval Shipyard (PSNS), located in Bremerton, Washington, on the Puget Sound, 32 kilometers west of Seattle. Approximately 10 500 active-duty naval personnel and 9000 civilian employees operate on the 77 hectares at PSNS. In addition to overhauling, maintaining, decommissioning and recycling naval vessels, PSNS is also the headquarters of Carrier Group Three, and a homeport for one aircraft carrier, three auxiliary oilers, two cruisers and other naval ships. PSNS is the only remaining US Navy full-maintenance shipyard on the mainland's Pacific coast.
- McChord Air Force Base, located adjacent to Tacoma, Washington, 64 kilometers south of Seattle. Approximately 4000 active-duty Air Force personnel are stationed there. The major units are two Airlift Wings of the Air Mobility command, currently flying the C–141 transport aircraft. The new C–17 will soon be deployed at McChord. McChord is also adjacent to Fort Lewis.
- Fort Lewis, also located near Tacoma, Washington. Consisting of 35 000 hectares and housing over 20 000 active-duty US Army personnel, Fort Lewis is the largest military installation in the US Pacific Northwest, and one of the largest and most modern military reservations in the United States. Fort Lewis is home to many Army units, including I Corps headquarters, brigades of the 25th and 2nd Infantry Divisions, the 1st Special Forces Group and the 2nd Ranger Battalion, all assigned to US Army, Pacific. In addition, Fort Lewis includes the sub-installation Yakima Training Center, 129 600 hectares in central Washington State used for realistic training by US Army, Marine Corps and allied troops, including those from Japan.

There have been a significant number of base closures and realignments in *California*, but that large state retains many key military installations. Among those with special relevance to the Asia–Pacific region are:

- Naval Air Station Lemoore, located in California's central San Joaqin Valley, 64 kilometers south of the city of Fresno. Approximately 5000 active-duty naval personnel are stationed there. NAS Lemoore's primary mission is to support fleet carrier squadrons. Commander, Strike Fighter Wing, US Pacific Fleet Headquarters is the major command. One carrier air wing staff, eleven strike fighter squadrons and a fleet readiness training squadron are homeported there. Lemoore also serves as a master training center for carrier-based strike fighter squadrons of the US Pacific Fleet, operating the F/A–18 aircraft.
- Fort Irwin, located in the High Mojave Desert midway between Las Vegas, Nevada, and Los Angeles, California. In 1981 the National Training Center (NTC) was established on the 2600 square kilometers of Fort Irwin. The NTC is considered to be the premier training site of the US Army. Although it has a small permanent staff, approximately 4000–5000 soldiers from other installations rotate through the NTC each month for intensive, technologically advanced combined arms training.
- Marine Corps Base (MCB) Camp Pendleton, located 97 kilometers south of Los Angeles and 48 kilometers north of San Diego on California's Pacific coast. Encompassing 27 kilometers of coastline and 50 625 hectares, Camp Pendleton is home to approximately 38 000 active-duty Marines and sailors. It is the site of the Marine Corps' largest amphibious training facility. The base is home of the I Marine Expeditionary Force, the 1st Marine Division, the 1st Force Service Support Group and many other units. It is the premier training and support facility for Fleet Marine Force Pacific.
- Naval Station San Diego is located on 31 hectares in downtown San Diego on the Pacific coast at the southern end of California. In addition to Shore Intermediate Maintenance, Shipbuilding Conversion and Repair, and Pacific Fleet surface ships, Naval Station San Diego is home to the Pacific Fleet Training Center. Over 43 000 US Navy personnel are assigned to the base.
- Marine Corps Air Station (MCAS) Miramar, located 24 kilometers north of San Diego. Formerly the home of the Navy's

'Top Gun' center of training for F–14 fighters, Miramar is being realigned to base the Marine Corps' 3rd Air Wing.
- Naval Air Station North Island is located adjacent to San Diego. Known as 'The Birthplace of Naval Aviation', NAS North Island is the largest aviation industrial complex on the US west coast. Together with two outlying facilities, North Island administers over 18 456 hectares in Southern California. Twenty-three naval air squadrons and 50 other tenant commands are based there, including headquarters for four major naval flag staffs including: Commander Naval Air Force, US Pacific Fleet, Commander Third Fleet, and Commanders Carrier Group One and Seven. Two aircraft carriers are homeported at NAS North Island. With all the ships in port, the total base population is over 30 000, including civilian personnel. Adjacent to NAS North Island is Naval Amphibious Base (NAB), Coronado. Twenty-seven tenant commands, mainly amphibious organizations, are housed there, with a base population of 5000 permanent military and civilian personnel and 7000 personnel rotating through. Among the major headquarters are Commander, Naval Surface Force, US Pacific Fleet, Naval Special Warfare Command, and Commander, Expeditionary Warfare. Naval Submarine Base San Diego is nearby, on 128 hectares of coastline. Seven nuclear attack submarines are currently based there.

The United States mainland has such an extensive Pacific coastline as well as Pacific island territories and other Pacific defense responsibilities (e.g. for the Republic of the Marshall Islands, the Federated States of Micronesia and Palau) that those factors alone are sufficient reason to guarantee a continuing interest in the region's security. Moreover, the fact that the last US territory to become a sovereign state is located in the middle of the Pacific Ocean only serves to emphasize the direct importance of the Asia–Pacific region to US security. Since the 1930s *Hawaii* has become perhaps the most important location on United States soil for military installations focused on the Asia–Pacific region. Among the most important installations there are:

- Naval Station Pearl Harbor, located 13 kilometers from the city of Honolulu on the island of Oahu. Famous as the site of the Japanese surprise attack on 7 December 1941, Pearl Harbor remains the site of several major and many minor commands. Over 20 000 active-duty personnel are stationed there. Pearl Harbor is the US Navy's largest forward base in the Pacific. Naval Station Pearl Harbor operates the harbor and provides berthing and shoreside facilities for surface ships. Submarine Base Pearl Harbor provides berthing and shoreside facilities for some 24 nuclear attack submarines (the great majority of those submarines in the Pacific are based there), along with maintenance and training facilities. It is the only intermediate maintenance facility for submarines in the Middle Pacific. Naval Shipyard Pearl provides overhaul, repair and conversion of both surface ships and submarines, up to the largest ships in the US Navy.

- Hickam Air Force Base, located 14 kilometers from Honolulu on the island of Oahu. The Headquarters of Pacific Air Forces (PACAF) is located on the 890 hectares of Hickam AFB. The 15th Air Base Wing is stationed there. The base's runway is 3769 meters long.
- Fort Shafter/ Schofield Barracks, located on 608 hectares north of Honolulu. It is home to the Headquarters, US Army Pacific (USARPAC), and two infantry brigades, an aviation brigade, division artillery, and division support command of the 25th (Light) Infantry Division, whose focus is low-intensity conflict throughout the Pacific.
- Marine Corps Base Hawaii (MCBH) Kaneohe Bay, located 19 kilometers northeast of the city of Honolulu. MCBH was established on 15 April 1994 by combining several Hawaii Marine Corps facilities into one entity on the site of the Marine Corps Air Station already in existence there. Approximately 6800 Marine and Navy personnel are stationed there. MCBH Kaneohe Bay is home to the Marine Corps Air Facility, the Third Marine Regiment of the Third Marine Expeditionary Force (whose headquarters, and two other regiments, are on Okinawa), Combat Service Support Group-3 and the Aviation Support Element First Marine Air Wing (MAW). The base's position in the Pacific makes it an ideal location for rapid strategic deployment of Marine forces further forward to the Far East.
- MCBH Camp H. M. Smith, now an administrative sub-installation of MCBH Kaneohe Bay, located on 89 hectares atop Halawa Heights above Pearl Harbor. Camp Smith contains the headquarters of the US Commander in Chief Pacific (USCINCPAC), the Commander, Marine Forces, Pacific, and Fleet Marine Force Pacific.

Figure 4.2 Deployment of US forces in Japan outside Okinawa

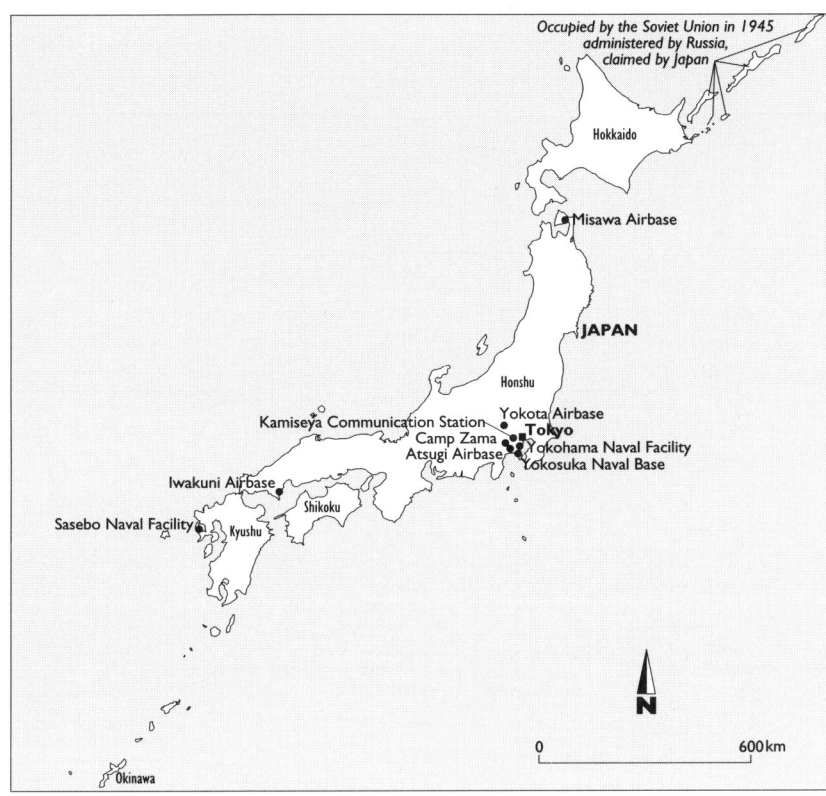

Source: *Strategic Assessment 1997*, Institute of National Strategic Studies, p. 65.

BASES IN THE WESTERN PACIFIC (WESTPAC)

The island of *Guam* is a territory of the United States at the southern end of the Marianas island chain, at 12 degrees 75 minutes north latitude and 144 degrees 47 minutes east longitude in the central Western Pacific, some seven hours by air from Honolulu and three hours by air from Tokyo. Some 48 kilometers long and 8 kilometers wide, nearly one-third of Guam's land once consisted of US military bases. Since the end of the Cold War several bases have been closed, but Guam retains the following important bases:

- Andersen Air Force Base, located on the northern end of the island. Approximately 2200 Air Force and 460 active-duty

Navy personnel are stationed there. The tenant units are the 13th Air Force headquarters, the 634 Air Mobility Support Squadron, and Navy Helicopter Combat Support Squadron Five. During World War II, the Korean conflict, the war in Vietnam and the 1991 Persian Gulf War, Andersen AFB served as a heavy bomber base. Although no combat units are currently stationed there, Andersen, with its 3324-meter runway, remains at readiness to support US global power projection efforts as the need arises.

- US Naval Forces Marianas, consisting of numerous commands at several locations on the island of Guam. A total of approximately 7500 active-duty Navy personnel are stationed on Guam. The largest single facility is the Ordnance Annex, consisting of some 3560 hectares in the south-central section of the island. Naval Activities Command provides waterfront, ordnance and other logistical support to visiting units of the Fifth and Seventh fleets, and to the four support ships homeported there. Other commands include detachments of Military Sealift Command, Fleet Imaging Center Pacific, the Naval Computer and Telecommunications Area Master Station WESTPAC, Pacific Meteorology and Oceanography Center West, and Special Warfare Unit One (Navy SEALS).
- US Marine Corps Afloat Prepositioning Squadron Two ships, and Army Afloat Prepositioning ships, at the island of Saipan, a short distance north of Guam.

As America's most important ally in Northeast Asia, the main islands of *Japan* have been the site of bases for forward-deployed US military units since the end of World War II, when US forces occupied the country after the end of hostilities.

The most important bases for US forces on the main islands include:

- Misawa Air Base, located 644 kilometers north of Tokyo on the northeastern part of Honshu, Japan's main island. The base is shared by the Japan Air Self Defense Force, the US Air Force's 35th Fighter Wing, a US Navy Maritime Patrol air squadron, and several US military intelligence units. Approximately 5300 active-duty US Air Force and Navy personnel are stationed there. US F–16 fighters and P–3 patrol aircraft operate from Misawa's 3050-meter runway.
- Yokota Air Base, located 45 kilometers northwest of Tokyo on the main island of Honshu. Approximately 3600 US Air Force personnel are stationed there. Yokota is the headquarters of

the 5th Air Force, Commander, US Forces Japan, and the 374th Airlift Wing, operating the C–130 aircraft, is based there. Yokota is the primary airlift resource for forward-deployed US Pacific Forces. Its runway is 3355 meters long.
- Commander Fleet Activities Yokosuka, a 234-hectare naval base located on a small peninsula in Tokyo Bay, about 48 kilometers southwest of Japan's capital city, Tokyo. Yokosuka is the most important US naval facility in the Western Pacific. The base is shared with the Japanese Maritime Self Defense Force. Approximately 9800 US Navy personnel are stationed there. As the home of the US Navy's Commander, Seventh Fleet, Yokosuka hosts thirteen afloat commands and more than 50 other shore commands and activities, including the major naval ship-repair facility in the Far East. The Seventh Fleet's command ship, USS *Blue Ridge*, is homeported at Yokosuka, and so is a US Carrier Battle Group, centered around the aircraft carrier *Kitty Hawk*—the only one homeported at a base on foreign territory. A nearby Ordnance Facility and off-base housing areas comprise another 344 hectares.
- Naval Air Facility (NAF) Atsugi, located on 486 hectares 35 kilometers southwest of Tokyo. Atsugi is the largest Naval Air Facility in the Pacific and is home to US Carrier Air Wing FIVE, the wing assigned to the US carrier homeported at Yokosuka. F–14 and FA–18 fighters constitute the main striking power of CAW–5. The Commander, US Fleet Air Western Pacific is headquartered at Atsugi. The base is shared with aviation elements of the Japanese Maritime Self Defense Force. The base's US population fluctuates greatly, depending primarily on the deployments of the carrier air wing, which consists of over 2000 US Navy personnel.
- Camp Zama, located 40 kilometers southwest of Tokyo. Camp Zama is headquarters for Commander, US Army Japan (USARJ) and the 17th Area Support Group. Numerous other small administrative and logistics commands, and a heavy weapons firing range, are located there. The base provides combat service support, forward presence, power projection and installation management for US Army forces in the Western Pacific theater. Approximately 900 US Army active-duty personnel are stationed there.
- Marine Corps Air Station (MCAS) Iwakuni, located 966 kilometers south of Tokyo and 48 kilometers from the city of Hiroshima at the southern end of Japan's main island of Honshu. Approximately 3200 active-duty US Marines are

stationed there. Iwakuni is home to units of the 1st Marine Aircraft Wing, operating F/A–18s and AV–8B fighters, and the 3rd Force Service Support Group. The base is shared with aviation units of the Japanese Maritime Self Defense Force.

- Commander Fleet Activities Sasebo, located on 405 hectares at the northwest corner of the Japanese island of Kyushu, 1450 kilometers southwest of Tokyo and 177 kilometers from Korea. Sasebo naval base is currently home to Commander, US Navy Amphibious Squadron Eleven and the six homeported ships (including support ships and ships of an Amphibious Ready Group). Sasebo is also a major logistics hub for forward-deployed US forces, and has major munitions and fuel storage facilities. Approximately 5000 US Navy personnel are stationed at the base, which is shared with ships of the Japanese Maritime Self Defense Force.

The Japanese island of *Okinawa*, located in the Ryukus island chain 1600 kilometers south of Tokyo, was the site of the last and most costly major battle in the Pacific theater of World War II. It remained under US control until 1972. The large US military presence on the island is planned to diminish somewhat in the future. However, Okinawa remains the location of many key US military bases, including several large training areas. Approximately 28 000 US military personnel—two-thirds of the total US force in Japan—are stationed there, on about 18 per cent of the island's total land area.

Although an Agreement concluded by the governments of Japan and the United States on 2 December 1996 will lead to the return of 21 per cent of the total area of the US facilities and areas in Okinawa (excluding joint-use facilities and areas),[3] the following major US bases remain in operation on Okinawa at the time of writing:

- Marine Corps Base (MCB) Camp Butler, consisting of five physically separated 'Camps', and one Marine Corps Air Station, spread over 80 kilometers of Okinawa. The major commands are the III Marine Expeditionary (MEF) (1st Marine Aircraft Wing, 3rd Marine Division and 3rd Force Service Support Group), the MCAS Futenma (scheduled to be closed by 2003 and perhaps replaced by a sea-based facility offshore), and Fleet Activities Okinawa. Approximately 20 000 US Marines and sailors are stationed on Okinawa, at Camps Courtney, Kinser, Hansen, Schwab, Gonsalves and Shields. The primary mission of the III MEF requires execution of

Figure 4.3 US bases on Okinawa

Source: *Strategic Assessment 1997*, Institute of National Strategic Studies, p. 66.

amphibious assault. In addition, the 31st Marine Expeditionary Unit (MEU) works as a contingent of the US Pacific forward presence, routinely deploying on board the ARG homeported at Sasebo in readiness for any regional contingency. There are also several large Training Areas on Okinawa, including White Beach, where amphibious operations are practiced and US naval ships visit.

- Kadena Air Base, located in the center of Okinawa. Kadena is home to the US Air Force's 18th Air Wing, which includes

F-15 fighters, KC-135 aerial refueling tankers, E-3 AWACS aircraft and HH-60G rescue helicopters. Approximately 7500 active-duty US military personnel, mostly from the Air Force, are stationed there. Kadena is one of the US Air Force's largest and most important overseas bases, with a runway over 3660 meters long.
- Torii Station, the main post for the US Army on Okinawa. The US Army on Okinawa is the smallest of the branches of service there, with approximately 900 active-duty personnel at several locations on the island. The main commands are the 1st Battalion, 1st Special Forces Group, Airborne (Green Berets), the only forward-deployed Special Forces Unit in the Far East, and the 10th Area Support Group. The Support Group's mission is to receive, stage, equip and deploy rerouted or diverted forces in the Western Pacific theater. Several other Army logistics and communications units are also located on Okinawa.

US BASES IN THE REPUBLIC OF KOREA (ROK)

Nearly 45 years after the cease-fire that ended active hostilities on the Korean peninsula, approximately 36 000 US military personnel remain in the Republic of Korea to help defend it against North Korea.

The major US military bases in South Korea as of 1998 include:

- Camp Hialeah, located in the port city of Pusan at the southeastern tip of South Korea, 483 kilometers southeast of the capital city of Seoul. Camp Hialeah is the most important US military logistical base in the ROK. Although there are only about 500 active-duty US military (mostly Army) personnel permanently stationed there, the base's population expands during exercises and crisis periods as units arrive in Pusan port. Camp Hialeah includes the Pusan Storage Facility, the largest within US Forces Korea, and the US Army 4th Quartermaster Detachment (Airborne), the largest in the Pacific region.
- Commander, Fleet Activities, Chinhae, located on 34 hectares next to the Republic of Korea Naval Base at Chinhae, a port city on the southeast coast of South Korea west of Pusan. Chinhae is the most significant US naval facility in the ROK, and the headquarters of US Naval Forces Detachment Chinhae.
- Camps Henry, Walker, George and Carroll, located on about 100 hectares in and around Taegu City, ROK, 320 kilometers south of Seoul. Taegu is headquarters of the US 19th Theater

Figure 4.4 US bases in the Republic of Korea

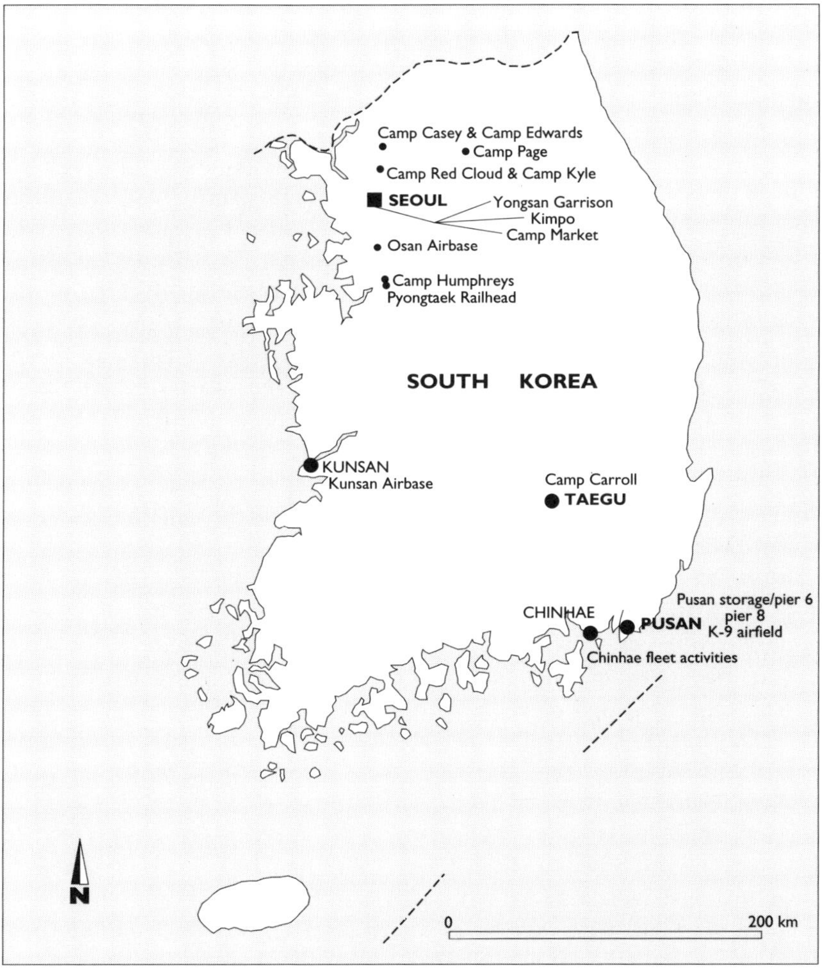

Source: US Forces Korea and Eighth US Army in the Republic of Korea 1996, p. 41

Army Area Command, the second largest command in US Forces Korea. The primary wartime mission of the Support Group's storage sites in these Camps is to provide for the reception, staging, onward movement and integration of US augmentation units arriving from the continental US and Pacific commands.
- Kunsan Air Base, located near Kunsan City on the west coast of the peninsula, about 320 kilometers south of Seoul. Kunsan is home to the US Air Force's 8th Fighter Wing, known as

'The Wolfpack'. Approximately 2650 US Air Force personnel are stationed there. The 8th Fighter Wing operates the F–16 strike fighter off the base's 2745-meter runway.
- Camp Humphreys, located on 5 square kilometers about 61 kilometers south of Seoul. Camp Humphreys is the headquarters location for support of the Eighth US Army and US Forces Korea operations south of Seoul and north of Taejon. Approximately 4500 US Army and Air Force personnel are stationed there. There is an Army airfield at Camp Humphreys.
- Osan Air Base, located on 634 hectares 55 kilometers south of Seoul. Osan Air Base is home to the headquarters of the US 7th Air Force and the 51st Fighter Wing, which operates F–16 and A–10 fighters from the 2745-meter runway there. Special Operations and U–2 aircraft are also based at Osan. There are approximately 6700 active-duty US Air Force personnel stationed there.
- Yongsan Garrison, located in the heart of Seoul, the Republic of Korea's capital city with a population of 13 million. Yongsan is the headquarters of Commander, US Forces Korea and the Commander, US Eighth Army.
- US Army Garrison Area I/2nd Infantry Division, located in 42 camps in an area of approximately 300 square kilometers in the northwestern section of the Republic of Korea, north of Seoul and south of the De-militarized Zone (DMZ) separating North and South Korea. More than 15 000 US Army personnel of the 2nd Infantry Division, known as 'The Warrior Division', are stationed in 31 of these camps, in a high state of readiness for any contingency involving a North Korean threat to the ROK. The bulk of the troops, about 9300, are stationed at Camps Casey and Hovey, near the town of Tongduchun. The Division's headquarters is located at Camp Red Cloud, near the town of Uijongbu, closer to Seoul. About 1700 US Army personnel are stationed there. The most forward-deployed US military unit in the Asia–Pacific region is the 1st Battalion, 506th US Army Infantry Regiment, located north of Freedom Bridge and the Imjin River, only two kilometers from the DMZ. Its motto is 'In front of them all'.

AUSTRALIA AND THE INDIAN OCEAN

Far to the south, about 200 active-duty US Air Force personnel of the 5th Space Warning Squadron are stationed together with

Australian personnel at the Joint Defense Facility Nurrungar (JDFN), in the 'outback' in south central Australia. Their primary mission is the detection of ballistic missile launches by means of satellite. During the Gulf War, Nurrungar alerted Coalition forces of Scud launches from Iraq.

Finally, some 1500 active-duty US military personnel from the Navy, Marines and Army are based on the 2700 hectares at Naval Support Facility (NSF) *Diego Garcia*, the largest island of the Chagos Archipelago in the heart of the Indian Ocean. The forces are there with the permission of the British government, which administers the island as part of the British Indian Ocean Territory. Following the overthrow of the Shah of Iran in 1979, Diego Garcia's strategic importance increased, and the base underwent the most dramatic buildup of any location since the Vietnam War, including the construction of a major air field. In addition to communications and support units, Diego Garcia is home to the US Navy's Patrol Wing One, which flies the P–3C maritime patrol aircraft, and to the Marine Corps' second Maritime Prepositioning Ships (MPS) Squadron. Diego Garcia played a major role during the 1991 Persian Gulf War and subsequent military operations in that region.

ACCESS AGREEMENTS

In addition to its remaining bases in the region, in recent years the United States has adopted a policy sometimes known as 'places, not bases', or more accurately, 'not bases but critical facilities access'. Thus, for example, Commander, US Logistics West Pacific, a small administrative detachment under a US Navy Rear Admiral, is located in Singapore, which also provides access to US air and naval forces. Access agreements have also been reached with Thailand (U Tapao airbase), Malaysia (Naval Base Lumut), Indonesia (Naval Base Surabaya) and Australia (training facilities in the north and east). The United States has also recently agreed with the Philippines government on the legal status of visiting military personnel, which (if ratified by the Philippines Senate) should facilitate access to Subic Bay and other facilities (see Chapter 9).

SUMMARY

This brief overview of only the major US bases in the Asia–Pacific region reveals the great size and complexity of the infrastructure necessary to support the 100 000 forward-deployed US forces in the region and augmentation units in the United States proper. With the end of the Cold War, the high financial cost of maintaining these installations will probably continue to result in some limited further reductions of this US infrastructure. In addition, the presence of US military bases on foreign soil is an increasingly sensitive political issue in those countries.

Nevertheless, for the foreseeable future the United States will certainly maintain a substantial base infrastructure on its own soil forward in the region, and retain substantial forces at sea. At this time, it also appears probable that, despite the financial and political costs, Japan and South Korea will continue to agree to the presence of some US bases in their nations, for the purpose of enhancing regional stability. This topic will be taken up again in Chapter 9 on the future of US military forces in the region.

5
US nuclear forces

In 1945, as part of the effort to defeat the Axis powers in World War II, the United States became the first nation to acquire—and thus far the only nation to employ in war—nuclear weapons. Today, over 50 years later, the United States, as one of the five nations (including Russia, the United Kingdom, France and China) with an acknowledged nuclear weapons capability, continues to believe that 'nuclear weapons will be part of the cornerstone of our deterrent strategy for some time into the future'.[1] Some analysts maintain that 'continuing uncertainty over the status of nuclear forces in Northeast Asia is the most dangerous feature of Asia–Pacific security'.[2]

Since the end of the Cold War, many aspects of US nuclear forces have undergone significant change. In order to understand the current situation, it is necessary to briefly review these changes.

One of the hallmarks of the Cold War was the nuclear 'arms race' and related nuclear arms control agreements between the United States and the Soviet Union. For example, concerning the most powerful nuclear forces, as of September 1990 the US strategic (i.e. long-range, intercontinental) nuclear forces consisted of nearly thirteen thousand nuclear warheads deployed on nearly two thousand land-, air- and sea-based launchers, including missiles and bombers.

At the same time, the Soviet Union had deployed nearly eleven thousand nuclear warheads on about 2500 strategic launchers, also distributed among land-, air- and sea-based forces, including missiles and bombers.

In late July 1991, following nine years of negotiations, the United States and the USSR (in its last few months of existence) signed a Strategic Arms Reduction Treaty (known as START), and

Table 5.1 US and Soviet/Russian strategic nuclear forces, July 1997

US strategic forces:	warheads by delivery system September 1990	warheads by delivery system July 1997	Soviet/Russian strategic nuclear forces:	warheads by delivery system September 1990	warheads by delivery system July 1997
ICBMs			ICBMs		
MX	500	500	SS-11	326	0
Minuteman III	1500	1845	SS-13	40	0
Minuteman II	450	55	SS-17	188	0
			SS-18	3080	1860
			SS-19	1800	1020
			SS-24 silo	560	100
			SS-24 rail	330	360
			SS-25	288	360
TOTAL	2450	2400	TOTAL	6612	3700
SLBMs			SLBMs		
Poseidon			SS-N-6		
(C-3)	1920	320		192	16
Trident I (C-4)	3072	1536	SS-N-8	280	192
Trident II (D-5)	768	1920	SS-N-17	12	0
			SS-N-18	672	624
			SS-N-20	1200	1200
			SS-N-23	448	448
TOTAL	5760	3776	TOTAL	2804	2480
BOMBERS			BOMBERS		
B-52 (ALCM)	1969	1620	Bear (ALCM)	672	512
B-52 (non-ALCM)	290	49	Bear (non-ALCM)	63	10
B-1	95	93	Blackjack	120	48
B-2	0	19			
TOTAL	2353	1781	TOTAL	855	570
TOTAL WARHEADS	10 563	7957	TOTAL WARHEADS	10 271	6750

Source: START I Memorandum of Understanding, 1 July 1997

began negotiations on a follow-on agreement, referred to as START II. As a result, by July 1997 US strategic nuclear forces had been reduced to 7957 warheads on 1162 launchers, and the strategic nuclear forces of the Russian Federation (following the demise of the Soviet Union in December 1991) had been reduced to 6750 nuclear warheads on 1257 launchers.

On 26 January 1996 the US Senate approved the START II treaty calling for further significant reductions by the year 2003, but at the time of writing the Russian parliament has not yet ratified that agreement. If that agreement, with an extension agreed upon by both parties in 1997, enters into force, by 2007 US strategic nuclear forces will have declined to 3500 nuclear warheads on 923 launchers, while Russia will probably be down to 3101 warheads on 1082 launchers. The details of this strategic nuclear drawdown are contained in Table 5.1.

This glimpse of post–Cold War strategic nuclear reductions only serves to introduce the changes that have affected US nuclear forces since the late 1980s. In documenting those changes and the current status of US nuclear forces, emphasis will be placed on their relevance to the Asia–Pacific region in the post–Cold War era.

CHANGES IN THE US NUCLEAR POSTURE, 1990–1994

The term 'US nuclear posture' encompasses the entire range of issues relating to US nuclear forces: policy, doctrine, force structure, operations, command and control, safety and security, and infrastructure.[3]

Reductions in strategic nuclear weapons resulting from formal arms control agreements between the United States and the USSR captured most of the attention at the end of the Cold War. However, another hallmark of the Cold War nuclear arms race had been the deployment of shorter-range 'tactical' nuclear weapons, both on land and at sea. At the end of the 1980s, the United States Navy had already begun to quietly remove a large portion (one unofficial estimate indicated around 1000) of the 'tactical' or 'non-strategic' nuclear weapons it had deployed at sea on surface ships in the form of air defense missiles and anti-submarine rockets. The process was to be completed by the end of 1989.

According to then Deputy Chief of Naval Operations Vice Admiral Henry C. Mustin, the unilateral withdrawal represented an evolution in US Navy thinking about nuclear weapons for war at sea: 'There is a recognition that if there is a nuclear war at sea, we have got more to lose than the Russians. The concept of nuclear war at sea is a concept whose time has passed. It is in the interest of the country to persuade the Soviets that the time has passed.'[4]

The attempted coup against President Gorbachev's leadership of the Soviet Union in August 1991 raised grave concerns in the United States about that country's future in general and particularly about nuclear command and control in the USSR—especially after it was learned that the Soviet defense minister and the chief of the General Staff had taken sides against Gorbachev.[5]

Partly in response to that event, on 27 September 1991 US President George Bush announced a series of unilateral nuclear reductions—and invited President Gorbachev to respond, which he did on 5 October. In summary, the Fall 1991 Bush initiatives and Gorbachev response resulted in:

- the mutual removal of all tactical nuclear weapons from US and Soviet surface ships, attack submarines and land-based naval aircraft (amounting to a total of over 4000 nuclear weapons from both forces);
- the mutual elimination of all US and Soviet ground-based tactical nuclear systems, including nuclear artillery shells, missile warheads and nuclear mines (including some 2000 US and 10 000 Soviet weapons);
- the mutual standing down of all US and Soviet strategic bombers from their 24-hour alert status;
- mutual proposals to go beyond the existing START agreement;
- mutual decisions by the United States and the USSR to place their nuclear forces under a single command structure.[6]

Although Europe was the primary focus, these initiatives had a significant impact on the presence of US nuclear forces in Northeast Asia. First, according to estimates by non-governmental analysts, during the mid-1980s the United States had stored approximately 150 nuclear warheads (down from a high of about 680 in the 1970s), including 21 land mines, 70 artillery shells and 60 gravity bombs, at Kunsan air base in South Korea. Since 1972 Kunsan had reportedly been the only forward base for US nuclear weapons storage in Asia.[7]

By 1991 the nuclear land mines had already been removed. Under the 27 September 1991 Bush initiative, the nuclear artillery shells were also scheduled for removal, reportedly without any prior notice to the South Korean government. At first, in keeping with the announced retention of forward-deployed nuclear gravity bombs in NATO, the United States informed South Korea that air-delivered nuclear weapons would not be removed.[8] In the end, however, *all* US nuclear weapons were also removed from South Korea, a fact first publicly confirmed by then South Korean President Roh Tae Woo on 18 December 1991, and later acknowledged by the United States.[9]

Second, throughout the Cold War the US Navy had strictly adhered to a policy of 'neither confirm nor deny' (NCND) regarding the presence of nuclear weapons on specific ships. Following the September 1991 Bush initiative, unnamed US Navy sources reportedly revealed that the 'standard loadout' for an aircraft carrier battle group had been around one hundred nuclear bombs, depth charges and cruise missiles.[10] This had presumably been the case for the carrier battle group homeported or operating out of Yokosuka, Japan, particularly in light of the fact, revealed under the US Freedom of Information Act, that on 5 December 1965 an A–4E *Skyhawk* bomber carrying a B–43 hydrogen bomb had fallen off the carrier USS *Ticonderoga* while it was some 320 kilometers off Okinawa on its way back to Yokosuka.[11]

In any event, on 2 July 1992 President Bush announced that all of the US nuclear weapons withdrawals announced in September 1991 were complete, indicating that 'all ground-launched tactical nuclear weapons have been returned to US territory as have all naval nuclear weapons'.[12] During the 1980s independent analysts had reported that the main stockpile for US nuclear weapons in the Western Pacific was located in the US territory of Guam.[13] More recently, analysts at the Natural Resources Defense Council in the United States claim that currently the only storage sites for US nuclear weapons in the Pacific region are located in the state of Washington on the US mainland's Pacific coast.[14] Officially, the US Department of Defense still maintains a 'neither confirm nor deny' policy with regard to nuclear weapons storage sites.[15]

In addition to continuing concern about Russia, the 1991 Persian Gulf War also had a serious impact on the US nuclear posture. The United States had long been aware of Iraq's efforts to achieve a nuclear weapons capability, and that Saddam Hussein's forces also possessed chemical and biological weapons as well as Scud-type ballistic missiles. Vigorous attempts were made during the initial air-war phase of Operation Desert Storm to eradicate those capabilities. However, both during and then after the war it became apparent that the United States had underestimated Iraqi capabilities and had failed to destroy them.[16]

In fact, as early as June 1990, then US Secretary of Defense Dick Cheney told the US Congress that the United States needed to maintain its strategic nuclear forces 'not only because the Soviets give every indication of wanting to maintain theirs ... but also, obviously, because there is a growing proliferation of weapons of mass destruction and sophisticated weapons technology in the Third World'.[17] Events in the Gulf War only reinforced that rationale. In Secretary Cheney's February 1992 annual report, he indicated that 'the possibility that Third World nations may acquire nuclear capabilities has led the Department to make adjustments to nuclear and strategic defense forces and to the policies that guide them'.[18]

Those adjustments had been made in the course of the first major post–Cold War review of US nuclear strategy conducted by a Deterrence Study Group established by General Lee Butler, commander of the Air Force's Strategic Air Command, and chaired by former Secretary of the Air Force Thomas C. Reed. The group came to be known as the Reed Panel and its January 1992 Report called for revisions in the basic US nuclear warfighting plan, called the Single Integrated Operating Plan or SIOP, to reflect the end of the Cold War and the growing danger of nuclear proliferation.[19]

The new circumstances called for a new form of command and control over US nuclear forces. In the ultimate sense, of course, US nuclear forces have always been under the direct control of the National Command Authority (NCA)—that is, the President—or his constitutional successors in the event of an emergency (see Chapter 3). In operational terms, however, in 1946 the US Air Force's Strategic Air Command (SAC) was established, with control of the US nuclear bomber force, and later the Intercontinental Ballistic Missile (ICBM) force. In the late 1950s the US Navy began developing nuclear ballistic missile submarines, and as a result the Joint Strategic Target Planning Staff (JSTPS) was established in 1960 as a single agency to plan and target all US nuclear forces.

On 1 June 1992 SAC and the JSTPS were dissolved, and the planning, targeting and wartime employment of US strategic forces came under the control of a single commander of the newly formed US Strategic Command (USSTRATCOM). The day-to-day operational training, equipping and maintenance responsibilities for its forces remained with the two individual services that still retain nuclear weapons—the Air Force and the Navy.[20] Basic nuclear weapons capabilities and nuclear weapons accident response training is conducted at the Defense Nuclear Weapons School at Kirtland Air Force Base in New Mexico, under the aegis of the Defense Special Weapons Agency, formerly called the Defense Nuclear Agency.[21]

Concerning the rationale for the retention of nuclear weapons, in August 1992 the US Joint Chiefs of Staff for the first time adopted the terminology of 'weapons of mass destruction' (WMD) when it stated, 'The purpose of [US] nuclear forces is to deter the use of weapons of mass destruction'.[22] In December 1992 USSTRATCOM formed a Strategic Planning Study Group (SPSG) 'to develop a flexible, globally-focused war-planning process known as the Strategic War Planning System (SWPS)' to produce 'a living SIOP'.[23]

The core SIOP began to undergo major changes due to the dramatic reduction in the nuclear arsenals of both the United States and the USSR/Russia resulting from arms control agreements and unilateral reductions. According to Bruce Blair of the Brookings Institution, from 1986 to 1995 the number of Soviet/Russian targets in the SIOP declined from 16 000 to 2500, and targets in China had been dropped from the SIOP in the early 1980s.[24]

Soon after the Clinton administration took office in 1993 the US Joint Chiefs of Staff published a new official, classified 'Doctrine for Joint Nuclear Operations', which was later released under the Freedom of Information Act. That document stated that:

> the fundamental purpose of US nuclear forces is to deter the use of weapons of mass destruction (WMD), particularly nuclear weapons, and to serve as a hedge against the emergence of an overwhelming conventional threat.
>
> ... US nuclear forces serve to deter the use of WMD across the spectrum of potential conflict. From a massive exchange of nuclear weapons to limited use on a regional battlefield, US nuclear capabilities must confront an enemy with risks of unacceptable damage and disproportionate loss should the enemy choose to introduce WMD in a conflict.[25]

With regard to regional contingencies, the Joint Chiefs stated:

> The proliferation of WMD technologies and industrial capabilities in the world may allow a potential aggressor to develop a WMD arsenal capable of being employed against US forces deployed to a regional crisis. WMD used on US forces would ... leave the United States with a difficult choice: to retaliate or not to retaliate. A selective capability of being able to use lower-yield weapons in retaliation, without destabilizing the conflict, is a useful alternative for the US National Command Authorities (NCA).[26]

The Joint Chiefs also noted that, in addition to the long-range strategic nuclear forces:

> Nonstrategic nuclear forces (NSNF) offer options short of strategic response in those situations where escalation control is desired. In addition, NSNF increases the overall deterrent value of US forces by their direct deterrence at regional level. Both strategic and nonstrategic nuclear weapons hold regional targets at risk.[27]

The October 1993 Department of Defense *Report on the Bottom-Up Review* was the Clinton administration's first comprehensive defense document (see Chapter 2). It is interesting to note that it listed the proliferation of weapons of mass destruction first among the 'Nuclear Dangers and Opportunities' facing the United States, with Korea and the Persian Gulf as possible theaters, and North Korea, Iran and Iraq as possible adversaries. The 'Former Soviet Union' received a secondary emphasis.[28]

This new emphasis on WMD proliferation led to several proposals by the Department of Defense, the Department of Energy, the Air Force and the Navy for the development of lower-yield nuclear warheads to be delivered with the same precision exhibited by US forces during the Gulf War. Critics in the United States, such as the anti-nuclear and environmental organization Greenpeace, warned that a new nuclear arms race could be the result.[29] Near the end of 1993 the US Congress passed a law banning any 'research and development which could lead to the production by the United States of a new low-yield nuclear weapon, including a precision low-yield nuclear weapon'.[30]

Following a summit meeting in Vancouver, Canada, between US President Clinton and Russian President Yeltsin in early 1993, the White House announced that the US had begun 'a comprehensive review of measures that could enhance strategic stability, including the possibility of each side reprogramming its nuclear missiles so they are not routinely aimed at each other'.[31] Concerning reprogramming missiles, the Defense Department and USSTRATCOM proceeded to prepare an option called 'broad open ocean area targeting'.[32]

The first result of this comprehensive review process was an agreement struck at the next Clinton–Yeltsin summit in January 1994 to implement a so-called 'detargeting' plan by 30 May 1994. Britain and China eventually joined this agreement to aim all their nuclear missiles away from their wartime targets and point them at the ocean or no targets at all.[33] Analysts point out that this agreement, while perhaps important with regard to the accidental launch of a single weapon, is primarily political in nature given the fact that most targeting can be restored in a short time, in some cases as little as a few seconds. Moreover, the agreement is not subject to verification.[34]

The second and far more significant result of the process first announced by President Clinton in 1993 was the comprehensive, classified *Nuclear Posture Review* (NPR) which was completed in September of 1994.

FROM THE 1994 *NUCLEAR POSTURE REVIEW* TO THE PRESENT

On 22 September 1994 the US Department of Defense announced the completion of its *Nuclear Posture Review*, the first comprehensive review of US nuclear policy, strategy and forces in over fifteen years. Although the results of the Review were classified, US officials did provide summaries in briefings to the US Congress and the media.

The Review began by answering the question 'Why [Do] We Have Nuclear Weapons?' with the following quotes from the 1994 *National Security Strategy of the United States*:

> Even with the Cold War over, our nation must maintain military forces that are sufficient to deter diverse threats. We will retain strategic nuclear forces sufficient to deter any future hostile foreign leadership with access to strategic nuclear forces from acting against our vital interests and to convince it that seeking a nuclear advantage would be futile. Therefore we will continue to maintain nuclear forces of sufficient size and capability to hold at risk a broad range of assets valued by such political and military leaders. A critical priority for the United States is to stem the proliferation of nuclear weapons and other weapons of mass destruction and their missile delivery systems.[35]

In addition to the new security environment that included the end of the Cold War, the emergence of regional threats, and the proliferation of weapons of mass destruction, the Review briefing also cited US budget constraints and a need to take stock of the impact of arms control agreements as part of the rationale for the process.

Long-range *strategic nuclear forces* were the keystone of the Cold War arms race between the United States and the Soviet Union/Russia, so the Review briefing addressed them first. Concerning the military requirements for US strategic nuclear forces, the Review briefing said that force plans to the year 2003 were based on 'projected military requirements', assuming the implementation of the START I and START II agreements between the United States and Russia.[36] In a press conference, then Deputy Secretary of Defense John Deutch elaborated on this point by stating that:

> The way we arrived at requirements for US nuclear force structure for this period of time through START II was to assess the capabilities of the former Soviet Union—the targets that are

there—and we looked at the kind of targeting and kinds of attack plans we might have, and also are prepared to deal with hostile governments not only in Russia, but in other countries.[37]

Deutch went on to state, as was noted above, that due to reductions in the nuclear force structure of the former Soviet Union, the number of targets included in the Single Integrated Operating Plan (SIOP) had gone down 'extraordinarily', to 'much more than 50 per cent reduction'.[38]

The fact that Russian targets, presumably including some in the Russian Far East such as the nuclear submarine bases at Vladivostok and Petropavlosk, remain in the SIOP is due to the fact that the United States 'must be prepared for possible emergence of [a] hostile government in Russia or failure of arms control process in the former Soviet Union'.[39] In other words, US strategic nuclear forces constitute a 'hedge' against a resurgent Russian threat.[40] Recent intelligence reports indicate that Russia continues to construct deep underground bunkers, subways and command posts to help Moscow's leaders survive a nuclear attack. Some see this activity as essentially defensive and non-threatening; others cite it as a reason for the United States to continue its 'hedging' nuclear policy.[41]

The SIOP is highly classified, of course. Independent analysts familiar with the subject report that US strategic nuclear forces are assigned two roles: (1) those on daily alert are committed to the primary target set of the SIOP, which now consists of some 2500 targets in Russia (China having been dropped in the early 1980s); and (2) others constitute a 'strategic reserve force' to be employed only *after* an initial nuclear exchange with Russia. Among the targets for this 'reserve force' are nations outside Russia who are considered to be potential wartime adversaries in the aftermath of such an exchange. The target set assigned to these forces reportedly includes a total of 'some 800 or so' targets in China, North Korea, Libya, Iran and elsewhere, with 'the vast majority' in China.[42]

According to Bruce Blair of the Brookings Institution, the authors of the September 1994 *Nuclear Posture Review* considered restoring China to the SIOP primary target set, but rejected that view, 'leaving China as the prime target set of the reserve force'.[43] Blair suggests that the continuing modernization of China's nuclear ballistic missile force might eventually prompt a reconsideration of this decision.[44] It is interesting to note that in February 1995 then US Defense Secretary Perry, when asked whether he thought China currently targets the United States with its long-range missiles, responded that 'I am not really sure what I can say in that category. I do not believe there is a current threat from Chinese missiles'.[45]

Recent press reports have revealed that the March 1996 crisis in the Taiwan Strait included undercurrents of nuclear menace and led to serious dialog about preventing unintended war. Among the results was the 27 June 1998 announcement by Presidents Clinton and Jiang Zemin that the United States and the People's Republic of China 'will not target the strategic nuclear weapons under their respective control at each other'.[46] Analysts were quick to point out that, like the previous 1994 US–Russian 'detargeting' agreement, this was a purely symbolic achievement, since the missiles can be quickly retargeted. Moreover, in effect the United States had *already* 'detargeted' China back in May 1994, since the mechanics of detargeting Russia at that time had meant the removal of *all* targets for US missiles because of the technology involved.[47]

All of these considerations flow from remaining US concerns about potential nuclear war with Russia. However, as noted above, since the end of the Cold War the potential of 'regional' aggression and the proliferation of weapons of mass destruction and ballistic missiles have added possible new dimensions to the role of US strategic nuclear weapons: counter-proliferation and regional deterrence.

There are several constraints on the use of any US nuclear weapons in such circumstances. First, with regard to declared policy and legally binding treaties, on 12 June 1978 then US Secretary of State Cyrus Vance declared a so-called US 'negative security assurance' at the UN Special Session on Disarmament in New York:

> The United States will not use nuclear weapons against any non-nuclear weapons state party to the [Nuclear Non-Proliferation Treaty] NPT or any comparable internationally binding commitment not to acquire nuclear explosive devices, except in the case of an attack on the United States, its territories or armed forces, or its allies, by such a state allied to a nuclear-weapons state or associated with a nuclear-weapons state in carrying out or sustaining the attack.[48]

On 5 April 1995 then Secretary of State Warren Christopher restated this US commitment at the NPT review and extension conference.[49]

Most recently, however, at an 11 April 1996 White House press briefing following the US signing of the protocol to the African Nuclear-Weapon-Free-Zone Treaty, which included a pledge not to use or threaten to use a nuclear weapon against any treaty party, the United States apparently added an exception to this non-use pledge. At that briefing, Robert Bell, special assistant to President Clinton and a senior director for defense policy and arms control at the US National Security Council, stated that the protocol 'will not limit options available to the United States in response to an attack by [a treaty] party using weapons of mass destruction'.[50] In other words, the United States has added an exception for biological and chemical weapons attacks to the US 'negative security assurance' policy. This amendment has received criticism from arms control advocates in the United States.[51]

In addition to the constraints of declaratory policy and treaties, there are pragmatic issues. The enormous destructive power and relative lack of precision (compared with conventional 'smart bombs' for example) of most US strategic nuclear weapons make it unlikely that they would be employed in either a counter-proliferation or a regional role. Thus in 1994 General Charles A. Horner, the US Air Force theater commander during the Gulf War, said:

> I just don't think nuclear weapons are usable . . . I'm saying that I have a nuclear weapon, and you're North Korea, and you have a nuclear weapon. You can use yours. I can't use mine. What am I going to use it on? What are nuclear weapons good for? Busting cities. What President of the United States is going to take out Pyongyang?[52]

There are other considerations as well. Analysts point out, for example, that although land-based ICBMs in the continental United States have the range to reach non-Russian targets in Northeast Asia including North Korea and China, they 'are not particularly relevant to the region because their flight paths would cross Russian territory and might inadvertently provoke a response from Moscow'.[53] This factor would not, however, necessarily affect either submarine or air-launched strategic nuclear weapons.

In any event, under the policy developed as a result of the 1994 *Nuclear Posture Review* and recently confirmed as part of the *Quadrennial Defense Review*, the United States possesses a 'triad' of strategic nuclear forces which, at the time of writing, consists of:

- 50 land-based Peacekeeper and 500 Minuteman III Intercontinental Ballistic Missiles (ICBMs), carrying a total of 2090 warheads, based at F. E. Warren Air Force Base, Wyoming, Grand Forks Air Force Base, North Dakota, Malmstrom Air Force Base, Montana, and Minot Air Force Base, North Dakota;
- 174 long-range B–1B, B–2 and B–52H bombers capable of carrying 3048 nuclear weapons, based at Barksdale Air Force Base, Louisiana, Minot Air Force Base, North Dakota, Dyess Air Force Base, Texas and Whiteman Air Force Base, Missouri—scheduled to decline to 67 B–52H and 20 B–2 bombers capable of carrying 1320 nuclear weapons by 2003;
- 408 Trident I(C–4)and Trident II(D–5) Submarine-Launched Ballistic Missiles (SLBMs), carrying 3048 nuclear warheads, on board 18 Trident Ballistic Missile Nuclear Submarines (SSBNs), eight based at Naval Submarine Base, Bangor, Washington, and ten at Naval Submarine Base, Kings Bay, Georgia—scheduled to decline to 336 Trident II SLBMs carrying 1680 warheads on board 14 Trident SSBNs by 2003.[54]

It is important to stress that at all times these weapons are under the control of the US National Command Authorities (NCA), which consist first and foremost of the personal civilian command of the US President or, in the event that the President is dead or disabled, his legal civilian successors: the Vice-President, then the Speaker of the House of Representatives, and then other civilian members of the Cabinet (see Chapter 2). Only the President or his legal successor can order nuclear strikes. The civilian office of the Secretary of Defense is next in the chain of command. Underground control centers exist both at the National Military Command Center at the Pentagon near Washington, DC, and at US Strategic Command headquarters near Omaha, Nebraska. Moreover, in the event of an emergency or destruction of ground command control centers, at least one E–4B National Airborne Operations Center (similar to a Boeing 747 airliner) is always on alert with a fully manned battle staff and sophisticated communications gear.[55]

In day-to-day operational terms, US strategic nuclear weapons come under the control of the US Strategic Command, formed in June 1992. Its responsibilities include: employing assigned forces, as directed; providing support to other combatant commanders, including the Commander in Chief of the US Pacific Command; conducting worldwide airborne reconnaissance in support of strategic missions; ensuring command, control, communications, computers and intelligence (C^4I) for strategic force employment.

The US Strategic Command is a 'unified' command consisting of some 2100 personnel from all the armed services, with the majority coming from the Air Force. The Commander in Chief (CINC) of USSTRATCOM is either an Air Force General or a Navy Admiral. USSTRATCOM headquarters is located at Offutt Air Force Base, Nebraska. The US Strategic Command's Command Center at that base is a large, heavily protected underground complex that is prepared to transmit National Command Authority directives to strategic aircraft, submarines and missile forces. An EC–135 'Looking Glass' Airborne Command Post (similar to a Boeing 707 airliner) is on 24-hour a day ground alert ready to receive orders from the National Command Authorities and then direct bombers and missiles from the air should USSTRATCOM's ground Command Center become inoperable.

Communication with strategic nuclear forces is maintained via satellites and radio networks (VLF, LF, UHF and HF). Several sophisticated detection and display systems provide the USSTRATCOM Command Center (and North American Air Defense Command Headquarters at Cheyenne Mountain in Colorado) with ICBM and SLBM attack warnings. Pending a Presidential decision, CINCSTRAT can take measures to *protect* strategic nuclear forces (e.g. launch aircraft for survival) but only the President can order nuclear strikes.

Concerning shorter-range *non-strategic US nuclear forces* (NSNF), the 1994 *Nuclear Posture Review* is built on the 1991 Bush–Gorbachev initiatives described above. Going beyond the removal of such weapons from US Navy surface ships, the 1994 NPR announced that the United States was 'beginning the process of removing the capability both in terms of the training of the individuals and the facilities on the ships themselves to deal with nuclear weapons on the surface vessels'.[56]

At the same time US defense officials emphasized that the US would retain two non-strategic nuclear weapons capabilities: Air Force fighter-bombers capable of carrying nuclear bombs, and nuclear attack submarines (SSNs) capable of launching the nuclear version of the Tomahawk sea-launched cruise missile, designated the TLAM-N. The SSNs would not routinely carry TLAM-N, but could load such weapons quickly if ordered. The 'dual-capable' bombers would remain stationed in NATO countries in Europe and in the continental United States, but they can be quickly re-deployed if necessary.[57]

According to analysts at the Brookings Institution, the United States possessed 1225 active non-strategic B–61 nuclear gravity bombs and W–80 warheads at the end of 1996.[58] Prior to the 1991 Bush initiative the United States possessed 367 nuclear Tomahawk cruise missiles, each with a range of 1350 nautical miles (2482 km) and carrying one W–80 nuclear warhead. By 1992 all the nuclear Tomahawks had been removed from the submarines to storage depots in US territory. One analyst estimates that 'the re-deployment of nuclear-tipped sea-launched cruise missiles on attack submarines would probably only take a few weeks to complete'.[59] At the time of writing, the 30 nuclear attack submarines assigned to the US Pacific Fleet in 1998 are based either at Pearl Harbor, Hawaii (24) or San Diego, California (6). All are capable of launching Tomahawk cruise missiles, although it is not evident how many have the necessary trained personnel and equipment to launch the nuclear version.[60]

As with strategic nuclear weapons, only the President can authorize the use of non-strategic nuclear weapons. The operational chain of command and control of the non-strategic weapons is less apparent. According to some sources, in late 1994 the US Strategic Command 'took responsibility for global planning of non-strategic nuclear weapons', despite some objections from US theater commanders.[61]

According to some reports, STRATCOM may have taken a major role in target planning against weapons of mass destruction located in areas other than the former Soviet Union, including the US Pacific Command. However, the regional Commander-in-Chief (CINC) would retain operational control of the weapons themselves.[62]

The 1994 *Nuclear Posture Review* also resulted in further changes in the Command, Control, Communications and Intelligence of US nuclear weapons. For example, some ballistic missile submarines were placed on 'modified-alert' as opposed to 'alert' status, and the airborne command and control aircraft described earlier ended in-flight alert status. Upgrades to communications, warning/attack assessment and intelligence systems were also announced.[63]

The infrastructure of the US nuclear weapons capability also received attention. With regard to delivery systems, the aging Minuteman ICBM force was slated for new guidance systems and new motors, the Trident D–5 missile would be kept in production, and the industrial base needed to maintain guidance systems and re-entry vehicles would be sustained.

Concerning nuclear weapons themselves, in the 1994 *Nuclear Posture Review* the Department of Defense instructed the Department of Energy to:

- maintain nuclear weapon capability (without underground nuclear testing or fissile material production), including the ability to refabricate and certify nuclear weapons in the stockpile, and maintaining a capability to design, fabricate and certify new warheads;
- ensure the availability of tritium, an element in nuclear weapons that decays fairly rapidly over time;
- refrain from any new-design nuclear warhead production.[64]

In fact, the United States had virtually ceased nuclear warhead production by 1989, due to a combination of factors including the end of the Cold War and growing concerns over the safety and environmental impact of nuclear weapons production sites. Controversy has, however, arisen over whether modifications to improve the hard target penetration capabilities of the existing B–61 nuclear bomb (e.g. the 'Mod–11' version) constitute 'new production'. In 1992 the United States ceased underground nuclear weapons tests and has renounced further detonation tests, but not computer simulations.[65]

Under the 'Stockpile Stewardship and Management Program' the US Department of Energy 'will maintain the core intellectual and technical competencies of the weapons plants and laboratories' and 'is maintaining the ability to resume underground testing at the Nevada Test Site and reconstitute weapons production capacities'.[66]

More recently, the United States has announced that, in order to replace obsolete warheads and preserve the effectiveness of its strategic nuclear forces, it plans to resume nuclear weapons production by the year 2003 in order to maintain a stockpile of about 6000 nuclear weapons. Specifically, the Energy Department plan calls for the Los Alamos National Laboratory in New Mexico to demonstrate the ability to make plutonium 'pits' or nuclear triggers in 1998, and to be ready for sustained production of up to 50 nuclear bombs a year by 2003.[67]

The 1994 *Nuclear Posture Review* next addressed the issue of US nuclear weapons Safety, Security, and Use Control. Throughout the Cold War, many analysts felt that inadvertent, accidental or unauthorized use of nuclear weapons was a greater danger than deliberate nuclear war between the superpowers.[68] In addition to the unilateral measures already documented above, the NPR also:

- reduced storage locations for US nuclear weapons by over 75 per cent
- cut the number of personnel with access to nuclear weapons by 70 per cent
- upgraded the coded control device (CCD) components (also referred to as 'Permissive Action Links' or PALs) on the B–52 bomber and Minuteman III ICBM systems
- began the installation of CCDs for the first time on US Trident ballistic missile submarines, to be completed during 1997.[69]

Concern about the safety and security of nuclear weapons in the former Soviet Union played a role in the adoption of these measures, with the United States desiring to set a positive example.

Finally, the 1994 *Nuclear Posture Review* outlined a series of 'Counterproliferation Initiatives' designed to improve US security in the face of the proliferation of weapons of mass destruction. These included initiatives to:

- develop effective theater defenses against ballistic missile and air-breathing threats (see Chapter 9)
- enhance conventional capabilities to counter the proliferation threat (e.g. non-nuclear weapons capable of destroying 'hard' underground targets)
- support international non-proliferation efforts and arms control agreements
- continue assistance to the former Soviet Union to enhance safety and security of nuclear weapons there.[70]

The 1994 *Nuclear Posture Review* came under criticism from both conservatives and liberals in the United States. Conservatives such as former Secretary of Defense Caspar Weinberger argued that the NPR went too far in dismantling the massive nuclear capability the United States had assembled by the late 1980s.[71] Arms control advocates asserted the opposite, claiming that the NPR was a missed opportunity to move decisively away from the Cold War nuclear arms race. For example, William Arkin of Greenpeace wrote that 'mid-level bureaucrats and one-star generals were allowed to push through the predictable result. Stagnation was assured'.[72] Some Asian observers also aired doubts about 'whether nuclear arms can deter [non-nuclear] threats and prevent proliferation'.[73]

RECENT DEVELOPMENTS THROUGH THE 1997 *QUADRENNIAL DEFENSE REVIEW*

Since 1990 an increasing, albeit still minority, number of military officers and defense officials have reached the conclusion that nuclear weapons are largely obsolete in the post–Cold War era and should be drastically reduced or even eliminated.[74] In keeping with this trend, on 14 August 1996 the Canberra Commission on the Elimination of Nuclear Weapons, which had been established by the Australian government in November 1995, released its report. The Commission, which included retired US Air Force General Lee Butler, who had been Commander In Chief of USSTRATCOM from 1992 to 1994, and former US Secretary of Defense Robert McNamara, called upon the United States, Russia, the United Kingdom, France and China to 'give the lead by committing themselves, unequivocally, to the elimination of all nuclear weapons' and outlined a series of steps by which this goal might be achieved. Among the immediate steps it called for were:

- taking nuclear forces off alert
- removal of warheads from delivery vehicles
- ending deployment of non-strategic nuclear weapons
- ending nuclear testing
- initiating negotiations to further reduce United States and Russian nuclear arsenals
- agreement among the nuclear-weapons states of reciprocal no-first-use undertakings, and of a non-use undertaking by them in relation to non-nuclear weapons states.[75]

On 4 December 1996 General Butler and retired General Andrew Goodpaster, former Supreme Allied Commander in Europe, released a joint statement also arguing in favor of the ultimate elimination of all nuclear weapons worldwide. The next day, 61 retired generals and admirals from 17 countries—including 19 from the United States—issued a similar statement, outlining a plan for the elimination of all nuclear weapons worldwide by the middle of the next century.

The official US response to these calls was ambivalent. In his 4 December press briefing, US State Department spokesman Nicholas Burns reiterated US support for the *eventual* elimination of nuclear weapons worldwide, but cautioned that the current international situation did not permit such an action. On the same day White House Press Secretary Michael McCurry wrote that '... we do not believe that removing nuclear weapons from alert status and placing warheads in controlled storage or further restricting US nuclear declaratory policy is in our security interests'.[76]

Some analysts and former government officials argued that the eventual elimination of nuclear weapons from the US arsenal could cause more harm than good in East Asia. Robert Oakley, former US ambassador to Pakistan and National Security Council assistant to President Reagan said:

> [Hasty disarmament] could be dangerous because others in East Asia will want to do at least what the Pakistanis and Indians have done. They might want to have nuclear warheads deployed on missiles or, at the very least, have the option of drawing on a nuclear capability. Otherwise they'd be naked, particularly with regard to the Chinese.

In a similar vein, a US State Department official stated, 'Obviously, we must honor our treaty obligations to allies in the region. Minus a wholesale adjustment in regional dynamics, this issue is a non-starter'.[77]

On 9 March 1997, however, there were reports to the effect that the United States was ready to negotiate deeper cuts in nuclear weapons with Russia, provided that the Russian parliament ratified the START II agreement.[78] In fact, at the Helsinki summit between Presidents Clinton and Yeltsin on 21 March 1997, the United States did indeed make such an offer.

In return for a pledge by President Yeltsin to facilitate the ratification of START II by the State Duma of the Russian Federation, the United States and Russia

> reached an understanding that START III will establish by December 31, 2007 a ceiling of 2000–2500 strategic nuclear weapons for each of the parties, representing a 30–45 per cent reduction in the number of total deployed strategic warheads permitted under START II . . .[79]

Furthermore, Clinton and Yeltsin agreed to include in START III measures relating to the transparency of strategic nuclear warhead inventories and the destruction of strategic nuclear warheads, and transparency in other nuclear materials.

Finally, in a matter of particular interest in regional terms, at the Helsinki summit non-strategic nuclear weapons were also included for the first time in proposed formal negotiations. Clinton and Yeltsin 'agreed to explore possible measures relating to long-range nuclear sea-launched cruise missiles and tactical nuclear systems'. These discussions will apparently include transparency and confidence measures and will take place 'separate from, but in the context of, the START III negotiations'.[80] In a later background briefing to the press, a senior US administration official answered a question about this matter.

> Q: The tactical weapons—that got thrown in that tactical weapons will be included in the START III negotiations. [sic] Could you give us some sense of the dimensions of this, what it means, is it a big deal? . . . And it's what Russia wants, isn't it?
> A: This is a classic SALT-START issue. It goes back to Vladivostok and before . . . This has to do with cruise missiles, which because they are on platforms that can move close to Russia and are, as the Russians say, effectively strategic. Because you have their range plus the range of the airplane or the ship that can bring them in.
> Q: But it's basically the Cruises?
> A: Yes . . .[81]

Predictably, these agreements were welcomed by arms control advocates who had urged Clinton to make gestures that would reinvigorate the stalled START process, but harshly criticized by conservative members of the US Congress and analysts. Some claimed, for example, that the inclusion of sea-launched cruise missiles was 'a long-standing Soviet-Russian demand resisted by every previous US administration and fraught with peril for the US Navy's operational flexibility and security'.[82]

Be that as it may, the Helsinki agreements were all predicated on the ratification of START II by the Russian Duma, which had not occurred at the time of writing.

Following information in a 12 December 1996 Department of Defense press briefing that the newly instituted *Quadrennial Defense Review* (QDR) would include nuclear forces, some commentators called for a deeper re-evaluation than had taken place during the 1994 *Nuclear Posture Review*. Morton Halperin, a former Pentagon and National Security Council official during the Carter administration, stated:

> It is my understanding that the same people who did the NPR are going to do the nuclear piece of the QDR and will take as their starting point the requirements that have been laid on them by past Presidents of what kind of nuclear forces they have and what kind of targeting is needed. You will not get from that kind of study a fundamental look at the basic issues which I think needs to be done in light of the end of the Cold War.[83]

In fact, the strategy section of the *Quadrennial Defense Review* contained the following statement:

> The primary role of US nuclear forces in the current and projected security environment is to deter aggression against the United States, its forces abroad, and its allies and friends. Although the prominence of nuclear weapons in our defense posture has diminished since the end of the Cold War, nuclear weapons remain important as a hedge against NBC (nuclear, biological, chemical) proliferation and the uncertain futures of existing nuclear powers, and as a means of upholding our security commitments to allies.
>
> In this context, the United States retains strategic nuclear forces sufficient to deter any hostile foreign leadership with access to nuclear weapons from acting against our vital interests and to convince such a leadership that seeking a nuclear advantage would be futile. Thus, for the foreseeable future, the United States will continue to need a reliable and flexible nuclear deterrent—survivable against the most aggressive attack, under highly confident, constitutional command and control, and safeguarded against both accidental and unauthorized use.[84]

The exact size and nature of US nuclear forces will continue to be most directly affected by the progress—or lack thereof—in the START process between the United States and Russia, as described above. For example, the further warhead reductions projected for START III could easily be reached on the US side by loading fewer warheads on the Trident II submarine-launched ballistic missiles.

In September 1997, in another effort by the United States to facilitate the Russian Duma's favorable consideration of the START II treaty, the United States and Russia signed a package of agreements that would give Russia an additional five years—until the end of 2007—to dismantle launching systems as required by START II, although the systems must still be 'disabled' by the original date of 2003.[85]

In December 1997 the *Washington Post* revealed that President Clinton had issued new classified guidelines, known as Presidential Decision Directive (PDD) 60, for the targeting of US nuclear weapons, replacing one signed by President Ronald Reagan in 1981. Although affirming that the United States will continue to rely on nuclear arms as a cornerstone of its national security for 'the indefinite future', the Directive reportedly drops any planning for a long nuclear war on the grounds that no nation would emerge as the victor in a nuclear exchange. Such a statement had already been made by Presidents Reagan and Gorbachev during the 1985 Reykjavik Summit, but the new PDD formally ends target planning for a protracted nuclear conflict—possibly due to the fact that the reductions already agreed to in the START process would leave 'too few' nuclear weapons to conduct such a long war. Robert G. Bell, special assistant to the President and senior director for defense policy at the National Security Council, told reporters that 'most notably the PDD removes from presidential guidance all previous references to being able to wage a nuclear war successfully or to prevail in a nuclear war'.[86]

Some reports also indicated that the new PDD removes Russian conventional forces and civilian targets from the target list, while broadening the list of sites that might be struck in a nuclear exchange with China to include that country's growing military-industrial complex and its improved conventional forces, despite improving US–China relations, but Bell refused to comment on the reports.

Finally, the PDD apparently demands general planning for potential strikes against other nations (so-called 'rogue states') that have what Bell called 'prospective access' to nuclear weapons and that are or may become hostile to the United States. Moreover, Bell indicated that the new nuclear targeting directive reflects 'much greater sensitivity to the threats' posed by chemical and biological attacks, and that if any nation uses any weapons of mass destruction against the United States it may 'forfeit' its protection from US nuclear attack under the US 'negative security assurance' pledge first made in 1978 and then re-stated in 1995 prior to the extension of the Nuclear Non-Proliferation Treaty (NPT).[87]

This last element rekindled the controversy, described above, over the role of US nuclear weapons in preventing or halting the proliferation of weapons of mass destruction. Further revelations about apparent US planning for such a role came in March 1998 when an arms control organization released a report based on US defense documents partially de-classified and released under the Freedom of Information Act. The Report cited a 1995 STRATCOM study detailing the post–Cold War shift toward targeting 'rogue' states such as Iraq, Libya, Syria, Cuba and North Korea. Other de-classified documents outline the ongoing 'modification' of existing nuclear weapons such as the B–61–11 bomb designed to destroy underground targets, as well as research into other possible ways to employ nuclear weapons in a counter-proliferation role.⁸⁸

Responding to arms control advocates who fear that this reported trend will undermine the NPT and actually lead to increased proliferation, Presidential Adviser Bell stated, 'I don't think there's a disconnect in principle between some level of general planning at STRATCOM and the negative security assurance and our goals relative to the Non-Proliferation Treaty'.⁸⁹

In the Asia–Pacific region, the two most salient issues affecting the US nuclear posture are the continuing concerns over North Korea's nuclear program, and the slow but steady modernization of China's nuclear weapons capability, which, according to CIA Director George Tenet, currently contains a 'small number of strategic missiles with sufficient range to target large urban areas in the United States'.⁹⁰

As the turn of the century approaches, unless there are further dramatic political changes in the global security environment, it seems clear in 1998 that by 2007 the United States will continue to deploy at least 2000 active strategic nuclear weapons with the range to reach any target on earth, and to possess hundreds of active non-strategic nuclear weapons—a fact that many will find reassuring, and many others will regard as dangerous.

6
US Navy and US Marine Corps

Both geography and history have made the United States Navy and its integral sea service, the US Marine Corps, nearly synonymous with (at least in the public perception) the term 'American military presence in the Asia–Pacific region' throughout this century, notwithstanding the major contributions of the Army and Air Force. From the great naval battles and the 'island-hopping' campaign across the South and Central Pacific during World War II, through the Inchon landing and other battles of the Korean Conflict, and throughout the ten-year trial in the jungles and skies of Vietnam, the Navy and Marine Corps have played critical roles. At the time of writing approximately 24 000 US Navy and 20 000 US Marine Corps personnel are 'forward deployed' throughout the region. This chapter examines the mission, organization, strategic vision, force structure and capabilities of the US Navy and the US Marine Corps, with a particular emphasis on the Asia–Pacific region.

MISSION AND ORGANIZATION

The US Navy was founded by an act of Congress on 13 October 1775. Today, nearly 225 years later, the mission of the Navy is 'to maintain freedom of the seas for the United States and its allies, to be prepared to conduct combat operations at sea in support of national interests of the United States, and to maintain the ability for power projection ashore'.[1]

The US Marine Corps was founded by Congress shortly thereafter, on 10 November 1775. By law, the mission of the Marine Corps is to:

- provide Fleet Marine forces of combined arms for service with

Figure 6.1 Organization of the Department of the Navy

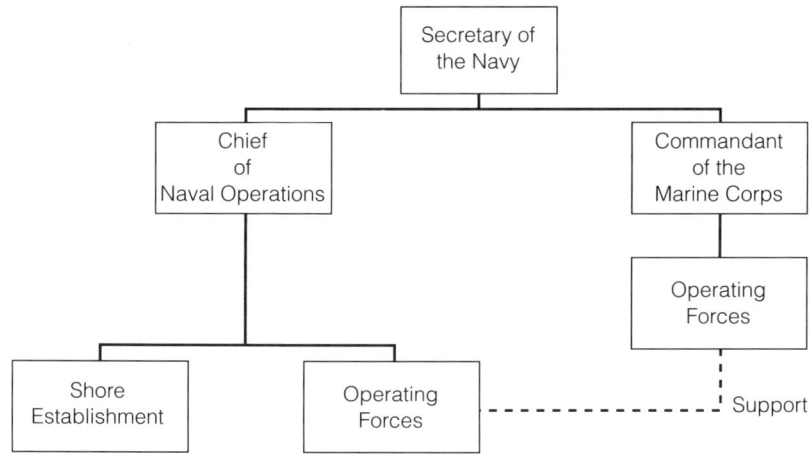

The dashed line marked 'Support' indicates the cooperative support of the Navy–Marine Corps team. Each of the operating forces supports the other.

Source: US Navy

    the fleet in the seizure or defense of advanced naval bases and for the conduct of such land operations as may be essential to the prosecution of a naval campaign
- develop tactics, techniques and equipment used by landing forces
- perform such duties as the President may direct.[2]

The US Navy and the Marine Corps are both 'sea services' under the jurisdiction of the Department of the Navy. The Department of the Navy is a major component of the Department of Defense, and comes under the civilian authority of the President, the Secretary of Defense, and then the Secretary of the Navy. The Department of the Navy has three principal components: the Navy Department, with its executive offices in Washington, DC; the Operating Forces, including the Marine Corps, the reserve components and, in time of war only, the US Coast Guard; and the Shore Establishment. The highest military officer in the US Navy is the Admiral appointed the Chief of Naval Operations (CNO); the highest military officer in the US Marine Corps is the General appointed Commandant of the Marine Corps. Both are by law official military advisers to the President and the Secretary of

Defense (see Chapter 3). Figure 6.1 presents an overview of the organization of the Department of the Navy.

At the end of 1997 the US Navy included a total of approximately 388 000 active-duty personnel, 125 000 in the Individual Ready Reserves, 93 000 in the Selected Reserves, and 202 000 civilian employees. The Operating Forces of the US Navy consist of the following:

- Naval Reserve Forces, New Orleans, Louisiana
- Operational Test & Evaluation Forces
- Naval Special Warfare Command, Coronado, California
- Military Sealift Command, Washington, DC
- US Naval Forces Europe, including the 6th Fleet, London, England
- US Naval Forces Central Command, including the 5th Fleet, Bahrain/McDill AFB, Florida
- Atlantic Fleet (LANTFLT), including Fleet Marine Forces and the 2nd Fleet, Norfolk, Virginia
- Pacific Fleet (PACFLT), including Fleet Marine Forces and the 3rd and 7th Fleets, Pearl Harbor, Hawaii.[3]

In addition, 'Type Commands' constitute an administrative chain of command within the Navy based on the 'type' of ship (e.g. destroyer, submarine, etc.). Figure 6.2 illustrates the organization of the Operating Forces.

The extensive Shore Establishment of the US Navy provides support to the operating forces, collectively known as 'the fleet'. Most of the Shore Establishment is located in the continental United States, especially the Washington, DC, area.[4] More information about individual bases and installations can be found in Chapter 4.

The US Marine Corps is organized in a similar fashion into three broad categories: the Operating Forces, the Supporting Establishment and the Marine Corps Reserve.

The Operating Forces constitute the combat power immediately available to the unified commanders in charge of the basic Unified Commands described in Chapter 3. The major elements are:

- Fleet Marine Forces
- Marine Corps Security Forces at naval installations and shipboard detachments
- the Marine Security Guard Battalion with detachments at embassies and consulates around the globe.

Figure 6.2 Organization of the Operating Forces of the US Navy

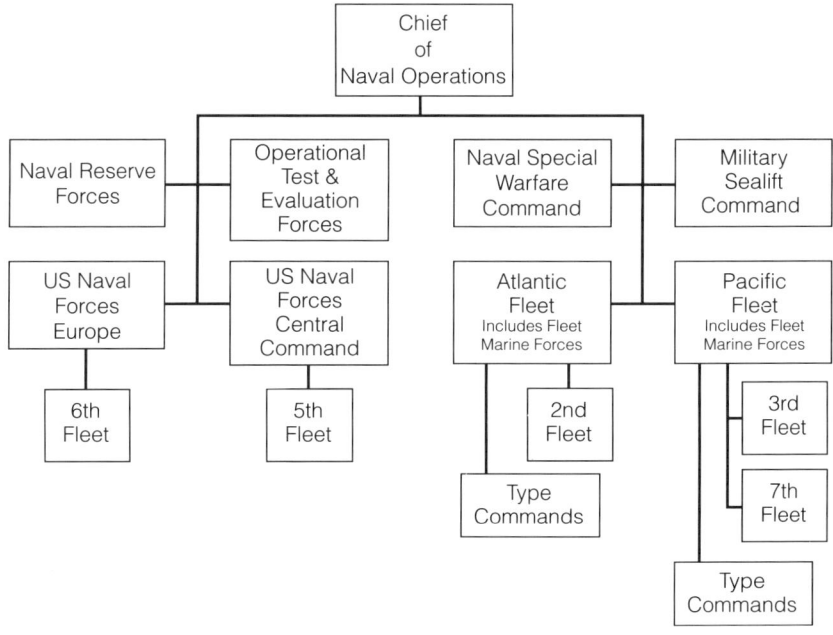

Source: US Navy

Operating forces that are available to the unified commanders are provided from Fleet Marine Force, Atlantic (FMFLant) and Fleet Marine Force, Pacific (FMFPac). These commands are under the operational control of the Commander in Chief of their respective fleets, and perform service component functions for the US Atlantic and Pacific Commanders in Chief.

The major combat force in FMFLant is II Marine Expeditionary Force (MEF), located in North and South Carolina in the United States. The major combat forces in FMFPac are I MEF, based in California, and III MEF, forward-based at Okinawa.

The Supporting Establishment includes Marine Corps Headquarters in Virginia, bases and stations, training activities and formal schools, etc. Its purpose is to build and support the Operating Forces. More information about individual bases and installations can be found in Chapter 4.

The Marine Corps Reserve, like the active forces, is a reservoir of balanced, combined arms forces. The major commands are the 4th Marine Division, 4th Marine Aircraft Wing and 4th Force Service Support Group. The Reserve provides both individuals and units in such a way as to integrate their capabilities into the active forces.

In 1997 the US Marine Corps consisted of approximately 174 000 active-duty personnel and 42 000 in the Reserve.[5]

STRATEGIC VISION

Within the overall context of the US National Security Strategy, National Military Strategy and Regional Security Strategy described in Chapter 2, the post–Cold War strategic vision of the Navy and Marine Corps represents a significant change from the US 'Maritime Strategy' of the 1980s. Following the end of the Cold War and the demise of the Soviet Union, in September 1992 the US Navy, together with the Marine Corps, published a White Paper entitled *From the Sea: Preparing the Naval Service for the 21st Century*. This seminal document and its 1994 supplement, *Forward . . . From the Sea*, summarize the Navy's post–Cold War strategy. In 1997 this strategy was fleshed out in operational terms in 'The Navy Operational Concept' and the Marine Corps 'Operational Maneuver from the Sea' Concept.

In order to fully appreciate the magnitude of the recent change in US naval strategy, it is necessary to briefly review its predecessor, the 'Maritime Strategy' of the 1980s. The most succinct review can be found in an earlier draft of the new US naval strategy.

> As our focus has shifted from global war to regional conflicts, we have recognized that the Maritime Strategy (published in 1986 to articulate the contribution of Naval forces to the Cold War effort which dominated training, acquisition and tactics) can no longer guide the Navy. The assumptions established under the Maritime Strategy envisioned a global war which would be at the initiative of the Soviet Union. The strategy called for Naval forces to *indirectly influence* events on the Central [European] Front by establishing and *defending the fleet's battlespace* in sea areas on the Soviet flanks, thereby threatening the Soviet homeland, and containing the Soviet fleet which otherwise would threaten our sea lines of communications. Under the old National Military Strategy, the task was *war at sea* through sea control. Naval operations on the Soviet flanks were *coordinated* with Army and Air Force operations on the Central Front.[6]

In other words, the old Maritime Strategy envisioned a 'forward defense' of NATO (and, although not explicitly mentioned, Japan and South Korea) against Soviet attack, by US naval forces operating on the 'Soviet flanks' (i.e. the Norwegian sea and the North Pacific). Such a 'forward defense' included the threat of US naval air and missile strikes against Soviet land bases before their aircraft and ships could attack the US fleet or convoys, and the option for 'strategic anti-submarine warfare' against Soviet ballistic missile submarines in their 'bastions' near the Soviet coasts. Although the North Atlantic was seen as the primary 'flank', throughout the 1980s the US Navy practiced the Maritime Strategy in a series of realistic exercises in the North Pacific—which some considered provocative.[7]

The failure of the attempted coup in Moscow in August 1991 and the dissolution of the Soviet Union in December of that year were the pivotal events that finally shaped the 'new US naval strategy' of the 1990s, first described in *From the Sea* in 1992. *From the Sea* was a watershed document. First, it is unequivocal in its declaration about the end of the 'Soviet' threat: 'With the demise of the Soviet Union, the free nations of the world claim preeminent control of the seas . . . As a result, our maritime policies can afford to de-emphasize efforts in some naval warfare areas'.[8]

Second, the document clearly states that as a result of the end of the Cold War, US national security strategy—and therefore its naval strategy and associated force structure—are undergoing a 'fundamental' shift: 'We must structure a *fundamentally* different naval force to respond to strategic demands . . . the *new* [strategic] direction of the Navy and Marine Corps team . . . represents a *fundamental* shift away from open-ocean warfighting *on* the sea toward joint operations conducted *from* the sea'.[9]

Finally, *From the Sea* spells out the new direction for the Navy–Marine Corps team. It is 'to provide the nation Naval Expeditionary Forces—shaped for Joint Operations operating forward from the sea—tailored for national needs'.[10]

After noting that the Navy still has 'a continuing obligation to maintain a robust strategic deterrence by sending ballistic missile submarines to sea' (see Chapter 5), the document fleshes out all four components of the new direction summarized above.

1. *'Naval Expeditionary Forces'* are:
    - swift to respond, on short notice, to crises in distant lands
    - structured to build power from the sea when required by national demands
    - able to sustain support for long-term operations

- unrestricted by the need for transit or overflight approval from foreign governments in order to enter the scene of action.[11]
2. Naval forces will be *'shaped for joint operations'* because 'the battlefield of the future will demand that everyone on the field be teammates'. Three examples are offered:
    - A naval force commander can command the joint task force while the operation is primarily maritime, and shift the command ashore later.
    - The Navy and Marine Corps can seize and defend an adversary's port, naval base or coastal air base to allow the entry of heavy Army or Air Force forces.
    - Sealift will provide the maritime bridge for the arrival of heavy forces.[12]
3. The Navy and Marine Corps will be *'operating forward, from the sea'* in order 'to project a positive American image, build foundations for viable coalitions, enhance diplomatic contacts, reassure friends, and demonstrate US power and resolve', in other words, 'to demonstrate United States commitment overseas and protect American interests'. In times of tension, these forces will attempt to 'contain crises', and if diplomacy fails, 'to project United States combat power'.[13]

From the Sea gives a new meaning to the term 'forward'. Under the Cold War Maritime Strategy, 'forward defense' primarily meant operating forward *on the high seas on the flanks of the Soviet Union* (i.e. the Norwegian Sea and the North Pacific). Now:

> Operating forward means operating in the littoral or 'near land' areas of the world. As a general *concept* we can define the littoral as comprising two segments of battlespace:
> Seaward: The area from the open ocean to the shore which must be controlled to support operations ashore.
> Landward: The area inland from the shore that can be supported and defended directly from the sea.[14]

From the Sea does not try to predict *which* 'near land' areas of the world are likely sites for future action. However, all the examples mentioned are 'regional' or 'third world' locations: Iraq, Iran, Kuwait, Bangladesh, Liberia and Somalia. In December 1992 the Marine Corps conducted a major war game entitled 'Operational Maneuver From the Sea' which focused on four scenarios: Cuba, Libya, Iran and Korea.[15]

4. Under the new strategy, naval forces will be *'tailored for national needs'*. The term 'package' is applied to the 'Naval Expeditionary Force' concept to indicate that a 'mix and match' approach to force composition will be taken, depending on the precise nature of each situation. One obvious conclusion is that 'The answer to every situation may *not* be a carrier battle group'.[16] Every element from maritime patrol aircraft to submarines, surface combatants, amphibious craft, mine warfare forces and Navy Special Warfare Forces will be considered.

In traditional terms, 'naval strategy' has meant the use of naval forces for the purpose of winning—or denying—command of the sea. In this era when the US Navy's command of the open sea is not under serious challenge, *From the Sea* may not represent a new naval 'strategy' in the traditional sense. Nevertheless, *From the Sea* does articulate a genuinely new strategic framework for linking US naval capabilities with national military goals in an era when the ability of the fleet to influence events *on land* is paramount. Developments since the publication of *From the Sea* leave no doubt about the basic change in the strategic direction of America's naval forces.

Following the Department of Defense's 1993 *Bottom Up Review* with its emphasis on 'regional conflict' (see Chapter 2), in November 1994 the Navy released an updated and expanded supplementary document entitled *Forward . . . From the Sea*. It emphasized the importance of maintaining forward-deployed *naval* forces, based on the premise that, in situations short of war, naval forces are *best* suited 'to be *engaged* in forward areas, with the objectives of *preventing* conflicts and *controlling* crises'.[17] This is so because: (1) naval forces represent a *unique* form of presence due to the fact that every US warship is sovereign US territory regardless of its location, and (2) US naval forces, operating from highly mobile bases at sea in forward areas, are free of the political encumbrances such as base access and overflight rights that might inhibit and otherwise limit the scope of land-based operations.[18]

Forward . . . From the Sea re-emphasizes the importance of *aircraft carrier battle groups* (CVBG) with versatile, multipurpose, naval tactical aviation wings, and *amphibious ready groups* (ARG) with special operations-capable Marine Expeditionary Units as the 'building blocks' of 'forward presence'. It reaffirms the traditional 'expeditionary' focus of the Naval Service, noting that 'expeditionary' implies 'a mindset, a culture, and a commitment to forces that are designed to be deployed forward and to respond swiftly'.[19]

In 1997 the Navy and the Marine Corps fleshed out this strategic vision in two documents on operational doctrine, *The Navy Operational Concept* (NOC) and *Operational Maneuver From the Sea* (OMFTS). In describing how the Navy operates, the NOC reaffirms the focus on 'operating in and from the littorals' with carrier battle groups and amphibious ready groups as the key elements. However, it also introduces the concept of 'network-centric' warfare in the following terms:

> We link dispersed units as an integrated force with command and control networks ... we take advantage of the reach of our sensors and weapons to project power over vast areas from a dispersed, networked force—concentrating combat power rather than our platforms and delivering firepower far inland when required by the mission.[20]

The Navy's *peacetime engagement* missions include:

- ensuring freedom of navigation on international trade routes, especially in the face of excessive maritime claims
- providing humanitarian assistance when disaster strikes
- engaging in a wide range of diplomatic activities, especially ship visits supporting peacetime coalition-building efforts.

Deterrence and conflict prevention are the second major mission category for the Navy. In addition to the nuclear deterrence embodied in ongoing ballistic missile submarine patrols, forward-deployed naval forces are a means of 'signaling US capabilities and resolve to friend and foe alike'. The NOC points out that the Navy possesses 'the unique capability of responding to ambiguous warning that either would not justify costly deployments from the continental United States, or might be insufficient to persuade nations in the region to host US forces on their soil'. The covert positioning of submarines is cited as one unique naval capability in that regard.[21]

When it comes to *crisis response* operations, forward-deployed naval forces 'shape the battlespace' and demonstrate a capability to defeat aggression by:

- enhancing US awareness of a potential aggressor's activities by deploying additional organic sensors overtly with ships and aircraft and covertly with submarines and Naval Special Warfare units
- shifting the strategic and operational situation in the favor of

the United States and its allies by forcing a potential aggressor to consider our combat capability when formulating his plans
- extending a protective shield over allies, potential coalition partners, and critical infrastructure ashore.[22]

The Navy's ultimate mission is, of course, to *fight and win*. In contingencies of limited size and duration, naval forces alone can project decisive power ashore. In larger conflicts, naval forces play a vital role throughout a joint campaign, from beginning to end, by:

- halting aggression early in a conflict by delivering a wide range of naval firepower far inland from dispersed, networked forces
- enabling the joint campaign by ensuring access to the theater for forces surging from the United States, supporting coalition forces to keep them in the fight, seizing or defending shore bases for land-based forces, and by extending defensive systems over early-arriving US joint forces ashore
- continuing all the above operations throughout the joint campaign, especially by using operational maneuver from the sea to establish operational and strategic advantages
- remaining on scene after the joint campaign concludes to enforce sanctions and to maintain a US presence for regional stability.[23]

Throughout its history the US Marine Corps has been the premier 'force in readiness' to respond to international disturbances. Although all military forces employ 'operational maneuver' in the search for a decisive effect on an adversary, what distinguishes the Marine Corps' 'Operational Maneuver From the Sea' (OMFTS) is 'the extensive use of the *sea* as a means of gaining advantage—an avenue of friendly movement that is simultaneously a barrier to the enemy and a means to avoid disadvantageous engagements'.[24] In summary form, the OMFTS concept replaces ship-to-shore maneuver with ship-to-objective maneuver. OFMTS:

- focuses on an operational objective
- uses the sea as maneuver space
- generates an overwhelming tempo
- pits strength against weakness
- emphasizes flexibility, intelligence and deception
- integrates all organic, joint and combined assets.

The 1950 capture of Seoul, South Korea, following the amphibious assault at Inchon, is cited as a 'classic example' of an OMFTS.[25]

Although OMFTS is applicable on a global basis, Asia is seen as a region of increasing importance. Marine Corps Commandant General Krulak notes that the US permanent overseas land-based presence is not likely to expand, 'particularly along the Pacific and Indian Ocean–Persian Gulf littoral' and that therefore 'the only feasible solution for maintaining presence in this region will be to maintain a capable naval power-projection capability'.[26]

FORCE STRUCTURE: US NAVY

In the early 1980s the US Navy successfully argued that a force structured around at least 15 deployable aircraft carrier battle groups, four battleship surface action groups and 100 nuclear attack submarines was essential. A '600 ship' combat fleet was the declared goal.[27] By 1988 the US Navy had essentially fulfilled the vision contained in the 'Maritime Strategy' and reached a strength of almost 600 ships—just as the threat it was designed to counter collapsed with a suddenness that surprised even the most seasoned analysts.

Faced with a diminished threat and declining budgets, in 1992 the US naval leadership reluctantly accepted the 450-ship, 12-carrier 'Base Force' proposed by the Bush administration. In 1993 the Clinton administration's *Bottom-up Review* of US defense strategy and force structure concluded that, since 'the threat posed by a blue-water Soviet navy has disappeared', by 1999 a 346-ship navy with eleven active and one reserve aircraft carriers, twelve amphibious ready groups and 45–55 nuclear attack submarines was sufficient to carry out a 'win two Major Regional Conflicts' strategy (see Chapter 2).[28]

The 1997 *Quadrennial Defense Review* retained the 12-carrier and 12-amphibious-groups requirement but called for further reductions in surface ship combatants from 128 to 116, and set the number of nuclear attack submarines at 50. The result will be a 1999 fleet numbering some 315 combat vessels, down from 347 at the end of 1997.[29]

In aggregate terms, Table 6.1 illustrates the dramatic reduction in the US Navy from its Maritime Strategy, Cold War strength in the late 1980s to the *Forward from the Sea*, regional conflict size envisioned by the end of the 1990s.

Table 6.1 Changes in US naval force structure

US naval strength	1989	1999
Aircraft carriers (CV/N)	15	12
Battle force ships	566	315
Aircraft	5400	3700
Personnel in uniform	782 000	568 000

Source: US Navy 1994 Posture Statement, p. 20, *1998 Report of the Secretary of Defense*, p. 30.

An examination of exactly *what* is being cut is much more revealing than aggregate figures. The fundamental strategic shift away from the old Maritime Strategy's vision of open ocean conflict with the Soviet Navy is being rigorously implemented in the new force structure. Frigates designed largely to escort and protect Europe-bound convoys from Soviet submarines were cut. Additional large cuts are being made in two ship categories (and future building plans) whose mission profiles were primarily defined by the Cold War: nearly half the 1989 total of 100 nuclear attack submarines (SSNs), and 27 nuclear-powered and older conventional guided missile cruisers designed to protect carriers from fleets of Soviet bombers and anti-ship missiles.

The only major warship categories to survive the transition to the post–Cold War security environment relatively unscathed are the large-deck aircraft carriers, the major aviation-capable amphibious assault ships (LHA/LHD) and landing ship docks and advanced Aegis air defense cruisers and destroyers. At one point during the intense (and ongoing) debate about the future of the carrier force, a low figure of six carriers was even suggested,[30] but both the *Bottom-up Review* and the *Quadrennial Defense Review* have concluded that in order to adequately fulfill the Navy's 'presence' requirements, plus the requirement to fight and win two nearly simultaneous Major Theater Wars, a force of eleven active carriers and one reserve carrier and ten active air wings and one reserve air wing is essential. To date, this figure is holding, although doubts have sometimes arisen about the Navy's long-term ability to sustain the air wings.

Cuts of this magnitude in ship and submarine numbers have already caused considerable controversy. However, in light of the agreement reached between the White House and the Congress in May 1997 calling for a balanced budget by 2002, the basic trend toward a smaller Navy is not likely to change in the foreseeable future.

The forces of the US Navy are basically divided into two

major 'force providing' components: *the Atlantic Fleet* (LANTFLT) and *the Pacific Fleet* (PACFLT). For reasons both of focus and space, only the most basic information on the Atlantic Fleet is provided here.

With its headquarters in Norfolk, Virginia, the Atlantic Fleet in 1997 is comprised of more than 142 000 Navy and Marine Corps personnel, 195 ships and submarines and almost 1360 aircraft, with 18 major shore stations. Six large-deck aircraft carriers and 48 nuclear submarines are included in the Atlantic Fleet's order of battle. The Atlantic Fleet is responsible for the area of the Atlantic Ocean from the North Pole to the South Pole; the Caribbean Sea and the waters around Central and South America extending to 92 degrees west longitude in the Pacific (the Galapagos Islands); the Norwegian, Greenland and Barents Seas; and the waters around Africa extending to the Cape of Good Hope.

The Atlantic Fleet provides forces to the Second Fleet in the Atlantic, the Sixth Fleet in the Mediterranean, and (along with the Pacific Fleet) to the Fifth Fleet in the Persian Gulf–Indian Ocean area. On a typical day, about one-third of the Fleet is deployed to meet peacetime requirements of US and NATO commanders.[31]

THE US PACIFIC FLEET

The Pacific Fleet's history dates back to 1821, with the establishment of the Pacific Squadron, the first permanent US Naval presence in the region (see Chapter 1). At its peak strength during World War II it numbered some 1970 ships. As of July 1998 the Pacific Fleet consisted of approximately 254 900 people, including 120 400 active-duty personnel in the Navy, 73 500 active-duty Marines, 35 000 Naval Reservists and 26 600 civilians.

In July 1998 the Pacific Fleet numbered some 193 ships (including Military Sealift Command ships), down from a strength of 283 in 1986. The Fleet included:

- 3 Nuclear Aircraft Carriers (CVN)
- 3 Conventional Aircraft Carriers (CV)
- 1 Nuclear-powered Guided Missile Cruiser (CGN)
- 13 Cruisers (CG)
- 12 Guided Missile Destroyers (DDG)
- 12 Destroyers (DD)
- 18 Guided Missile Frigates (FFG)
- 30 Nuclear Attack Submarines (SSN)
- 8 Ballistic Missile Submarines (SSBN)

- 2 Fleet Flagships (1 Amphibious Command & Control Ship [LCC] and 1 Amphibious Transport Dock Ship [AGF])
- 2 Amphibious Assault Ships (LHD)
- 3 Amphibious Assault Ships (multipurpose) (LHA)
- 8 Dock Landing Ships (LSD)
- 6 Amphibious Transport Dock Ships (LPD)
- 1 Tank Landing Ship (LST)
- 12 Auxiliary Ships (cargo, fuel, etc.)
- 4 Patrol Craft
- 2 Mine Countermeasure Vessels (MCM)
- 55 Military Sealift Command Ships.

The Pacific Fleet also included approximately 1432 aircraft of the following types:

- US Navy:
  - 357 Tactical (fighters/bombers)
  - 203 Helicopters
  - 73 P-3 (maritime patrol)
  - 158 other
- US Marine Corps:
  - 197 Tactical (fighters/bombers)
  - 404 Helicopter
  - 40 other.[32]

With its headquarters at Pearl Harbor, Hawaii, the Pacific Fleet's mission is to support the US Pacific Command's theater strategy (see Chapters 2 and 3), and to provide interoperable, trained, combat-ready forces to USCINCPAC and other US unified commands. The Pacific Fleet's area of responsibility covers more than 50 per cent of the earth's surface, encompassing over 250 million square kilometers in the Pacific, Indian and Arctic Oceans, from the west coast of the United States to the Arabian Gulf.

Figure 6.3 illustrates the organization of the US Pacific Fleet.

The Pacific Fleet provides forces to its two 'numbered' fleets, the *Third Fleet* and the *Seventh Fleet*.

The Commander of the *Third Fleet* is headquartered aboard the USS *Coronado* (AGF-11) operating from San Diego, California. Its area of responsibility includes the eastern and northern Pacific Ocean areas including the Bering Sea, Alaska, the Aleutian Islands and a sector of the Arctic, with the International Dateline as its western boundary. The primary wartime mission of the Third Fleet is the defense of the western sea approaches to the

Figure 6.3 Organization of the US Pacific Fleet

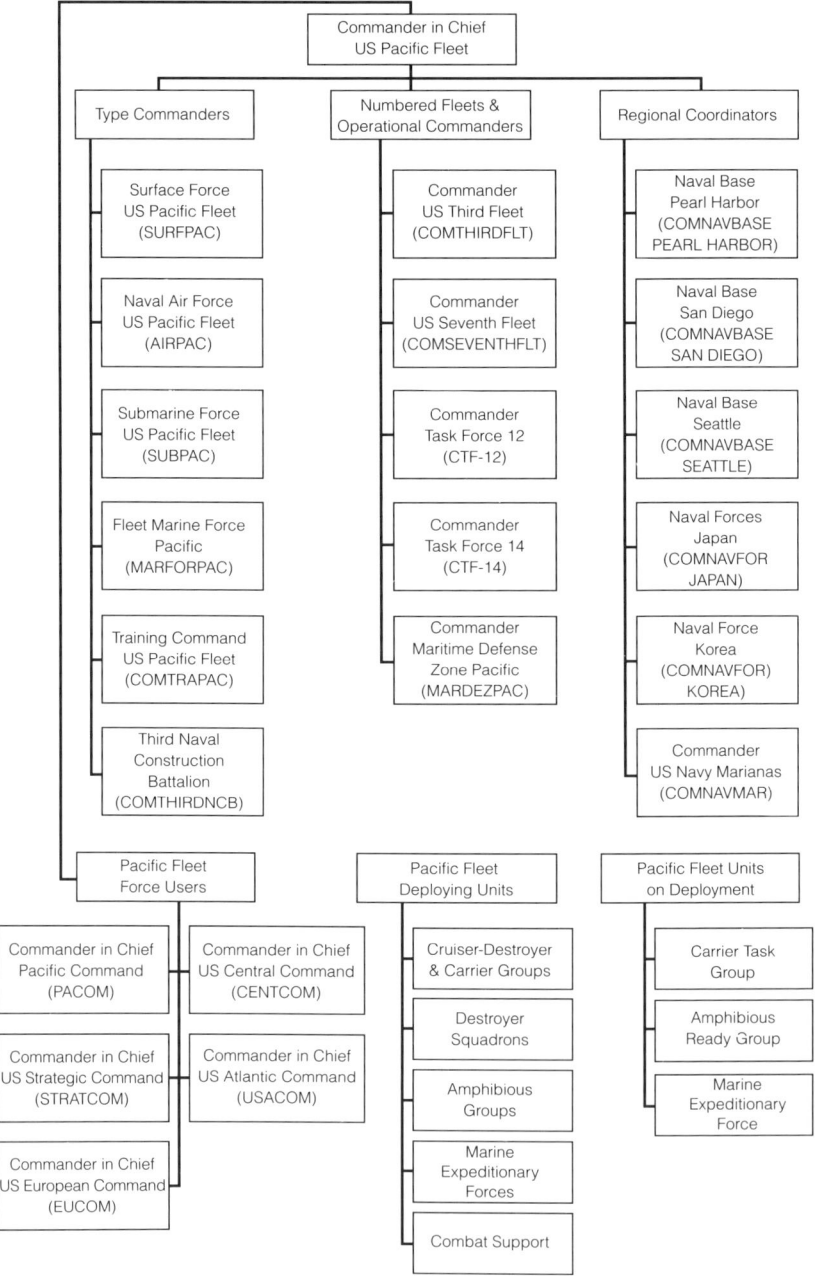

Source: US Pacific Fleet

United States, including Alaska and the Aleutian Islands. In addition, the Third Fleet may be assigned to respond to a specific crisis event or contingency, with its Commander acting as a Joint Task Force Commander. For this purpose the Third Fleet maintains a Ready Battle Group. This battle group consists of an aircraft carrier and a tailored mix of surface warships, submarines and support ships, ready to respond to any emerging contingency within 96 hours.

The Third Fleet also maintains other *Carrier Battle Groups* (CVBG) and *Amphibious Ready Groups* (ARG), plus service support ships and nuclear attack submarines. A Carrier Battle Group consists of a carrier, surface combatants, submarine escorts and logistics ships. An Amphibious Ready Group usually consists of a Multi-purpose Amphibious Assault Ship (LHD/LHA), a Landing Platform, Dock (LPD), and a Landing Ship, Dock (LSD). A Marine Expeditionary Unit (MEU) consisting of about 2000 Marines and their equipment embark in ARG shipping to complete the ARG/MEU team.

In normal peacetime, the Third Fleet continually trains Navy and Marine Corps forces for the expeditionary warfare mission. Naval forces trained and certified 'ready to deploy' by the Third Fleet normally deploy to the Western Pacific/Indian Ocean for duty with the Seventh Fleet, and to the Arabian Gulf region for duty in support of Commander, Fifth Fleet/Commander, US Naval Forces Central Command.[33]

The *Seventh Fleet* was first established in 1943. Today, it constitutes the largest forward-deployed fleet in the US Navy, with 50–60 ships, 350 aircraft and 60 000 Navy and Marine Corps personnel. The Commander of the Seventh Fleet is headquartered aboard the USS *Blue Ridge* (LCC–19) forward-based from Yokosuka, Japan. The Seventh Fleet's area of responsibility includes over 130 million square kilometers of the Pacific and Indian Oceans, stretching from the International Dateline westward all the way to the east coast of Africa, and from the Kurile Islands in the North Pacific to the Antarctic in the south.

Approximately twenty of the Seventh Fleet's ships operate from US facilities in Guam and Yokosuka and Sasebo, Japan. Other ships are deployed on a rotating basis from bases in Hawaii and on the US west coast. On any given day, about 50 per cent of the Seventh Fleet forces are deployed at sea throughout the area of responsibility. The Seventh Fleet operates the most advanced weapons systems in the US naval arsenal. A representative composition of the Seventh Fleet on a typical day includes:

- *Ships*:
  - 1 or 2 large-deck aircraft carriers
  - 3 or 4 cruisers
  - 18–20 destroyers and frigates
  - 5 or 6 submarines
  - 1 amphibious command and control ship (Seventh Fleet Flagship)
  - 5–8 amphibious transport and landing ships
  - 18 mobile logistics and support ships
  - 16 Maritime Prepositioned Force (MPF) ships
- *Naval aircraft*:
  - 200 aboard aircraft carriers and other ships
  - 22 shore-based maritime patrol aircraft
  - 10 shore-based utility aircraft
  - 150–160 Marine Corps aircraft
- *Marine air and ground forces:*
  - A Marine Expeditionary Force composed of a Marine Division, Marine Aircraft Wing, Marine Expeditionary Brigade, Force Service Support Group and afloat Marine Expeditionary Unit (see below)
- *Personnel*:
  - US Navy—38 000
  - US Marine Corps—22 000.

These forward-deployed units embody the US Navy–Marine Corps 'Forward Presence' in the Asia–Pacific region, directly supporting three principal elements of the US national security strategy: deterrence, forward defense and alliance solidarity.[34]

FORCE STRUCTURE: US MARINE CORPS

In keeping with its 'expeditionary' mission as the nation's 'ready force', the Marine Corps task organizes for operations into *Marine Air-Ground Task Forces* (MAGTF). Once Fleet Marine commanders have been assigned a mission, they organize appropriately tailored MAGTFs by drawing ground, aviation and combat service support capabilities from Fleet Marine forces. In terms of size, MAGTFs are categorized in the following four types:

- Marine Expeditionary Force (MEF)
- Marine Expeditionary Brigade (MEB)
- Marine Expeditionary Unit (MEU)
- Special Purpose MAGTF (SPMAGTF).[35]

Since the end of the Cold War the US Marine Corps has undergone a 12 per cent reduction in its ranks, from approximately 200 000 to 174 000 active-duty personnel (plus another 42 000 in the Reserves), but it has retained its basic structure of three active and one reserve *Marine Expeditionary Forces* (MEF), each composed of a division, an air wing and a force support group. The MEF is the Marine Corps' primary 'standing' MAGTF, and its principal warfighting organization, particularly for a larger crisis or contingency. Every MAGTF is composed of a Command Element (CE), Ground Combat Element (GCE), Air Combat Element (ACE) and Combat Service Support Element (CSSE).

The Command Element of an MEF includes the headquarters, communications, surveillance, reconnaissance and intelligence elements necessary to provide C^{4}I support to the MEF.

The *Ground Combat Element* of an MEF ranges in size from a partial Marine Division (MARDIV) to a complete Marine Division. A complete MARDIV consists of the following:

- Two Infantry Regiments
- One Combined Arms Regiment
- Tank Battalion
- Reconnaissance Battalion (Light Armored)
- Assault Amphibian Battalion
- Combat Engineer Battalion.

In approximate terms, the major weapons of a Marine Division include:

- 58 Tanks
- 184 Assault Amphibious Vehicles
- 110 Light Armored Vehicles
- 72 155 mm Howitzers
- 48 105 mm Howitzers
- 72 81 mm mortars
- 81 60 mm mortars
- 144 TOW launchers
- 216 Dragon Trackers

The *Air Combat Element* of an MEF is composed of the appropriate assets of a Marine Air Wing, which may include:

- Rotary Wing Aircraft Group
- Fixed Wing Aircraft Group
- Marine Wing Support Group
- Tactical Electronic Warfare Detachment

- Aerial Refueler Transport Assets
- Tactical Reconnaissance Assets

The aircraft/launchers of a Marine Aircraft Wing consist of:

- 40 AV–8B fighter-bombers
- 72 F/A–18C/D fighter-bombers
- 10 EA–6B electronic warfare
- 12 KC–130 transports
- 32 CH–53D/E helicopters
- 54 AH–1W/T helo gunships
- 24 UH–1N helicopters
- 16 Hawk missile launchers
- 90 Stinger missile teams.

The *Combat Service Support Element* of an MEF contains the units and supplies necessary to support an MEF's 30 000–60 000 personnel in a wide range of amphibious and ashore operations for 60 days.[36]

The First Marine Expeditionary Force (I MEF) is home-based on the US west coast at Camp Pendleton in California, the II MEF is home-based at Camp Lejeune, North Carolina, and the III MEF is home-based on Okinawa, Japan.

The next size of MAGTF is the *Marine Expeditionary Brigade* (MEB) which is about two-thirds the size of a full division and is normally composed of a reinforced infantry regiment, a Marine Aircraft Group and a Brigade Service Support Group. An MEB is accompanied by 30 days of supplies for its approximately 4000–18 000 Marines (typically 15 000). An MEB may be deployed as the lead element of a larger MEF, or as a 'stand alone' MAGTF. There are three types of MEBs: Amphibious, with that organic capability, Maritime Prepositioning Force (MPF), with personnel to be airlifted and matched up with equipment on MPF ships, and the Norway Air-Landed MEB. The ships of MPS Squadron–3 (MPSRON) stationed at Guam and MSP Squadron–2 stationed at Diego Garcia each contain supplies and equipment for an entire MEB.

The *Marine Expeditionary Unit* (MEU) is the Marine Corps' immediately responsive, sea-based MAGTF routinely deployed to meet forward presence and limited power projection requirements. The MEU is normally composed of a reinforced infantry battalion, a helicopter squadron reinforced with fixed wing AV–8B fighter-bombers, and an MEU service support group. All forward-deployed MEU have completed specialized training and evaluation and are designated 'special operations capable' (SOC). Although MEUs can be the lead element of a larger MAGTF, their special training and composition dictates their normal use as a rapid, initial response to a crisis. The MEU deploys with 15 days of supplies for its 1000–4000 Marines (typically 2000). In addition, each Maritime Prepositioning Squadron also includes two ships that each contain the equipment and supplies to support an airlifted MEU in excess of fifteen days. The US Navy maintains forward-based MEUs on ships in the Mediterranean, Persian Gulf and Western Pacific regions. In the Pacific, the III MEF's MEU is usually forward-based on the ships of an Amphibious Ready Group homeported at Sasebo, Japan, and additional equipment and supplies are on ships of MPSRON-3 based at Guam.

Finally, smaller Special Purpose MAGTFs are organized to accomplish specialized missions or for unique instances for which another MAGTF would be inappropriate or too large. These units are normally given a designation according to their mission location, for example SPMAGTF (Liberia).[37]

US MARINE FORCES IN THE PACIFIC

US Marine Forces Pacific (MARFORPAC), with its Headquarters at Marine Corps Base Hawaii (MCBH), is the largest field Command in the US Marine Corps. MARFORPAC is a Service Component Headquarters that reports directly to USCINCPAC, to the Commander of the US Central Command (USCINCCENT), and to the Commander in Chief, United Nations Command, Korea (CINCUNC). This means that both of the identified potential major regional contingencies—Korea and the Persian Gulf—lie within MARFORPAC's area and scope of responsibility.

The Force Commander commands roughly 80 000 Marines and associated sailors (medical support, etc.) forward deployed, both ashore and afloat, and forces stationed in the United States, as noted above. MARFORPAC's two major subordinate commands are I MEF, headquartered at Camp Pendleton, California, and III MEF, headquartered on Okinawa. Marine Corps Bases in the Asia–Pacific Region are described in Chapter 4. The Fleet Marine Force Pacific (FMFPAC), also headquartered at MCBH, is responsible for providing Marine forces to Naval Aviation and to deploying Navy fleets.

MARFORPAC maintains two rapidly deployable Alert Contingency MAGTFs (ACM)—one in I MEF and one in III MEF—each consisting of a lightly armed, battalion-sized force on standby alert, ready to be airlifted into a crisis area. In the event of a major crisis in Korea, the MARFORPAC commander and headquarters would deploy there and become Commander, Marine Forces, Korea. Together with the Republic of Korea Marine Corps, MARFORPAC would form the Combined Marine Forces Command and play a decisive role in ending hostilities on the peninsula. Under the Maritime Prepositioned Force Concept, more than 17 000 Marines and associated sailors could fly into a benign or secured airfield to link up with MPS ships on fewer than 250 aircraft sorties.[38]

CAPABILITIES AND LIMITATIONS

The US Navy–Marine Corps team possesses a very powerful capability in all three realms of naval combat operations—naval strike warfare, naval undersea warfare (USW) and naval expeditionary warfare—plus a host of peacetime engagement capabilities. Only the most significant of those capabilities—and limitations—will be outlined here. The US Navy's role in nuclear deterrence is covered in Chapter 5.

In the realm of *Naval Strike Warfare*, no other nation on earth operates even one large-deck aircraft carrier of the size, power and sophistication of the twelve currently operating in the US Fleet, and no other nation possesses anything close to the US Navy's sea-based air force.

For example, the aircraft carrier USS *Independence* (CV–62) which was forward-based out of Yokosuka, Japan, until mid-1998 was, at over 79 000 tons displacement, the *smallest* of the US carriers. The seven operational nuclear-powered *Nimitz*-class carriers (CVN–68 to 74) are the largest warships in the world, over 317 meters in length, with a flight deck over 76 meters wide. Despite their enormous displacement of approximately 97 000 tons (87 300 metric tons), their nuclear power plants enable them to travel at a speed of over 30 knots (55.5 kilometers per hour), and they can do so for years without refueling.

Each US aircraft carrier has a ship's crew of over 3000 sailors and Marines, plus an air wing complement of 2480 Navy and Marine personnel. Each carrier is equipped with four steam-powered catapults capable of thrusting a 22 000 kilogram 'conventional take-off' aircraft 92 meters, from zero to 265 kilometers per hour in two seconds. The flight deck crew can launch two aircraft and land one every 37 seconds in daylight, and one per minute at night. No other aircraft carriers in the world have such a capability.[39]

Although they are equipped with close-in air defense weapons such as the NATO *Sparrow* guided surface-to-air missile and the 20 mm *Phalanx* cannon, the strike power of US aircraft carriers is contained in their onboard *carrier air wing*. Each carrier air wing consists of 75–85 aircraft. In addition to Fleet Air Reconnaissance, Logistics Support, Helicopter Antisubmarine and Helicopter Support Squadrons, each carrier air wing includes Fighter, Strike Fighter, Sea Control, Tactical Electronic Warfare and Carrier Airborne Early Warning Squadrons.[40]

US Navy *Fighter Squadrons* (VF) are equipped with the F–14 *Tomcat*, made famous in the movie *Top Gun*. In service since the early 1970s, the frequently upgraded F–14 is a supersonic, twin-engine, variable sweep wing, two-place fighter designed primarily to attack and destroy enemy aircraft around the clock in all weather conditions. It remains one of the world's premier air defense fighters. Capable of speeds over Mach 2 above 15 000 meters, the Tomcat can track up to 24 targets simultaneously with its advanced weapons control system, and attack six with long-range *Phoenix* AIM–54A missiles, equipped with both semi-active and active radar homing guidance, at a range in excess of 100 nautical miles (184 km). The F–14 also carries the medium-range radar-guided AIM–7 Sparrow air-to-air tactical missile, and its successor, the improved AIM–120 *AMRAAM*, which has an all-weather, beyond-visual-range capability, an active radar and inertial reference unit, and a range of over 48 kilometers. The Tomcat can also mount the short-range, heat-seeking AIM–9 *Sidewinder* air-to-air missile, one of the oldest, least expensive and yet most successful missiles in the entire US weapons inventory. Over 27 other nations also employ the AIM–9, and continuous improvements such as all-angle attack capability and better defense against infrared countermeasures have kept it effective. An MK–61A1 *Vulcan* 20 mm cannon rounds out the F–14's air-defense armament.[41]

In addition to its superior air-defense capability, ongoing modifications are giving upgraded F–14s a strike capability, and these aircraft have been informally called the 'Bombcat'. The modifications include Low Altitude Navigation and Targeting Infrared for Night (LANTIRN) pods, which are being installed on a total of 197 F–14s, giving them the capability to deliver laser-guided bombs. Finally, when equipped with the latest digital Tactical

Airborne Reconnaissance Pod System (TARPS), Tomcats can perform target identification before, and near real-time bomb damage assessment after, a strike.[42]

No US-piloted Tomcat has ever lost an air-to-air combat, and at the time of writing it remains highly effective, especially given the high level of training accorded US naval aviators—the highest in the world, according to many observers. But the aircraft are aging, and production has ceased.

With the 1997 retirement of the Vietnam-era *Intruder* long-range, all-weather medium bomber, the F/A–18 *Hornet* strike-fighter provides the bulk of the US Navy/Marine Corps air strike force. First deployed in 1983, the Hornet is an all-weather fighter and attack aircraft, designed for traditional strike missions such as interdiction and close air support without compromising its fighter capabilities. The F/A–18 is a twin-engine, mid-wing, multi-mission tactical aircraft capable of attaining speeds of Mach 1.7+ at over 15 000 meters. About 1000 FA/18C/D aircraft are currently operating in 37 tactical US Navy and Marine Corps squadrons from air stations worldwide, and from all aircraft carriers.

When configured as an air-defense fighter, the F/A–18 has a maximum one-way range of 1379 nautical miles (2537 km) with external fuel tanks, and, as is the case with all US combat aircraft, is capable of in-air refueling. In terms of air-defense weapons, when configured as a fighter the Hornet lacks only the F–14's long-range Phoenix missile capability.

When configured as an attack bomber, the F/A–18 has a lesser range of 1333 nautical miles (2453 km), and can carry a wide range of guided and unguided missiles, bombs, mines and rockets. Among them are the *Harpoon* and *Harpoon/SLAM* missiles. The AGM–84D Harpoon is an all-weather, over-the-horizon, anti-ship missile with active radar guidance and sea-skimming cruise trajectory over a range in excess of 90 kilometers. The AGM–84E SLAM is an infrared Stand-Off Land Attack missile used for long-range precision strikes, and is equipped with an inertial navigation system with Global Positioning System (GPS) connectivity. An extended-range version, the SLAM-ER, is nearing deployment. The F/A–18 can also carry *Maverick* missiles (see Chapter 7) and will be capable of launching the coming Joint Stand-Off Weapon (JSOW) and Joint Direct Attack Munition (JDAM) in the near future.

The Hornet was effective and versatile during the Persian Gulf War. F/A–18s shot down two Iraqi planes without loss, subsequently bombing targets with the same aircraft on the same mission, and meanwhile breaking all records for tactical aircraft in availability, reliability and maintainability. The aircraft also proved highly survivable, taking direct hits from surface-to-air missiles, recovering, being quickly repaired, and flying again the next day.[43]

The Hornet has its limitations as an attack aircraft, however. It lacks the 'stealth' characteristics of the Air Force's F–117 and B–2 bombers. Compared with its predecessor, the venerable *Intruder*, it has a limited fuel capacity and combat radius. Moreover, most versions of the F/A–18 are single-seat, requiring a great deal of the pilot in high-threat situations. The C and D models delivered since 1989 include an improved night-attack capability, but earlier models have limitations in that role.

A significantly larger and improved evolution of the F/A–18 C and D models is undergoing flight testing at the time of writing. The F/A–18 E/F *Super Hornet* will reportedly be able to:

- fly up to 40 per cent farther on a typical interdiction mission
- remain on station 80 per cent longer during a typical combat air patrol scenario
- bring back approximately three times the amount of payload (unused ordnance)—an important feature given the expense of 'smart' weapons.[44]

By the end of the next decade, the F–14s will all be retired and the future air defense/strike aircraft mix on aircraft carriers will begin to reflect the eventual inclusion of F/A–18 E/Fs and the even newer Joint Strike Fighter (JSF) (see Chapter 9).

All-weather *airborne early warning and command and control* functions for the carrier battle group are provided by the E–2C *Hawkeye* aircraft, in addition to surface surveillance coordination, strike and interceptor control, search and rescue guidance and communications relay. In service since 1973, the Hawkeye has undergone frequent upgrades to its computerized sensors, including electronic surveillance and radar, and has an advanced tactical data and communications system. With its two turboprop engines, the E–2C can attain a speed of 300+ knots (552 km) per hour, and has a range of 1000 nautical miles (1850 km) and a ceiling of 9100 meters. Although the Hawkeye is unarmed, its five-person crew provides a critical component of naval strike warfare. For example, E–2Cs provided the command and control for many successful land attack and combat air patrol missions over Iraq, including the shoot-down of two Iraqi MiG–21 aircraft by carrier-based F/A–18s early in the Persian Gulf War.[45]

The Hawkeye's main limitation is its size, due to the carrier takeoff requirement. In comparison with the much larger ground-based AWACS aircraft (see Chapter 7), the E-2C has a limited fuel capacity/range/loiter time, and its smaller crew has a more limited endurance. Thus, for example, the E-2Cs aboard a single aircraft carrier are not normally tasked to round-the clock airborne patrol over a carrier battle group. Nevertheless, the E-2C is the most effective sea-based airborne warning and control system in the world, and will continue to play a major role in the Navy's evolution toward 'network-centric' warfare.

Airborne *electronic countermeasures* for US Navy/Marine strike aircraft and ships are provided by the EA-6B *Prowler* aircraft, a modification of the basic A-6 Intruder airframe. The Navy and Marine Corps currently operate 19 EA-6B squadrons (fourteen Navy, one Navy Reserve and four Marine Corps). With the 1998 retirement of the last of the Air Force's EF-111 aircraft, the Prowlers now also provide joint support to regional CINCs. The EA-6B is a fully integrated electronic warfare system combining long-range, all-weather capabilities with advanced electronic countermeasures to jam enemy radar, electronic data links and communications. First deployed in 1971, the twin-engined Prowler can reach a speed of over 500 knots (920 km) per hour, with a range of over 1000 nautical miles (1840 km) and a ceiling of 11 300 meters. In addition to operating its countermeasures, the EA-6B's crew of four can launch the AGM-88A High-Speed Anti-Radiation Missile (HARM). The HARM is an air-to-surface tactical missile designed to seek out and destroy enemy radar-equipped air defense systems. In service since 1983, the HARM has a range of over 90 kilometers and travels at a speed of 1220+ kilometers per hour. This weapon proved to be very effective during the Persian Gulf War.[46]

The US Navy possesses a sea-based airborne strike capability unmatched by any other nation. However, many nations are acquiring increasingly advanced integrated air defense systems (IADS) consisting of sensors, aircraft and missiles that may pose a serious threat to that capability over the next 10 to 15 years.[47]

Partly in response to that phenomenon, the US Navy possesses another powerful strike capability in the form of the land-attack version of the Tomahawk subsonic cruise missile (TLAM). Made famous by its combat performance during and after the Persian Gulf War and in Bosnia, the Tomahawk can be launched at land targets under all weather conditions from many of the over 70 US submarines and 120 surface ships, thus 'spreading out' the US

Navy's long-range strike capability far beyond its complement of piloted aircraft on twelve aircraft carriers.

The conventional land-attack Tomahawk can carry a 1000 pound warhead over a range of 600 nautical miles (1104 km) at about 880 kilometers per hour. The Tomahawk's small size and low-altitude flight make it difficult to detect. Several different types of warhead can be mounted, including a submunitions dispenser with combined effect bomblets. The missile has inertial and terrain contour matching guidance (TERCOM). TERCOM uses a stored map reference to compare with the actual terrain to determine the missile's position and correct its course if necessary, thus making the weapon extremely accurate. During the Persian Gulf War, about 85 per cent of the roughly 300 missiles fired from two battleships, 11 other surface ships and at least two attack submarines reportedly hit and damaged their targets, one even clipping a television tower in Baghdad. Later versions include a Global Positioning System (GPS) receiver to allow in-flight updates and Time of Arrival control. The US Navy has planned the procurement of about 4000 Tomahawks.[48]

Because of its devastating accuracy and the fact that it is unmanned, the Tomahawk is becoming a weapon-of-choice in the US naval inventory when the target is heavily defended, as first seen in the 1991 Persian Gulf War and more recent deployments in limited attacks against Iraqi and Bosnian Serb targets. However, the Tomahawk does have its limitations. At over $600 000 per unit, it is very expensive and therefore unsuitable for use against large-area targets. Earlier versions can only attack fixed targets that have been mapped. The Tomahawk's conventional warhead has a very limited ability to penetrate hardened targets. Still, the missile has greatly increased the US Navy's strike capability and improved 'smarter' versions (with an ability to attack mobile targets) have been proposed.

Naval Expeditionary Warfare has long been a major capability of the US Navy, and the *raison d'être* of the US Marine Corps. Naval Expeditionary Warfare comprises 'military operations mounted from the sea, usually on short notice, consisting of forward deployed, or rapidly deployable, self-sustaining naval forces tailored to achieve a clearly stated objective'.[49] These operations fall across the full range from peacetime engagement to deterrence and conflict prevention, on to 'fight and win' warfare.

US naval expeditionary forces are the largest and most capable in the world. They are centered around twelve Amphibious Ready Groups (ARG), described above. As an expeditionary force approaches a hostile littoral, the first challenge it usually faces is air and missile attack. In addition to the air defense provided by any present carrier air wings as outlined above, US forces at sea are protected by the most advanced air defense in the world, the *Aegis Combat System*.

The Aegis system is a total weapons system, from detection to kill. The heart of the system is an advanced, automatic detect and track, multi-function phased array radar, the AN/SPY-1. This high-powered radar is able to perform search, track and missile guidance functions simultaneously with a track capacity of about 200 targets, out to a range of 250 nautical miles for high-altitude objects and 45 for sea-skimming targets. The computer-based command and decision element is the core of the system. First tested at sea in 1974, the system has undergone several upgrades, especially to the computers. The Aegis system is deployed on all 27 *Ticonderoga*-class guided missile cruisers (CG–47 class), including the 13 in the Pacific Fleet (two forward-based at Yokosuka), and an improved lighter version is deployed on the 21 operational *Arleigh Burke*-class guided-missile destroyers (DDG–51 class), including the ten in the Pacific Fleet (two at Yokosuka), with 36 more under construction or planned. At the time of writing only one other Navy, Japan, deploys the Aegis system (on a total of four *Kongo*-class guided missile destroyers), although Spain has also purchased a smaller version for its new guided missile frigates.[50]

The 'business end' of the Aegis weapons system is the *Standard* surface-to-air and surface-to-surface missile. Earlier versions (SM–1MR, SM–2MR) are also deployed on non-Aegis ships. The latest SM–2 Aegis Extended Range (ER) Block IV missile is equipped with both a semi-active homing radar and an infrared sensor and has a reported range of 200 nautical miles and an altitude of up to 29 000 meters. It is being deployed on all US Aegis ships that utilize the versatile Mark 41 Vertical Launch System (VLS) which can also fire Tomahawks. Since its first deployment in 1970, the Standard missile has proven to be the most reliable in the Navy's inventory. Counting the non-Aegis vessels, the Standard missile is deployed on more than 100 US Navy ships, and is used by many other nations, including Australia, Japan, South Korea and Taiwan.[51]

The Aegis system and Standard missile have proven to be extremely effective against both surface and air targets, but they are very expensive (Aegis cruisers cost around $1 billion each and each Standard missile costs over $400 000), and that limits the number of ships that can be equipped with it. It is *theoretically* possible to 'saturate' an Aegis defense, for example with very large numbers of high-speed anti-ship missiles, but few nations have anything approaching that capability. Moreover, the US Navy's increasing ability to 'network' its ships and aircraft decreases this potential vulnerability.

The system's actual operational limitations are: (1) the vulnerability of its sensors/computer to battle damage, as revealed during a mine attack on an Aegis cruiser in the Gulf War; (2) the imperfections of its human operators in rapid, intense littoral situations, as in the tragic accidental shoot-down of the mis-identified Iranian civilian airliner in the crowded skies over the Persian Gulf by the USS *Vincennes* in 1988; and (3) the current system's inability to 'kill' intermediate-range or *theater ballistic missiles* (TBMs), which pose an increasing threat to US expeditionary forces. In March 1996 China fired a series of TBMs into the ocean near Taiwan. The Aegis cruiser USS *Bunker Hill* was sent to the area and recorded each missile flight in detail, but did not yet have a missile on board that could have intercepted the threat. On 24 January 1997 the US Navy successfully demonstrated a Theater Ballistic Missile Defense (TBMD) capability when a *Lance* ballistic missile target was shot down over the White Sands Missile Range in New Mexico with an SM–2 Block IV-A missile, the 'next generation' of the Standard missile. When operational, this further development of the Aegis system will complete the Navy's Area Theater Ballistic Missile Defense System (see Chapter 9).[52]

Mines pose a widespread, serious and relatively inexpensive threat to naval expeditionary forces. Fourteen of the 17 US warships that have suffered combat damage since 1945 were mine victims, including the Aegis cruiser *Princeton* and the amphibious assault ship *Tripoli*—serving as the mine-clearing command ship— in the Persian Gulf War. The US Navy employs a variety of *mine countermeasures* (MCM) to meet this challenge, including the 14-ship *Avenger* class (MCM–1) 1300-ton ocean mine countermeasures vessel and the 12-ship *Osprey*-class (MHC–51) 900 ton coastal minehunter. Both classes are equipped with sophisticated mine detection sonars and sweeping devices.

The primary airborne mine countermeasures mission is accomplished by several versions of the H–53 *Sea Stallion* heavy helicopter, capable of towing the sophisticated *Sea Dragon* mine-clearing sled at a high speed. The RH–53 Sea Stallion has a crew of seven and can fly at a speed of 294 kilometers per hour over a range of 578 nautical miles (1064 km). However, the Navy possesses only 29 of these aircraft.

Some analysts believe that mine countermeasures are the US Navy's 'weak link' due to insufficient resources being devoted to a mission that is not 'glamorous'. Despite the fact that the MCMs and MHCs are new ships, problems remain. The MCMs—two of which have been permanently forward deployed to Sasebo, Japan, since 1996, with two others at Bahrain in the Persian Gulf—continue to be plagued by engine problems. The rest of the MCMs and all MHC ships are based at Corpus Christi, Texas, very distant from overseas theaters, and would require dedicated fast sealift to deploy in time. Another concern is the obsolescence of the US Navy's own offensive mining capability.[53]

After the release of the *Quadrennial Defense Review*, the Chief of Naval Operations directed an assessment of the MCM force's capability to support the 'win two Major Theater Wars' requirement. That CNO study confirmed that the US Navy's current 'dedicated' MCM response capability is unsatisfactory for regional enemy mine threats. Consequently, the US Navy has decided to adopt 'organic' MCM, defined as a 'capability that is carried in deployed forces to allow early MCM operations and . . . to conduct MCM operations en route.'[54] It will take considerable time to develop and field the family of 'organic' MCM systems essential to such a capability.

A crucial element of naval expeditionary warfare is the *ship-to-shore movement of US Marines*, who pioneered the modern form of 'amphibious' warfare prior to World War II and then employed it so effectively across the Pacific during that conflict. The US Navy–Marine Corps team remains the world's largest and most capable amphibious force.

The core of the US Navy's capability consists of its fleet of twelve *amphibious assault ships*—LHA, LHD and LPH. These ships somewhat resemble in appearance previous medium-size straight-deck, conventional takeoff and landing aircraft carriers, but are designed to perform as primary landing and support ships for the assault operations of Marine Air and Ground Task Forces against defended positions ashore. At over 253 meters in length, the newest *Wasp* class (LHD–1) are the largest amphibious ships in the world, with a displacement of 40 500 tons (36 450 metric tons). Capable of making 20+ knots (37.8 kilometers per hour), these ships carry a crew of over 1100 sailors, plus a Marine Detachment of 1894, close to a typical Marine Expeditionary Unit (MEU).

The US Navy deploys 27 other major amphibious landing craft. Eleven *Austin*-class Amphibious Transport Docks (LPD) each displace 17 000 tons, travel at 21 knots (38.7 kilometers per hour) and are capable of launching up to six CH–46 helicopters and carrying 900 Marines. A total of 16 *Anchorage*-, *Whidbey*- and *Harpers Ferry*-class dock landing ships (LSD), displacing 14 000–17 000 tons, can travel at 20+ knots and can carry 330–400 Marines. When configured for an assault role, these ships use a combination of air-cushion landing craft, conventional landing craft and helicopters (and, eventually, the MV–22 VTOL aircraft) to move Marine assault forces ashore.

The 87-ton *Landing Craft, Air Cushioned* (LCAC) is a high-speed, over-the-beach, fully amphibious landing craft capable of carrying a 60–75 ton payload at a speed of 40+ knots (73 kilometers per hour) over a range of 320 kilometers. A typical load might consist of 24 fully equipped troops or 1 M–1 Main Battle Tank. The air cushion allows this vehicle to reach more than 70 per cent of the world's coastline, whereas conventional landing craft can land at only 15 per cent of the coasts.

The current Assault Amphibian Vehicle Personnel Model 7A1 (AAVP7A1) is an armored assault, amphibious full-tracked landing vehicle that carries troops through rough water and the surf zone, and then on to inland objectives ashore. The AAVP7A1, in service since 1983, can carry 21 combat-equipped Marines or 4540 kilograms of cargo through the water for seven hours at 10 kilometers per hour, and is armed with machine guns.

US Marines can also employ *airlift* into battle in a maneuver known as 'vertical envelopment'. The transport version of the *Sea Stallion* helicopter (see above) has fulfilled the Marine Corps requirement for heavy airlift since 1966. The upgraded CH–53E *Super Stallion* can carry 56 Marines at a speed of 170 knots per hour (315 km/h) to an unrefueled range of 230 nautical miles (425 km). A fleet of over 130 is operational. The Marine medium-lift assault helicopter is the aging CH–46 *Sea Knight* helicopter. In service since the mid-1970s, the CH–46 can carry fourteen troops plus two aerial machine gunners at a speed of 267 kilometers per hour to a range of 132 nautical miles.[55]

This is an impressive force, but the Sea Knight medium-lift helicopter fleet is nearing the end of its service life, and its relatively low speed makes it vulnerable in modern combat environments. The revolutionary new MV–22A Osprey 'tiltrotor' aircraft, the expected replacement, is still undergoing testing. With its ability to operate as a helicopter when taking off and landing and then converting to a high-speed (522 kilometers per hour) turboprop airplane for horizontal flight, the Osprey will eventually provide a greatly improved medium-lift capability. The very slow speed and limited range of the current Assault Amphibian Vehicle is another serious limitation. A new generation, the *Advanced Amphibian Assault Vehicle (AAAV)*, is under development and will reportedly have a water speed of 20 knots and increased armor.[56]

Once ashore, the combat capability of the US Marines is legendary, and their performance in the Persian Gulf War added to their reputation, although they did not engage in an amphibious assault. First they played a central role in defeating the Iraqi assault on Khafji, Saudi Arabia, on 29 January 1991. Then, on the night of 24 February, the 1st and 2nd Marine divisions stormed through the heavy Iraqi defenses of the 'Saddam Line' at the Saudi–Kuwait border in what Theater Commander General Schwarzkopf later described as a 'textbook operation'. They then proceeded to liberate Kuwait City within three days. Moreover, the mere presence of a Marine Expeditionary Brigade-size landing force in the Gulf tied down many Iraqi troops along the coast, enabling the main assault to flank them.[57]

US Marine infantry forces employ much of the same weaponry used by the US Army, which is described in Chapter 8. The Marines also employ the *Light Armored Vehicle 25* (LAV–25), an eight-wheeled, all-terrain vehicle with night capabilities that can carry six troops plus its crew of two. The LAV–25 can travel at a speed of up to 99 kilometers per hour.

Marine air wings operate the F/A–18C/D Hornet (see above) in common with the Navy, plus the AV–8B *Harrier II* short-take-off-and-landing (STOVL) attack fighter, and the AH–1 *Cobra* attack helicopter. The latest version of the Harrier is an around-the-clock interdiction and close support aircraft capable of operating from ships or almost any type of ground landing site. It can carry a wide variety of air-to-air and air-to-ground weapons at subsonic speeds to a range of 163 nautical miles with 30 minutes on station. During the Gulf War, Marine Harriers flew 3380 sorties for a total of 4083 flight hours while maintaining a mission capable rate in excess of 90 per cent. At the peak of the ground war, their average 'turnaround' time between missions was 23 minutes. The latest version of the AH–1W *Super Cobra* attack helicopter can travel at a speed of 147 knots over a range of 256 nautical miles (473 kilometers) in its basic attack configuration, which includes a 20 mm turreted cannon and four external wing stations that can carry a wide variety of rockets and precision-guided missiles. During the Gulf War, Marine Cobras destroyed 97 tanks, 104 armored personnel carriers and vehicles, 16 bunkers and two anti-aircraft artillery sites without the loss of a single aircraft.[58]

The United States has an unmatched naval expeditionary warfare capability. However, US forces have not conducted a large-scale amphibious assault against a defended coast since the 1950 landing at Inchon, South Korea—cited as 'the example' of the Marine Corps 'Operational Maneuver From the Sea' Concept. During the Gulf War the original plan called for a two-Brigade assault on the Kuwaiti coast. However, after learning that 28 days of necessary preparation to soften up defenses for the landing would delay the main ground assault, and after considering both the potential damage to Kuwait City and Marine casualties, the amphibious assault was called off by US commanders. This has caused some to conclude (probably prematurely) that the concept of amphibious assault is obsolete in an era of high-tech weaponry that includes anti-ship and ballistic missiles.

Once ashore, Marine forces suffer some of the same limitations as do the US Army's 'Light' divisions (see Chapter 8): they lack heavy weaponry and cannot sustain heavy combat for an extended period by themselves. However, as interventionary forces in low-intensity situations, or as an 'enabling' force for follow-on heavy units, the US Navy–Marine Corps team is the best in the world.

Naval Undersea Warfare was often said to be the US Navy's 'top priority' during the last phase of the Cold War, due to the serious threat posed by the Soviet Union's then large and capable submarine force, both conventional and nuclear. Following the demise of the Soviet Union, Russia's submarine fleet has decreased considerably in size because of severe economic constraints, but it remains a potent force. Nevertheless, the political-strategic relationship between the two countries has led to a significantly diminished threat in the eyes of US national leadership. As a result, the US force of *nuclear attack submarines* (SSNs) is being reduced from a late-1980s high of nearly 100 boats to a total of 50 by the year 2000, and their primary mission is now said to be countering the threat of Third World countries acquiring modern state-of-the-art non-nuclear submarines. Moreover, their role in power projection, strike and special operations missions is being increased.

The newest *Seawolf* class nuclear attack submarine (SSN–21) was originally designed to meet the Soviet submarine threat, but the changed situation has led to multi-mission modifications and the limiting of the extremely expensive class to three units. The Seawolf is reportedly capable of 35 knots submerged, while remaining very quiet at speeds of 20 knots, and to be capable of reaching a depth of about 610 meters. Its weaponry includes up to 48 of the Advanced Capability Mark 48 torpedoes with a speed of 55 knots and range of 32 000 meters, or 48 Tomahawk or Harpoon cruise missiles (or any combination thereof) internally launched, and the third submarine is also reportedly capable of carrying 50 special operations troops. The Seawolf's advanced sonars, both internal and towed array, and its BYS–2 combat system are said to give it a three-fold increased anti-submarine warfare mission effectiveness over the next best US SSN, the *Improved Los Angeles* Class (SSN–688I). The Los Angeles-class boats can reportedly reach a submerged speed of 32 knots and a depth of 450 meters. A total of 26 weapons can be tube-launched, and boats numbers 719 and above also have a small external VLS with 12 launch tubes. The last 22 units of the 62-boat Los Angeles-class are designated 'Improved' because of their enhanced quietness, better under-ice capabilities and extended reactor core life. Older versions are being retired well short of their nominal 30-year life spans on the way to a 50-boat fleet.[59]

This submarine fleet, with its advanced technology and superbly trained elite crews, possesses the best anti-submarine capability in the world. However, in the post–Cold War era, these boats are also capable of performing other missions such as covert reconnaissance/surveillance, insertion of special forces, and cruise missile strike. During the Gulf War nine Los Angeles-class submarines performed a variety of missions, and two of them fired Tomahawk missiles from the eastern Mediterranean.

Many US surface ships, including Aegis cruisers, Arleigh Burke destroyers, and *Perry*-class frigates (FFG–7) also perform anti-submarine warfare missions. The *Spruance*-class destroyers (DD–963) were designed primarily for that mission, although 22 of the 31 ships of this class are being equipped with a VLS to enable them to launch a variety of missiles. Although equipped with advanced internal and towed array sonars and Mark 46 torpedoes, this ship's (and indeed the entire surface fleet's) most effective anti-submarine weapons system are its two onboard SH–60 *Seahawk* LAMPS III helicopters, equipped with sonobuoys and Mark 46 or Mark 50 torpedoes. Capable of flying at a maximum of 180 knots over a range of 380 nautical miles (600 km), these helicopters can detect and kill submarines before they can get close to US ships.

Two other airborne assets round out the Navy's undersea warfare capabilities. The carrier-based S–3B *Viking* is a twin jet-engine aircraft equipped with a high-speed computer that processes information generated by its acoustic and non-acoustic sensors, including an Inverse Synthetic Aperture Radar (ISAR). Able to attain a speed of 834 kilometers per hour and with a range of 2300+ nautical miles (4232 km), the Viking can carry nearly 4000 pounds of weapons, including guided missiles, torpedoes, mines, rockets and bombs. Its in-air refueling capability greatly enhances its effectiveness. In addition to its ASW role, the S–3B can also perform reconnaissance and refueling missions, making it one of the most versatile aircraft in the US naval inventory.

The P–3C *Orion* is a long-range land-based, four-engine propeller maritime patrol aircraft. Its crew of twelve operates advanced submarine detection sensors such as directional frequency and ranging sonobuoys (DIFAR) and magnetic anomaly detection (MAD) equipment. With a cruise speed of 649 kilometers per hour, on a typical mission the Orion can remain aloft for 10–12 hours up to a ceiling of 30 000 feet. Once it detects a target, it can deliver a variety of weapons from its large payload of 20 000 pounds (9 metric tons). Future upgrades will enhance the Orion's effectiveness in surface surveillance and targeting.[60]

The US Navy retains the most sophisticated undersea warfare capability in the world. However, the declining size of the SSN fleet, and the difficulties of detecting modern conventional submarines in the shallow waters of the littoral mean that this will remain an area of concern for US planners.

SUMMARY

For the present and through the mid-term, the US Navy–Marine Corps team is the most potent in the world. A brief review of the highlights of the US Pacific Fleet's 1996/97 operations reveals some measure of its effectiveness and readiness.

The Pacific Fleet conducts some 125 exercises annually with over 14 nations in the Asia–Pacific region. Regional stability in Southeast Asia is supported by the Fleet's Cooperation Afloat Readiness and Training (CARAT) which features several months of operations each year in the South China Sea region. In 1996 six other nations took part: Brunei, the Philippines, Indonesia, Malaysia, Thailand and Singapore. Rim-of-the-Pacific (RIMPAC) is a biennial exercise designed to enhance interoperability and proficiency of multinational and bilateral forces operating in response to short-notice littoral missions. More than 28 US ships and 1200 Marines—including the *Independence* and *Kitty Hawk* carrier battle groups, and the *Essex* (LHD–2) amphibious ready group with the 11th MEU(SOC) embarked—took part in and around Hawaii in RIMPAC 96. An additional 29 ships from Australia, Canada, Chile, Korea and Japan also participated.

In March–April 1996 the US Seventh Fleet engaged in a 'Taiwan Strait Flexible Deterrent Option' to monitor Chinese military live-fire missile exercises off the coast of Taiwan. The forward-deployed *Independence* carrier battle group took up station off the eastern coast of Taiwan. These forces provided a visible sign of US commitment to stability in the region. The *Nimitz* carrier battle group transited at high speed to arrive in the South China Sea within days, intensifying the signal of US resolve.[61]

However, the strain on naval and Marine Corps personnel and machines in an era of declining fleet size is becoming an issue. Since 1986, the US Pacific Fleet has gone from 283 ships to 192, while maintaining a full slate of commitments throughout the Asia–Pacific region. The seriousness of the situation reportedly prompted US Chief of Naval Operations Admiral Jay Johnson to declare in a June 1997 Naval War College forum: 'We're out of the "do more with less" business. We can do less with less, or we can do more with more, but we no longer will do more with less!'[62] In light of recurring procurement shortfalls and assuming a continued US strategy of engagement in the vital Asia–Pacific region, that remains a challenge. One thing is certain. For the foreseeable future, the US Navy–Marine Corps team will continue to carry the main burden of US military presence in the region.

7

US Air Force and US Space Command

In 1997 the US Air Force celebrated its 50th anniversary as a separate service. Due to highly publicized aspects of its performance during the 1991 Persian Gulf War, the Air Force has often been the premier symbol of American military superiority in the post–Cold War era. This chapter examines the mission, organization, strategic vision, force structure and capabilities of the US Air Force and the related US Space Command, with a particular emphasis on the Asia–Pacific region.

MISSION AND ORGANIZATION

In 1947 the Air Force ended a 40-year association with the US Army to become a separate service, as mandated by the National Security Act of that same year. The mission of the US Air Force is 'to defend the United States through control and exploitation of air and space'.[1] Teamed with the Army, Navy and Marine Corps, the Air Force is prepared to fight and win any war if deterrence fails. In keeping with its mission, the Air Force is responsible for providing:

- aircraft and missile forces necessary to prevent or fight a general war
- land-based air forces needed to establish air superiority, interdict the enemy and provide air support of ground forces in combat
- the primary aerospace forces for the defense of the United States against air and missile attack
- the primary airlift capability for use by all of the nation's military services

- major space research and development for the Department of Defense
- assistance to the National Aeronautics and Space Administration to conduct the space program.[2]

The Department of the Air Force incorporates all elements of the US Air Force. It is administered by a civilian Secretary appointed by the President and is supervised by a military Chief of Staff. The Secretariat and Air Staff help the Secretary and the Chief of Staff direct the Air Force mission.

The Chief of Staff, US Air Force, is appointed by the President, with the consent of the Senate, from among Air Force general officers, normally for a four-year term. The Chief of Staff serves as a member of the Joint Chiefs of Staff (JCS). In that capacity, the Chief of Staff is one of the military advisers to the President, the National Security Council and the Secretary of Defense. The Chief of Staff is also the principal adviser to the Secretary of the Air Force.

In 1997 the Department of the Air Force consisted of approximately 382 000 active-duty personnel organized into eight major commands, 37 field operating agencies, three direct reporting units and their subordinate elements, 96 major installations in the United States and overseas, plus an additional 187 000 Air Force Reserve, Air National Guard and civilian personnel.

Major commands are organized on a functional basis in the United States and a geographic basis overseas. They are generally assigned specific responsibilities based on functions. In descending order of command, elements of major commands include numbered air forces, wings, groups, squadrons and flights.

The basic unit for generating and employing combat capability is the wing, which has always been the Air Force's prime warfighting instrument. Composite wings operate more than one kind of aircraft, and may be configured as self-contained units designated for quick intervention anywhere in the world. Other wings continue to operate a single aircraft type ready to join air campaigns anywhere they are needed. Air base and other specialized mission wings also support the basic mission of the Air Force.

In 1997 the US Air Force consists of the following major commands:

- Air Combat Command, headquartered at Langley Air Force Base (AFB), Virginia
- Air Education and Training Command, Randolph AFB, Texas
- Air Force Materiel Command, Wright-Patterson AFB, Ohio

- Air Force Space Command, Peterson AFB, Colorado
- Air Force Special Operations Command, Hurlburt Field, Florida
- Pacific Air Forces, Hickam AFB, Hawaii
- United States Air Forces in Europe, Ramstein Air Base, Germany.[3]

STRATEGIC VISION

Throughout the Cold War the US Air Force played a key role in both nuclear deterrence and global containment of the Soviet Union. During that time the US Air Force was heavily committed in two 'limited' wars in the Asia–Pacific region: Korea from 1950 to 1953, and Indochina from 1963 to 1973 (see Chapter 1).

As the Cold War drew to a close, the Air Force, faced with declining budgets and the loss of such overseas bases as Clark Air Base in the Philippines, began to recast its doctrine in terms of crisis response and 'presence'. The first attempt at a reformulation of doctrine was contained in the 1990 publication entitled *The Air Force and National Security: Global Reach—Global Power*. As part of a US-based 'Contingency Force' the Air Force would be 'on call' to meet regional threats. In order to become more flexible and responsive, the Air Force combined the former Tactical Air Command and some elements of the Strategic Air Command into a single Air Combat Command including 26 active and reserve fighter wings, down from a Cold War high of 36. Overseas-based Air Force units were seen as a vital element of US 'presence'.

With the 'Global Reach—Global Power' statement, the Air Force sent a clear signal that in an era of diminished threats and declining budgets it was prepared to enter into a debate over roles and missions with the US Navy and Marine Corps, the two services that had previously claimed the 'crisis response' and 'presence' missions as their own.[4]

Faced with continuing change, on 21 November 1996, after an 18-month effort, the Air Force released its current strategic vision statement entitled *Global Engagement: A Vision for the 21st Century Air Force*. Shaped by the guidance document *Joint Vision 2010* published by the Chairman of the Joint Chiefs of Staff (see Chapter 2), *Global Engagement* addresses the entire Air Force—people, capabilities and infrastructure—and attempts to chart the future course of the Air Force into the first quarter of the 21st century. A 'Long-Range Plan' of implementation is under development.

Global Engagement describes the current US Air Force as 'the world's most powerful air and space force', which already offers 'an alternative to the kind of military operation that pits large numbers of young Americans against an adversary in brute, force-on-force conflicts'. The Air Force embodies a 'new way of war' that 'leverages technologically superior US military capabilities to achieve national objectives'. At the same time, *Global Engagement* acknowledges that 'technology and tactics only go so far' and that 'quality people define the Air Force'.[5]

Following the common direction for all US military services outlined in *Joint Vision 2010*, the Air Force has a key role to play in achieving that document's call for 'the capability to dominate an opponent across the range of military operations—Full Spectrum Dominance', which comprises four operational concepts: Dominant Maneuver, Precision Engagement, Full-Dimensional Protection and Focused Logistics. *Global Engagement* states that these concepts form 'a lens through which the Air Force looks to the first quarter of the 21st Century' and then offers a glimpse into the future:

What the Nation Will Need from Its Military in 2025
WHAT?
- Protect the nation's interests, wherever and however they are threatened
- Respond to new challenges and new missions
- Hedge against surprises
- Support national information needs
- Provide strategic and operational choices
- Respond to changing science and technology

WHERE?
- In non-traditional environments
- In the shadow of NBC (nuclear, biological, chemical) weapons, or after the use of NBC weapons
- Increasingly from the CONUS (Continental US)
- Global infosphere

HOW?
- To win the nation's wars decisively by dominating the battlespace
- With minimal human losses
- With minimal collateral damage
- With reasonable demands on the nation's resources
- In accordance with the nation's values
- As partners in joint-combined and regional operations

WHEN?
- Immediately, when called upon.[6]

Modern air and space power is described as having inherent strengths that are critical to 'Full Spectrum Dominance': speed, global range, stealth, flexibility, precision, lethality, global/theater situational awareness and strategic perspective.

Global Engagement reveals that in pursuit of continuing effectiveness, the Air Force is going through 'a transition of enormous importance. We are now transitioning from an air force into an air and space force on an evolutionary path to a space and air force'.[7] It is clear from this statement that the Air Force regards space as the ultimate 'high ground' from which to exercise battlespace dominance.

All US military forces already depend heavily on space assets to support their missions with regard to intelligence, surveillance and reconnaissance, warning, position location, weapons guidance, communications and environmental monitoring, as became apparent during the 1991 Persian Gulf War. In 1985 the Joint Chiefs of Staff activated a distinct joint command—the US Space Command (USSPACECOM)—to help normalize the use of space in support of US defense forces.

Headquartered at Peterson Air Force Base near Colorado Springs, Colorado, USSPACECOM conducts joint space operations in accordance with Unified Command Plan missions:

- Space Forces Support
- Space Force Enhancement
- Space Force Application
- Space Force Control.

In addition, USSPACECOM is responsible for planning and executing ballistic missile defense of North America.

Space Forces Support operations include launch and on-orbit satellite command and control operations which are provided by the Air Force, Army and Naval Space Commands, with primary launch sites located at Cape Canaveral Air Station, Florida, and Vandenberg Air Force Base, California.

Space Force Enhancement occurs by means of space systems which provide direct support to air, sea and land forces. Defense Support Program satellites provide ballistic missile warning—a capability that warned of Scud attacks during the Gulf War. Communications are provided by several satellite systems. During the Gulf War these satellites carried over 90 per cent of the communications into and out of the theater of operations. Weather data is provided by the Defense Meteorological Satellite Program. The Global Position System (GPS) and Navy Navigation Satellite System provide navigation and positioning information—another capability that proved vital in the featureless deserts that characterized the Gulf War battlefield.

In the future, *Space Force Application* will be performed through the planned acquisition of theater ballistic missile defense systems. *Space Force Control* will eventually become essential to the success of future US air, sea and land military operations. Assured access to and unimpeded operation in space, and the denial to an enemy of the same, are the key tenets of space control operations. USSPACECOM's worldwide Space Surveillance Network is already tasked to detect, track, identify and catalog all space objects to ensure that space operations are conducted without interference. Its Space Control Center, located underground within Cheyenne Mountain, Colorado, provides warning to US space systems operators to protect their satellites from potentially hostile situations or dangerous natural events.[8]

While the Army and the Navy play significant roles in USSPACECOM and have their own Space Commands, USSPACECOM is commanded by an Air Force general who also commands the Air Force Space Command and the North American Aerospace Defense Command (NORAD). The Air Force is the major participant, and clearly intends to 'sustain its stewardship of space' because 'the nation will expect the Air Force to be prepared to defend US interests in space when necessary'.[9]

It follows that when *Global Engagement* enumerates the *core competencies* that provide a bridge between Air Force doctrine and the acquisition and programming process, *air and space superiority* is listed first. 'Air and space superiority' means control over what moves through air and space in order to allow US forces freedom *from* attack and freedom *to* attack. Gaining air and space superiority is said to be operationally important—and a strategic imperative for protecting American lives. Everything on the battlefield is at risk without it. If air and space dominance is achieved, then joint US forces 'can operate with impunity throughout the adversary's battlespace'. Defense against ballistic and cruise missiles is described as 'an increasingly important element of Air and Space Superiority'.[10]

The second core competency laid out in *Global Engagement* is *global attack*, the 'ability to attack rapidly anywhere on the globe at any time'. During the Cold War the Air Force's long-range bombers and ICBMs primarily fulfilled that role in the nuclear deterrence mission. Although concern over Russia has diminished, there is a growing risk of proliferation. Consequently, Air Force units continue to fulfill the deterrence mission under the control of the US Strategic Command (see Chapter 5).

In the post–Cold War era, however, the Air Force's short- and long-range attack capabilities primarily support the deterrence of *conventional* war stemming from a regional crisis by providing versatile, responsive combat power that is able to intervene decisively when necessary. At present over a quarter of Air Force active-duty personnel are deployed overseas at any one time. *Global Engagement* notes that, over time, 'technological change, threats to forward bases, asymmetric strategies by adversaries who seek to deny entry to US power projection forces, and growing budgetary pressures will likely change the way the Air Force carries out its presence and power projection missions'.[11]

At this point the Air Force introduces a controversial new concept: the *Air Expeditionary Force* (AEF) based in the continental United States. Such an expeditionary force is said to be 'tailored to meet the needs of the Joint Force Commander, both for lethal and non-lethal applications, and can launch and be ready to fight in less than three days',[12] to deploy forward and provide sustained combat power in a crisis. The concept is controversial because the term 'expeditionary force' has previously been ascribed primarily to naval carrier battle groups and amphibious ready groups and sometimes to rapidly deployable ground forces, especially the US Marines and Army paratroop units. In November 1996 the Chief of Staff of the Air Force defended the notion in the following terms:

> We stress this expeditionary aspect not because we're trying to replace carriers, but because there are a finite number of carriers and they will always be in demand. We have to learn to work together and augment each other. There will be times and circumstances where carriers will be at a disadvantage. There will be places that land-based air will be at a disadvantage, so we'll need those carriers. There will be times when we need carriers in other parts of the world and it's better to deploy land-based air, which is cheaper and can sustain a greater sortie rate over a longer period of time. We're not trying to pit one organization against another. Instead, we're trying to support *Joint Vision 2010*.[13]

The concept remains controversial. Perhaps partly in response, in February 1997 the US Navy announced that it was testing a new concept called 'Revolution in Strike Warfare' in which an increased number of naval carrier-based fighters will operate around the clock for four days in 'an effort to demonstrate our part in the kind of scenario that demands high intensity operations and where you have a requirement to halt an invasion very quickly'.[14]

For its part, in 1996 the Air Force exercised the AEF concept three times in the Middle East with deployments to Bahrain, Qatar and Jordan in which the first simulated combat sorties were flown with less than 72 hours of notification to deploy, and the force provided a balanced capability for air superiority, precision attack and suppression of air defenses.[15]

The third core competency is *rapid global mobility*. When an operation must be carried out quickly anywhere in the world, airlift and aerial refueling forces are critical. These forces will be in great demand as the number of forward-deployed forces declines.

Precision engagement, the fourth core competency, is defined as the capability 'that enables our forces to locate the objective or target, provide responsive command and control, generate the desired effect, assess our level of success, and retain the flexibility to re-engage with precision when required'.[16]

Technology has clearly driven this definition. According to the Air Force, 'in the 21st Century, it will be possible to find, fix or track and target anything that moves on the surface of the earth'.[17] The delivery of overwhelming yet selective and discriminating power is the essence of this competency.

The pace and extent of technological change in the realm of information has led to the need for the fifth core competency: *information superiority*. The ability of future US joint forces to achieve dominant battlespace awareness will depend heavily on the ability of the Air Force's air- and space-based assets to provide global awareness, intelligence, communications, weather and navigation support.

To this end, future Battle Management/Command and Control (BM/C^2) systems will enable real-time control and execution of all air and space missions. The Air Force will also exploit the technological promise of Unmanned Aerial Vehicles (UAVs) over the full range of combat missions, beginning with Intelligence, Surveillance and Reconnaissance, and possibly extending into suppression of enemy air defenses.

Even as it develops its offensive Information Warfare (IW) capabilities, the Air Force will also aggressively expand its efforts in defensive IW capabilities, which are already operational in the defense of computer systems.

The final core competency listed in *Global Engagement* is *agile combat support*. The key concept here is 'time-definite resupply'. In the past, including the 1991 Gulf War, the slow establishment of huge—and vulnerable—forward supply depots was necessary to support the extended overseas deployment of substantial US combat forces. Under 'time-definite' resupply, 'when combat commanders require an item, the system will reach back to the continental United States and deliver it where and when it is needed'. Such a capability will greatly reduce the vulnerability of the logistics train of US power projection forces by reducing its size while increasing its responsiveness. At the heart of such a system are new information technologies that provide, for example, the ability to know the location of critical parts, no matter which service or agency holds them.[18]

For all of its emphasis on technology and hardware innovation, *Global Engagement* puts equal emphasis on people. 'People are at the heart of the Air Force's military capability,' it proclaims. Maintaining the high quality of its men and women, and providing a good quality of life for them and their families, will remain a high priority.

Core values of integrity, service and excellence are reinforced in all aspects of the Air Force's education and training, and result in 'cohesive units, manned with people who exhibit loyalty, who want to belong, and who act in a manner consistent with Air Force core values, even under conditions of high stress'.[19]

Global Engagement concludes with a summary Vision Statement: 'Air Force people building the world's most respected air and space force . . . global power and reach for America'.[20]

FORCE STRUCTURE

The United States Air Force is the world's largest and best equipped modern force. As of 1998 it operates approximately 550 intercontinental ballistic missiles (see Chapter 3), 142 long-range bombers, 906 active forces primary tactical combat aircraft (plus over 549 in the Reserve), 100 reconnaissance and command aircraft, 720 airlift transport aircraft, 526 in-flight refueling tankers, plus training aircraft. In addition, during a crisis the Air Force can call upon some 400 long-range commercial airliners in the Civil Reserve Air Fleet.[21]

The great majority of these aircraft, including all the long-range bombers and nearly all of the tanker aircraft, are based in the continental United States as part of the five numbered air forces of Air Combat Command (ACC) and the two numbered air forces of Air Mobility Command (AMC). However, it must be remembered that, because nearly all US combat aircraft are capable of in-flight refueling by the Air Force's large tanker fleet, they can deploy anywhere in the world, many of them in a matter of hours.

Two major Air Force combat commands are located outside of the 48 contiguous states of the continental United States: the US Air Forces in Europe (USAFE) and the Pacific Air Forces (PACAF).

The USAFE in 1997 consisted of two numbered air forces comprised of approximately 33 000 personnel, deploying 175 fighters, supported by 30 airlift aircraft and 9 aerial tankers, primarily based in Germany, the United Kingdom and Italy.[22]

THE US AIR FORCE IN THE PACIFIC

The Pacific Air Force (PACAF) traces its history back to World War II with the activation of Far East Air Force (FEAF) on 3 August 1944 at Brisbane, Australia. FEAF was then subordinate to the US Army Forces Far East. By 1945 three numbered air forces—5th, 7th and 13th—were supporting operations in the Pacific.

After World War II, FEAF and 5th AF remained in Japan, 7th AF operated from Hawaii and 13th AF operated from the Philippines. FEAF was designated the theater air force for the Far East Command, and all air forces in the Asia–Pacific region were placed under one commander for the first time.

During the Korean War, FEAF engaged in heavy combat with its 5th, 13th and 20th air forces operating out of South Korea, Japan and the Philippines. In 1957, four years after the Korean War armistice, FEAF was redesignated Pacific Air Forces and its headquarters transferred to Hickam Air Force Base in Hawaii, where it remains to this day.[23]

From 1961 to 1975 Pacific Air Forces were heavily involved in the war in Southeast Asia, including Vietnam, Thailand, Laos and Cambodia. During that war the US Air Force expended 6.162 million tons of air munitions, and suffered 2118 killed and 3460 wounded in action, along with the loss of 2257 aircraft.[24]

Today, PACAF is responsible for most Air Force units, bases and facilities in the Pacific and Alaska. PACAF's primary mission is to plan, conduct and coordinate offensive and defensive air operations in the Pacific and Asian theaters. PACAF's area of responsibility extends across more than half the earth's surface—from the west coasts of the Americas to the east coast of Africa, and from the Arctic to the Antarctic.

The command has approximately 44 000 military and civilian personnel serving in nine major locations and numerous smaller facilities, primarily in Hawaii, Alaska, Guam, Japan and South Korea. There are approximately 300 fighter and attack aircraft assigned to the command, and another 80 non-combat aircraft.[25]

PACAF's major units and aircraft are:

- 5th Air Force—Headquarters at Yokota Air Base, Japan, 16 000 personnel
- 18th Wing—Kadena AB, Japan (F-15C/D, HH-60G, E-3C, KC-135R)
- 35th Fighter Wing—Misawa AB, Japan (F-16C/D)
- 374th Airlift Wing—Yokota AB, Japan (C-130E/H, C-9A, UH-1N)
- 7th Air Force—Headquarters at Osan AB, South Korea, 9000 personnel
- 8th Fighter Wing—Kunsan AB, South Korea (F-16C/D)
- 51st Fighter Wing—Osan AB, South Korea (F-16C, A/OA-10A, C-12J)
- 11th Air Force—Headquarters at Elmendorf AFB, Alaska, 11 000 personnel
- 3rd Wing—Elmendorf AFB, Alaska (F-15, C-130H, C-12J, E-3B/C, F-15E)
- 13th Air Force—Headquarters at Andersen AFB, Guam, 2000 personnel
- 36th Air Base Wing—Andersen AFB, Guam
- 15th Air Base Wing—Hickam AFB, Hawaii (KC-135).[26]

PACAF is not large in numbers. However, its commander cites four advantages of air power that are perfectly suited to PACAF's enormous area of operations:

- *Mobility:* The speed and range unique to air power meets this essential requirement in a region of vast distances.
- *Responsiveness:* A potential aggressor in the Asia–Pacific region needs to be aware that PACAF can and will respond

quickly to acts of aggression, disrupting an aggressor's cycle of military operations.
- *Flexibility:* PACAF has the ability to mix a variety of air assets into a spectrum of combinations to meet developing conditions.
- *Versatility:* PACAF's force structure includes F–15s, F–16s, E–3 *Sentries*, airlifters and tankers already present in the region.[27]

In addition to keeping its own forces in a high state of readiness, PACAF devotes considerable effort to building solid relationships with other regional air forces in support of the USCINCPAC Cooperative Engagement strategy. PACAF forces regularly train with Asia–Pacific air units during exercises such as COPE NORTH in Japan, PITCH BLACK in Australia, COPE WEST in various Southeast Asian nations, COBRA GOLD in Thailand, COMMANDO SLING with Singapore, COPE TAUFAN in Malaysia, and FOAL EAGLE in South Korea. Although most of these exercises are bilateral given the absence of any overarching regional alliance, in 1995 PACAF joined the air forces of Thailand and Singapore in COPE TIGER. COPE THUNDER, an exercise held three times a year on the vast air combat ranges around Eielson Air Force Base in Alaska, is also a multilateral effort involving participation in recent years by forces from Japan, Thailand, Australia, New Zealand and Singapore, in addition to Great Britain and Canada. In all, the Pacific Air Forces are involved in a total of 32 different exercises annually with allies and friends throughout the region.[28]

As the air forces of the Asia–Pacific region grow in size and capability, these exercises are taking on an added significance. Many observers have noted the steady acquisition of significant numbers of advanced multi-role fighters such as the F–16, F–18, SU–27 and MiG–29 by many countries in the region. Some estimate that during the decade of the 1990s, as many as 3000 new fighters and strike aircraft may have been procured throughout the Asia–Pacific region, and an equal number upgraded with new avionics and armaments. Indeed, as one Asia–Pacific military analyst has stated, 'when it comes down to fighting and winning wars—as opposed to conducting peace-time activities such as maritime surveillance and patrolling, or monitoring dissidents—advanced strike aircraft are now the weapons of first choice'.[29]

Seen in this context, the Pacific Air Force's efforts in the 'Cooperative Engagement' program are an important element in its contribution to regional security. In April 1997, air force chiefs from 87 countries gathered at Nellis Air Force Base in Nevada to discuss the role of air power in the 21st century at a conference to mark the 50th anniversary of the US Air Force. In a paper delivered at that conference, Major-General Goh Yong Siang, the Republic of Singapore's Chief of the Air Force, stated:

> Nations in the Asia–Pacific region are beginning to share a common vision of the Pacific Century . . . In this process, regional countries will continue to share a similar air environment of large distances and limited air resources. This must ultimately impact on broader air power. The special characteristics of air power will mean that air forces are well placed as instruments in fostering closer defense cooperation.[30]

PACAF's commander stresses the importance of stability:

> In the midst of change, stability is a precious resource. As the air force component of USCINCPAC, PACAF with its commitment to forward presence and cooperative engagement will continue to help provide that stability. PACAF's combination of high quality people and modern weapons systems has served and will continue to serve as powerful deterrents to aggression in the Asia–Pacific region.[31]

THE CURRENT CAPABILITY AND LIMITATIONS OF THE US AIR FORCE

The US Air Force has incurred significant reductions in base infrastructure and force structure since 1990, with more to come. Nevertheless, in 1998 and for the near to mid-term future, no air force in the world can or will match the capability of the US Air Force, because of three factors: (1) its size, (2) its advanced weaponry, and (3) its highly trained personnel. The only air force in the world that presented a serious challenge in all three categories was the former Soviet Air Force. That force has declined so dramatically in both size and quality since the end of the Cold War, in large part because of Russia's economic troubles, that its Commander is worried that the Russian Air Force will cease to exist as an independent branch of that country's armed forces. Two of its four aviation commands have been disbanded, only 50 per cent of its aircraft are serviceable, and the average annual flying hours for front-line pilots in 1996 fell to 19—too low even to assure basic flight safety, as demonstrated by 12 air crashes in 1996.[32]

This brief survey of the capabilities of the US Air Force will examine four categories: (1) command, control, communications, computers, intelligence, surveillance and reconnaissance (C⁴ISR); (2) air superiority and suppression of enemy air defenses; (3) strike; and (4) airlift. The US Air Force's important contributions to Special Operations are covered in the section on the US Special Operations Command (USSOCOM) in Chapter 8. Emphasis will be placed on the Asia–Pacific region where appropriate.

In the realm of *command, control, communications, computers, intelligence surveillance and reconnaissance (C⁴ISR)*, the USAF has access to an unequaled set of space assets. Of the 500 satellites currently in earth orbit, 200 of them belong to the United States, and 100 are dedicated to military use.[33] This fleet of satellites includes intelligence-gathering satellites with visual (KH–11, KH–12, AFP–731), electronic (Chalet, Magnum, Jumpseat), infrared (DSP) and radar sensors (OSUS, Lacrosse) that provide a level of surveillance that no other nation possesses. The National Reconnaissance Office controls these satellites and the details of this capability are highly classified. During the 1991 Gulf War, satellites provided the Coalition forces with a detailed picture of the battlefield, and gave accurate and nearly instantaneous warning of Iraqi Scud launches.[34]

As powerful as these satellites are, they have a number of limitations. Darkness and bad weather degrade the capabilities of some sensors. Thus, during the Gulf War US satellite reconnaissance failed to detect the fact that civilians were taking shelter in the Al Firdos command and control bunker in Baghdad at night, and in the ensuing attack many of them were killed.[35] The orbits of some satellites are fixed and predictable. Those satellites with the most precise capabilities can only cover so much territory, and their numbers are limited. The commander of the US Marines in Operation Desert Storm was so frustrated by the lack of satellite photos of the Iraqi defenses in front of him that he sent in reconnaissance teams on the ground.[36] Finally, these satellites may eventually become vulnerable to countermeasures, such as laser 'blinding' or electronic jamming, and even to physical destruction in the event another nation develops an anti-satellite system.

In addition to its access to satellites, the US Air Force operates several types of highly sophisticated intelligence-gathering and command and control aircraft. The E–3 *Sentry* airborne warning and control system (AWACS) is a modified Boeing 707/320 commercial airframe with a large rotating radar dome that permits surveillance from the Earth's surface up into the stratosphere, over land or water. The radar has a range of more than 320 kilometers for low-flying targets and farther for aerospace vehicles flying at medium to high altitudes. The AWACS radar and identification friend or foe (IFF) subsystems enable it to look down to detect, identify and track enemy and friendly low-flying aircraft by eliminating ground clutter returns that confuse other radar systems. The AWACS also contains advanced computer and video display systems that together with the radar enable it to gather and present broad and detailed battlefield information and communicate to US forces in the field and to the national command authorities. Foremost among these is the latest version of the Joint Tactical Information Distribution System (JTIDS).

Most of the 33 US AWACS aircraft operate out of Tinker Air Force Base in Oklahoma, ready for assignment. However, Pacific Air Forces has a total of four E-3 Sentries stationed at Kadena Air Base in Japan and Elmendorf Air Force Base in Alaska. Additionally, NATO operates 17 AWACS, the United Kingdom has acquired 7 of the aircraft, Saudi Arabia 5, and France 4. Japan has ordered four AWACS based on the newer Boeing 767 airframe with delivery of the first two taking place in March 1998. South Korea has asked to purchase four of the new AWACS aircraft.[37]

During the Gulf War, AWACS were among the first to deploy during Operation Desert Shield to establish an around-the-clock radar screen to defend against Iraqi aggression. During Desert Storm, E-3s flew more than 400 missions with more than 5000 hours of on-station time. E-3 controllers assisted in 38 of the 40 air-to-air kills recorded during the Gulf War.[38]

The RC-135 *Rivet Joint* electronic reconnaissance aircraft is also based on the Boeing 707 airframe. Its elongated nose contains an extensive array of signals intelligence (SIGINT) antennae that provides vital real-time battle management information to US commanders. Two squadrons of Rivet Joint aircraft are based at Offutt Air Force Base in Nebraska, on call for global deployment. RC-135s were in constant use during the Gulf War and more recently completed 1000 missions in support of Operation Southern Watch enforcing sanctions against Iraq. An equal number of Rivet Joint missions have been flown since 1992 in support of operations Provide Promise, Deliberate Force and Joint Endeavor in Bosnia.[39]

The most recent addition to the Air Force's manned reconnaissance fleet is the Joint Surveillance and Target Attack Radar System (JSTARS) E-8C aircraft, also based on remanufactured Boeing 707 airframes. Developed in cooperation with the Army, JSTARS can deliver a picture of the ground situation equivalent to what AWACS provides in the air and space situation. The aircraft operates a side-looking synthetic aperture radar (SAR) and a moving target indicator radar to obtain data on stationary objects as well as locating and tracking moving targets without flying directly overhead. Although still under development, an early version of JSTARS was employed in Desert Storm with devastating effect, giving coalition forces a detailed picture of Iraqi ground force positions and movement.[40]

More recently, the first fully operational JSTARS aircraft played a key role in enforcing the Dayton Peace Agreement in Bosnia. Using ground station modules mounted on trucks, US Army commanders requested real-time radar information on specific areas from the JSTARS. JSTARS enabled the commanders on the ground to detect enemy troop movements and convoys virtually as they occurred, in almost any weather.[41]

The US Air Force plans to acquire a fleet of up to 19 JSTARS aircraft by 2005, at a rate of two per year.[42]

The oldest flying asset in the US Air Force manned reconnaissance fleet is the venerable U–2, which has been constantly upgraded since it entered into operation in 1956. The current U–2R and S models are capable of flying more than 11 000 kilometers at very high altitude, while collecting multi-sensor photo, electro-optic, infrared and radar imagery around the clock in any weather. The 9th Reconaissance Wing's 36 U–2s operate out of Beale Air Force Base, California. A forward operational detachment with at least one U–2R is maintained on a rotational basis at Osan Air Base in South Korea.[43]

The limitations of this airborne reconnaissance fleet are twofold. First, none of these aircraft are armed, and thus can only operate in low-threat areas or with fighter protection. Second, they are limited in numbers due to their high cost. An E–3 AWACS, for example, costs US$270 million.

In partial response to these factors, following the lead of the Israeli armed forces the USAF has deployed its first unmanned aerial vehicle (UAV), the Tier II Medium Altitude/Endurance *Predator*. The Predator is small (8.2 × 15 meters), and can loiter for up to 40 hours at a ceiling of 25 000 feet while cruising at low speed. It carries an infrared and electro optical sensor package and a synthetic aperture radar package and relays real-time imagery via satellite to air or ground commanders. Predators have been deployed over Bosnia. Because they are unmanned and *relatively* inexpensive (US$3 million each), they can more readily be deployed to high-threat areas. Two other UAVs, the High

Endurance 'Global Hawk' and the stealth High Endurance 'Dark Star', are currently under development. Clearly the role of UAVs will increase in importance in future US Air Force operations.[44]

Air and space superiority are seen as the key capability of the US Air Force.

With regard to space, during the Cold War the Anti-Ballistic Missile (ABM) Treaty between the United States and the former Soviet Union prevented, and still prevents, the deployment by either side of full-scale defenses against long-range ballistic missiles. Consequently, at present the United States has no defense against intercontinental ballistic missiles. The topic of national ballistic missile defense is covered in Chapter 8, inasmuch as the Army has the primary responsibility for that role.

Because of similar agreements against the deployment of active anti-satellite (ASAT) systems, the United States also lacks any defense against physical attack on its satellites. Research continues in this area, in the event that any other nation should develop an ASAT capability. A more near-term threat to US satellites lies in the potential for disruption of the computers essential to their operation. The US Space Command is looking at technology that will help provide better warning and characterization of an attack against US satellites.[45] In 1995 the US Air Force established its first Information Warfare Squadron at Shaw Air Force Base in South Carolina to protect Air Force information systems both in garrison and when deployed.[46]

In the realm of *air-to-air combat*, the US Air Force is second to none. Linked with the C⁴ISR assets described above, USAF fighter pilots have demonstrated an ability to establish complete air supremacy over the battlefield—a level beyond 'superiority'.

At present the premier US air superiority fighter is the F-15C/D *Eagle*, an all-weather, extremely maneuverable, tactical fighter that can carry AIM-7F/M Sparrow radar guided missiles, AIM-120 Advanced Medium Range Air-to-Air Missiles (AMRAAM), the AIM-9L/M infrared guided Sidewinder missile, and an internal 20 mm machine gun with 940 rounds of ammunition. Although it first flew in 1972, with constant upgrades the F-15, which is capable of speeds up to mach 2.5 at sea level, remains the best operational air superiority aircraft deployed in significant numbers in the world today. Its multimission avionics set the aircraft apart: they include a head-up display, advanced radar, inertial navigation system, UHF communications, tactical navigation system, an internally mounted tactical electronic warfare system, an 'identification friend or foe' system, electronic countermeasures, and a central digital computer.

The head-up display projects on the windscreen all essential flight information gathered by the integrated avionics system. This display, visible in any light condition, provides the pilot with the information necessary to track and destroy an enemy aircraft without having to look down at the cockpit instruments.

During the 1991 Gulf War, the 120 F-15C/Ds deployed in support of Operations Desert Shield and Desert Storm with AWACS support proved their combat superiority with a confirmed 26:0 kill ratio over the Iraqi Air Force, including five modern MiG-29s, during 5900 sorties.[47] Although equipped with several modern fighter types such as the Mirage F-1, the MiG-29 and the SU-24, the Iraqi pilots were no match for the United States because they had little training, were under strict ground control and lacked any AWACS capability. Apparently only one coalition aircraft, a US Navy FA-18, was downed by the Iraqi Air Force, although the evidence is inconclusive.[48]

This achievement did not come without intense effort. The Air Force was very dissatisfied with the two-to-one air combat exchange ratio that resulted from the war in Southeast Asia. Beginning in the 1970s the US Air Force conducted a series of exhaustive studies, war games, tests and combat exercises examining air-to-air combat in World War II, Korea, Southeast Asia, and the Middle East in 1967, 1973 and 1982 and finally, the 1991 Gulf War, culminating in a massive and unusually objective study commissioned on 22 August 1991 and two years in the making called the *Gulf War Air Power Survey*. One of that study's authors, himself a former Air Force pilot, drew the following conclusions from that large body of evidence:

- Surprise in the form of the unseen attacker is pivotal in over 80 per cent of air-to-air kills.
- This surprise results from a pilot's failure to be sufficiently aware of what is taking place in the combat area around him to avoid being hit by enemy fire.
- This failure is called a breakdown in 'situation' or 'situational awareness' (SA) which is defined as the ability of opposing aircrews to develop and sustain accurate representations of where all the participants in or near the air combat area are, what they are doing, and where they are likely to be in the immediate future.

- Therefore 'situation awareness' is 'the single most important factor affecting engagement outcomes'.
- Superior technology does not necessarily determine engagement outcomes—'situation awareness' is the bottom line.
- If the superior information technology is focused on root problems of situational awareness such as sorting—the timely and effective targeting of opponents—then such technology confers a strong advantage to its possessor.
- The US Joint Tactical Information Distribution System (JTIDS) recently deployed on front-line F–15C/Ds, by providing an integrated, all-aspect identification of friendlies and hostiles, including targeting decisions by others in one's flight, confers a *spectacular* (four- or five-fold) improvement in the air-to-air effectiveness of US pilots by improving their SA.
- Superior tactics, training, employment concepts or even organizational concepts may provide similar margins of superiority, although this remains to be proven.[49]

The final conclusion explains why, in addition to their superior information technology, US Air Force pilots receive air-to-air combat training that is second to none. Fighter pilots receive 208 hours of basic training. At the Air Warfare Center at Nellis Air Force Base, Nevada, 'home of the fighter pilot', they train intensively on the 31 000 square kilometers of flight ranges available, along with pilots from allied and friendly air forces, in such exercises as Red Flag and Coalition Green Flag. Front-line US fighter pilots fly approximately 240 hours annually. Two US Air Force pilots recently celebrated 3700 hours flying an F–16, and 1000 hours in the stealth F–117A. As with air forces everywhere, the US Air Force faces budgetary restrictions on its flying time. For the foreseeable future, however, in the realm of air-to-air combat the US Air Force, along with the fighter pilots of the US Navy and Marines (see Chapter 6), will remain the world's best trained—and therefore the most capable.[50]

Still, the F–15 is coming up to 30 years of service, and while constant upgrades have kept it at the cutting edge of performance, further improvements are likely to be marginal. For example, PACAF is equipping and training its F–15 pilots with night-vision goggles. A new generation of Russian aircraft widely available for export, including the MiG–29 and the SU–27, approaches the F–15 in aerodynamic performance, although not in avionics. Following a USAF exercise against Malaysian MiG–29s that had been in service for only six months, PACAF's commander reported 'Our guys were surprised—[we] did not totally dominate that exercise'.[51] In the near future another generation of fighters, including the Eurofighter 2000, the French Rafale and the Russian SU–37 can probably outperform the F–15 in some circumstances.

The US Air Force's answer is the F–22 *Raptor*, the next generation 'air-dominance' fighter currently under development by a team from the Boeing and Lockheed Martin companies. The prototype first flew in 1990, and the first production test model 'rolled out' on 9 April 1997. The F–22 will reportedly incorporate the following features:

- first look/first kill in all environments, with a cockpit design and avionics fusion to improve the pilot's 'situation awareness'
- reduced observables or 'stealth', building on the experience gained with the F–117 and B–2
- supersonic persistence: high-thrust engines that will allow the F–22 to efficiently cruise at supersonic speeds without using afterburner
- increased maneuverability: aero-design and high thrust-to-weight ratio will provide the capability to outmaneuver all current and projected threat aircraft
- improved reliability and maintainability
- weapons: AMRAAM, Sidewinder, M61 internal 20 mm gun, internal bay for two 2000 pound 'smart' weapons.[52]

If it lives up to these claims, the F–22 will ensure continuing air superiority for the US Air Force well into the next century. However, the F–22 is expensive, with a cost estimated at over US$80 million each. The Air Force had hoped to acquire 438, but the 1997 Department of Defense *Quadrennial Defense Review* reduced that number to 339, which means that the Air Force would de-activate one fighter wing, leaving it with a reduced total of 12 active and eight Reserve fighter wings.[53]

Strike warfare is the ultimate test of any air force. The ability to effectively hit enemy surface targets is essential to deterrence and successful warfighting. The televised performance of the US Air Force in the 1991 Persian Gulf War advertised its strong capability in this area of operations—and also oversold it, as the Air Force's own *Gulf War Air Power Survey* later demonstrated.

The first revelation concerned the first publicized employment of the F–117 *Nighthawk* 'Stealth Fighter', whose all-black color and unorthodox shape added an element of awe to its appearance. The F–117 was the world's first operational aircraft designed to exploit 'low-observable' or 'stealth' technology—a combination of shape, composition, exterior coating and countermeasures that render the aircraft extremely difficult to detect. The Air Force operates 54 of these aircraft, which are home-based at Holloman Air Force Base in New Mexico. The ability of the F–117 to penetrate Baghdad's heavy defenses on the first night of the air war and hit key targets with devastating accuracy without a single loss made a great impression. The impression was created that the F–117 was an utterly invisible plane that flew through Baghdad's defenses alone and hit every target it aimed at.

However, 'low observable' does not mean 'no observable'. In fact, the Air Force, in the midst of great internal controversy, put a great deal of effort into the 'suppression of enemy air defenses' (SEAD) to prepare the way for the F–117s (and of course for other non-stealthy aircraft that also hit Iraq that night). This effort included attacks on key elements of Iraq's *Kari* air defense system by air and sea-launched cruise missiles, helicopter gunships, and F–16s shooting high-speed anti-radiation missiles (HARM) at Iraqi missile sites. In particular, electronic jamming was provided by Air Force EF–111 *Raven* electronic countermeasures aircraft that accompanied the F–117s sent to Baghdad that first night, and the same procedure was followed occasionally thereafter during the air war.

US intelligence later determined that Iraq's Chinese-made *Nanjing* low-frequency radars did detect the F–117s but were unable to determine their altitude. Also, bad weather and smoke from bomb detonations limited the F–117s bombing effectiveness. The F–117 utilized a very accurate laser bombing system—but clouds or smoke interfere with it. Consequently, 18 of the F–117s never attempted to drop their GBU–10 and GBU–27 laser-guided bombs because of poor visibility caused by bad weather. During the three waves of attack on that first night, F–117s attacked about half of their assigned targets, scoring 27 hits out of 49 attacks. This was not the picture of perfection presented at press briefings, but it was an 'order of magnitude' improvement in bombing heavily defended targets, and not a single F–117 was shot down during the war.[54]

The televised effectiveness of the precision-guided munitions (PGMs), the so-called 'smart bombs' deployed by the F–117s and a limited number of other US bombers during the Gulf War, left a lasting impression. Guided or 'smart' bombs were first used by the German Luftwaffe in World War II. The US Air Force first used smart bombs in 1972, near the end of the war in Southeast

Table 7.1 Increasing precision/effectiveness of US Air Force weapons

Era	Circular Error Probability (CEP)[a]	Number of 2000 lb bombs necessary for 90 per cent probability of kill
World War II (B-17)	3300 feet	9070
Vietnam War (F-4)	400	176
Desert Storm (F-117)	10	1

Notes: [a] CEP = the circle within which there is a 50 per cent probability the bomb will land.
Source: Defense Intelligence Agency, cited in *Strategic Assessment 1996*, Institute for National Strategic Studies, p. 197.

Asia. Their success resulted in the development of the next generation, which was employed during the Gulf War.

In essence, current smart bombs consist of a normal unpowered glide bomb, generally ranging in weight from 500 to 2000 pounds, with a guidance section attached to the nose. That section contains either a television guidance system for daytime, or an imaging infrared system for night or limited, adverse weather operations. A data link in the tail section sends guidance updates to the control aircraft that enables the weapons system operator to guide the bomb remotely by sending signals that move its tail fins in such a way as to guide the bomb to the target.[55]

The increased accuracy of smart bombs is startling. During the planning for the Gulf War air campaign, Air Force leaders used the above table, based on studies of bombing accuracy, to demonstrate the difference. CEP is the radius, in feet, of the area in which a bomb is likely to land 50 per cent of the time. The right-hand column shows the number of bombs that would have to be dropped to ensure destruction of a point target.

PACAF's commander illustrates the difference this way: 'We can recall the multi-bomber formations of World War II, which dropped thousands of bombs to hit a point target. Today, we can hit the same target with only one pass and with only one bomb (WWII: 1500 B-17 sorties; Gulf War: 1 F-117, 1 bomb = same target)'.[56]

However, not all the bombs hit their targets, the bombs were in short supply, and during the Gulf War most American bombers were not equipped to guide smart bombs. Only the F-117s, F-111s and F-15Es normally dropped smart bombs. In all, the Air Force dropped 7400 tons of precision-guided munitions during the Gulf War, about 10 per cent of the total tonnage dropped, while aging B-52 heavy bombers dropped nearly 26 000 tons of 'dumb' bombs, 41 per cent of the total. Still, the Gulf War demonstrated the US

Air Force's outstanding capability to conduct strike warfare against heavily defended targets, and there is a general consensus that the air war so devastated the Iraqi army in Kuwait that coalition ground forces easily drove them out of Kuwait in four days.[57]

In addition to the F–117 Stealth fighter, the US Air Force operates many other types of strike aircraft. Only the most significant will be described here.

Three long-range bombers are included in the Air Force inventory. The oldest is the B–52H *Stratofortress*, originally designed to carry out a nuclear deterrence role. Although more than 30 years old, all of the 56 active B–52s have been constantly upgraded to enable them to perform a variety of roles in conventional conflict as well. The B–52 has an unrefueled range of nearly 15 000 kilometers and can carry 70 000 pounds of weapons, including nuclear and conventional air-launched cruise missiles. On the first day of the Gulf air war, B–52s flew for 35 hours non-stop, with three aerial refuelings, from Barksdale Air Force Base in Louisiana, to launch conventional cruise missiles at Iraqi targets. During Operation Desert Storm B–52s flew a total of 1624 missions on targets in Kuwait and Southern Iraq. In September 1996 B–52s flew for 34 hours non-stop from Andersen Air Base in Guam to launch 13 conventional cruise missiles against Iraqi targets during Operation Desert Strike.[58]

The B1-B *Lancer* long-range bomber was also designed to fulfill nuclear missions during the Cold War, but the entire fleet is currently being re-configured to a conventional role, with the process to be completed by 1999. The B–1's low radar cross-section makes it considerably more difficult to detect than the B–52, it can fly lower, faster, and carry a larger payload over intercontinental distances unrefueled, and it has enhanced electronic countermeasures. All 72 active B–1s will be upgraded to drop cluster bombs, and further enhancements will enable it to field precision guided munitions.[59]

On 1 April 1997 the Air Force's newest long-range bomber, the B-2 *Spirit*, reached its Initial Operational Capability (IOC). At that time the commander of the Air Force's Air Combat Command stated, 'The B–2's combination of low observability, large payload capacity, bombing accuracy and long range gives America a unique, unprecedented military capability'.[60] In October 1996 three B–2s destroyed 16 test targets from 12 000 meters using a new type of smart bomb guided with the assistance of global positioning satellites, called the GPS-Aided Munition

(GAM).⁶¹ Due to its extremely high cost of over US$1.3 billion each, only 21 B-2s have been ordered, down from an original 75 planned before the Cold War ended.

On 6 February 1997 the B-2 made its Asian debut at the opening ceremonies for the Asian Aerospace '96 show at Changi Airport in Singapore, flying in from Andersen Air Force Base on Guam. The stealth bomber's unique all-black flying-wing shape is startling. US Air Force Chief of Staff General Fogelman said of the B-2's 90-minute appearance, 'The B-2 stole the show . . . When you see a B-2 show up in Singapore—a long way from Missouri [Whiteman Air Force Base, the B-2's home]—it's a very visible presence that lets people know we can *reach* out and touch them anywhere in the world in a matter of hours'.⁶² The B-2 has been very controversial because of its cost and doubts about its effectiveness. Its advocates, such as retired Gulf War Air Force theater commander General Charles Horner, insist that the B-2 'is the only weapon in the US inventory free of range, survivability, and lethality limitations' and could be the 'only practical option for projecting truly decisive power in future regional crises' and should thus be acquired in larger numbers.⁶³ Skeptics, especially those in the US Navy, remain unconvinced and point to the aircraft's unproved performance in actual conflict.

The F-16C/D *Fighting Falcon*, much improved from the version which first flew in 1976, remains the Air Force's premier strike fighter, with over 1300 in the current total inventory. An extremely capable air combat fighter, the F-16 can withstand maneuvers that cause up to nine times the force of gravity with internal fuel tanks filled—greater than any other current fighter aircraft. The F-16 can also fly strike missions with a radius of 800 kilometers. The F-16s flew more missions during the Gulf War than any other aircraft, but was hampered by its inability to launch PGMs other than HARMS. The latest Block 50 version, recently deployed to Misawa Air Base in Japan, has state-of-the-art avionics and PGM guidance capability.⁶⁴

The F-15E *Strike Eagle* is a ground-attack version of the air superiority fighter described above, with a PGM guidance capability. During the Gulf War F-15Es flew more than 2200 sorties, carrying GBU-15 smart bombs on one mission to seal flaming oil pipeline manifolds sabotaged by Iraqi troops. There are approximately 200 F-15Es in the US Air Force inventory.⁶⁵

The A-10/OA-10 *Thunderbolt II*, more commonly known to its pilots as the *Warthog*, is a close air support aircraft first fielded in 1975, and carrying a devastating 30 mm Gatling gun anti-tank cannon in its nose. The aircraft is designed to fly low and slow for a long time, absorb punishment—and inflict heavy damage on enemy ground forces, especially armored vehicles. In addition to its cannon, the Warthog can carry bombs, and Maverick and Sidewinder guided missiles. Despite several attempts to retire the aircraft, its performance in the Gulf War, where it demonstrated a mission-capable rate of 95.7 per cent and flew 8100 sorties, gave it a second lease on life. Seven squadrons remained in service in 1997, one of them located at Osan Air Base in South Korea.[66]

This large strike force is the world's most capable, but it does have limitations. Chief among them is the Air Force's dependence on fixed—and therefore vulnerable—land bases near the location of conflict. Such bases are increasingly difficult to sustain both politically and economically. The Air Force is quite aware of this. It has developed the Air Expeditionary Force concept in response, and points to the global reach of its US-based long-range bombers, especially the new B–2. Also in development is the next generation of strike fighter, designed for all three services and known as the Joint Strike Fighter (JSF), which will have stealth, increased range and an advanced PGM capability (see Chapter 9). Critics still doubt that the Air Force can sustain the necessary number of sorties over a battlefield without access to nearby land bases.

Although the Air Force has doubled the number of aircraft capable of delivering smart bombs, many of its aircraft are still not equipped to deliver them, and the current generation of smart weapons does not perform well in bad weather or smoke. An entire family of next-generation precision guided munitions with all-weather capability and longer standoff range is on the boards, with two, the Joint Direct Attack Munition (JDAM) and the already mentioned GAM, near operational deployment. The performance of these weapons is dependent on their access to GPS satellites, which could prove vulnerable.

The Gulf War experience also revealed that the element of strategic surprise remains potent even given the US armed forces' information superiority. The Iraqis overran Kuwait before the Air Force could intervene. Furthermore, inadequate intelligence resulted in a failure to locate and target much of Iraq's nuclear infrastructure, and its mobile Scud launchers. Finally, despite heavy damage to Iraq's military machine, its command and control system and its economy, the regime did not fall, and large numbers of ground troops were employed to retake Kuwait. US air power did not win the war by itself, nor did it topple Saddam Hussein's regime.[67] But it did destroy (or grounded) Iraq's air force and render much of its ground force impotent with astonishing speed.

Airlift is the final major capability examined here. The US Air Force maintains the world's largest force of dedicated military long-range transport aircraft, including 143 C–141B Starlifters, 104 C–5A Galaxies, 54 KC–10s, 388 C–130 Hercules, and the newest addition, the C–17 *Globemaster III*. This new aircraft can lift a maximum payload of 170 000 pounds, fly 8400 kilometers at 450 knots without refueling, and land on runways as short as 900 meters and as narrow as 27 meters. Thirty-four, of an eventual total of 120, are already in service.[68] The strategic airlift to the Persian Gulf was the largest since World War II. By the cease-fire, the US Air Force had moved 482 000 passengers and 513 000 tons of cargo to the Gulf. This was equivalent to repeating the famous Berlin Airlift—which lasted 56 weeks—every six weeks. That effort required 90 per cent of the C–5s and 80 per cent of the C–141s.[69]

This formidable fleet has two main limitations. First, it must have somewhere to land and unload. Second, any large power projection conflict requires extremely large and heavy equipment such as tanks and trucks, and huge amounts of basic supplies—fuel, ammunition, food, water, etc. Airlift cannot move those items in sufficient quantity, leaving most less-critical items to sealift. For all of its accomplishments, airlift only brought in 4 per cent of the cargo sent to the Persian Gulf during the war.

The final limitation, as already noted with regard to the Navy–Marine Corps team, is the strain on equipment and, more importantly, on people in an era of declining force structure and increasing commitments. Since 1986 the US Air Force's endstrength has declined by 40 per cent and its forward basing has declined by 66 per cent. Nevertheless, since 1989 the Air Force's deployment requirements have quadrupled.[70] This has had predictable consequences: equipment is breaking down and skilled personnel, especially pilots, are leaving for less stressful and more lucrative civilian employment. In response, the length of planned overseas deployments has recently been reduced from 90 to 45 days, and 'reducing operations tempo is a top priority'.[71] Critics and some Air Force officials remain concerned about the future, despite assurances that force readiness remains high.

SUMMARY

In summary, in every facet of operations the US Air Force is the world's most capable and will undoubtedly remain so into the mid-term future. With its forward presence in Northeast Asia and the global reach of its forces based in the United States, the Air Force remains a key component in the US Pacific Command's deterrent and warfighting force in the Asia–Pacific region. In the long term, it remains to be seen to what extent the US Air Force can meet the challenges of keeping access to forward bases, of sustaining the high cost of maintaining its current technological lead as aerospace and information technology spreads throughout the world, and of balancing the procurement of new technology with the need to sustain a large force of well-trained and supported personnel.

8

US Army and US Special Operations Command

Although US air and naval forces are often associated with the Asia–Pacific region in public perception, the United States Army was heavily engaged in four serious conflicts in the region during the 20th century: the Philippines at the beginning of the century, the entire region during World War II, the Korean War and the Vietnam War. At the time of writing, approximately 29 000 US Army personnel remain forward deployed in South Korea and Japan. This chapter examines the mission, organization, strategic vision, force structure and capabilities of the US Army and the US Special Operations Command, the majority of whose forces come from the Army, with a particular emphasis on the Asia–Pacific region.

MISSION AND ORGANIZATION

The US Army traces its origin to an act of the Continental Congress in 1775. Today, nearly 225 years later, the US Army mission is to:

- Preserve the peace and security, and provide for the defense of the United States, the Territories, Commonwealths, and Possessions, and any areas occupied by the United States
- Support national policies
- Implement national objectives
- Overcome any nations responsible for aggressive acts that imperil the peace and security of the United States.[1]

The US Army's combat and services forces are organized, trained and equipped primarily for prompt and sustained combat incident to operations *on land,* although it does include some organic aviation and water transport elements.

In 1997 the US Army consisted of three basic force components: 495 000 personnel in the active-duty regular forces, 367 000 in the Army National Guard and, by the end of Fiscal Year 1998, 208 000 in the Army Reserve Forces. In addition, there are over 200 000 civilian personnel working for the US Army.[2]

As with the other US armed services, the Department of the Army is a major component of the Department of Defense, and comes under the civilian authority of the President, the Secretary of Defense and then the Secretary of the Army. The highest military officer in the US Army is the general appointed the Chief of Staff of the Army, who is by law an official military adviser to the President and the Secretary of Defense (see Chapter 3).

The US Army is organized into major commands (MACOMs) including:

- Eighth US Army, Republic of Korea, the Army component of the separate US Forces in Korea (USFK) command
- Forces Command (FORSCOM), Georgia, United States, the Army's largest command and the Army component of US Atlantic Command
- Military Traffic Management Command, Virginia, United States
- US Army Materiel Command, Virginia, United States
- US Army South, Panama, the Army component of US Southern Command
- US Army Corps of Engineers, United States
- US Army Criminal Investigation Command, Virginia, United States
- US Army Europe (USAREUR) and 7th Army, Germany
- US Army Intelligence and Security Command, Virginia, United States
- US Army Military District of Washington, DC
- US Army Pacific Command (USARPAC), Hawaii, United States, the Army component of US Pacific Command
- US Army Recruiting Command, Virginia, United States
- US Army Reserve Command, Georgia, United States
- US Army Signal Command, Georgia, United States
- US Army Special Operations Command, North Carolina, United States
- US Army Tank-Automotive and Armaments Command, Michigan, United States

- US Army Training and Doctrine Command, Virginia, United States
- US Total Army Personnel Command, Virginia, United States
- US Army Central Command (USARCENT) and Third Army, Georgia, United States, the Army component of the US Central Command.[3]

STRATEGIC VISION

On 13 November 1996 General Dennis J. Reimer, Chief of Staff of the US Army, released *Army Vision 2010*, described as 'the blueprint for the Army's contributions to the operational concepts identified in the Department of Defense document *Joint Vision 2010*.'[4] In the introduction to *Army Vision 2010* General Reimer adds that the document is the 'conceptual template' for how the Army will achieve new levels of effectiveness as the land component of the US joint warfighting team. The *fundamental competency* that the US Army contributes to joint operations is described as *the ability to conduct prompt and sustained operations on land throughout the entire spectrum of crisis*.[5]

In an era when air and naval forces are often seen as the most modern and relevant, *Army Vision 2010* answers the question 'Why an Army?' by pointing out that, with regard to fighting and winning wars, land forces have the 'power to exercise direct, continuing, and comprehensive control over land, its resources, and its peoples'. That control 'allows land power to make permanent the otherwise transitory advantages achieved by air and naval forces'.[6]

The versatility of land forces is said to make a primary contribution to 'preventive defense' in 'Military Operations Other Than War' (MOOTW), ranging from peacetime engagement in nation-building to military-to-military contacts, responding to disasters and intervening in civil disturbances. According to *Army Vision 2010*, 'In a dynamic and unpredictable geostrategic environment, the US Army provides a full range of choices to the Nation and a hedge against uncertainty—a unique asset'.[7]

Perhaps the document's most trenchant answer to the question 'Why an Army?' is its assertion that, when it comes to deterring aggression, 'the deployment of land forces is the gravest response that can be made, short of war, to demonstrate the national will to prevent conflict'. Or, to put it another way, '*Committing the Army commits the Nation*' in a way that no other single gesture does.⁸ Indeed, this very perception lies at the heart of the debate about the significance of US land forces in support of the US National Security Strategy (see Chapter 2).

Moreover, *Army Vision 2010* cites the fact that the US Army has deployed overseas 25 times since 1990 as evidence that *the significance of land power continues to rise* in the post-Cold War geostrategic environment, for several reasons. First, *Army Vision 2010* predicts that, given the lack of a major US global adversary for the near to mid-term, most future military operations will occur on the *lower and middle portions of the continuum of military operations*. Second, the document notes that in 11 out of 16 recent major overseas joint US military operations, ranging from Operation Just Cause in Panama in 1989 to the 1997 presence in Bosnia as part of Operation Joint Endeavor, *US Army personnel have constituted the highest percentage of the committed joint forces*. Third, *Army Vision 2010* again cites Bosnia as evidence of the fact that, despite a naval blockade and a no-fly zone in the Balkans, the NATO peace plan ultimately required a large, visible contingent of US ground troops. Finally, the document notes that the overwhelming majority of military forces throughout the world are predominantly *armies*, so that military engagement in those countries normally means army-to-army contact.

Although it puts more emphasis on the increased demand for land forces 'at the lower end of the contingency spectrum', *Army Vision 2010* points out the continuing danger of major theater wars in two regions after the Cold War: the 'Euro-Middle East' and the 'Asian Arc'. These regions are said to be in a 'transitional zone' characterized by numerous nations 'on their way to participating democracies and/or advanced economies', resulting in 'inherent instability'.⁹ These nations have access to the most advanced military technology, including very sophisticated and 'asymmetric' capabilities, thus making a conflict with them very dangerous.

According to *Army Vision 2010*, the Asian Arc, which is described as 'stretching from Petropavlosk to India/Pakistan' and containing one-half of the world's population, is characterized by 'a shortage of food and arable land' that poses increasing challenges in the next century. In the region, war will continue to be viewed by some as 'a viable means of achieving or protecting their national interests'. The disparate cultures, terrain and climates of the Asian Arc nations 'will drive significant differences in their force structures, tactics, and warfighting strategies'.¹⁰

This geostrategic environment, with its demands for decisive US operations across the full spectrum of crisis from humanitarian aid to defending or liberating territory in a major theater war, is said to have the following implications for US forces:

- We must have a military capable of deterring or defeating an emerging competitor.
- A regional focus is required for rapid response to crises in the 'transitional zone', where the nation's vital interests are most at risk.
- The frequency of demands for land forces will increase due to calls on the Army to take part in peacetime engagement activities and crises on the lower end of the crisis spectrum.
- Technology will play an important role in enabling the Army to conduct 'full-spectrum' operations.[11]

Following the overarching strategic vision of the Joint Chiefs of Staff as contained in their document *Joint Vision 2010*, the Army will fulfill its role in achieving the 'full spectrum dominance' called for by the Joint Chiefs as the land component of the joint team. Specifically, the Army elements will execute their responsibilities through 'a deliberate set of patterns of operations' which serve to focus the Army's many tasks. Perhaps responding to some criticism of the Army's performance at the close of the 1991 Gulf War, *Army Vision 2010* makes it clear that these patterns 'are not phases, nor are they sequential'.[12]

The six patterns are: Project the Force, Protect the Force, Shape the Battlespace, Decisive Operations, Sustain the Force and Gain Information Dominance. The first five of these patterns of operation are said to 'align precisely' with the *Joint Vision 2010* operational concepts of Dominant Maneuver, Precision Engagement, Focused Logistics and Full Dimensional Protection in the following way:

Project the Force	→ Dominant Maneuver
Decisive Operations	→ Dominant Maneuver &
	→ Precision Engagement
Shape the Battlespace	→ Dominant Maneuver &
	→ Precision Engagement
Protect the Force	→ Full Dimensional Protection
Sustain the Force	→ Focused Logistics

The sixth operational pattern, Gain Information Dominance, is described as 'fundamental' to the other five Army patterns of operation.[13]

The land component of Dominant Maneuver consists of two elements: strategic and operational. Strategic maneuver equates to the Army's requirement to *project the force*. Throughout the latter phases of the Cold War, the US Army maintained a massive overseas presence of heavy units in Europe amounting to 31.8 per cent of its strength in 1989. By 1996 that presence had been reduced by over 250 000 soldiers, Army civilians and family members, leaving only 11.1 per cent of the US Army in Europe.[14] In contrast, the US Army's post–Cold War *power projection force* is largely based in the continental United States and is equipped with lighter, more durable, multipurpose warfighting systems, augmented with critical equipment pre-positioned where the need is most likely. Air and naval components of the joint force will transport this more versatile, tailorable and modular Army 'within hours of the decision to deploy'. It is interesting, however, to note that although the US Army's presence in Europe has greatly diminished, as of 1997 the percentage of the US Army forward deployed on the ground in the Asia–Pacific region has actually risen to 11.1 per cent from its previous 10.7 per cent.

At the operational level, *decisive operations* are those which 'force the enemy to decide to give in to our will'. In today's US Army, decisive operations are 'vastly enhanced' by the precision fire, precise information and precise detection capabilities inherent in 'precision engagement'. Armed with this superior 'situation awareness' the US Army conducts decisive operations by 'positioning combat power throughout the battlefield'.[15]

However, decisive operations require much more than mere positioning of forces throughout the battlefield. In the language of *Army Vision 2010*, the conditions for success are set by *shaping the battlespace*, which is defined as 'the unambiguous integration of *all* combat multipliers—feints, demonstrations, limited attacks, command and control warfare (C2W), mobility/countermobility, deception, and all available fires—with the scheme of maneuver to achieve simultaneity and thus overwhelm the enemy'.[16] Shaping the battlespace begins with early Intelligence Preparation of the Battlefield (IPB) which identifies the enemy's main effort and enables the Land Component Commander (LCC) to *detect* and track targets, *decide* which of them are critical high-value targets, and then assign the appropriate weapon system to *deliver* the correct munitions to destroy those targets. The sharing of 'real time' information among all US armed services, allies and coalition partners is essential to shaping the battlespace.

In order to assure freedom of maneuver at both the strategic and the operational level, the US Army must *protect the force*, as part of *Joint Vision 2010*'s call for 'full dimensional protection'. According to *Army Vision 2010*, an array of fused sensors and area defenses will have the capability to protect critical, high-value operational and strategic assets from enemy air, land and sea attack. The US Army will also 'provide the teeth' of a 'missile engagement capability to protect the US land mass against its most serious external threat—missile attack'.[17]

In order to *sustain the force*, the US Army's version of 'focused logistics' will be 'the fusion of logistics and information technologies, flexible and agile combat service support organizations, and new doctrinal support concepts' that will provide 'rapid crisis response to deliver *precisely* tailored logistics packages directly to each level of military operations'.[18] Once again, 'technology' is called the 'great enabler' of this capability. Although this capability is not very glamorous, *Army Vision 2010* points out that focused logistics is the most applicable operational concept across all six patterns of operation, at all levels of the crisis spectrum.

Finally, all the patterns of operation require Information Operations (IO) conducted to *gain information dominance*. These operations consist of both offensive and defensive efforts to create a disparity between what is known about the battlespace and operations within it and what the enemy knows about the battlespace. Technologies ranging from the new Global Command and Control System (GCCS, see Chapter 3) to very small, mobile tactical sensors and satellite transceivers assist US Army forces in understanding the battlespace.

In short, *Army Vision 2010* foresees 'a capabilities-based Army with the proper mix of heavy, light and Special Operations Forces (SOF) focused on the Euro-Middle East and Asian Arc regions of the world—a force trained, ready and equipped to conduct full-spectrum operations, to do what needs to be done across the entire spectrum of crisis'.[19]

FORCE STRUCTURE

Since the end of the Cold War in 1989 the US Army has undergone a major transformation from a large, forward-deployed force to a smaller, capabilities-based power projection force based largely in the United States. Since 1989 the Army has reduced its endstrength by 469 000 soldiers to a total of 495 000, its Active Component from 18 to 10 divisions, and its Army National Guard from 10 to 8 divisions and from 23 brigade equivalents to 15 enhanced brigades, as called for by the 1993 *Bottom-Up Review* (see Chapter 2).[20]

The Army is currently in the process of re-evaluating its basic structure, within the limitations of the defense budget and with a view to implementing the current US National Military Strategy (see Chapter 9). As of 1997, however, the US Army retains a traditional force structure. In ascending order of size, the US Army is organized for combat into the following basic types of units:

Company	90–200 troops
Battalion	500–900 troops
Brigade	3000–5000 troops
Division	10 000–18 000 troops
Corps	2–5 Divisions
Field Army	2–5 Corps

The main component unit is the *division*. As of 1997, the US Army consisted of two categories of divisions: 'heavy' and 'light'. Heavy divisions include Armored and Mechanized Infantry divisions, which are designed and equipped for sustained, intensive combat, possess the greatest firepower and protection, are tactically mobile, but require a large support element or 'logistic tail'.

Light divisions include:

- Infantry Division: light, responsive, designed and equipped for a range of combat from low-to-high intensity, but with limited tactical mobility and a requirement for reinforcement for sustained combat
- Air Assault Division: highly responsive and tactically mobile, designed and equipped for a wide range of employment, including anti-tank combat, but with a considerable 'logistic tail'
- Airborne Division: capable of quick reaction mobility at the strategic level, including forcible entry, but with limited tactical mobility and anti-armor capability
- Light Infantry Division: rapidly deployable for low-to-mid intensity conflict, with a 'high foxhole strength ratio', but with limited tactical mobility and anti-armor capability and a requirement for reinforcement for sustained combat.

Each division consists de facto of a combined arms formation composed of three relatively fixed combat brigade task forces (BTFs), an aviation brigade and a small division base. Each BTF

Table 8.1 Weapons density by type of US Army division

Type	M1 Abrams main battle tanks	M2/3 Bradley APCs[a]	TOW anti-tank missile launchers	AH–64 Apache attack helicopter	Mortars	Artillery
Armor	348	216	48	44	60	72[b]
Mechanized Infantry	290	270	60	44	60	72[b]
Infantry	58	106	156	8	116	90
Airborne	0	0	36+	30	90	72
Air Assault	0	0	36+	84	90	72
Light Infantry	0	0	36	30	90	96

[a] M2/3s carry TOW launchers.
[b] Also has a Multiple Launch Rocket System (MLRS) with nine launchers.
Source: 'US Army Organization for Combat', US Naval War College Operations Department 1996.

has a mix of infantry and tank battalions, a direct support artillery battalion, an engineer battalion, a composite service forward-support battalion, and companies and detachments to provide reconnaissance, signal and other support capability. In approximate terms, the comparative strengths of the six types of divisions are shown in Table 8.1.[21]

In 1997 the US Army's 10 active divisions were organized into Four Corps:

- The XVIII Airborne Corps is based in the continental US and consists of two 'light' divisions, the 101st Air Assault Division at Fort Campbell, Kentucky, and the 82nd Airborne at Fort Bragg, North Carolina, plus the 'light' 2nd Armored Cavalry Regiment, and one 'heavy division', the 3rd Infantry Mechanized at Fort Stewart, Georgia.
- The V Corps is primarily forward deployed in Germany and consists of two 'heavy' divisions, the 1st Armored and 1st Mechanized, each with two brigades in Germany and one at Fort Riley, Kansas.
- The III Corps is based in the continental United States and consists of two 'heavy' divisions, the 1st Cavalry (Armored) and 4th Infantry Mechanized at Fort Hood, Texas, one 'light' division, the 10th Mountain at Fort Drum, New York, and the 3rd Armored Cavalry Regiment.
- The I Corps, which is both forward deployed in the Asia–Pacific Region and based in the western United States, consists of one 'heavy' division, the 2nd Infantry with two

brigades in South Korea and one at Fort Lewis, Washington, and one 'light' division, the 25th Light Infantry, with two Brigades at Fort Shafter, Hawaii, and one at Fort Lewis.[22]

In addition to the above Active Component forces, the US Army maintains one active Light Infantry Brigade in Alaska, and 15 separate, non-divisional 'enhanced' National Guard Combat Brigades with high priority for resources, based throughout the United States and ready to begin deploying within 90 days of mobilization, as called for in the 1993 *Bottom-Up Review*. Finally, the US Army's Special Forces Command consists of over 30 000 active and reserve troops. They are described in the later portion of this chapter dedicated to the US Special Operations Command.

THE US ARMY IN THE ASIA–PACIFIC REGION

At the end of Fiscal Year 1996, the US Pacific Command included over 58 000 US Army personnel. Of those, approximately 29 000 were 'forward deployed', with about 27 000 in South Korea and 2000 in Japan, including Okinawa. Of the remainder, some 15 000 were stationed in the western United States, with approximately 7000 in Hawaii, 7000 in Alaska and 6500 in Washington State.[23]

The 27 000 US Army troops in South Korea are part of the US Eighth Army, which is the Army component of the all-service Subordinate Unified Combat Command called US Forces in Korea (USFK). Due to the unique history stemming from the Korean War (see Chapter 1), the US Forces in Korea command supports the United Nations Command (UNC) established in 1950 to repel the North Korean invasion. At the same time, USFK supports the Republic of Korea–United States Combined Forces Command (ROK–US CFC) established in 1978 as the warfighting headquarters whose role is to deter, or defeat if necessary, outside aggression against the ROK. The CFC is headed by a four-star American General as Commander in Chief (who is 'triple-hatted' also as CINCUNC and Commander, USFK), with a four-star ROK army general as deputy. Throughout the command structure bi-national manning is maintained, although the US commander retains operational control (OPCON) of US forces as directed by the US CINCPAC. In addition, all CFC components are tactically integrated through continuous combined and joint planning, training and exercises. Although the major biannual field training exercise Team Spirit has been canceled in recent years to reduce tensions with North Korea, numerous smaller exercises continue.[24]

The great majority of US Army troops in South Korea are assigned to the *2nd Infantry Division*, known as 'the Warrior Division', whose motto is 'Second to None!' In this post–Cold War era, the division describes itself as 'the most powerful, most forward-deployed division in the US Army'.[25]

The Warriors of the 2nd Infantry Division are spread out across the western Korean peninsula south of the Demilitarized Zone (DMZ) along the 38th parallel (see Chapter 4). The division has six subordinate commands. The 1st and 2nd Brigades are the maneuver brigades, and have a total of two M1A1 Abrams tank battalions, two Mechanized Infantry battalions equipped with the M2A2 Bradley Fighting Vehicle, and two air assault infantry battalions. The other major commands are the Aviation Brigade, the Division Artillery, the Engineer Brigade and the Division Support Command. As noted above, the division's 3rd Brigade is located at Fort Lewis, Washington, ready to be airlifted from the nearby McChord Air Force Base.

Of particular note is the fact that the 2nd Division's Artillery component (DIVARTY) is 'the largest in the Army and contains more Multiple-Launched Rocket Systems than any other DIVARTY'. This capability reportedly means that the 2nd division 'possesses more combat power than any other division within the coalition forces'.[26] The Warrior Division receives continuous equipment upgrades to maintain that capability.

In addition to the strength of its weapons, the 2nd Infantry Division has given its number-one priority to combat readiness in light of its location near the Demilitarized Zone. The Division conducts frequent combined and joint exercises with South Korean forces ranging from Pony Express no-notice roll-out exercises for platoon-size units to Warsteed brigade and battalion evaluation exercises. A major computer simulation command post exercise called the 'Warfighter Exercise' is conducted annually, and smaller simulations take place each quarter.[27]

The forward deployment of the US 2nd Infantry Division represents a major commitment on the part of the US to the Republic of Korea and to the broader region. The economic and political costs of this commitment, together with the changing political situation in the Korean peninsula, pose one of the largest questions facing the United States and its Asia–Pacific allies in the future.

All other US Army troops in the Asia–Pacific region are assigned to the US Army Pacific (USARPAC), which is the Army Component Command (outside Korea) of the US Pacific Command (see Chapter 3) and has its headquarters at Fort Shafter, Hawaii. Established in its current form in 1990, USARPAC commands and supports assigned and attached active US Army and US Army reserve units, installations and activities in Alaska, Hawaii, Japan, and in possessions and trust territories administered by USPACOM. Although based in the Asia–Pacific region, USARPAC provides trained and ready Army forces worldwide in support of military operations and peacetime engagements in order to 'contribute to decisive victory and promote regional stability'.[28] USARPAC's major Subordinate Commands are:

- US Army Japan
- 25th Infantry Division (Light), Hawaii
- US Army Alaska/1st Brigade, 6th Infantry Division (Light)
- 516th Signal Brigade
- US Army Chemical Activity Pacific, Johnston Island
- 9th Army Reserve Command.

The 2000 US Army troops forward deployed in Japan are assigned to the US Army Japan/9th Theater Army Area Command (USARJ/9th TAACOM), which is a major subordinate command of US Army Pacific (USARPAC). The USARJ is headquartered at Camp Zama near Tokyo, and its history dates from the days of the US occupation of Japan under the command of General Douglas MacArthur. Today, of course, the presence of the USARJ is upheld by the 1960 Treaty of Mutual Cooperation and Security between the United States and Japan.

The USARJ/9th TAACOM is comprised of two major subordinate commands, the 10th and 17th Area Support groups, nine other assigned units and a host of changing attached and other units and activities. Most of these forces perform logistical support missions for the US Pacific Command and the US Army's I Corps, in addition to conducting operations with the Japan Ground Self Defense Force. The US Army Japan soldiers work at 39 different locations on the Japanese islands of Honshu, Hokkaido, Kyushu and Okinawa (see Chapter 4). The largest combat unit is the 1st Battalion, 1st Special Forces Group stationed on Okinawa.[29]

In addition to its forward-deployed forces, the US Army maintains significant forces in the Pacific region of the United States, assigned to USPACOM. In the far North, the bulk of the 7000 troops of the US Army Alaska constitute the separate 1st Brigade of the 6th Light Infantry Division (and its only existing component). They are stationed at Fort Wainwright, Alaska, near Fairbanks. The 'Arctic Warrior' Brigade is the only unit in the

US Army specifically trained and equipped to operate in arctic conditions.[30]

In the middle Pacific, the 25th 'Tropic Lightning' Light Infantry Division at Fort Shafter forms the combat nucleus of the 15 000 troops assigned to the US Army Hawaii. The Division's 1st Brigade is located at Fort Lewis, Washington. The inherent global strategic mobility of this light division enabled it to play a major role in Haiti in late 1994, when fully one-half of the division was deployed there in the multinational effort to restore democracy in that country.[31]

CAPABILITIES AND LIMITATIONS OF THE US ARMY

In public perception, the enormous capability of the US Army was demonstrated during the 1990/91 Persian Gulf War, which was widely viewed at the time as an unqualified victory for the United States and its coalition partners. On the other hand, the very real limitations of the Army in the post–Cold War world were also widely publicized during the last phase of the multinational operation in Somalia in 1994, which was viewed as a failure when US forces were withdrawn. As is usually the case in large and complex historical events, hindsight has revealed that neither event was a complete victory or a complete failure.

The Persian Gulf War has already been subjected to a large body of analysis, and only a concise summary of those findings will be offered here. In effect, the timing, nature and location of the Persian Gulf War enabled the US Army to deploy the cream of its (pre-drawdown) Cold War-era force in very favorable conditions—conditions unlikely to be repeated. Still, that experience serves as the best available indication of the US Army's capability at the high end of the crisis spectrum: major theater war.

Although Iraq's invasion of Kuwait on August 1990 caught US leadership (but not its intelligence agencies) by surprise, the US military had long had plans for intervention in the region. Although these plans were initially primarily focused on a possible Soviet threat to the region's oil fields, as far back as 1979 the Pentagon had studied possible responses to a crisis involving Iraq. Also, Saudi Arabia's port and air-base facilities were better than most in the region, and were thus able to receive the hastily organized arrival of deploying US forces.

At the time of the Iraqi invasion, the 2nd Brigade of the Army's 82nd Airborne Division at Fort Bragg, North Carolina, was on call as the 'ready brigade', prepared to deploy anywhere in the world on only several hours' notice. Even given the enormous airlift capability of the US Air Force, it took four days to transport the entire Brigade to Saudi Arabia—and the forces that arrived were lightly armed and seriously short of artillery and antitank ammunition. The US commander, General Norman Schwarzkopf, later admitted that the 82nd Airborne amounted to only a symbolic 'tripwire' force, capable of signaling US resolve and commitment but not of stopping a determined Iraqi armored assault. In his estimate, it was not until the arrival of the first of the Army's heavy armored divisions on 24 September—more than seven weeks after the invasion—that he was confident he could repulse an Iraqi attack.[32] Even then the force was highly dependent on air power. This experience highlights both the strength and the weakness of the Army's 'light' forces: they are fairly quickly deployable over vast distances but do not have a great deal of combat power. They may be fully capable in low-to-mid intensity conflicts, but not at the 'high' end, especially against tanks. Improved air-delivered munitions are on the way to help protect light forces. Meanwhile, the Army itself is currently trying to address this inadequacy by improving the anti-armor capabilities of its helicopters and artillery forces (see below).

Following the rapid deployment of the 82nd Airborne, the effort to move heavier US Army forces to the Gulf for operation Desert Shield took longer and proved to be harder than anyone had anticipated. The Army's official history of the Persian Gulf War revealed the difficulties encountered in transporting the 24th Mechanized Division's 1574 armored vehicles on eight SL-7 'fast sealift' ships, expected to be ready to sail within four days. Three of the ships were delayed an average of ten days by unscheduled repairs, and another carrying the division's critical helicopter brigade and its maintenance and supply system broke down in mid-Atlantic. The replacement ship did not arrive until 23 September.[33] Moreover, there were considerable difficulties in supplying the newly arrived divisions with adequate ammunition in the early phase of Desert Shield.

The Army was quick to point out that the Navy was responsible for funding and supplying sealift capability during the Gulf War. For its part, the Army has recently put a great emphasis on 'prepositioning' equipment both ashore and afloat in a manner similar to that already adopted by the US Marines. The Army has established an armored brigade set of equipment afloat in 14 ships, based in the Indian and Pacific Oceans, which are available to be sent to either Southwest Asia or Northeast Asia. By 2001 this force will increase to 16 ships with double the current capacity. In addition, the Army has prepositioned one brigade equipment set ashore in Kuwait, is establishing a second heavy brigade set (with headquarters equipment) in Qatar, and has a heavy armor brigade set in South Korea. The other services are making similar improvements.[34] These enhancements will improve the US Army's 'power projection' capability, but they will not eliminate the many difficulties of moving large military forces great distances.

Although there is little evidence to support the view that Iraq in fact planned to continue its 1990 invasion into Saudi Arabia, the fact that Iraq halted its invasion and then allowed the coalition six months to build up its forces for a counteroffensive must be seen as another unique facet of the Persian Gulf War— one unlikely to be repeated. Eventually, US Army Special Forces helped to pave the way for the devastating six-week-long air campaign against Iraq and its forces in Kuwait from 16 January to 24 February 1991 (see below, and Chapter 7). The bombing campaign wreaked such havoc that some airpower advocates remain convinced that it alone 'won' the war. The fact remains, however, that Iraq refused to leave Kuwait unconditionally, and a ground offensive was ultimately necessary to finish the task of reversing the invasion.

The combat performance of the US Army in Operation Desert Storm was very impressive. While US Marines made a frontal attack into eastern Kuwait (see Chapter 6), the Army sent two full corps on a gigantic flanking attack through western Kuwait, with a view to cutting off and destroying Iraq's elite Republican Guard units.

The XVIIIth Airborne Corps' 116 000 troops included the 82nd Airborne, 101st Air Assault and the 24th Mechanized Divisions, which formed the far-left element of the attack and swept all the way into southern Iraq within four days.[35] Complete air supremacy over the battlefield had been achieved during the initial air-war phase of Desert Storm. Consequently, the XVIIIth Airborne Corps was able to fully demonstrate *the combat power of its helicopter forces*. Transport and gunship helicopters had played a central role during the Vietnam War, of course. Now a new generation of helicopters dominated the battlefield. The Gulf War marked the combat debut of the AH–64 *Apache* attack helicopter. The Apache is a day/night, adverse-weather-capable airborne weapons system with a cruising speed of 147 kilometers per hour and a crew of two. It is armed with *Hellfire* anti-armor air-to-ground guided missiles, a 30 mm M230 chain gun and *Hydra* 70 (2.75 inch) rockets. In addition, the Apache is heavily armored and highly survivable. By 1996 the Army had procured approximately 820 Apaches, equipping 25 battalions with 24 Apaches in each. An even more capable version of the Apache, known as the *Longbow Apache*, equipped with a much improved air/ground targeting system and an improved fire-and-forget *Hellfire II* missile, is currently being deployed.[36]

During Desert Storm, Apaches, sometimes called 'flying tanks', knocked out Iraqi air defense radars at the beginning of the air war, occasionally defeated and even captured whole Iraqi units, and penetrated into Iraq—all without direct infantry or tank support.[37] Their performance marked a milestone in military history. No other army in the world today possesses such a formidable attack helicopter capability. The only serious limitation on this force is the requirement that air superiority has first been achieved over the battlefield.

The US Army also demonstrated significantly improved mobility during Desert Storm with the performance of the UH–60 *Black Hawk* light utility and assault helicopter. First introduced in 1978, the Black Hawk's troop capacity and cargo lift capability are much superior to the UH–1 'Huey' of Vietnam War fame. The Black Hawk can carry 11 fully-equipped soldiers or a 105 mm howitzer and 30 rounds of ammunition, plus its crew of three. It is highly survivable and easy to maintain. The Black Hawk is armed with two 7.62 mm machine guns. Over 1330 of these aircraft are in the Army inventory.[38] The Black Hawk performed countless missions successfully during the Gulf War, especially for the airborne divisions.

The main punch of the Army's 'left hook' into Kuwait was delivered by the VIIth Corps, comprised of the 'heavy' 1st and 3rd Armored Divisions from Europe and the 1st Mechanized Infantry from the United States. Their assault against what were believed to be heavy Iraqi forces in fixed defenses was preceded by a massive artillery barrage. Thought to be in some respects inferior to the Iraqi capability, the artillery of the US Army nevertheless proved to be very effective. Between 20 and 23 February 1991 about 24 000 artillery shells and 1600 rockets were fired into the area in front of VIIth Corps. In the 30 minutes immediately prior to the attack, over 6000 rounds and 400 rockets were fired.[39]

In addition to standard M119A1 105 mm and M109 155 mm

artillery (with new versions and new 'smart' ammunition currently under development), the Army employed two new systems in combat for the first time in the Gulf War. The *Multiple Launch Rocket System* (MLRS) is a free-flight, area-fire, artillery rocket system that delivers very large volumes of firepower in a short time, over a range of 31.8 kilometers, with a variety of ammunition types. The Army has procured over 700 MLRS launchers, and an improved version with a 50 kilometer range, improved aim and faster loading time is being deployed. As noted above, the 2nd Infantry Division in South Korea possesses a high number of MLRS launchers. The *Army Tactical Missile System* (Army TACMS) provides long-range, surface-to-surface fire support. The Army TACMS are ground-launched missile systems consisting of a guided missile with an anti-personnel/anti-materiel warhead, used to attack enemy missile sites, air defense systems, logistics and command, control and communications systems at a range 'well beyond the capability of existing cannons and rockets'. Army TACMS are fired from modified MLRS launchers. The Army intends to procure over 4000 TACMS missiles, including the improved Block IA version now entering service with double the range of the original and an enhanced Global Positioning System (GPS) accuracy.[40]

The wide open terrain of the Kuwait desert provided almost ideal conditions for the deployment of the armor of the US Army. In Desert Storm, the performance of the Army's M1 *Abrams* main battle tank was outstanding. For example, in one climactic 45-minute armored battle with dug-in forces of the Iraqi 'Medina' Republican Guard Division on 27 February, the M1 tanks of the 2nd Brigade and supporting helicopters of the US 1st Armored Division annihilated 60 T–72 tanks, 9 T–55 tanks, and 38 Iraqi armored personnel carriers, often at a range of over 2200 meters. The Abrams had a superior gun, superior targeting system, superior armor protection—and superior crews—and didn't suffer a single loss from enemy fire. While this particular battle stands out in terms of size and duration, it was otherwise typical of the US Army's tank performance in the Gulf War. In fact, the only weakness exhibited by the Abrams concerned its enormous fuel consumption rate, which caused several delays during the offensive—despite prodigious efforts that included the use of inflatable fuel storage tanks and huge tanker trucks. It is true that the Iraqis were not equipped with some top-of-the-line Soviet armor and their crews were less well-trained, but the M1's performance was outstanding.[41]

Weighing in at over 67 tons, the Abrams in its current version M1A1 has a 120 mm cannon that fires dense depleted uranium ammunition capable of penetrating any known armor. The M1's thermal imaging, laser-ranging and gyro-stabilization systems give it unparalleled accuracy. The Abrams' 1500 horsepower turbine engine is capable of propelling it at speeds of up to 66.8 kilometers per hour. Its crew of four is protected by heavy composite armor and an NBC protection system that provides additional survivability in a contaminated environment. A new M1A2 version with a distributed data and power architecture and other 'digital battlefield' enhancements is being deployed, and about 1000 older M1 tanks are being upgraded to the M1A2 configuration. The Abrams is widely regarded as the best main battle tank in the world today, and further upgrades are planned.[42]

US Army troops were carried into battle by the M2/M3 *Bradley* Fighting Vehicle. Capable of a road speed of 60 kilometers per hour and armed with a 25 mm cannon, TOW (Tube-launched, Optically tracked, Wire command-link) guided long-range heavy anti-tank missiles and a 7.62 mm coaxial machine gun, Bradleys fought side by side with M1 tanks during the offensive, providing full-tracked cross-country mobility, mounted firepower and protection from artillery and small-arms fire for its mounted infantry troops. The Army has procured over 6700 Bradleys, and over 3000 are the improved A2 High Survivability models.[43]

In the final analysis, the individual US Army volunteer professional soldier on the ground with small arms was still necessary to take and hold ground in the Gulf War. Although some were equipped with GPS navigation gear, night vision devices, laser range finders and other 'high-tech' weaponry, it was the high quality of the personnel, enhanced by intensive training, that made US Army troops completely victorious over the Iraqis in a mere 100 hours. Over against the expected figure of thousands of American casualties, there had been a total of 613 US battle casualties: 146 killed and 467 wounded. Of these, 35 were killed and 72 wounded by fire from 'friendly' forces—indicating a need for better 'identification of friend or foe' (IFF) systems on a battlefield where 'fire and forget' weapons are employed.[44]

Although the US Army demonstrated an astonishing measure of superiority in conventional warfare, *limitations* were also revealed at the tactical and operational levels when it came to *defending against the enemy's actual or potential employment of unconventional or 'asymmetric' means of war*. While there is to this day no hard evidence that Iraq ever actually employed *chemical or biological weapons* against coalition forces, it became apparent throughout the conflict that US forces were ill-equipped to deal with such a threat. Detection and decontamination systems were nearly non-existent and had to be called in from allies. Experimental preventive antidotes were administered to troops in the field without their informed consent—a matter that continues to cause controversy. Protective gear was not always supplied in a timely manner and in adequate quantities, and proved difficult to wear in the field, etc. The Army is working on this issue, but there are no easy solutions.[45] Ironically, the major exposures of US troops to Iraqi chemical weapons apparently took place after the war, when US forces blew up an Iraqi ammunition dump at Khamisiyah, Iraq, in March 1991, unaware that it contained such weapons. Possible lingering effects among US Gulf War veterans from these and other exposures, known collectively as the 'Gulf War Syndrome', remain a source of controversy.[46]

Of greater immediate—and possibly long-term—significance during the Gulf War was *the inability of US forces to prevent or completely defend against ballistic missile attacks.* Missile defense at both the national and theater levels is obviously a matter of joint concern and involvement for all of the US armed forces, but the Army is charged with the primary responsibility on land. At the outset of the Gulf War, Iraq possessed a number of Soviet-designed theater or 'short-range' ballistic missiles (SRBMs), codenamed 'Scuds' by NATO, thought capable of carrying nuclear, chemical and biological warheads in addition to conventional explosives.

Despite intense bombing raids, Special Forces ground surveillance and attacks, and the hurried deployment of a new version of the *Patriot* air-defense missile thought to be more capable of theater ballistic missile interception, Iraq fired over 80 Scuds, about half at Israel and half at Saudi Arabia. The attacks nearly brought Israel into the war, nearly hit the US helicopter carrier *Tarawa* as it docked at Al Jubail on the Saudi east coast, and produced the largest single American casualty toll in the war when a Scud hit a temporary US barracks at Al Khobar on 25 February, killing 29 US troops and wounding another 98. Early media coverage led to the impression that the Patriot missile system was successfully intercepting Scuds. But the version deployed to Saudi Arabia and to Israel was designed to defend small 'point' targets like air bases, not entire cities. Moreover, the poor construction of the Scuds caused them to break apart upon re-entry, thus producing inadvertent 'decoys' that made it extremely difficult for the Patriots to hit the incoming warheads. At the war's end, the US Defense Intelligence Agency concluded that the coalition had failed to knock out any of Iraq's elusive, mobile Scud launchers, had failed to permanently degrade its Scud command and control capability, and that Iraq retained an ability to re-target and launch Scuds even in the last days of the war.[47]

This was perhaps the greatest 'wake-up call' of the Gulf War, and has led to a vigorous US effort to improve its ability to defend against theater ballistic missiles. A new version of the Army's Patriot missile system, the PAC–3, with improved ballistic missile defense capability, is to be deployed in US forces in the continental United States, Europe, Southwest Asia and Korea. Japan is participating in a Patriot acquisition program along with Israel, Kuwait, Saudi Arabia, Germany and the Netherlands. Furthermore, the Army is developing an entirely new theater missile defense (TMD) system known as the Theater High Altitude Area Defense (THAAD), which will consist of missiles, launchers and Battle Management/Command, Control, Communications, Computers and Intelligence (BM/C⁴I) elements. However, THAAD has encountered serious technical problems and its deployment date was shifted from 2004 to 2006 in the 1997 *Quadrennial Defense Review* (QDR).[48] The Navy and the Air Force are also involved in the Theater Missile Defense development effort, which will be covered in Chapter 9.

The Army also bears primary responsibility for *National Missile Defense* (NMD) of US territory. Since the end of the Cold War, the Strategic Defense Initiative of the Reagan era to defend the United States against a massive Soviet intercontinental ballistic missile (ICBM) attack, also popularly known as 'Star Wars', has been de-emphasized. However, research is continuing in the effort to protect the United States from limited ICBM attacks by reducing the lead time to deploy a single site system capability that is compliant with the 1972 ABM Treaty. The QDR declared NMD to be a 'high priority' and allocated additional funds toward 'creating the option to make a decision on deployment possible as early as fiscal year 2000, if the threat warrants', while noting that NMD remains a program of 'high schedule and technical risk'.[49]

At the strategic level, the US Army's experience in the Gulf War raised at least three important issues.

First, the US doctrine of employing only *overwhelming force* to achieve a decisive victory was used to great effect in the Gulf

War. However, overwhelming force cannot—and perhaps should not—necessarily be employed in all conflict circumstances, especially those at the lower end of the crisis spectrum. Over-reliance on this doctrine may cause problems in the future, leading either to a reluctance to become involved or an over-reaction.

Second, the successful outcome of the Gulf War may have created, among the public and political leaders, *unrealistic expectations regarding casualties* in future conflicts where US forces may be employed.

Third, it now appears in retrospect that the early termination of the Gulf War by the coalition allowed a major portion of the Iraqi Republican Guard forces to escape intact and play a subsequent role in the brutal suppression of Shiites in Iraq and in the continued existence of Saddam Hussein's regime. The issue of an *exit strategy for US ground forces committed to a conflict* was highlighted by the unsatisfactory aftermath of the Gulf War, and became even more acute during operations in Somalia in 1994.

SOMALIA, 1992–1994

The American mission in Somalia beginning in August 1992 and terminating in 1994 was an illustration of military involvement at the 'low' end of the crisis spectrum—unlike the 'high' end of the Gulf War. US forces were first sent to Somalia in a purely humanitarian role in Operation Provide Relief, under the authority of a United Nations Security Council Resolution. An expeditionary force of US Marines was sent in order to protect relief supplies of water, food and medicine from theft by bandits or confiscation by the warring clans and factions in what amounted to a civil war.

The security situation worsened to the point of a relief ship being driven out of the harbor of Mogadishu under fire in November 1992. Subsequently a second UN Resolution authorized a larger multinational military United Nations Task Force to restore order in southern Somalia until a UN peacekeeping force could take over. Some 28 000 US troops took part in Operation Restore Hope. In March 1993 a third UN Security Council Resolution, number 814, mandated the first-ever UN peacekeeping operation under the Chapter VII enforcement provisions of the United Nations Charter—including the requirement for disarming the warring Somali clans. Moreover, this Resolution explicitly endorsed the objective of rebuilding the political and economic institutions of Somalia, in effect nation-building. Finally, the Resolution called for building a secure environment throughout the entire country, including the northern region that had declared its independence.[50]

Although US participation in this phase was to be largely logistical in nature, the United States was asked by the UN to provide a 'Quick Reaction Force' (QRF). Around 1150 soldiers from the US Army's 10th Mountain Division formed the QRF, under the tactical control of the Commander, US Forces Somalia, Army Major General Thomas Montgomery. These developments, especially the disarming of clan warriors, apparently endangered the power base of prominent clan warlord Mohammed Aideed to such an extent that his forces began ambushing members of the multinational peacekeeping force, killing 24 Pakistani soldiers on 5 June 1993. The United States played a major role in drafting UN Security Council Resolution 837, passed the next day, which called for the immediate apprehension of those responsible.[51]

This resulted in a de facto change of mission for the US forces: a manhunt for Aideed, which translated into expanded operations for the QRF. Armed helicopters of the 10th Mountain Division were engaged, as were Special Operations AC–130 gunships (see below). As the manhunt intensified, so did the violence when the QRF clashed with Aideed's followers. This in turn led to the commitment of a US military 'strategic asset', a unit of Special Operations troops consisting of the US Army Rangers of Bravo Company, 3rd Ranger Battalion, designated 'Task Force Ranger'. As a strategic asset, Task Force Ranger operated under its own chain of command headed by Army Major General William F. Garrison and extending directly back to the US Central Command (CENTCOM)—but not through the existing UN and US in-country commands.[52]

Although Task Force Ranger succeeded in capturing several of Aideed's high-level leaders, the warlord himself eluded them and their searches were encountering increased resistance. The US commander of the QRF requested the addition of US armored forces to back up Task Force Ranger, but the request was denied by Secretary of Defense Les Aspin. Then on 3 October 1993 Task Force Ranger conducted a daylight raid on a clan stronghold in the middle of Mogadishu. In the words of the Army's official Special Forces history:

> the men of Task Force Ranger came under heavy fire as they rushed to complete their mission to capture some high level

leaders of General Aideed's faction. Then . . . a supporting helicopter was shot down. The Rangers quickly ran to guard the site and rescue the crewmen. Cut off by heavy enemy fire, the Rangers established perimeters of defense and, with the assistance of mini-gun fire from friendly helicopters, held on until morning. Their harrowing ordeal lasted until the next day . . . They fought their way out of the trap with the assistance of a ready reaction force of the 10th Infantry Division (Mountain).[53]

As recorded in their official history, troops of the 10th Mountain Division's 14th Infantry Battalion were dispatched to secure a ground evacuation route for the Rangers. They had to call in armor from Malaysian and Pakistani UN forces and took three hours to fight their way in from the gates of the Port to the Ranger perimeter at the Olympic Hotel. Then began a long withdrawal under fire along a route secured by Pakistani forces. The 12-hour ordeal had resulted in 29 wounded and one killed among the 10th Mountain rescue troops. The Rangers had fared much worse: they suffered 19 killed, 57 wounded and—fatefully—one captured.[54]

Media coverage of the aftermath was extensive. Pictures first of a dead Ranger being dragged through the dusty streets of Mogadishu, and then of the captured Ranger (who was eventually released), magnified the event for US audiences. Shortly thereafter President Clinton announced a phased withdrawal of all US troops from Somalia, to be concluded by 31 March 1994.[55]

This incident has been described in detail because some analysts regard it as far more typical of likely US military involvement in the post–Cold War world than the Gulf War was. In fact, since 1989 US forces have frequently become involved in similar situations, and at the time of writing some 8000 US Army troops are on the ground in Bosnia enforcing the Dayton Peace Agreement.

The commitment of 'light' Army forces, especially Special Operations forces, in Somalia ultimately raised many of the same issues that the Gulf War did: the limits of the 'overwhelming force' doctrine, the concern about US casualties, and the necessity of crafting a clear 'exit' strategy. Perhaps the clearest lesson to come out of the Somalia experience was that in so-called peacekeeping or peace enforcement operations, 'If the disarmament of the population becomes an objective, then there should be no mistaking the fact that the troops given this mission have been committed to combat'. The term 'mission creep' has been coined to describe crossing over a line like this one without clearly admitting it. General Montgomery summed up Somalia this way: 'If this isn't combat, then I'm sure having a helluva nightmare.'[56]

The increasing number of low-intensity conflicts and crises that have marked the post–Cold War era has meant a commensurate increase in the use of US Special Forces (SOF) troops abroad. These forces are the subject of the next section.

US SPECIAL OPERATIONS COMMAND (USSOCOM)

The US Special Operations Command was activated in 1987 and is one of the eight unified combat commands in the US armed forces. USSOCOM has its headquarters at MacDill Air Force Base, Florida. The command has approximately 44 000 active, reserve and National Guard forces from the Army, Navy and Air Force.

The components of USSOCOM include the US Army Special Operations Command at Fort Bragg, North Carolina, the Air Force Special Operations Command at Hurlburt Field, Florida, the Naval Special Warfare Command at Coronado, California, and the Joint Special Operations Command at Fort Bragg. Each of these services has its own Special Warfare schools. In actual operations, service component units are normally employed as part of a joint force by the theater CINCs through the theater Special Operations Command.

'Special Operations' are defined as 'operations conducted by specially trained, equipped and organized Department of Defense Forces against strategic or tactical targets in pursuit of national military, political, economic, or psychological objectives'.[57] SOCOM's primary mission is to provide combat-ready forces for rapid reinforcement of other US unified combat commands worldwide, as was the case with Task Force Ranger in Somalia. However, Special Operations may also be undertaken *independently* when the use of conventional forces is either 'inappropriate or infeasible'.[58]

First formed and deployed during World War II, US Special Operations Forces have a dual heritage. They are the nation's penetration and strike force, capable of responding to specialized contingencies across the conflict spectrum with stealth, speed and precision. At the same time, they are also 'warrior-diplomats' capable of influencing, advising, training and conducting operations with foreign forces, officials and populations in peacetime and during conflict.

As of 1997 US Special Operations Forces (SOF) have the following prioritized missions:

- Counter-proliferation (CP): efforts to combat proliferation of nuclear, biological and chemical weapons across the full range of military, intelligence, diplomatic, arms control and export control activities
- Combating Terrorism (CBT): precluding, preempting and resolving terrorist actions throughout the entire threat spectrum
- Foreign Internal Defense (FID): organizing training, advising and assisting host national and para-military forces to enable them to protect their society from subversion, lawlessness and insurgency
- Special Reconnaissance (SR)
- Direct Action (DA): conducting short-duration strikes and other small-scale offensive actions to seize, destroy, capture, recover or inflict damage on designated personnel or material
- Psychological Operations (PSYOP): inducing or reinforcing foreign attitudes and behavior favorable to the originator's objectives by conveying selected information to foreign audiences to influence their emotions, motives, reasoning and ultimately their behavior, as in convincing Iraqi troops to surrender during Desert Storm
- Civil Affairs (CA): assisting commanders by establishing, maintaining, influencing or exploiting relations between military forces and civil authorities and the civil population in a friendly, neutral or hostile area of operations
- Unconventional Warfare (UW): organizing, training, equipping, advising and assisting indigenous and surrogate forces in guerrilla warfare, evasion and escape, and subversion and sabotage operations, normally of long duration
- Information Warfare (IW)/Command and Control Warfare (C^2W): actions taken to achieve information superiority by affecting adversary information, information-based processes, information systems and computer-based networks while defending one's own
- Special Operations Forces are also involved in a host of 'collateral activities' ranging from combat search and rescue operations to counterdrug activities and humanitarian operations.[59]

The *US Army's Special Operations Command* (ARSOC) includes five active and two reserve Special Forces Groups of approximately 1400 troops each. The Special Forces are widely known by their distinctive *green berets*, first worn during the Vietnam War era. The first battalion of the 1st Special Forces Group is based at Torii Station, Okinawa. Its other two battalions are at Fort Lewis, Washington. The 12 trooper 'A' team remains the basic Green Beret tactical unit, trained and equipped for a wide variety of special operations.[60]

A regiment of US Army *Rangers* forms the main light infantry component of US Special Operations Forces. The 75th Ranger Regiment has its headquarters at Fort Benning, Georgia. One of its three battalions is stationed at Fort Lewis, Washington.

In addition, the Army's Special Operations Command includes one active Special Operation Aviation regiment, two active and one reserve PSYOP groups, and one active and 24 reserve Civil Affairs battalions, all based in the United States.[61]

The Naval Special Warfare Command's forces are organized into two Naval Special Warfare Groups and two Special Boat Squadrons. Each Naval Special Warfare Group is composed of three Sea, Air, Land (*SEAL*) teams with ten platoons each and a team equipped with underwater *SEAL Delivery Vehicles* (SDV), a type of miniature submarine. SEAL teams One, Three and Five are based at Coronado, California, and SEAL Delivery Vehicle Team One is based at Pearl Harbor, Hawaii. Each Group is assigned one Naval Warfare Special Unit (NSWU), a small command and control element. NSWU One is stationed on Guam.[62]

SEAL teams go through what is considered by some to be the most challenging military training in the world. A 'typical' SEAL mission is described as: 'free fall parachuting at 10 000 feet, traveling by small rubber boat for 100 miles, conducting a mission, then traveling 30 miles out to sea to rendezvous with a submarine'. After 30 weeks of training, SEALS must be capable of running four miles in boots in 30 minutes, running 14 miles, and swimming two miles in the open ocean with fins in 75 minutes.[63]

The Special Boat Squadrons and their subordinate units operate a variety of vessels such as high-speed boats and patrol coastal ships. Six of a planned twenty 82-foot Mark Five Special Operations Craft have been delivered. Thirteen 170-foot *Cyclone*-class Patrol Coastal (PC) Ships are also in the Naval Special Warfare inventory, each equipped with two SEAL raiding craft and a diver launching platform. In addition, several nuclear attack submarines have been modified to carry dry deck shelters for launching

SDVs, and several others have been modified to carry and deliver SEALs.[64]

The US *Air Force Special Operations Command* (AFSOC) has its headquarters at Hurlburt Field, Florida. AFSOC has approximately 9700 people, 22 per cent of whom are stationed overseas. These forces are organized into one active and two reserve/National Guard Special Operations Wings, two Special Operations Groups based overseas, and one active Special Tactics Group.

The 353rd Special Operations Group, with headquarters at Kadena Air Base, Okinawa, Japan, is the Air Force component for Special Operations Command Pacific. Its 1st Special Operations Squadron (SOS) flies the MC–130E *Combat Talon*, a four-engine transport craft highly modified to provide day, night and adverse weather capability to airdrop and airland personnel and equipment in support of special operations forces, and with a capability to refuel deep penetration helicopters; in addition, the 17th SOS at Kadena flies the similar MC–130P *Combat Shadow*, whose primary mission is clandestine night aerial refueling of special forces helicopters; the 31st SOS is based at Osan Air Base, Korea, and flies the MH–53J *Pave Low* helicopter, a heavy lift aircraft described as 'the most technologically advanced helicopter in the world'. The Pave Low is designed for low-level penetration, made possible by terrain-following and terrain-avoidance radar and infrared sensors, and a projected map display. Equipped with armor plating and several machine guns, the Pave Low can transport 38 troops and has an external cargo hook with a 9000 kilogram (20 000 pound) capacity, over an 880 kilometer range, and is capable of in-flight refueling. Other AFSOC units fly the lighter MH–60G *Pave Hawk* and the AC–130H *Spectre* gunship, with its devastating complement of two 20 mm Vulcan cannons with 3000 rounds, one Bofors cannon with 256 rounds and one 105 mm howitzer with 100 rounds.

In 1996 US Special Operations Forces conducted over 1240 overseas missions in 136 countries and five territories. With the exception of the Korean peninsula and Japan, the deployment of main units of US ground troops to Asian territory is not a very probable development for the foreseeable future in this post–Cold War era. However, the role of Special Operations Forces in the theater may actually be on the increase. The high versatility and relatively low political and economic cost of SOF are a distinct advantage. In 1993 Special Operations Forces took part in joint-combined exercise training in 27 Asia–Pacific nations and territories, and in 1994 the program was expanded to include Russia. This was in addition to SOF participation in such annual exercises as Cobra Gold in Thailand. SOF humanitarian and Civil Affairs personnel responded to the destruction caused by the eruption of Mount Pinatubo in the Philippines in 1991. Since 1993 US Army PSYOP and Special Forces troops have been involved in instructing Cambodian military personnel in the difficult—and increasingly visible—task of mine-clearing. Some analysts see a potential for a wide range of operations in the region at the request of host nations. It is particularly interesting to note that the recently confirmed Chairman of the Joint Chiefs of Staff, Army General Henry Shelton, previously held the position of Commander, US Special Operations Command.[66]

The United States possesses the largest, best-trained and best equipped modern Special Operations Forces in the world today. In the years to come they may increasingly make their presence felt in the Asia–Pacific region.

SUMMARY

The US Army and Special Forces are second to none in the world in terms of effective ground forces. Although the likelihood of major ground combat outside of Korea is low, US Army and Special Forces will continue to play an important role in Asia–Pacific security for many years.

9

The future of US armed forces

The size and complexity of this chapter's topic make any attempts at prediction quite unrealistic. By way of comparison, few experts foresaw the financial crisis that swept through much of East Asia in the latter half of 1997, and even those few tended to underestimate its breadth and severity. Still, the great amount of interest in the future of US military forces in the Asia–Pacific region warrants an attempt at examining the major foreseeable factors, beginning with US strategy in the region.

US INTERESTS AND STRATEGIC POLICY

The US Department of Defense has not issued any new documents comparable with its 1995 East Asia Strategy Report, described in Chapter 2. At its broadest level, the US national security strategy for the Asia–Pacific region will continue to envision a 'new Pacific community' that links security interests with economic growth and a commitment to democracy and human rights.

However, during his early 1998 visit to the region, US Secretary of Defense William Cohen delivered an address entitled 'Continuity, Change and Commitment: America's Asia–Pacific Security Strategy'. In that address, he first noted three *'enduring features of the Asian security landscape'*.[1]

First and foremost are the 'high stakes' involved. Asia remains a concentration of powerful states with sizable militaries, some with nuclear weapons. It is a region of great global economic importance. The East Asian financial crisis of 1997–98 has served to emphasize the growing importance of the region to the US economy. For example, a November 1997 US State Department fact sheet highlighted the following facts:

- Over the last decade, the East Asia and Pacific region has surpassed Western Europe to become the largest regional trading partner of the United States, both as a supplier of US imports and as a market for its exports. In 1996 US trade with the Asia–Pacific region totaled $982.6 billion, roughly 68 per cent of US trade with the entire world.
- US direct investment in ASEAN has grown to more than $35 billion.
- Air traffic on Pacific routes has overtaken Atlantic traffic on a passenger-kilometer basis. By the year 2000 the Pacific market is projected to account for almost half of international traffic.[2]

Although at the time of writing the full ramifications of the region's 1997–98 financial crisis are not yet known, there is no doubt that in the long term the United States will retain a very large economic interest in the Asia–Pacific region.

The region's vital sea lanes with their numerous navigational choke points form the final element of the 'high stakes' noted by Cohen.

Because the stakes are so high, they lead directly to the second enduring feature of the region's security landscape from the US perspective: 'the integral role of American military power as a stabilizing force in the region'. As the February 1998 Annual Report of the Secretary of Defense clearly stated, 'The United States is committed to maintaining its current level of military capability in East Asia and the Pacific Rim. This capability allows the United States to play a key role as security guarantor and regional balancer.' Again and again, in the 1997 US National Security Strategy, the *Quadrennial Defense Review* and other official statements, the United States expands on this capability in referring to its 'continued commitment to maintain approximately 100 000 US personnel forward-deployed in the Asia–Pacific'. However, some qualifying remarks have begun to appear. Cohen, for example, states that the '100 000 troops' commitment is 'shorthand for a panoply of measures of our security engagement and military capability in the region' and that efforts to enhance them will introduce 'new technologies, operational concepts and organizational structures that will transform [US] forces in the coming decade and beyond'.[3] It is conceivable that this 'transformation' will mean a force with fewer personnel but equal—or greater—capability. This will be discussed in greater detail later in this chapter. Moreover, on this issue the US Deputy Assistant

Secretary of Defense for Asian and Pacific Affairs stated in early 1998:

> During the Cold War we had over 150 000 troops in the region . . . currently we have about 100 000, and in our most recent public statements . . . one of the conclusions was that 100 000 continues to be about the right number.
>
> We have stated on a variety of occasions that when there are important strategic developments in the Asia–Pacific region, then we will adjust our forces accordingly. So it is difficult to predict the future . . .[4]

The May 1997 US National Security Strategy confirms this by stating:

> Our military presence has been essential to maintaining the stability that has enabled most nations in the Asia–Pacific region to build thriving economies for the benefit of all. To deter regional aggression and secure our own interests, we will maintain an active presence . . . our commitment to keeping 100 000 US military personnel in the region serve[s] as the foundation for America's continuing security role.[5]

The third enduring feature that defines the regional security landscape is the crucial role of strong bilateral relationships. The US treaty alliances with Japan, South Korea, Australia, Thailand and the Philippines remain firm.

Concerning the future of US–Japan security relations, the September 1997 Review of the US–Japan Defense Guidelines has been described by some observers as 'the Asian corollary of NATO expansion' and a 'very important strategic innovation in Asia'.[6] Under the overall authority of the 1960 US–Japan Security Agreement, these Guidelines were first negotiated in 1978 as the basis of military cooperation between the United States and Japan under normal circumstances and in the event of a war or other crises in or near Japan. In other words, they provide guidance for political leaders and military planners in terms of roles and missions about how the US and Japan would cooperate militarily. The April 1996 'US–Japan Joint Declaration on Security' reconfirmed that the US–Japan security relationship remains the cornerstone for achieving common security objectives' and for maintaining a stable and prosperous environment in the Asia–Pacific region.'[7]

Although the Guidelines focus primarily on the defense of Japan itself and cover a broad area of military cooperation, media attention focused on the section concerning 'Situations in areas surrounding Japan that will have an important influence on Japan's peace and security'. While stating that 'US Forces will conduct operations to restore the peace and security affected by situations in areas surrounding Japan', the new Guidelines also state that the Self Defense Forces of Japan 'will conduct such activities as intelligence gathering, surveillance and minesweeping, to protect lives and property and to ensure navigational safety' and will provide 'temporary' use of Japanese bases and civilian facilities by US forces and 'rear area support' for them as well.[8]

US Secretary of Defense Cohen said that '[t]hese guidelines that are being updated are designed to help face the challenge not of the past but of the future'. China was quick to issue warnings that 'a stronger US–Japan alliance was a provocation that would threaten peace and stability throughout the region', despite American and Japanese reassurances about cooperating with—not 'containing'—the People's Republic of China.[9] It seems clear that closer—and broader—cooperation between the armed forces of the United States and Japan's Self Defense Forces will form a central part of US strategy in the region.

Secretary Cohen went on to describe several *patterns of change* that mark the Asia–Pacific security landscape.

First, the emergence of multilateral frameworks for discussion and cooperation, including the ASEAN Regional Forum, several trilateral dialogs and the Four-Party Talks on the Korean peninsula, marks a change from the mostly bilateral framework of the Cold War era. On this matter, Cohen states:

> The United States views multilateral mechanisms as important, and having a greater role to play in the future. But we also believe that they will be successful only if they are built upon the foundation of solid bilateral relationships and a continued US forward presence in the region. That is why the United States does not support efforts that intentionally or otherwise constrain our military posture or operational flexibility—efforts that would only undermine, rather than contribute to, the region's security.[10]

The growing importance of Southeast Asia is the second element of change listed by Cohen. The US looks forward to Southeast Asia 'as an increasingly important partner and facilitator of the US forward presence through such activities as port calls, repair, training and logistics support'.[11]

Third, the most anticipated change in Asia has been the

emergence of China. In a speech at the Academy of Military Sciences in Beijing in January 1998, US Secretary of Defense Cohen outlined America's policy of 'strategic engagement' with China, which he described as 'an essential pillar of our regional strategy'.[12] Cohen noted the important agreements already reached within the past year between the United States and China:

- Chinese assurances to the United States regarding exports of cruise missiles and nuclear technology
- military exchanges and reciprocal ship visits
- steps to increase mutual confidence and decrease miscalculation, in particular the Military Maritime Consultative Agreement, the first direct agreement between the US military and the People's Liberation Army, which will help to avoid incidents at sea and create a venue for dialog between Chinese and American operational naval officers
- a strategic dialog between policy officials of the United States and Chinese ministries.

In the future, Cohen called for a 'threefold approach to engagement—*deepening* our current joint efforts, modestly *broadening* them into new areas, and *advancing* from confidence-building to real-world cooperation'.[13] Greater military/strategic transparency, possible exchanges of officials from nuclear rocket forces, and future military cooperation in humanitarian disaster relief were among the examples he gave.

Only time will tell the degree to which a US strategy of engagement with China will succeed in enhancing the region's peace and prosperity.

The fourth element of change in the region cited by Cohen is the evolving situation in Korea. The US government is convinced that the decline of the North Korean regime is irreversible and that change is inevitable. The concern is that the change occur in a peaceful and orderly way—and not with a desperate military effort by the Democratic People's Republic of Korea. In the South, the election of former dissident Kim Dae-jung to the Presidency seems to strengthen that nation's democracy, but the economic crisis will present a major challenge to his administration and may decrease the ROK's defense 'burden sharing' contribution to the cost of maintaining US forces there. In early interviews Kim Dae-jung reportedly had this to say on the issue of the presence of US troops in his country: 'Please tell North Korea that insisting on US withdrawal is not wise. In the struggle between Japan and

China, left alone, Korea would be a small shrimp caught between two whales. And if the US were to withdraw, our defense budget would skyrocket.'[14] He later added, 'Without the presence of American troops, there won't be any stability or military balance of power. The presence of US troops will continue for the national interest of both the US and Korea.'[15]

As of 1998 then, it is apparent that substantial US military forces will remain in the Asia–Pacific region for the foreseeable future to defend US interests and those of its allies. The size, nature and location of those forces are subject to significant change over the mid to long term, however. They will depend on the extent of the ongoing 'transformation' of the armed forces of the United States in light of the 'Revolution in Military Affairs' (RMA), changing threat perceptions and budgetary limitations.

THE IMPACT OF THE REVOLUTION IN MILITARY AFFAIRS

At the time of writing there is not a consensus within the national security apparatus of the United States concerning the implications and impact of the so-called revolution in military affairs (RMA). There is something of a common definition: 'RMA centers on developing the improved information and command and control capabilities needed to significantly enhance joint operations. With the support of an advanced command, control, communications, computers, intelligence, surveillance and reconnaissance (C^4ISR) common backbone, the United States will be able to respond rapidly to any conflict; warfighters will be able to dominate any situation; and day-to-day operations will be optimized with accurate, timely and secure information.'[16]

What this means for American armed forces in the future is still a matter of debate. Looking ahead to the 1997–2015 period, the 1997 US *Quadrennial Defense Review* stated that the fundamental challenge is to 'maintain the ready, versatile forces necessary to meet the challenges of shaping and responding in the near term, [and] at the same time be transforming our forces, capabilities, and support structures to be able to shape and respond effectively in the future'.[17]

In notional terms, in 1997 the US National Defense University outlined three alternative 'Force Design Paths' for the future of US armed forces, including basic assumptions, pros and cons and summary descriptions. The first of these paths is the *Recapitalized Force*. Its basic assumptions are:

- current trends continue
- moderate modernization will occur
- minimum structural change.

The pros and cons are:

- promises little disruption
- but may miss opportunities for more effective force postures.

In summary, the Recapitalized Force would seek to maintain current force structure patterns while modernizing at a moderate rate. It would continue to introduce advanced information technologies and precision weapons, and add new generations of tactical aircraft (such as the F–22) and ships. The primary focus, however, would be on meeting and alleviating the need to recapitalize the force on the assumption that the defense budget will not rise significantly. Such a force in 2007 would be marginally smaller than in 1997 but basically similar.

The *Full Spectrum Force* is the second force design path. Its assumptions are:

- many current trends continue
- accelerated modernization occurs
- moderate structural change takes place
- tiered readiness is a basic concept.

The pros and cons of this middle-of-the-road approach are said to be:

- promises improvements and low risk
- but would be expensive.

In summary, the Full Spectrum Force would seek to maintain a relatively robust force structure while pushing rapid force modernization. The size of US naval and air forces would be maintained at about today's levels while advanced technologies would be integrated into the forces. There would be increased efforts to move to shared situation awareness and quick response with longer-range standoff weapons of greater precision and accuracy.

The third force design path is the *Accelerated RMA Force*. It assumes:

- strategic lull allows rapid modernization
- accelerated modernization occurs
- rapid structural change takes place
- active and reserve forces experience divergence.

The pros and cons of this path are:

- promises dramatic leaps in force efficiency
- but would be risky and disruptive.

In summary, the Accelerated RMA Force model assumes a concerted, systematic effort to speed delivery of the 'system of systems' technologies to a force structure altered to take full advantage of these technologies. Force reductions, possibly significant ones, would be consistent with this model, not to reduce defense spending but as a means to shift that spending to speed the transition to an RMA force. There would be major structural changes to US ground forces and their operational doctrine, with reserve components embodying older elements. Organizational changes to naval and air forces would be less dramatic, although there would also be some force reductions.[18]

From the vantage point of late 1998, it appears from the conclusions of the 1997 *Quadrennial Defense Review* (QDR) that US decision-makers have chosen the middle-of-the-road model, the so-called 'Full Spectrum Force'—and that choice has come under strong criticism from proponents of the other two paths.

On the one hand, there are those most concerned with the affordability of any future US force in the light of approaching 'block obsolescence' of major weapons systems early in the 21st century and a limited defense procurement budget. They note that the Department of Defense has established a goal of increasing weapons procurement funding to approximately $60 billion by fiscal year 2001. However, the Electronic Industry Association's most recent 10-year defense budget forecast predicts that spending on weapons systems will climb to slightly more than $50 billion, up from $43.2 billion now, but well below that $60 billion figure necessary to fund something approaching a 'full spectrum' force. In particular, their analysis forecasts 'insufficient funding for all of the aircraft modernization sought by the military services, as spelled out in the QDR'.[19]

Those most concerned by this phenomenon strongly urge the closing of unnecessary US military bases, especially those located in the continental United States, to free up funds for procurement. However, base closings are unpopular with nearby local populations who place considerable political pressure on their elected representatives in Congress to keep them open. So it is unclear whether that approach will succeed. Currently, nearly two-thirds of all US defense spending goes to operations, maintenance and personnel. Others advocate further reductions in the force structure to free up procurement funds—but only if there is a commensurate reduction in commitments abroad. For the foreseeable future this trend toward isolationism does not appear likely to grow, but any funds freed up by major force reductions would be claimed by those seeking to address domestic problems in the United States.

Criticism from another angle has come from the group of high-ranking retired military officers and civilian defense experts established to critique the *Quadrennial Defense Review*, the National Defense Panel (NDP). After describing the current period in international relations as 'a relatively secure interlude following an era of intense international confrontation', the NDP began its criticism with a negative assessment of the 'win two nearly simultaneous major theater wars' strategy first introduced in the 1993 *Bottom-Up Review* and reaffirmed in the QDR. The NDP called that 'an unlikely contingency' and 'a low probability scenario' that served primarily to justify an existing force structure, at the cost of future forces.[20]

The NDP went on to declare that

> in the 2010–2020 time frame our military forces will need capabilities very different from those they currently possess . . . Current force structures and information architectures extrapolated to the future may not suffice to meet successfully the conditions of future battle . . . the procurement budgets of the services are focused primarily on current systems and do not adequately support the central thrust of their visions. In light of these factors the Panel questions the procurement plans for Army equipment, Navy ships, and tactical aircraft of all services.[21]

Instead, the NDP urged a much more rapid 'transformation' of US armed forces at *every* level, including the basic structure of the Department of Defense and intelligence services established by the 1947 National Security Act. The Unified Command Plan would be restructured, adding, for example, Pakistan to the Pacific Command's Area of Responsibility. The forces themselves should be reduced significantly in size but transformed in capability to fit something like the 'accelerated RMA' model outlined above, because 'technology will play an ever-increasing and imperative role in America's security policy and programs in the future'. If this transformation does not take place, 'the current and planned structure, doctrine, and strategy—that is to say, our current security arrangements—will not be adequate to meeting the challenges of the future'.[22]

In his response to this sweeping criticism, US Secretary of Defense Cohen was polite, and promised to take it seriously—but he rejected its main points. Stating that the NDP 'incorrectly characterizes our approach to sizing forces' Secretary Cohen reaffirmed the 'win two major theater wars' strategy in the following terms:

> Given America's enduring global interests and today's serious security challenges on the Korean Peninsula and in Southwest Asia . . . I believe that maintaining a capability, in concert with our allies, to fight and win two major theater wars in overlapping time frames remains central to credibly deterring opportunism and aggression in those critical regions.[23]

However, he did go on to note that if threats of large-scale regional aggression grow or diminish significantly, it would be prudent and appropriate for the United States 'to reevaluate our theater warfighting requirements'.

Cohen said the NDP's warnings about the gap between service visions and the procurement budget 'merits consideration', but the Department of Defense Budget for fiscal year 1999 still confidently predicts reaching the QDR fiscal year 2001 goal of a $60 billion procurement budget,[24] despite growing doubts among outside analysts about the feasibility of that figure.

Perhaps most significantly, Cohen rejected the NDP's call for a rapid acceleration to an RMA-inspired transformation of the entire US defense structure. He asserted that the Department of Defense has recognized the challenges of transforming the US forces and is already engaged in the process. Then he added, 'However, in the face of very real near-term demands to protect US interests and within the constraints of available resources, we must pursue this transformation *prudently*.' Afterward, the NDP's Chairman noted that it is very difficult for an enormous bureaucracy like the US Department of Defense to change dramatically and that, consequently, the real impact of the NDP's critique will probably not be felt until the next scheduled Quadrennial Defense Review in 2001, by which time the NDP's views will be 'conventional wisdom'.[25]

In summary, as of 1998 it seems clear that the US Department of Defense remains committed to something like the 'full spectrum' force design model outlined above and spelled out in the QDR which actually uses that term, with its support for both immediate readiness and cutting-edge technology. Only time will tell if that choice is affordable. US armed forces will retain their current basic organizational structure for the foreseeable future. They will continue to shrink somewhat in size, with the expectation that their capability will be undiminished or even enhanced due to the technological superiority of a coming new generation of weapons. The Revolution in Military Affairs is not the only factor affecting the future of US armed forces in the Asia–Pacific region, however. Changing threat perceptions will play an important role.

THE IMPACT OF CHANGING THREAT PERCEPTIONS

Following the end of the Cold War, the major threat perceptions in the Asia–Pacific region centered around a series of possible 'flashpoints' involving major or regional powers. In something like a descending order of probability and magnitude with regard to US military involvement they include, but are not limited to:

- Korea—the threat of invasion by North Korea, possibly including weapons of mass destruction
- Taiwan—the threat of attack or blockade by the People's Republic of China
- South China Sea—the threat of disruption of vital sea lanes due to territorial disputes between China and several Southeast Asian nations.

Although these potential regional 'flashpoints' remain matters of great concern, the 1997 *Quadrennial Defense Review* and the subsequent report by the National Defense Panel also took a new approach to threat assessment in light of the Persian Gulf War and the Revolution in Military Affairs. Instead of focusing on specific potential adversaries in particular geographic locations, the QDR and the NDP began with the basic assumption that potential adversaries have learned from the Gulf War two basic lessons: (1) that the US has an overwhelming conventional military superiority based on precision guided weapons and every effort should be made to acquire similar capabilities; and (2) that since it will not be possible to completely eliminate the US lead in conventional weaponry, every effort should be made to circumvent and undermine US strengths and exploit any existing vulnerabilities by using 'other' means of warfare—called 'asymmetric threats' by US defense planners.

These 'lessons' extend across the full spectrum of US national security, including defense of the US homeland. For the purposes of this chapter, however, the discussion will be limited to factors directly affecting US armed forces in the Asia–Pacific region.

With regard to the first factor, efforts to prevent proliferation include the 1996 Wassenaar Arrangement on Export Controls for Conventional Arms and Dual-Use Goods and Technologies approved by 33 co-founding states, including the US. This agreement may mitigate the problem, but the proliferation of advanced conventional weaponry is to some extent inevitable, due to the realities of the international arms market, the 'dual use' nature of much of the essential technology, and the growth of indigenous weapons production capabilities, some of it resulting from 'offset' agreements that transfer production technology as part of arms sales. Consequently, US forces in the future will be faced with some of the same precision guided weapons and advanced delivery systems that they now employ, albeit probably inferior versions. These would include, for example, theater ballistic missiles such as the Scuds employed by Iraq, third-generation strike aircraft carrying guided munitions, cruise missiles, modern conventional submarines capable of deploying 'smart' mines, and increasingly sophisticated Integrated Air Defense Systems (IADS).

In the future, US forces will respond to these developments by improving both their defensive and their offensive capabilities. Because of the limitations of space, only the most important of these developments will be described here.

With regard to offensive forces, the ability of the United States to project power in the littoral lies at the heart of the 'forward presence' posture in the Asia–Pacific region. In order to maintain their ability to conduct successful strike warfare against heavily defended inland targets, US forces are developing: improved unmanned aerial vehicles (UAVs) to conduct reconnaissance, surveillance and battle damage assessment; improved versions of the Tomahawk cruise missile; a new generation of stealthy aircraft; and improved 'stand-off' precision-guided munitions that can be launched at greater distances from the intended target.

The most important—and expensive—elements of this 'next generation' strike warfare capability are two aircraft: the Air Force's F–22 *Raptor* air dominance fighter, and the multi-service *Joint Strike Fighter* (JSF).

The F–22, which will replace the current F–15C/D air superiority fighter, is described in detail in Chapter 7. The F–22 will begin production in 1999. By 2012 the Air Force will procure a total of 339 of this fourth-generation fighter jet.[26]

The centerpiece of future US manned strike warfare is the

Joint Strike Fighter, which will be the Department of Defense's largest acquisition program in the first two decades of the next century. Since this aircraft will eventually replace the F–16, the AV–8 and the FA–18C/D, the Department of Defense plans to buy 2852 JSFs, with procurement to begin in 2005 and peak at 194 aircraft per year in 2012. The aircraft is currently in its 'concept demonstration phase' until 2001. Two aerospace companies, Boeing and Lockheed Martin, were selected in November 1996 to compete for the huge $200 billion contract.

In general terms, the JSF 'is anticipated to have a substantial mission radius, high survivability, and will use advanced-technology design, materials, and manufacturing techniques'.[27] All three US services (and the British Royal Navy) will employ the aircraft. Although the precise characteristics of the final version to be chosen are not yet known, some idea of the advertised capabilities of the aircraft can be found, for example, in Boeing's assertion that their version's capabilities, compared with existing strike aircraft, will include:

- combat radius: up to 33 per cent farther
- acceleration: 27 per cent quicker
- agility: 33 per cent better
- sustained 'G' turns: 13 per cent greater
- specific excess power: up to 51 per cent better
- radar and infrared signature: highly survivable.

Lockheed Martin makes very similar claims, of course.

It remains to be seen if these claims can be met, and if the US can afford to buy the desired total, which has already experienced one reduction in projected numbers and an extension in procurement schedules. Nevertheless, as of 1998 the Joint Strike Fighter appears to be *the* critical element of future US manned strike warfare capability through to the middle of the next century.[28]

With regard to projecting ground power ashore, a great change is already taking place under the Marine Corps 'Operational Maneuver From The Sea' (OMFTS) concept described in detail in Chapter 6. In essence, the United States is aware that the previous concept of moving ships close to shore, landing a force to seize a beachhead and then moving inland to seize objectives will not be adequate in the future in the face of improving enemy defenses. Instead, the Navy–Marine Corps team is moving toward a sea-based, rapid ship-to-objective concept. Two of the key pieces of equipment in this approach, the new MV–22 *Osprey* tiltrotor medium-lift aircraft and the Advanced Amphibious Assault Vehicle (AAAV), are described in Chapter 6. Another critical component, the new *LPD–17 Transport Dock*, will first enter the Fleet in 2002 and will ultimately include 12 state-of-the-art vessels.

The LPD–17 *San Antonio*-class ships will displace approximately 25 000 tons fully loaded, and travel at a speed in excess of 22 knots (38.7 kilometers per hour). It will be equipped with advanced self-defense weapons and C4 systems, and will incorporate 'reduced signature' technologies. Capable of carrying 720 Marines, two air-cushioned landing craft (LCAC) and either four helicopters or two MV–22 Ospreys, the LPD–17, along with the LHA/Ds described in Chapter 6, will form the heart of amphibious ready groups far into the future.[29]

However, the US Marine Corps is studying a more radical concept of 'sea-basing' that 'will lead to an entirely new method of supporting littoral power projection'. In a Concept Paper entitled 'MPF2010 and Beyond' Marine Corps Commandant General Charles Krulak has proposed a new role for Maritime Prepositioned Forces (MPF). In essence this concept proposes a new generation of MPF ships that will truly be 'at sea' bases that provide 'advanced facilities for tactical employment of assault support aircraft, surface assault craft, advanced amphibious vehicles, and the ships' organic lighterage in conditions of at least sea state three (wave heights greater than 1.6 feet, but less than 4.1 feet)'. By conducting operations from 'over the horizon', such sea bases would be better protected than current forces from anti-ship missiles, ballistic missiles and terrorists.[30]

It remains to be seen if this concept is accepted and leads to such a new class of MPF ships, but 'sea-basing' is clearly a major component in official thinking about the future of US amphibious forces. (A related but grander earlier concept was that of very large 'mobile offshore bases' (MOB) that might one day combine the strike and support capabilities of aircraft carriers, amphibious ships and MPF vessels.) The US Army is also developing a 'Strategic Meeting Engagement' concept that would require projection of a force capable of achieving operational objectives over strategic distances, so-called 'CONUS to combat'.[31]

In addition to these new technologies and concepts to deal with improved enemy conventional weapons, US defense planners are devoting great attention to the second future-threat category listed above, 'asymmetric threats'. First and foremost among these are the proliferation of weapons of mass destruction (WMD), whether nuclear, biological or chemical weapons, and the means to deliver them, especially ballistic missiles.

The overall US approach to this very serious threat is twofold: prevention and protection. The Department of Defense makes many contributions to the prevention effort, beginning with the deterrence afforded by its own nuclear forces (see Chapter 5), but also including funding for the Cooperative Threat Reduction (CTR) program with countries of the former Soviet Union and funding and intelligence implementing and inspecting for treaties such as SALT and START (see Chapter 5), the Non-Proliferation Treaty (NPT), the Missile Technology Control Regime (MTCR) and the Framework Agreement with North Korea, whose details are beyond the scope of this chapter.

In the realm of protection, the greatest single effort is being devoted to ballistic missile defense. Although this includes research aimed at a possible US 'homeland' National Missile Defense (NMD) against a limited attack by intercontinental ballistic missiles (ICBMs), the discussion here will be limited to the defense against shorter-range missiles, that is, *Theater Ballistic Missile Defense* (TBMD), as it directly affects the Asia–Pacific region.

Russia and China both possess theater ballistic missiles and a full range of weapons of mass destruction that can be delivered by them. North Korea possesses theater ballistic missiles and may possess deliverable NBC weapons.[32] Consequently, the United States is developing the means to protect its forces—and those of its allies—from ballistic missile attack. To begin with, protection for specific limited sites or small 'areas' containing joint and coalition troops is the goal. Eventually, a 'theater-wide' capability to defend civilian populations and larger troop concentrations is the goal.

Area ballistic missile defense (sometimes referred to as 'lower tier') currently consists of two deployed elements: the improved PAC–2/GEM version of the Army's *Patriot missile system* of Gulf War fame (described in Chapter 8) and the Marine Corps *Hawk* system, both older air defense systems with limited TBMD capabilities. A much more capable version of the Patriot, the PAC–3 with a new interceptor missile and a new non-explosive kill mechanism, is due to begin deployment in 1999. It will reportedly feature much-improved coverage and lethality.

The second 'area' system, the *Navy Area Defense System*, will consist of an advanced version of the Navy's *Aegis/Standard missile system* (described in Chapter 6). In 1997 a target simulating a ballistic missile was successfully engaged by the prototype of this system. An Operational Evaluation System will be in place on two Hawaii-based Aegis-equipped cruisers by the end of fiscal year 1999, and if all goes well the system could become operational by the end of 2001. One major advantage of this Navy system will be its global mobility without the need for a land base.

The last of the area defense systems is the *Medium Extended Air Defense System* (MEADS) being developed in conjunction with NATO nations including Germany and Italy. It is the only theater missile defense system under consideration to provide maneuver forces with 360-degree protection against ballistic missiles, cruise missiles and unmanned aerial vehicles. Under design to be rapidly transportable by C–130 aircraft, MEADS would replace the Hawk system and some portion of Patriot. The program is currently only funded through fiscal year 1999.

Farther into the future, theater or 'upper tier' systems are being developed. The Army's *Theater High-Altitude Area Defense System* (THAAD) was thought to be the 'most mature', but has run into technical problems and its original goal of a fully operational capability by 2004 has been pushed back to 2006. The *Navy Theater-Wide System* features an even more improved version of the Aegis/Standard missile system, with longer-range coverage over a wider area and exo-atmospheric intercept capabilities. Unlike other TBMD systems that target the end-phase of a ballistic missile's trajectory, this system will also offer ascent-phase and mid-course intercept capabilities in those cases where the Aegis ship can be positioned near the launch point or between the launch point and the target area. Because of the difficulties encountered by THAAD, funding for the Navy system has been increased, and an initial test flight intercept is scheduled to take place in early 2000.

The final element in TBMD is the *Airborne Laser* (ABL), a powerful laser mounted in a modified Boeing 747 commercial aircraft. The ABL is designed to destroy theater ballistic missiles in their most vulnerable early 'boost' phase of flight, hundreds of kilometers away from their targets and while still over enemy territory. Current plans call for an initial test aircraft to be deployed in 2002 and, if successful, to be available for urgent deployment in a manner similar to the deployment of test JSTARS aircraft during the 1991 Persian Gulf War.[33]

Among the other defensive measures the United States is developing to protect its forces and those of its allies from WMD are:

- strategic and operational intelligence, including early warning data

- advanced automated and deployable command, control and communications
- continuous, wide-area ground surveillance
- stand-off and point biological and chemical detection, identification, warning and response
- improved individual NBC protective equipment for ground forces.[34]

In addition to these defensive measures, a major *offensive* military program for protection from the WMD threat is being developed as part of the overall effort termed 'counter-proliferation'. This program consists of two main elements:

- development of a capability to attack an adversary's nuclear, biological and chemical infrastructure, including a capability to defeat hard/and or deeply buried targets
- increased funding for Special Operations Forces counter-proliferation activities.[35]

With regard to the first capability, a standing mission need statement exists for US combat air forces to detect, characterize and defeat NBC/missile facilities with minimal collateral effects, and to destroy 'hardened' targets, (i.e. structures reinforced by placing materials atop a structure after its construction and/or targets in tunnels and deep shafts). During the Gulf War the United States learned that it did not possess an adequate capability in this regard. The US Air Force's Agent Defeat Weapon (ADW) program to achieve this mission began its 'concept exploration' phase in 1997. The Department of Defense is also conducting the Hard and Deeply Buried Target Defeat Capability (HDBTDC) Acquisition activity to develop strike concepts.

Several weapons for these purposes have entered Advanced Concept Technology Demonstrations as of 1997. They include:

- a munitions effectiveness assessment tool for weapons employment and combat assessment, deployed to multiple warfighting commands
- a hazard prediction assessment capability for prediction of collateral effects, deployed to multiple warfighting commands
- a hard-target smart fuse which will optimize weapon detonation to maximize lethality with minimum collateral effects, tested successfully in 1997 in live drops by Air Force and Navy aircraft against surrogate targets
- a new inertial terrain-aided guidance capability, a weapon-borne sensor, and tactical unattended ground sensors

- an improved version of the GBU–24B laser-guided penetrating bomb.[36]

Facilities housed in tunnels tens of meters below the surface are invulnerable to direct attack by conventional means, and following the Gulf War a 'clear worldwide trend in tunneling to protect facilities' has been noted by US defense planners. The US Department of Energy has continued to work on new or modified designs for nuclear weapons such as the B–61 bomb, possibly to increase its capability to destroy facilities deep underground.[37] However, serious political and moral inhibitions against the use of nuclear weapons continue to restrict their usefulness in this regard. Consequently, the Defense Special Weapons Agency is engaged in a variety of research efforts to defeat hard and deeply buried targets without nuclear weapons, including:

- geomechanical modeling to identify key aspects of geology that affect strike weapon penetration and damage propagation
- advanced simulation and testing to improve understanding of weapons effects/target coupling
- development of an automated target planning tool for tunnel defeat
- development of improved capabilities to understand target characteristics to identify specific vulnerabilities that may be exploited.

A Tunnel Defeat Demonstration Program will include a series of tunnel facilities, of varying design and function, to be constructed at the Nevada Test Site as demonstration sites.[38]

Another element of the 'asymmetric' threat to US forces might be said to consist of a 'low' and a 'high' component: terrorism on the one hand, and information/space warfare on the other.

The successful terrorist attacks against US troops in Beirut in 1983 and at the Khobar towers in Saudi Arabia in 1996 (and the New York World Trade Center and Oklahoma City Federal Building bombings) have greatly heightened awareness of this threat. The US Army's classified *Delta Force* is an elite, dedicated, on-call anti-terrorist unit trained to defeat conventional terrorist attacks.[39] Among the other efforts under way to defeat conventional terrorism are several state-of-the-art development programs, including: systems to detect, assess and disable large vehicle bombs; stand-off explosive detection capabilities; pre- and post-construction blast mitigation techniques for physical structures; capabilities to maintain surveillance of and tag harmful materials that can be used in terrorist attacks; and improvements to robotics vehicles used in counterterrorism operations.[40]

The 1995 use of sarin nerve gas in the Tokyo subway by a cult group highlighted the growing threat of NBC terrorist attacks. Following a 1995 Presidential Decision Directive on US Policy on Counterterrorism, the Department of Defense began to develop a national interagency terrorism response system. In the Asia–Pacific region, Department of Defense response forces will be employed either under the operational control of the Joint Special Operations Task Force or a Response Task Force assigned to Commander in Chief, US Pacific Command. Among the units trained to respond to a terrorist incident with a 24-hour, on-call emergency response capability in chemical or biological incidents are:

- the US Army Technical Escort Unit, with missions of escorting the movement of chemical or biological material, and finding and destroying chemical or biological munitions
- US Marine Corps Chemical and Biological Incident Response Force (CBIRF), which is capable of performing chemical or biological consequence management following a terrorist attack; CBIRF is most effective when forward deployed in response to a credible threat to domestic or overseas installations
- the US Air Force's rapid response unit under the 820th Security Forces Group, trained in NBC defense measures.[41]

With regard to protecting America's vital lead in *information warfare and space assets*, the *Quadrennial Defense Review* announced several long-term programs to improve defensive and offensive capabilities. In particular, the US lead in space, which is already vital, is sure to grow in importance in the future. For example, the US Defense Advanced Research Projects Agency (DARPA) is 'investigating a satellite constellation, known as "Starlite", that can provide on-demand radar imagery anywhere and in near real-time to the theater commander, and a "Situational Awareness System" that will link the Internet to the warfighter via an arm-mounted terminal'. Also, US defense planners are devising means to better monitor foreign use of space-based assets, to protect US systems and to deny hostile use of space by an adversary.[42]

As important as these 'asymmetric' threats are, there is a final one that has figured heavily in failed US military efforts: *urban warfare*. Dense modern urban environments present a severe challenge to US forces because those environments negate or degrade many of the strengths of what some have come to call 'the American way of war'. As events in Vietnam, Beirut, Panama and most recently

Somalia have demonstrated, urban environments foil or degrade many sensors, including satellite systems, and tall buildings and associated wind currents endanger flight operations. Moreover, narrow streets and ruins inhibit maneuver, especially of heavy vehicles, indirect fire is extremely difficult, civilian refugees confuse a dangerous situation, and command and control is difficult to maintain as units become separated and communications devices fail.

Given the increasing urbanization of the world, this is a serious challenge to current US forces which are optimized for operations in open terrain, such as the deserts of the Middle East. It is true that in the Asia–Pacific region several key US allies (for example Japan and Australia) have island homelands where urban conflict is unlikely. However, there are several potential urban battle sites in the region, the most obvious being Seoul, South Korea, which was the scene of bitter fighting twice during the 1950–53 Korean War. Since that time Seoul has increased enormously in size and population, and the threat from nearby North Korean forces persists.

Although several services are addressing this issue, the US Marine Corps has taken the lead in improving US capabilities to conduct military operations in urban terrain (MOUT) with its two-year-long 'Urban Warrior' program. This program stresses the fact that, in the end, urban warfare is an infantry fight in which technology can provide some advantages but will not prove decisive. Among the technological innovations the Marines are employing is a modified version of a popular commercial computer game called *Doom* that simulates urban warfare at a tactical level. One of the main problems facing the 'Urban Warrior' program is the lack of realistic 'urban' training facilities. To compensate for this the Marines have begun conducting exercises, with advance notice, in urban areas in the United States. The program concentrates on the fact that the role of small unit leaders is paramount in this type of combat. Critics charge that not enough resources are being devoted to this issue. Given the increasing concentration of the world's population in cities in the littoral, it is almost certain that US forces will be called upon to engage in urban terrain in the future.[43]

THE BOTTOM LINE: BASES AND TROOPS

Two things should be apparent from the preceding information. First, substantial US armed forces will remain in the Asia–Pacific region well into the 21st century. Second, a variety of trends point to the probability that this force will consist of somewhat fewer personnel and fewer ground bases, yet equal or improved capability.

The basic implication of the Revolution in Military Affairs points toward smaller, dispersed, mobile, high-tech sea and air forces—and away from large, concentrated, fixed, land-based forces with heavy equipment. When the financial and political ramifications of maintaining the older style of force structure are factored in, this trend becomes even more clear.

It is not wise to speculate, but interest in this topic means that some effort to indicate specific developments is called for, with the keen awareness that things could change very rapidly, before the ink is dry on these pages.

The status of US forces based in Korea and Japan is at the heart of the matter. The presence of *any* US forces in these countries depends on the continuing consent of the host nations, of course. At the time of writing, it seems likely that US bases and some ground forces will continue to exist in both nations well into the 21st century. However, unless there is a dramatic worsening in the geo-strategic situation, some reductions will probably occur.

In Korea, any changes in the US force structure would only occur with very close consultation between the United States and the ROK. Should the situation on the peninsula improve dramatically, presumably involving some sort of peaceful reunification of the North and the South, the US force most likely to undergo restructuring, reduction or withdrawal is the 'heavy' 2nd Infantry Division north of Seoul. It should be recalled that the first version, in 1990, of the US *Strategic Framework for the Asian-Pacific Rim* said that a restructuring of the 2nd Infantry Division would be considered as a part of Phase II US reductions, although that plan was shelved in November 1991 due to the deteriorating situation concerning North Korea's nuclear weapons program. Moreover, in its 1997 Strategic Assessment the US National Defense University concluded that

> Ideally, US force structure on the peninsula following reunification would:
>
> - reflect a regional, rather than a peninsular, orientation
> - emphasize quick-reaction forces with the lift and mobility to project power over long distances
> - rely more on air and maritime forces and less on heavier

assets like the 2nd Infantry Division currently deployed between Seoul and the DMZ.[44]

Such a force would ideally continue to feature US land-based air power in Korea, and either a portion of a 'restructured' 2nd Infantry Division or perhaps a more mobile 'Light' Infantry force (see Chapter 8).

With regard to Japan, controversy over US bases on Okinawa continues, despite the 1996 agreements (see Chapter 4). For example, at the time of writing the agreement to eventually close the Marine Corps Air Station at Futenma and replace it with an offshore facility near the city of Nago appears to have run afoul of elements of Okinawan public opinion, still angry in the aftermath of a terrible 1995 incident wherein three US servicemen raped a 12-year-old Okinawan schoolgirl. In December 1997, in a non-binding referendum, 54 per cent of Nago voters rejected the heliport proposal and ousted a pro-base mayor. In February 1998 the governor of Okinawa Prefecture rejected the offshore heliport as part of a policy pursuing a 'base-free, pacifist prefecture'. It is impossible to predict the final outcome of this particular dispute, and Nago citizens elected a new pro-base mayor later in February 1998. What seems clear, however, is that opposition to the heavy US military presence on Okinawa remains strong.[45] In addition, the bursting of the Japanese 'bubble economy' in the early 1990s and the recent devaluation of the yen have put heavy pressure on Japan's 'burden-sharing' support for US bases.

It seems likely that, at the very least, some 'restructuring' of the US military presence in Japan will continue to occur, possibly with a shift of some forces from Okinawa to the main Japanese islands. As with the situation in Korea, the force most likely to be affected by the several trends noted above is the ground force, in this case the 3rd Marine Division based on Okinawa. It is possible that elements of this division would eventually be 'restructured' or reduced in Okinawa, and key elements relocated to Guam, Hawaii and the US West Coast. As long as the threat of conflict on the Korean peninsula persists, major relocation of US forces from Okinawa is unlikely. However, once the need for proximity and readiness for Korean contingencies is gone, US and Japanese political and economic pressures for significant restructuring of Marine forces on Okinawa will intensify.

In any case, the United States will certainly continue to seek to maintain the air and naval bases that it now operates from in Japan (see Chapter 4), and to have access to other Japanese facilities, in a manner consistent with the 1997 Guidelines Review discussed above. These bases will continue to be seen as essential platforms for US forces to maintain a forward presence necessary to fulfill their broader role in maintaining regional stability.

With its withdrawal from Vietnam and the Philippines, the United States ceased to have any Southeast Asian bases after 1992. It is not likely that it will ever replace those bases. However, in recent years the United States has negotiated 'access' agreements for its naval and air forces with several nations in the region—and that trend is growing. In January 1998 the United States and Singapore concluded an agreement allowing US aircraft carriers and other warships to dock at a new port in Singapore beginning in the year 2000. Although a previous agreement allowed smaller US ships maintenance access, carriers had to anchor offshore. Also in January 1998 representatives of the US government and the government of the Philippines initialed a Visiting Forces Agreement, which, if confirmed by the Philippine Senate, will enable the United States and the Philippines to resume major military exercises, combined training, and ship visits, thus restoring some measure of the access it lost in 1992.[46]

SUMMARY

Nearly all the major trends—strategic, military/technological, political and economic—point to an enduring, equally or more capable, smaller, more dispersed, high-tech US forward military presence in the Asia–Pacific region well into the 21st century, with a greater emphasis on mobile air and naval forces and a lesser emphasis on heavy, fixed, land-based ground combat units. This force will seek to deploy a new generation of advanced weaponry that will maintain the US lead in that regard, while maintaining readiness to respond to crises. The main constraints will be economic, but the strong US economy should be able to sustain a substantial presence in the region for a long time. An improving geo-strategic situation will result in a smaller US force, of course. Should that situation deteriorate badly, the United States, with permission where appropriate, will retain or even increase the forward-deployed forces necessary to sustain its firm commitment to peace and prosperity in the region.

10

Conclusion

Only a few years ago, following the withdrawal of US armed forces from the Philippines in 1991, it seemed to many that the 'high water mark' of US military presence and influence in the Asia–Pacific region had been reached and that a steady decline was inevitable. The economic troubles of the United States, the end of the Cold War and the economic dynamism of many nations in the Asia–Pacific region all seemed to confirm that trend.

As of 1998 it is apparent that the predicted 'inevitable decline' has not occurred, and probably will not occur for the foreseeable future.

This chapter very briefly summarizes the information in the rest of the book with regard to US armed forces, especially those present in the Asia–Pacific region under the US Pacific Command. It can, to some extent, be read as an 'executive summary' of the preceding chapters. Documentation of the concise information contained in this chapter is contained in earlier chapters, along with a much greater depth and scope of information on all the topics briefly described here. In particular, it should be pointed out, as noted in the preceding chapters, that a large portion of the US armed forces has global mobility, and that in the event of a major conflict in the Asia–Pacific region those forces would augment the forces of the US Pacific Command which are the main focus of this summary chapter.

HISTORY OF US ARMED FORCES IN THE REGION

The armed forces of the United States have been present in the Asia–Pacific region for nearly two centuries. The voyage of the USS *Essex* to the Western Pacific in the year 1800 marked the first venture of US military forces into the region. By 1835 the US Navy's 'East India Station' established a fairly continuous US 'forward presence'. The annexation of California and Oregon in 1848 extended the US homeland boundary to the Pacific Ocean, making the United States a 'Pacific nation' forever. The purchase of Alaska, including the Aleutian Islands, in 1867 greatly extended the US presence in the north Pacific.

The voyage of US Navy Commodore Perry to Japan in 1854 resulted in a treaty of peace and trade between the United States and Japan. In 1882 a similar agreement was reached with Korea by US Navy Commodore Shufeldt. Thus the foundations of US economic interests in the region were laid by US military representatives.

The war with Spain that broke out in 1898 led to the first substantial deployment of US military forces to the region because the Philippines was a Spanish colony. Eventually some 50 000 US troops fought Spanish and then indigenous forces for over four years in the Philippines, which was ceded to the United States by Spain, along with Guam, in 1898. Together with the annexation of Hawaii that same year, the United States had acquired major island territories in the Central and Western Pacific.

Throughout the first three decades of the century small forces of US Army and Marine Corps troops were deployed to China to protect US citizens and property during a period of great instability. But it was not until Japan joined the Axis in 1940 that the strategic importance of the region to US security became fully apparent.

Japan's December 1941 attack on Pearl Harbor, Hawaii, marked the beginning of US involvement in the Pacific theater of World War II. After three and a half years of brutal struggle, over 2 million Americans had served in the Pacific theater and 90 000 died in achieving total victory. In terms of size and duration, legitimacy, public attention and national passion, World War II marked a permanent turning point in the importance of the Asia–Pacific region to US security. Following the war, the United States made a commitment to maintaining strong military forces in the region to deal with future threats—a commitment that remains to this day. The most visible legacy is a series of military bases in the region.

The Cold War between the West and the Soviet Union would mark the next 40 years. Although Europe was the central focus of the Cold War, the invasion of South Korea by the Soviet-supported North in June 1950 led to the eventual involvement of over 225 000 US troops there. In that bloody three-year conflict nearly 34 000 Americans died. The Korean War ended with an armistice, but no peace agreement, a situation which persists to this day. The importance of US forces on the ground in Korea and on bases in Japan became apparent. At the time of writing some 37 000 US troops remain stationed in Korea, with another 54 000 in Japan or afloat.

The next major involvement of US forces in the region began with the dispatch of US advisers in 1961 to South Vietnam which was engaged in fighting an insurgency supported by communist North Vietnam. At the height of US involvement, over half a million American military personnel were deployed in Vietnam, and over 57 000 were killed during the long and bitter war. Although US forces were never defeated militarily, the Vietnam War was not a classic military struggle. The United States, and especially its South Vietnamese allies, never established an effective strategy for dealing with the insurgency. By 1972 the United States withdrew its forces, and three years later South Vietnam fell to the forces of North Vietnam.

The United States drew some important lessons from this defeat, subsequently declaring that it would not commit its military forces unless: (1) there is a national consensus that clear and vital issues are at stake; (2) the nations receiving US military help are stable and able to help themselves; (3) US leaders have a clear and declared goal and timeline; and (4) every effort is made to keep US casualties to a minimum and use overwhelming force.

The withdrawal of US forces from Southeast Asia led many to question US commitment to the security of the region. Throughout the 1980s, however, US forces in Northeast Asia and the North Pacific played a major deterrence role in the last phase of the Cold War. The end of the Cold War in 1991 and the withdrawal of US forces from the Philippines again raised questions about US commitment. However, as the 20th century draws to a close, that commitment, embodied in 100 000 forward-deployed troops, remains in force due to continuing US strategic interests in the Asia–Pacific region.

US INTERESTS AND STRATEGIC POLICY

Although the end of the Cold War removed a clearly identified military threat to US security and that of its allies in the Asia–Pacific region, the United States retains strong interests there, and bases its strategy on those interests.

The US National Security Strategy of 'engagement and enlargement' aims at achieving peace and prosperity by enabling the spread of democratic government and free market economies. In Northeast Asia the spread of democracy and market economics to Japan and South Korea stand as examples. The Philippines is an example in Southeast Asia. In situations where those conditions do not fully exist, as with the People's Republic of China, a strategy of 'engagement' is employed in the hope that it will strengthen ties and lead to peaceful change.

As it looks to the future, the US military strategy has three major strategic goals: (1) shaping the international environment as outlined above; (2) responding to the full spectrum of crises that may arise; and (3) preparing now for an uncertain future.

In recent years the economic importance of the Asia–Pacific region to the United States has grown tremendously due largely to increasing trade. US trade with the Asia–Pacific region exceeds that with Europe by more than 50 per cent, and totals more than $300 billion annually. Many jobs in the United States depend on this trade. Strong US efforts to ameliorate the East Asian financial crisis of 1997–98 are a good indication of the region's economic importance.

Within this context, the *US National Military Strategy* lists two 'ends': (1) promote stability; and (2) defeat adversaries. Four strategic concepts are seen as 'ways' to implement the strategy: (1) strategic agility—the timely concentration and employment of US military power anywhere on earth; (2) overseas presence—visible US forces and infrastructure positioned forward in key regions; (3) power projection—the ability to rapidly and effectively deploy and sustain US forces in and from many dispersed locations; and (4) decisive force—the commitment of enough superior military force to overwhelm all armed resistance.

Concerning 'means', the National Military Strategy, following the recent *Quadrennial Defense Review*, calls for the following active conventional forces by 1999:

- Army—four active corps, ten active divisions—six heavy and four light—and two armored cavalry regiments
- Navy—12 aircraft carrier battle groups and 12 amphibious ready groups, with ten active and one reserve air wings, and a combat fleet of 315 ships
- Marine Corps—three Marine Expeditionary Forces, each com-

prising a command element, a division, an aircraft wing and a service support group
- Air Force—just over twelve active and eight reserve fighter wing equivalents and four air defense squadrons, plus a fleet of 187 bombers and a large number of tanker and airlift aircraft.

US nuclear forces, the vast majority of which are assigned to the US Strategic Command and based in the United States, are determined both by national strategy and international arms control agreements. Assuming that Russia ratifies the START II agreement, by 2007 US nuclear forces will consist of:

- 500 nuclear warheads on 500 intercontinental ballistic missiles
- not over 1750 warheads on sea-launched ballistic missiles on board 14 ballistic missile submarines
- 1250 nuclear bombs on 92 strategic bombers
- several hundred non-strategic nuclear warheads deliverable by fighter aircraft or Tomahawk cruise missile.

As of 1998 there were 1.45 million American men and women under arms. At around US$250 billion, the defense budget amounts to 15 per cent of the national budget and 3.2 per cent of the US Gross National Product.

COMMAND AND CONTROL

The United States was founded by people who had suffered under authoritarian governments often maintained by military force. Consequently, the principle of civilian command and control of the military is enshrined in the US Constitution and subsequent legislation.

The elected President of the United States (or his legal successor in an emergency) is the Commander in Chief of US Armed Forces. The President and the civilian Secretary of Defense form the National Command Authorities (NCA). The Departments of the Army, Navy and Air Force are also headed by civilian Secretaries. The highest ranking military officer in each service is a member of the Joint Chiefs of Staff, who are by law military advisers to the President. The Chairman of the Joint Chiefs of Staff is the President's primary military adviser. In that capacity, the Chairman and the Joint Chiefs of Staff have outlined their vision of the future of US military operations in a 'template' document, *Joint Vision 2010*, which is described in Chapter 3. In addition, the National Security Council is the primary body or senior cabinet of advisers to the President.

A fully-equipped national command post aircraft is on constant alert near Washington, DC, to carry the National Command Authorities in case of an emergency.

Since 1986, the operational chain of command has run from the National Command Authorities directly to the combatant commanders of the nine US Unified Combatant Commands, which include:

- US Pacific Command
- US European Command
- US Atlantic Command
- US Southern Command
- US Central Command
- US Space Command
- US Special Operations Command
- US Transportation Command
- US Strategic Command.

These Commands are connected to the National Command Authorities by the Global Command and Control System, a rapid, highly sophisticated, computerized global automated information system.

THE US PACIFIC COMMAND

In the operational chain of command, all US armed forces stationed in the Asia–Pacific theater are assigned to the US Pacific Command (USPACOM), the Unified Combatant Command for the region.

In 1997 USPACOM celebrated its 50th anniversary as America's first unified command, an outgrowth of the Pacific Ocean Area and Southwest Pacific Area command structure used during World War II.

Today, from USPACOM headquarters at Camp H. M. Smith in Hawaii, the Commander in Chief, US Pacific Command (USCINCPAC) has responsibility for the largest geographical area of any of the US unified commands. This area equals about 50 per cent of the earth's surface—more than 250 million square kilometers—including 45 countries, ten US territories and twenty territories and possessions of other countries, containing over 60 per cent of the world's population. USPACOM's Area of Responsibility extends from the west coast of the United States mainland to the east coast of Africa, from the Arctic to the Antarctic, and includes the states of Alaska and Hawaii.

As of March 1998 the USPACOM total force consisted of some 300 000 military personnel from the Army, Navy, Air Force and Marines (about 20 per cent of all active-duty US military forces). This force consists of service components, subordinate unified commands and standing Joint Task Forces.

The Service Components are follows:

- US Army Pacific (USARPAC)
- US Pacific Fleet (PACFLT), including Marine Force Pacific (MARFORPAC)
- US Pacific Air Forces (PACAF).

The subordinate unified commands consist of forces from all the services and include:

- US Forces Japan, headquartered at Yokota Air Base Japan, which conducts the activities of the 44 000 US Air Force, Navy, Marine Corps and Army personnel stationed at 97 locations in Japan;
- US Forces Korea, headquartered in Seoul, Republic of Korea (ROK), which conducts the activities of 37 000 US Army, Air Force and Navy personnel in more than 120 locations in South Korea; the Commander of US Forces in Korea also serves as Commander in Chief of the United Nations Command and of the ROK/US Combined Forces Command;
- Special Operations Command Pacific, which exercises operational control over Army, Navy and Air Force Special Operations Forces assigned to USCINCPAC (see Chapter 8);
- Alaskan Command, headquartered at Elmendorf Air Force Base outside Anchorage, which is responsible for the unified defense of Alaska's land and territorial waters, including the Aleutian Islands, and includes nearly 18 000 Army, Navy and Air Force personnel.

Standing Joint Task Forces include:

- Joint Interagency Task Force West, which supports national counterdrug initiatives in USPACOM;
- Joint Task Force-Full Accounting, which conducts field operations to achieve the fullest possible accounting for Americans

still unaccounted for in Southeast Asia as a result of the Vietnam War;
- other contingency Joint Task Forces as necessary.

In addition, eight designated representatives, known by the acronym CINCPACREP, report directly to USCINCPAC for other areas in the region as of 1997.

USPACOM THEATER STRATEGY

The Pacific Command's military strategy derives from two fundamental premises: (1) the political, economic and military aspects of security are interdependent; and (2) military security undergirds the stable conditions that are prerequisite for economic growth and prosperity.

USPACOM's strategy consists of three levels of activities and operations:

- peacetime engagement
- crisis response
- fight and win a major theater war.

USPACOM FORCES AND BASE INFRASTRUCTURE

Since 1992 there have been no US nuclear weapons deployed in the Asia–Pacific region, with the exception of the submarine-launched ballistic missiles aboard Trident submarines on regular deterrent patrols. Nuclear attack submarines are capable of deploying nuclear Tomahawk cruise missiles, but do not normally carry them (see Chapter 5).

The US Pacific Fleet takes its post–Cold War strategic direction from the US Navy's key documents, *From the Sea* and *Forward from the Sea*, which emphasize the role of naval expeditionary forces in providing presence and power projection in the littoral regions of the world. As of July 1998 the US Pacific Fleet consists of approximately 254 900 people, including 120 000 active duty in the Navy, 73 500 active-duty Marines, 35 000 Naval Reservists and 26 600 civilians. The Pacific Fleet numbers some 193 ships (including Military Sealift Command ships), down from a strength of 283 in 1986. The Fleet includes:

- 3 Nuclear Aircraft Carriers (CVN)
- 3 Conventional Aircraft Carriers (CV)

- 1 Nuclear-powered Guided Missile Cruiser (CGN)
- 13 Cruisers (CG)
- 12 Guided Missile Destroyers (DDG)
- 12 Destroyers (DD)
- 18 Guided Missile Frigates (FFG)
- 30 Nuclear Attack Submarines (SSN)
- 8 Ballistic Missile Submarines (SSBN)
- 2 Fleet Flagships (1 Amphibious Command and Control Ship [LCC] and 1 Amphibious Transport Dock Ship [AGF])
- 5 large Amphibious Assault Ships (LHD/LHA)
- 15 medium Amphibious Ships (LSD/LPD/LST)
- 12 Auxiliary Ships (cargo, fuel, etc.)
- 4 Patrol Craft
- 2 Mine Countermeasure Vessels (MCM)
- 55 Military Sealift Command Ships.

The Pacific Fleet also includes approximately 1432 aircraft of the following types:

- US Navy:
  - 357 Tactical (F–14 and F/A–18 fighters/bombers)
  - 203 Helicopters
  - 73 P–3 (maritime patrol)
  - 163 other.
- US Marine Corps:
  - 197 Tactical (F/A–18 and AV8-B fighters/bombers)
  - 404 Helicopter
  - 40 other.

With its headquarters at Pearl Harbor, Hawaii, the Pacific Fleet's mission is to support the US Pacific Command's theater strategy (see Chapters 2 and 3), and to provide interoperable, trained, combat-ready forces to USCINCPAC and other US unified commands. The Pacific Fleet provides forces to its two 'numbered' fleets, the Third Fleet and the Seventh Fleet.

The Commander of the Third Fleet is headquartered aboard the USS *Coronado* (AGF–11) operating from San Diego, California. The primary wartime mission of the Third Fleet is the defense of the western sea approaches to the United States, including Alaska and the Aleutian Islands. In addition, the Third Fleet may be assigned to respond to a specific crisis event or contingency. For this purpose the Third Fleet maintains a Ready Battle Group. This battle group consists of an aircraft carrier and a tailored mix of surface warships, submarines and support ships, ready to respond to any emerging contingency within 96 hours.

The Third Fleet also maintains other Carrier Battle Groups (CVBG) and Amphibious Ready Groups (ARG), plus service support ships and nuclear attack submarines. A carrier battle group consists of a carrier, surface combatants, submarine escorts and logistics ships. An amphibious ready group usually consists of a Multi-purpose Amphibious Assault Ship (LHD/LHA), a Landing Platform, Dock (LPD), and a Landing Ship, Dock (LSD). A Marine Expeditionary Unit (MEU) consisting of about 2000 Marines and their equipment embark in ARG shipping to complete the ARG/MEU team. In normal peacetime, the Third Fleet continually trains Navy and Marine Corps forces for the expeditionary warfare mission.

The US Seventh Fleet constitutes the largest forward-deployed Fleet in the US Navy, with 50–60 ships, 350 aircraft and 60 000 Navy and Marine Corps personnel. The Commander of the Seventh Fleet is headquartered aboard the USS *Blue Ridge* (LCC–19) forward-based from Yokosuka, Japan. The Seventh Fleet's area of responsibility includes over 132 million square kilometers of the Pacific and Indian Oceans, stretching from the International Dateline westward all the way to the east coast of Africa, and from the Kurile Islands in the North Pacific to the Antarctic in the south.

Approximately 20 of the Seventh Fleet's ships operate from US facilities in Guam and Yokosuka and Sasebo, Japan. A CVBG is homeported at Yokosuka and an ARG is homeported at Sasebo. Other ships are deployed to the Seventh Fleet on a rotating basis from bases in Hawaii and on the US west coast. On any given day, about 50 per cent of Seventh Fleet forces are deployed at sea throughout the area of responsibility. The Seventh Fleet operates the most advanced weapons systems in the US naval arsenal, including nuclear-powered large-deck carriers and attack submarines, advanced strike aircraft, Tomahawk missiles and the Aegis air defense system.

US Marine Forces Pacific (MARFORPAC), with its headquarters at Marine Corps Base Hawaii (MCBH), is the largest field Command in the US Marine Corps. MARFORPAC is a Service Component Headquarters that reports directly to USCINCPAC, to the Commander of the US Central Command, and to the Commander in Chief, United Nations Command, Korea. This means that both of the identified potential major regional contingencies—Korea and the Persian Gulf—lie within MARFORPAC's area and scope of responsibility.

Under its concept of 'Operational Maneuver From the Sea' the Marine Corps is emphasizing rapid movement from ship to inshore objective in a crisis or war. The Marine Force Pacific Commander commands roughly 80 000 Marines and associated sailors forward deployed, both ashore and afloat, and additional forces stationed in the United States. MARFORPAC's two major subordinate commands are I Marine Expeditionary Force (MEF), headquartered at Camp Pendleton, California, and III MEF, headquartered on Okinawa. Each MEF operates well-equipped ground, air and support forces. The Fleet Marine Force Pacific, also headquartered at MCBH, is responsible for providing Marine forces to Naval Aviation and to deploying Navy Fleets.

MARFORPAC maintains two rapidly deployable Alert Contingency Marine Air-Ground Task Forces—one in I MEF and one in III MEF—each consisting of a lightly armed, battalion-sized force on standby alert, ready to be airlifted into a crisis area. Under the Maritime Prepositioned Force Concept, more than 17 000 Marines and sailors could fly into a benign or secured airfield to link up with MPS ships on fewer than 250 aircraft sorties. In the event of a major crisis in Korea, the MARFORPAC commander and headquarters would deploy there and become Commander, Marine Forces, Korea, which would play a decisive role in ending hostilities on the peninsula.

The Pacific Air Forces (PACAF) is responsible for most Air Force units, bases and facilities in the Pacific and Alaska. PACAF's primary mission is to plan, conduct and coordinate offensive and defensive air operations in the Pacific and Asian theaters. Under the US Air Force strategic vision contained in the document *Global Engagement*, PACAF stands ready to achieve air and space superiority anywhere on the globe, utilizing rapid mobility, superior information and precision weapons.

PACAF has approximately 44 000 military and civilian personnel serving in nine major locations and numerous smaller facilities, primarily in Hawaii, Alaska, Guam and South Korea. There are approximately 300 fighter and attack aircraft assigned to the command, and another 80 non-combat aircraft.

PACAF's major units and aircraft are:

- 5th Air Force—Headquarters at Yokota Air Base, Japan, 16 000 personnel

- 18th Wing—Kadena AB, Japan (F-15C/D, HH-60G, E-3C, KC-135R)
- 35th Fighter Wing—Misawa AB, Japan (F-16C/D)
- 374th Airlift Wing—Yokota AB, Japan (C-130E/H, C-9A, UH-1N)
- 7th Air Force—Headquarters at Osan AB, South Korea, 9000 personnel
- 8th Fighter Wing—Kunsan AB, South Korea (F-16C/D)
- 51st Fighter Wing—Osan AB, South Korea (F-16C, A/OA-10A, C-12J)
- 11th Air Force—Headquarters at Elmendorf AFB, Alaska, 11 000 personnel
- 3rd Wing—Elmendorf AFB, Alaska (F-15, C-130H, C-12J, E-3B/C, F-15E)
- 13th Air Force—Headquarters at Andersen AFB, Guam, 2000 personnel
- 36th Air Base Wing—Andersen AFB, Guam
- 15th Air Base Wing—Hickam AFB, Hawaii (C-135).

PACAF is not large in numbers. However, it has four advantages of air power that are perfectly suited to PACAF's enormous area of operations.

- Mobility: The speed and range unique to air power meets this essential requirement in a region of vast distances.
- Responsiveness: A potential aggressor in the Asia–Pacific region needs to be aware that PACAF can and will respond quickly to acts of aggression, disrupting an aggressor's cycle of military operations.
- Flexibility: PACAF has the ability to mix a variety of air assets into a spectrum of combinations to meet developing conditions.
- Versatility: PACAF's force structure includes F-15s, F-16s, E-3 Sentries, airlifters and tankers already present in the region.

In addition to keeping its own forces in a high state of readiness, PACAF devotes considerable effort to building solid relationships with other regional air forces in support of the USCINCPAC Cooperative Engagement strategy.

The US Army is an important element of the US presence in the Asia–Pacific region. Under the guidelines of its document *Army Vision 2010*, the US Army continues to refine and improve the air-land battle concept that it employed so effectively during the Persian Gulf War. At the end of fiscal year 1996 the US Pacific

Command included over 58 000 US Army personnel. Of these, approximately 29 000 were forward deployed, with about 27 000 in South Korea and 2000 in Japan, including Okinawa. Of the remainder, some 15 000 were stationed in the western United States, with approximately 7000 in Hawaii, 7000 in Alaska and 6500 in Washington state.

The 27 000 US Army troops in South Korea are part of the US Eighth Army, which is the Army component of the all-service Subordinate Unified Combat Command called US Forces in Korea (USFK). Due to the unique history stemming from the Korean War (see Chapter 1), the US Forces in Korea command supports the United Nations Command established in 1950 to repel the North Korean invasion. At the same time, USFK supports the Republic of Korea–United States Combined Forces Command (ROK–US CFC) established in 1978 as the warfighting headquarters whose role is to deter, or defeat if necessary, outside aggression against the ROK. The CFC is headed by a four-star American General as Commander in Chief, with a four-star ROK army general as deputy. Throughout the command structure bi-national manning is maintained, although the US commander retains operational control of US forces as directed by the US CINCPAC.

The great majority of US Army troops in South Korea are assigned to the 2nd Infantry Division, known as 'the Warrior Division'. The Warriors of the 2nd Infantry Division are spread out across the western Korean peninsula south of the Demilitarized Zone along the 38th parallel (see Chapter 4). The division has six subordinate commands. The 1st and 2nd Brigades are the maneuver brigades, and have a total of two M1A1 Abrams tank battalions, two Mechanized Infantry battalions equipped with the M2A2 Bradley Fighting Vehicle, and two air assault infantry battalions. The other major commands are the Aviation Brigade, the Division Artillery, the Engineer Brigade and the Division Support Command. The Division's 3rd Brigade is located at Fort Lewis, Washington, ready to be airlifted from the nearby McChord Air Force Base.

The 2nd Division reportedly possesses more combat power than any other division within the coalition forces. It receives continuous equipment upgrades to maintain that capability, and engages in numerous exercises to maintain readiness.

The forward deployment of the US 2nd Infantry Division represents a major commitment on the part of the United States to the Republic of Korea and to the broader region. The economic and political costs of this commitment, together with the changing political situation in the Korean peninsula, pose one of the largest questions facing the United States and its Asia–Pacific allies in the future.

All other US Army troops in the Asia–Pacific region are assigned to the US Army Pacific (USARPAC), which is the Army Component Command (outside Korea) of the US Pacific Command (see Chapter 3) and has its headquarters at Fort Shafter, Hawaii. Established in its current form in 1990, USARPAC commands and supports assigned and attached active US Army and US Army reserve units, installations and activities in Alaska, Hawaii, Japan and possessions and trust territories administered by USPACOM. Although based in the Asia–Pacific region, USARPAC provides trained and ready Army forces worldwide in support of military operations and peacetime engagements in order to contribute to decisive victory and promote regional stability. Some of USARPAC's major subordinate commands are:

- US Army Japan
- 25th Infantry Division (Light), Hawaii
- US Army Alaska/1st Brigade, 6th Infantry Division (Light).

The 2000 US Army troops forward deployed in Japan are assigned to the US Army Japan/9th Theater Army Area Command (USARJ/9th TAACOM), which is a major subordinate command of US Army Pacific. The USARJ is headquartered at Camp Zama near Tokyo. The presence of the USARJ stems from the 1960 Treaty of Mutual Cooperation and Security between the United States and Japan.

The USARJ/9th TAACOM is comprised of two major subordinate commands, the 10th and 17th Area Support groups and a host of other units and activities. Most of these forces perform logistical support missions for the USPACOM and the US Army's I Corps, in addition to conducting operations with the Japan Ground Self Defense Force. The US Army Japan soldiers work at 39 different locations on the Japanese islands of Honshu, Hokkaido, Kyushu and Okinawa (see Chapter 4). The largest combat unit is the 1st Battalion, 1st Special Forces Group stationed on Okinawa.

In addition to its forward-deployed forces, the US Army maintains significant forces in the Pacific region of the United States, assigned to USPACOM. In the far North, the bulk of the 7000 troops of the US Army Alaska constitute the separate 1st Brigade of the 6th Light Infantry Division (and its only existing component). They are stationed at Fort Wainwright, Alaska, near

Fairbanks. The 'Arctic Warrior' Brigade is the only unit in the US Army specifically trained and equipped to operate in arctic conditions.

In the middle Pacific, the 25th 'Tropic Lightning' Light Infantry Division at Fort Shafter forms the combat nucleus of the 15 000 troops assigned to the US Army Hawaii. The Division's 1st Brigade is located at Fort Lewis, Washington. The inherent global strategic mobility of this Light Division enables it to play a role at great distances from its home base.

CAPABILITIES AND LIMITATIONS

Although Russia still possesses a vast nuclear arsenal that is in some aspects equivalent to US nuclear forces, there is a broad consensus that at this time the conventional armed forces of the United States are, at all levels, the most powerful and effective in the world and are without, at least for the near future, serious challenge. The collapse of the Soviet Union, the subsequent decline of Russian conventional forces, and the performance of US forces in the 1991 Persian Gulf War have made US superiority apparent.

This superiority is most apparent in areas dominated by high technology, such as intelligence gathering, air-to-air combat, precision strike warfare, carrier and submarine operations, amphibious operations, armored combat and special operations. However, it is equally true that the quality, training and morale of US military personnel are essential to US superiority.

This does not mean that US forces are without their limitations. For example, strategic air and sealift capability is still somewhat short of stated requirements. Some types of current US combat aircraft are seeing their capabilities approached or matched by new generations of foreign-built planes. US conventional weapons cannot currently destroy targets deep underground. The US Navy has not done enough with regard to mine countermeasures. Much of the Marine Corps' amphibious equipment is aging and needs to be replaced. Other examples are illustrated in various chapters of this book.

Perhaps the greatest day-to-day limitation has to do with the fact that, although US armed forces have declined by 40 per cent since 1986, US international commitments have not declined and smaller forces are being asked to do more. No matter how effective, a ship, plane, tank or soldier can only be in one place at one time. The strain on personnel and equipment from a high tempo of operations is severe. The US armed forces are beginning to experience some difficulty in retaining trained, qualified personnel essential in an all-volunteer force.

In the broader context of future threats, it is acknowledged that America's potential adversaries have learned from the Gulf War and will attempt to employ 'asymmetric means' to circumvent or undermine US capabilities. Chief among these is the threat of weapons of mass destruction, whether nuclear, chemical or biological, delivered by theater ballistic missiles—against which no complete defense currently exists. Terrorism is another threat in this category, as is 'information warfare' against the high-tech systems that the US military is increasingly dependent on. Also, warfare in urban terrain presents a serious challenge even to well-equipped US forces, as was seen in Somalia. The United States is devoting considerable research and development resources to meeting these concerns.

The final limitation is US concern over casualties. In an era of instant global communications, people in a democracy become quickly aware of the cost of combat in human terms. Any conflict seen as unnecessary, ill-defined, or poorly and unsuccessfully conducted, will quickly lose popular support. On the other hand, at key periods throughout their history the American people have demonstrated the will to accept even high casualties in a competently conducted defense of truly vital interests. Potential adversaries should know that they would undoubtedly do so again if such a circumstance were to arise.

THE FUTURE

Even assuming an improving international climate in the Asia–Pacific region, including an eventually peaceful reunification of Korea and a successful United States engagement with China, it is still likely that substantial American forces will remain in the region for the foreseeable future in the role of regional balancer and keeper of stability. This presence, in the case of overseas ground bases, would continue only at the continuing request of host Asian nations. US forces on the high seas would remain in any case.

However, the political and economic cost of this presence and the trends occurring under the rubric of the 'Revolution in Military Affairs' mean that these forces will probably be somewhat smaller in number and more dispersed—yet equally or even more capable due to continued US superiority in equipment and training.

There is no doubt that America will remain Asia–Pacific's premier military power well into the 21st century.

Appendix

SUMMARY OF FORCES IN THE WESTERN PACIFIC REGION, INCLUDING ALASKA AND HAWAII

Note: a more comprehensive and detailed list of forces is contained in the chapters devoted to the individual military services, and bases are described in Chapter 4.

Nuclear Forces

Strategic nuclear forces
No US long-range (i.e. strategic) nuclear weapons are based in the Asia–Pacific region, here defined as the Western Pacific including Alaska and Hawaii. However, 8 *Ohio*-class Trident ballistic missile submarines (SSBN) of Submarine Group Nine are based at Bangor, Washington state, near the Pacific coast. In 1998 each of these submarines carried 24 Trident I C–4 submarine-launched ballistic missiles (SLBM), and each missile carried 8 W–78 nuclear warheads, for a total of 192 warheads for each submarine and 1536 for the entire force. At any given time at least three of these boats are at sea: one on patrol in the Pacific, one returning to base, and one heading out to the patrol area. Of course, nearly all US strategic nuclear weapons based in the continental United States can reach targets in the Asia–Pacific region.

As a result of the 1994 US *Nuclear Posture Review*, the four oldest Ohio SSBNs, all based at Bangor, are scheduled for decommissioning (although some non-nuclear role may yet be found for them). Three newer Trident SSBNs, equipped with the improved Trident II (D–5) missile, will replace them. In addition, the rest of the Bangor-based SSBNs will be upgraded to enable them to deploy the newer missile, which features greater accuracy. The number of warheads deployed may be reduced if the START II treaty enters into force. See Chapter 5 for details.

Theater/Tactical nuclear forces
As a result of mutual agreements between Presidents Bush and Gorbachev in September 1991, all medium- and short-range US nuclear weapons were removed from US ground, sea and air forces in the Asia–Pacific region by July 1992, according to the US government. Moreover, all the equipment, personnel and training procedures necessary for US Navy surface ships to deploy nuclear weapons have been removed, again according to official US sources. However, an unspecified number of the US Pacific Fleet's 30 nuclear attack submarines (SSN) retain the *capability* to deploy the nuclear version of the Tomahawk cruise missile (TLAM-N), with a range of 2482 kilometers, but they do not normally carry them.

Navy–Marine Corps

At the end of 1997 the US Navy and Marine Corps forces stationed in the Western Pacific, including Hawaii, consisted of the Seventh Fleet and the Third Marine Expeditionary Force. The *Seventh Fleet* is the largest forward-deployed Fleet in the US Navy, with 50–60 ships, 350 aircraft and 32 000 Navy plus 28 000 Marine Corps personnel. The Seventh Fleet's command ship and an aircraft carrier battle group (CVBG) are homeported at Yokosuka, Japan, and an Amphibious Ready Group (ARG) is homeported at Sasebo, Japan. Approximately 20 Seventh Fleet ships operate from Yokosuka, Sasebo and Guam. Others are deployed on a rotating basis from Hawaii and the US west coast.

On a typical day, the Seventh Fleet includes:

Ships
- 1 or 2 large-deck carriers (including the *Kitty Hawk* homeported at Yokosuka, Japan)
- 3 or 4 cruisers
- 18–20 destroyers and frigates
- 5–6 nuclear-powered attack submarines
- 1 amphibious command and control ship
- 5–8 amphibious transport and landing ships
- 18 mobile logistics and support ships
- 16 Maritime Prepositioned Force (MPF) ships.

Naval aircraft
- 200 aboard aircraft carriers and other ships, including F–14s, F/A–18s, EA–6Bs, E–2Cs, S–3 and SH–60
- 22 shore-based P–3 maritime patrol aircraft
- 10 shore-based utility aircraft
- 150–160 Marine Corps aircraft, including F/A–18s, AV–8Bs, AH–1s, CH–47s.

The Third Marine Expeditionary Force (III MEF) is composed of about 20 000 Marines in a Marine Division, Aircraft Wing, Expeditionary Brigade, Force Support Group and afloat Marine Expeditionary Unit. III MEF is based on Okinawa and its aircraft wing is based at Iwakuni AB, Japan. About 5000 Marines, including the Headquarters of Marine Forces Pacific (MARFORPAC) and Fleet Marine Forces Pacific, are located at Marine Corps Base Hawaii.

US Air Force

The US Pacific Air Force (PACAF) has approximately 44 000 military and civilian personnel serving in nine major locations and numerous smaller facilities, primarily in Hawaii, Alaska, Guam, Japan and South Korea. There are approximately 300 fighter and attack aircraft assigned to the command, and another 80 non-combat aircraft.

PACAF's major units and aircraft are:

- 5th Air Force: Headquarters at Yokota Air Base, Japan, 16 000 personnel
- 18th Wing: Kadena AB, Japan (F–15C/D, HH–60G, E–3C, KC–135R)
- 35th Fighter Wing: Misawa AB, Japan (F–16C/D)
- 374th Airlift Wing: Yokota AB, Japan (C–130E/H, C–9A, UH–1N)
- 7th Air Force: Headquarters at Osan AB, South Korea, 9000 personnel
- 8th Fighter Wing: Kunsan AB, South Korea (F–16C/D)
- 51st Fighter Wing: Osan AB, South Korea (F–16C, A/OA–10A, C–12J); Operational Detachment, 9th Reconnaissance Wing (U–2R)
- 11th Air Force: Headquarters at Elmendorf AFB, Alaska, 11 000 personnel
- 3rd Wing: Elmendorf AFB, Alaska, (F–15, C–130H, C–12J, E–3B/C, F–15E)

- 13th Air Force: Headquarters at Andersen AFB, Guam, 2000 personnel
- 36th Air Base Wing: Andersen AFB, Guam
- 15th Air Base Wing: Hickam AFB, Hawaii (F–15, KC–135) See Chapter 7 for more details.

US Army

Approximately 51 000 US Army troops are stationed in the Asia–Pacific region, including Alaska and Hawaii. The major units are:

- 27 000 members of the US Eighth Army in South Korea, most of them in two brigades of the 'heavy' 2nd Infantry Division located between the DMZ and Seoul. The 2nd Division's forces include two M1A1 tank battalions, two mechanized infantry battalions equipped with M2A2 fighting vehicles, two air assault infantry battalions with AH–64 helicopters, and an artillery component with more Multiple-Launched Rocket Systems than any other US division.
- 2000 soldiers in the US Army Japan in 39 locations, including Okinawa
- 15 000 soldiers in two brigades of the highly mobile 25th 'light' Infantry Division at Fort Shafter, Hawaii
- 7000 troops of the US Army Alaska in the 1st Brigade of the 6th 'light' Infantry Division at Fort Wainright, specifically trained and equipped to operate in arctic conditions.

For more details, see Chapter 8.

Notes

Abbreviated references are to books or book chapters, journal articles and official documents listed in the Bibliography.

INTRODUCTION

1 Cf., for example, *The Pacific Century: America and Asia in a Changing World* by Frank Gibney, New York, Scribner's, 1992, and 'A US Strategy for the Asia-Pacific' by Douglas T. Stuart and William T. Tow, *Adelphi Paper* 299, IISS, Oxford University Press, 1995.
2 Conetta and Knight 1997, p. 1.
3 'Clinton Directive Changes Strategy on Nuclear Arms', *Washington Post*, 7 December 1997, p. A01.
4 'START I Memorandum of Understanding,' 1 July 1997.

CHAPTER 1

1 Schratz 1980, p. 127.
2 Swartz 1996.
3 Hagan 1973, p. 111.
4 Wiley 1990, p. 213.
5 Swartz 1996.
6 Schratz 1980, note, p. 266.
7 ibid. p. 128.
8 Dingman 1980, note, p. 21.
9 Trask 1981.
10 Gates 1980, pp. 79–91.
11 Dingman 1980, p. 22.
12 Swartz 1996.
13 Schratz 1980, note, p. 130.
14 Dingman 1980, pp. 25–27.
15 Schratz 1980, note, p. 130.

16 Kaufman 1990.
17 Flint 1980, pp. 148–59; Simmons 1980, pp. 172–76.
18 Friedman 1968.
19 Dingman 1980, pp. 30–31.
20 Swartz 1996.
21 Morison 1963, pp. 38–39.
22 Spector 1985.
23 Smurthwaite 1995, p. 136.
24 Morison 1963, p. 586.
25 Swartz 1996.
26 Sunderman 1962.
27 Dingman 1980, p. 32.
28 Dower 1986.
29 Dingman 1980, pp. 32–33.
30 ibid., p. 34.
31 Converse 1984, p. 10.
32 Hayes et al. 1986, p. 19.
33 Payne 1951, p. 251.
34 Converse 1984, p. 176.
35 'US Requirements for Post-War Air Bases', 1943, p. 101 053.
36 ibid., p. 101 057.
37 Allen and Polmar 1995; Alperovitz 1995.
38 'Overall Effects of Atomic Bomb on Warfare and Military Organization', 1945, p. 6.
39 Swartz 1996.
40 Dingman 1980, p. 36.
41 *New York Times*, 30 December 1949.
42 Dingman, 1980, p. 37.
43 ibid., p. 39.
44 Schlight 1980, p. 161.
45 Myers 1996, pp. 34–36; Johnson 1996, pp. 37–39.
46 Leckie 1962, p. 30; Hayes et al. 1986, p. 400.
47 Strategic Air Command 1982, p. 44.
48 Leckie 1962, p. 31; Hayes et al. 1986, p. 37.
49 Leckie 1962, p. 30.
50 Graebner 1980, p. 59.
51 Leckie 1962, pp. 154–99.
52 ibid. pp. 200–33.
53 Acheson 1971, p. 129.
54 Schlight 1980, p. 167, note 14.
55 Donovan 1982, pp. 308–10; Hayes et al. 1986, pp. 53–54.
56 Rumbaugh et al. 1951.
57 'International Defense Commitments in the US Pacific Command', 1996.
58 Halperin 1966 , p. 53.

59 'Off Taiwan, US Sailors Are Unworried', *New York Times*, 19 March 1996.
60 Spector 1980, pp. 109–15.
61 Sheehan et al. 1971, p. 81.
62 ibid., pp. 234–306.
63 ibid., p. 385.
64 Karnow 1991, pp. 536–65.
65 ibid., pp. 628–85.
66 Maclear 1981, p. 312.
67 *A National Security Strategy of Engagement and Enlargement* 1995, pp. 12–13; *National Military Strategy of the United States of America: A Strategy of Flexible and Selective Engagement* 1995, pp. 13–16; see Chapter 2.
68 Berger 1977, p. 366.
69 Lavalle 1980.
70 Kissinger 1979, pp. 222–25.
71 Solomon and Kosaka 1986.
72 Eden and Miller 1989.
73 Watkins 1986; Hattendorf 1988, pp. 7–28.
74 Department of the Navy 1992, pp. 13–14.
75 Weinberger 1982, pp. 1–17.
76 Sakitt 1988; Stefanick 1987.
77 *The 600 Ship Navy and the Maritime Strategy: Hearings Before the Seapower and Strategic Materials Subcommittee of the House Armed Services Committee* 1986.
78 Kerr 1991.
79 Hersh 1987.
80 Mack and Keal 1988; Meconis and Wallace 1990.
81 Tritten 1992.

CHAPTER 2

1 *A Strategic Framework for the Asian Pacific Rim: Looking Toward the 21st Century* 1990, pp. 1–2.
2 ibid., p. 9.
3 ibid., pp. 3–6.
4 ibid., p. 8.
5 ibid.
6 ibid., pp. 9–10.
7 ibid., pp. 10–14.
8 ibid., pp. 15–21, emphasis added.
9 ibid., p. 22.
10 *A Strategic Framework for the Asian Pacific Rim: Report to Congress 1992*, pp. 13–14.
11 Tritten 1992, see Chapter 1.
12 ibid., pp. 29–30.

13 '1992 Joint Military Net Assessment', p. 22.
14 Tritten 1992, p. 27.
15 *A Strategic Framework for the Asian Pacific Rim: Report to Congress 1992*, pp. 1, 5.
16 ibid., pp. 13–22.
17 ibid., pp. 10–11.
18 ibid., pp. 8–9.
19 ibid., p. 28.
20 Aspin 1993, p. iii.
21 ibid., p. 7.
22 ibid.
23 ibid., emphasis added.
24 ibid., p. 19.
25 ibid., p. 13.
26 ibid., pp. 30–31.
27 ibid., pp. 23–24; 'US Naval Chief Rejects Idea of Asian Arms Race', Reuters, 2 May 1995.
28 Aspin 1993, p. 24.
29 ibid., p. 108.
30 *A National Security Strategy of Engagement and Enlargement* 1994, pp. i–iii.
31 *A National Security Strategy of Engagement and Enlargement* 1995, p. 8.
32 ibid., emphasis added.
33 ibid., pp. 3, 9.
34 ibid., p. 9.
35 ibid., p. 20.
36 *New York Times*, 20 November 1993.
37 *A National Security Strategy of Engagement and Enlargement* 1995, p. 28.
38 ibid.
39 ibid., p. 29.
40 *United States Security Strategy for the East Asia-Pacific Region* 1995, p. 5.
41 ibid., pp. 6–7.
42 Montaperto 1995, p. 18.
43 *United States Security Strategy for the East Asia-Pacific Region* 1995, p. 7.
44 ibid., p. 10.
45 ibid., pp. 10–12.
46 ibid., pp. 12–14.
47 'China Imports Reach New High', *Seattle Post-Intelligencer*, 20 February 1997.
48 *United States Security Strategy for the East Asia-Pacific Region* 1995, pp. 14–15.
49 ibid., pp. 15–16.

50 ibid., p. 20.
51 'US Policy on Spratly Islands and South China Sea', 1995.
52 *United States Security Strategy for the East Asia-Pacific Region* 1995, pp. 18–20.
53 ibid., pp. 16–17.
54 ibid., pp. 16–17, 20–22.
55 ibid., p. 23.
56 ibid., pp. 23–24.
57 ibid., pp. 25–29.
58 ibid., p. 29.
59 ibid., p. 32.
60 *National Military strategy of the United States of America: A Strategy of Flexible and Selective Engagement* 1995, preface.
61 ibid., pp. 4–5.
62 ibid., pp. 6–8.
63 ibid., pp. 8–9.
64 ibid., p. 10.
65 ibid., pp. 10–11.
66 ibid., p. 11.
67 ibid., p. 12.
68 ibid., p. 13.
69 ibid., p. 15.
70 ibid.
71 ibid., p. 16.
72 ibid., pp. 17–18.
73 ibid., p. 19.
74 'News Briefing on the Quadrennial Defense Review', 1996; *A National Security Strategy for a New Century*, 1997, pp. 5–13.
75 Cohen 1997a, Section III, pp. 8–10.
76 ibid., p. 7.
77 ibid., p. 15.
78 ibid., The Secretary's Message, pp. 6–7.
79 ibid., Section III, p. 11.
80 'News Release: Secretary Cohen Appoints National Defense Panel', 6 February 1997, p. 1.
81 'National Defense Panel: Assessment of the May 1997 Quadrennial Defense Review', 20 May 1997, p. 1; *Transforming Defense: National Security in the 21st Century*, 1997.
82 *National Military Strategy of the United States* 1997, pp. 11, 9.
83 ibid., pp. 19–20.
84 ibid., p. 18.

CHAPTER 3

1 *The Constitution of the United States of America: Literal Print* 1996, p. 9.

2 ibid., p. 13.
3 House Committee on Foreign Affairs 1994.
4 ibid.
5 *Hearings on Crisis in the Persian Gulf Region: US Policy Options and Implications* 1990, p.701.
6 'Overview of National Security Structure', 1997, p. 1.
7 *Goldwater-Nichols Department of Defense Reorganization Act 1986.*
8 'The Unified Combatant Commands', 1997
9 'Overview of National Security Structure', 1997, pp. 3–4.
10 'The Joint Chiefs of Staff (JCS)', 1997, p. 1.
11 *Joint Vision 2010* 1996, Introduction.
12 ibid., p. 1.
13 ibid., p. 20.
14 ibid., p. 21.
15 Owens 1995, p. 135.
16 *Joint Vision 2010* 1996, pp. 22–24.
17 ibid., p. 24.
18 ibid., pp. 24–25.
19 ibid., pp. 8–9.
20 ibid., p. 9.
21 'US Pacific Command 50th Anniversary' 1997, p. 2; 'USCINCPAC at a Glance', 1996, p. 3.
22 'USCINCPAC at a Glance',1996, p.1.
23 ibid., p. 2; 'Statement of Admiral Joseph W. Prueher, US Navy, Commander in Chief US Pacific Command', 4 March 1998, pp. 21–22.
24 'About GCCS', 1997.
25 ibid.
26 Conoley 1997, slide 3.
27 ibid. slides 5, 8–9.
28 ibid. slides 15.
29 ibid. slide 18.
30 ibid., slide 16.

CHAPTER FOUR

1 *Challenges to Naval Expeditionary Warfare* 1987, p. 7.
2 'Eielson AFB, Installation Overview', 1998, Office of the Secretary of Defense, online SITE database. Unless otherwise indicated, all the base information in this chapter comes from this official database. Its Internet address as of January 1998 is: http://dmdcu1.dmdc.osd.mil/sites/
3 'Special Action Committee on Okinawa Final Report', 1996.

CHAPTER 5

1. 'Press Briefing', White House, 11 April 1996.
2. Segal 1997, p. 305.
3. Aspin 1993, p. 57.
4. 'Navy Phasing Out Nuclear Rockets for Close Combat', *New York Times*, 30 April 1989; Ball 1985, pp. 103–31.
5. Blair 1995, pp. 20–21.
6. 'Presidential Initiative on Nuclear Arms', 27 September, 1991; CISSM 1991. With regard to the command structure issue, the US responded by placing all strategic nuclear weapons completely under the control of the newly formed US Strategic Command. The US Navy may have objected somewhat to this development, because it removed US ballistic missile submarine operations from direct naval command. Of course, the actual release of nuclear weapons themselves had always been, and remains, under the control of US National Command Authorities. From the US perspective, the main issue was central control of *Soviet* nuclear weapons following the attempted 1991 coup.
7. Arkin and Fieldhouse 1985, pp. 120, 231.
8. 'Airborne US A-Arms to Stay in South Korea', *Washington Post*, 12 October 1991.
9. 'No A-arms in S. Korea, Roh Says', *Washington Post*, 19 December 1991; 'Seoul Says It Now Has No Nuclear Arms', *New York Times*, 19 December 1991; *A Strategic Framework for the Asian Pacific Rim: Report to Congress 1992*; Lockwood 1994, p. 21; Lockwood 1997, p. 323. Further confirmation of the removal of all US nuclear weapons from South Korea is contained in the recently declassified portion of the 'USCINCPAC Command History 1991, Volume I', pp. 90–93, released under the Freedom of Information Act to the Nautilus Institute in October 1997.
10. 'Naval Nuclear Cuts', *Navy Times*, 14 October 1991.
11. 'US Navy Lost H-Bomb Off Okinawa in 1965', *Mainichi Daily News*, 9 May 1989.
12. 'President Bush's Nuclear Weapons Initiative on Nuclear Arms', 1992.
13. Arkin and Fieldhouse 1985, p. 221.
14. Arking, Norris and Handler 1998, pp. 70–71.
15. 'Naval Nuclear Cuts', *Navy Times*, 14 October 1991.
16. Gordon and Trainor, 1995.
17. Cheney 1990, p. 304.
18. Cheney 1992, p. 59.
19. Reed and Wheeler 1992.
20. 'United States Strategic Command: the Forces', 1997.
21. 'Defense Nuclear Weapons School', 1997.
22. '1992 Joint Net Military Assessment', p. 12.
23. Butler 1994, pp. 77, 79.

24 Blair 1995, p. 73.
25 'Doctrine for Joint Nuclear Operations', 1993, pp. I–2, I–3. Released under the Freedom of Information Act.
26 ibid., p. I–3.
27 ibid., p. II–2.
28 Aspin 1993, p. 6.
29 Kristensen and Handler 1995.
30 'Prohibition on Research and Development of Low-Yield Nuclear Weapons', 1993.
31 'Statement by the President on Advancing US Relations with Russia and the Other New Independent States', 1993.
32 'US Is Considering Aiming Its Missiles Away From Russia', *New York Times*, 6 December 1993.
33 'UK, Russia Agree to End Targeting', *Jane's Defence Weekly*, 26 February 1994.
34 Blair 1995, pp. 78–81; Ball and Richelson 1986.
35 *Nuclear Posture Review* Briefing Slides 1994, slide 2.
36 ibid., slide 15.
37 'Press Conference with Secretary of Defence William J. Perry, General Shalikashvili, Chairman, JCS, Deputy Secretary of Defence John Deutch, Mr Kenneth H. Bacon', 22 September 1994, p. 7.
38 ibid., p. 14.
39 *Nuclear Posture Review* Briefing Slides 1994, slide 15.
40 Aspin 1994, p. 59.
41 'Moscow Builds Bunkers Against Nuclear Attack', *Washington Times*, 1 April 1997.
42 Blair 1995, pp. 6–8, notes 10–14, p. 77.
43 ibid., p. 8, note 14.
44 ibid., p. 7.
45 Quoted in *Jane's Defence Weekly*, 18 February 1995 p. 56.
46 'Press Availability by President Clinton and President Jiang' Office of the Press Secretary, Beijing, 27 June 1998, p. 1. Concerning the 1996 Taiwan Strait Crisis, cf. the two articles by Barton Gellman in *The Washington Post*, 'US, China Nearly Came to Blows in '96', 21 June 1998, and 'Reappraisal Led to New China Policy' 22 June 1998.
47 'US already directed its missiles from China' *Seattle Post-Intelligencer*, 2 July 1998.
48 'Statement of Secretary Cyrus Vance', 1978, p. 52.
49 'Statement of Secretary Warren Christopher', 1995.
50 'Press Briefing', Office of the Press Secretary, 11 April 1996.
51 Bunn 1996, pp. 7–10.
52 'Air Force General Calls for End to Atomic Arms', *Boston Globe*, 16 July 1994.
53 Lockwood 1994, p. 22.
54 'United States Strategic Command: The Forces', 1997.
55 ibid.

56 'Press Conference with Secretary of Defense William J. Perry, General Shalikashvili, Chairman, JCS, Deputy Secretary of Defense John Deutch, Mr Kenneth H. Bacon', 22 September 1994, p. 8.
57 ibid., pp. 3–4, 8.
58 Brookings Institution 1997.
59 Blair 1995, p. 71, note 123; Friedman 1994, p. 15; as of March 1998, analysts at the Natural Resources Defense Council estimate that the United States retains 320 nuclear Tomahawks, cf. Arkin, Norris & Handler 1998.
60 'Navy Fact File', 1997.
61 Blair 1995, pp. 6–7, note 11; 'STRATCOM Offers to Play Role in Counterproliferation Target Planning', *Inside the Pentagon*, 15 December 1994.
62 'STRATCOM Sees New Role in WMD Targeting', *Jane's Defence Weekly*, 14 January 1995.
63 *Nuclear Posture Review* Briefing Slides 1994, slides 23–24.
64 ibid., slides 26–27.
65 'Factfile: Fifty Years of Nuclear Testing', 1995, pp. 33–35; 'Air Force Deploys "New" Earth-Penetrating Warhead', 1997, p. 29. In the face of US technological superiority with regard to destroying surface targets, potential adversaries are moving more of their vital assets to deep underground locations that may prove invulnerable to even the most accurate conventional weapons. Among the US responses, in the face of legislation barring 'new production' of nuclear warheads, is the version 11 modification of the B–61 nuclear bomb, which reportedly 'focuses' the warhead's explosive power in such a way as to achieve very deep underground penetration and destruction, while limiting 'collateral damage' to the surrounding surface area. Critics argue that this development amounts to a circumvention of the will of Congress.
66 'Opening Statement of Secretary of Energy Designate Federico Pena to the Committee on Armed Services', 1997.
67 'US Nuclear Weapons Plan Under Fire', *Los Angeles Times*, 19 February 1997.
68 Gottfried and Blair, eds 1988; Posen 1991.
69 *Nuclear Posture Review* Briefing Slides, September, 1994, slides 29–30. The installation of PALs on US ballistic missile submarines had long been sought by arms control advocates, and resisted by the US Navy.
70 ibid., slide 32.
71 Weinberger and Schweizer 1996.
72 Arkin 1995, p. 80; Blair 1995; Lockwood 1994b, pp. 27, 32.
73 Morimoto 1996, p. 132.
74 McNamara 1996.
75 'Report of the Canberra Commission on the Elimination of Nuclear Weapons', 1996, pp. 35–37.

76 'Retired Generals Re-Ignite Debate Over Abolition of Nuclear Weapons', 1996, p. 14; 'Move Grows to Ban All Nuclear Weapons—For All Time', *Boston Globe*, 25 December 1996.
77 'Denuclearization Drive May Imperil East Asian Security', *Defense News*, 6–12 January 1997.
78 'US Tells Russians It Is Ready to Negotiate Deeper Cuts in Nuclear Weapons', *New York Times*, 9 March 1997.
79 'Fact Sheet: Joint Statement on Parameters on Future Reductions in Nuclear Forces', 1997.
80 ibid.
81 'Background Briefing by a Senior Administration Official', 1997.
82 Gaffney 1997.
83 Quoted in *Inside the Navy*, 10 February 1997, pp. 1, 16–17.
84 Cohen 1997a, Section III, p. 6.
85 'US and Russians Agree to Put Off Arms Deadline Until 2007', *New York Times*, 27 September 1997.
86 'Clinton Directive Changes Strategy on Nuclear Arms', *Washington Post*, 7 December 1997.
87 ibid.
88 Kristensen 1998.
89 'Study Backed "Irrational View" on Nuclear Policy', *Seattle Post-Intelligencer*, 2 March 1998.
90 Quoted in 'Clinton Directive Changes Strategy on Nuclear Arms', *Washington Post*, 7 December 1997

CHAPTER 6

1 'Navy Organization: Mission of the Navy', 1997.
2 Title 10, US Code.
3 'Navy Organization: The Operating Forces', 1997; 'Status of the Navy', 2 March 1998.
4 'Navy Organization: The Shore Establishment', 1997.
5 'The United States Marine Corps: Roles and Missions, Organization' in *Forces/Capabilities Handbook Volume I: Organizations* 1993, pp. 5–1, 5–2; Cohen, 1997, p. 167.
6 'Power from the Sea', 27 August 1992, unpublished draft.
7 Watkins 1986. The Maritime Strategy generated a wide-ranging debate about its feasibility and desirability. For a comprehensive annotated bibliography, see Swartz and Breemer eds, 'The Maritime Strategy Debates: A Guide to the Renaissance of US Naval Strategic Thinking in the 1980s', 1989; also see Pauline Kerr 1991 for a survey of 1980s US naval operations in the North Pacific.
8 *From the Sea* 1992, p. 2.
9 ibid.
10 ibid.
11 ibid., p. 3.

12 ibid., p. 4.
13 ibid., p. 5.
14 ibid., p. 5.
15 Cushman 1993, p. 47.
16 *From the Sea* 1992, p. 6.
17 *Forward ... From the Sea* 1994, p. 1.
18 ibid., p. 5.
19 ibid., pp. 1, 8.
20 'The Navy Operational Concept', 1997, p. 3.
21 ibid., pp. 3–4.
22 ibid., pp. 5–6.
23 ibid., pp. 7–8.
24 Krulak 1997, p. 4.
25 ibid., p. 5.
26 Krulak 1997b, p. 27.
27 *The 600 Ship Navy and the Maritime Strategy: Hearings Before the Seapower and Strategic Materials Subcommittee of the House Armed Services Committee* 1986.
28 Aspin 1993, p. 28.
29 Cohen 1997a, Section V, p. 1; 1998b, p. 30. Some analysts predict a 300 ship US Navy by the year 2000.
30 *Navy Carrier Battlegroups: The Structure and Affordability of the Future Force* 1993.
31 'US Atlantic Fleet Fact Sheet', 1997.
32 'Status of the US Pacific Fleet as of July 24, 1998'.
33 'Third Fleet: Mission and Capability, Area of Responsibility, Assets, Operations, Carrier Battle Group, Amphibious Ready Group', 1997.
34 'US Seventh Fleet: Facts, Composition, Forward Deployed Units, Forward Presence', 1997.
35 *US Marine Forces Pacific Command Brief* 1998, p. 5; *Forces/Capabilities Handbook Volume I: Organizations* 1993, section 5, pp. 3–4.
36 ibid., pp. 5–7.
37 ibid., pp. 9–12; *US Marine Forces Pacific Command Brief* 1998, p. 6.
38 *US Marine Forces Pacific Command Brief* 1998, pp. 4–22.
39 'Carrier: Powerhouse of the Fleet', 1997, pp. 1–2; 'Navy Fact File: Aircraft Carriers—CV, CVN', 1997, pp. 1–7.
40 'Carrier Air Wings and Squadrons', 1997.
41 'Navy Fact File: F–14 *Tomcat*; Aim–7 *Sparrow* Missile; AIM–9 *Sidewinder* Missile; AIM–120 Advanced Medium Range, Air-to-Air Missile (AMRAAM)', 1997.
42 Kennedy 1997, p. 126; Bathrick 1997, p. 74.
43 'Navy Fact File: F/A–18 *Hornet*; *Harpoon* and *Harpoon/SLAM* Missile Systems', 1997.
44 'F/A-18-E/F *Super Hornet* ... Leading Naval Aviation into the 21st Century', 1997.
45 'Navy Fact File: E–2C *Hawkeye*', 1997.

46 ibid., 'EA–6B *Prowler*'; 'AGM–88 HARM Missile System', 1997.
47 *Worldwide Challenges to Naval Strike Warfare* 1997.
48 'Navy Fact File: *Tomahawk* Cruise Missile'; Friedman 1991, pp. 120–22, 809–10.
49 *Challenges to Naval Expeditionary Warfare* 1997, p. 4.
50 'Navy Fact File: Aegis Combat System; Cruisers CG-CGN; Destroyers DD-DDG', 1997; Friedman 1991, pp. 337–38.
51 'Navy Fact File: Standard Missile'; Friedman 1994, pp. 42–43.
52 'Investigation Report: Formal Investigation into the Circumstances Surrounding the Downing of Iran Air Flight 655 on 3 July 1988' 1988; 'Navy Intercepts Ballistic Missile; Accelerated TBMD Program' 1997.
53 'Navy Fact File: Mine Countermeasures Vessels; CH–53A/D and RH–53D *Sea Stallion*', 1997; Truver 1997, pp. 90–94. Many US Navy officers believe that the real solution to the mine problem is to equip all Navy combatant ships as soon as possible with new technologies for integral mine detection and avoidance. Consequently, the US Navy has decided to begin 'mainstreaming' mine countermeasures by spreading elements of that capability across the fleet, chiefly by giving the widely used SH–60 helicopter an MCM capability. With regard to offensive mining, the need for a new medium-depth littoral mine is being addressed.
54 Broughton and Burdon 1998, pp. 56–57.
55 'Navy Fact File: 'Amphibious Assault Ships'; 'Amphibious Transport Dock-LPD'; 'Dock Landing Ship', 1997.
56 'Navy Fact File: Landing Craft, Air Cushioned; V–22A *Osprey*', 1997; 'United States Marine Corps Fact File: Assault Amphibian Vehicle Personnel Model 7A1; CH–46E *Sea Knight* Helicopter', 1996; *Challenges to Naval Expeditionary Warfare* 1997, p. 31.
57 Gordon and Trainor 1995, pp. 355–74.
58 'United States Marine Corps Fact File: Light Armored Vehicle–25; AV–8B *Harrier II*; AH–1W *Super Cobra*', 1995.
59 'Navy Fact File: Attack Submarines', 1997; Sharpe 1994, pp. 772–74.
60 'Navy Fact File: SH–60 *Seahawk*; S–3B *Viking*; P–3C *Orion*; Torpedoes', 1997; *Submarine Challenges* 1997.
61 'Command Brief CincPacFlt Plans and Policy', 1997, slides 1–37; *1997 Posture Statement: The Navy-Marine Corps Team, Enduring Impact...From the Sea* 1997, section III, pp. 6, 9. Recent press reports have revealed the seriousness of this crisis in detail. Cf. 'US, China Nearly Came To Blows in '96', *The Washington Post*, 21 June 1998.
62 Truver 1997, p. 90.

CHAPTER 7

1 'Organization of the United States Air Force', 1995, p. 2.
2 ibid.
3 ibid., pp. 3–6.

4 Tritten 1992, p. 97.
5 'Global Engagement: A Vision for the 21st Century Air Force', 1996, p. 2.
6 ibid., p. 2.
7 ibid., p. 3.
8 *On Orbit: United States Space Command* 1997.
9 'Global Engagement: A Vision for the 21st Century Air Force', 1996, p. 4.
10 ibid., Appendix 1.
11 ibid., p. 5.
12 ibid.
13 Fogelman 1996, pp. 5–6.
14 'US Navy Exercise to Assess Firepower of Carriers', *Defense News*, 24 February–2 March, 1997, pp. 3, 18.
15 'Global Engagement: A Vision for the 21st Century Air Force', 1996, Appendix 2; *Air Force Issue Book 1997*, Part Two, pp. 8–10; 'USAF Air Power Move into Qatar is "Routine"', *Jane's Defence Weekly*, 12 February 1997, p. 5.
16 'Global Engagement: A Vision for the 21st Century Air Force', 1996, Appendix 4.
17 ibid.
18 'Global Engagement: A Vision for the 21st Century Air Force', 1996, Appendix 6.
19 ibid., pp. 5–6.
20 ibid., p. 8.
21 Cohen 1998b, Appendix C.
22 'United States Air Forces in Europe', 1997.
23 Air Force News Service 1995a, 'Pacific Air Forces'.
24 Berger 1977, pp. 366–67.
25 Air Force News Service 1995a, 'Pacific Air Forces'; Lorber 1996, p. 18.
26 'Pacific Air Forces', *Airman*, January 1997, vol. 13 no. 1, online version; Lorber 1996, online version, p. 19.
27 ibid., p. 18.
28 Lorber 1996a, pp. 16–25; 1996b, online version.
29 Stephens 1997, pp. 26–27; Ball 1993, pp. 78–112. As the decade draws to a close, the figure of 3000 seems to be unrealistically high, especially in the light of the 1997/1998 financial crisis in East Asia. The basic point remains valid, however.
30 'Regional Security through Air Power diplomacy', *The Straits Times*, 1 May 1997, online version.
31 Lorber 1996a, pp. 24–25.
32 Novichkov and Mann, 1997; IISS 1996, p. 105.
33 Estes 1997.
34 Gordon and Trainor 1995, pp. 26, 228.
35 ibid., p. 325.
36 ibid., p. 338.

37 Boeing Company, 'E-3 AWACS in Service Worldwide', Seattle, Washington, 13 May 1997, pp. 1-10; '767 AWACS' 13 May 1997, p.5; 'Boeing wins orders worth $3 billion: S. Korea, Kuwait buying military aircraft', *Seattle Post-Intelligencer*, 4 September 1997; 'Japan takes delivery of first Boeing 767 AWACS', *Jane's Defence Weekly*, 18 March 1998. The South Korean AWACS procurement has been postponed due to the regional economic crisis. *Jane's Defence Weekly*, 18 February 1998, p. 21.
38 Air Force News Service 1996c, 'E-3 *Sentry* (AWACS)', pp. 1-3.
39 'Mildenhall Units Reach Flying Milestone', Air force News Service, 17 October 1996; 'Gen. Moorman Flies Rivet Joint', Air Force News Service, 5 February 1997; 'RC-135 Flies 1000th Mission in SWA', Air Force News Service, 22 February 1997.
40 Gordon and Trainor 1995, pp. 237, 267, 278, 363, 383, 406, 436.
41 'Joint STARS: Opening the Door to the Future', 1996; 'Joint STARS Returns from First Deployment', Air Force News Agency, 30 January 1997.
42 Cohen 1997, pp. 21, 179; 'USA Seeks Larger Force for Ground Surveillance' *Jane's Defence Weekly*, 18 March 1998, p. 8.
43 Air Force News Service 1996e, 'U-2R/U-2S'; Ball 1995, pp. 30-31; *Airman*, June 1996, online version.
44 US Air Force UAV Battlelab 1997, 'Endurance UAVs'; 'Air Force Unveils *Predator* UAV', Air Force News Agency, 31 January 1997. Note: In 1997 the Air Force News Service changed its name to Air Force News Agency, but for the sake of clarity the former name has been retained in these notes and in the bibliography.
45 'One on One with General Howell Estes—Commander in Chief US Space Command', *Defence News*, 6 May 1997.
46 *Air Force Issues Book 1997* Part 3, p. 18.
47 Air Force News Service 1991, 'Airpower in Operation Desert Storm', Special Edition.
48 Gordon and Trainor 1995, pp. 105-105, 218-19.
49 Watts 1996, pp. 93-104.
50 Air Force News Service 1997c, 'Air Education and Training Command'; 'F-117 Pilot Logs 1000 Hours', Air Force News Service, 2 November 1996; 'Pilot with Most F-16 Flying Hours Honored', Air Force News Service, 10 December 1996.
51 *Aviation Week and Space Technology*, 10 February 1997, p. 22.
52 Boeing Company, 'F-22 Air Dominance Fighter', 5 November 1996, pp. 1-4.
53 Cohen 1997a, Introduction, p. 7.
54 Air Force News Service 1996a, 'F-117A *Nighthawk*'; Gordon and Trainor 1995, pp. 117-18, 205-20, 495, note 6; 'Nighthawks over Iraq: A Chronology of the F-117A Stealth Fighter in operations DESERT SHIELD and DESERT STORM', 1991.
55 Air Force News Service 1994, 'GBU-15'.

56 Lorber 1996, p. 4.
57 Air Force News Service 1991, 'Airpower in Operation DESERT STORM' Special Edition; Gordon and Trainor 1995, pp. 473–74; Keaney and Cohen 1993.
58 Air Force News Service 1996b, 'B–52 Stratofortress'.
59 Air Force News Service 1997a, 'B–1B *Lancer*'. These aircraft would not be available for nuclear missions on short notice, but they could be returned to a nuclear role given sufficient time and a requirement to do so. Cf. Cohen 1997, p. 209.
60 'B–2 Reaches Initial Operational Capability', Office of the Assistant Secretary of Defense (Public Affairs), 1 April 1997.
61 ibid.
62 Air Force News Service 1997b, 'Stealth Bomber Makes Asian Debut'. In March 1998, two B–2s were forward deployed to Andersen Air Force Base on Guam for one week of training. *Jane's Defence Weekly*, 25 March 1998.
63 Horner 1997, p. 6.
64 Air Force News Service 1991, 'Airpower in Operation DESERT STORM,' Special Edition; 1992,'F–16 *Fighting Falcon*'.
65 Air Force News Service 1991, 'Airpower in Operation DESERT STORM,' Special Edition, 1991; 1992a, 'F–15 *Eagle*'.
66 Air Force News Service 1996f, 'A–10/OA–10 *Thunderbolt II*'; Smallwood 1993.
67 Gordon and Trainor 1995; Keaney and Cohen 1993.
68 Cohen 1998b, Appendix C.
69 Air Force News Service 1991, 'Airpower in Operation DESERT STORM,' Special Edition.
70 *Air Force Posture Statement 1988*, p. 21.
71 ibid.; 'Air Force Admits It's Running Out of Spare Parts', CNN, 7 August 1997; 'Pilots Stressed—Air Force Cutting Down Their Flights', *Seattle Post-Intelligencer*, 20 August 1997; 'It's Raining on US Air Force Parade', Reuters, 18 September 1997.

CHAPTER 8

1 'Army Mission and Vision', 1997, p. 1.
2 West and Reimer 1997, Chapter 2, p. 4.
3 'US Army Major Commands (MACOM) Online', 1997.
4 'Army Mission and Vision', 1997, p. 1.
5 *Army Vision 2010* 1997, p. 1.
6 ibid., p. 2.
7 ibid., p. 3.
8 ibid., pp. 3–4.
9 ibid., pp. 5–7.
10 ibid., p. 7.
11 ibid., pp. 8–9.

12 ibid., p. 10. A 1993 article in *US Naval Institute Proceedings* by retired US Air Force Colonel James G. Burton charged that the US Army failed to completely destroy the elite Iraqi Republican Guard at the end of the Gulf War due to its insistence on 'synchronization', a carefully phased, sequential advance of forces. The article ignited an intense six-month debate in that journal's subsequent issues. Cf. Burton, J. 'Pushing Them Out the Back Door', *US Naval Institute Proceedings*, vol. 119/6/1084 (June 1993), pp. 37–42, and following issues through January 1994.
13 *Army Vision 2010* 1997, p.10.
14 West and Reimer 1997, Chapter 2, pp. 1–2.
15 ibid.; *Army Vision 2010* 1997, p. 11.
16 ibid., pp. 12–14.
17 ibid., pp. 14–15.
18 ibid., pp. 15–16.
19 ibid., pp. 17–18.
20 West and Reimer 1997, Chapter 2, p. 1.
21 Brinkerhoff 1997, pp. 60–63; 1996, pp. 4–7; 'A Handout on US Army Organization for Combat', 1995, pp. 1–8.
22 Brinkerhoff 1996, pp. 4–7; Armylink online divisional information.
23 *PACOM Digest* 1996.
24 'USFK Mission Statement, United Nations Command History, Combined Forces Command History, USFK History', 1997.
25 '2nd Infantry Division: Mission and Training, History', 1997, online version.
26 ibid.
27 ibid.
28 'United States Army Pacific: America's Army in the Pacific', 1997; 'US Army Japan and 9th Theater Army Area Command', 1997.
29 ibid.
30 'Arctic Warrior Brigade', 1997.
31 '25th Light Infantry Division', 1997.
32 Gordon and Trainor 1995, pp. 54–57.
33 *Certain Victory: The US Army in the Gulf War* 1993, pp. 87–88.
34 Cohen 1997, pp. 22–23.
35 Gordon and Trainor 1995, pp. 375–432.
36 *United States Army Weapons Systems*, 1995, 'Air-to Ground Missile System', '*Apache*', '*Hellfire* II Missile', '*Longbow Apache*'.
37 Gordon and Trainor 1995, pp. 209–10, 340, 403, 411–12.
38 *United States Army Weapons Systems*, 1995, '*Black Hawk* UH–60'.
39 Gordon and Trainor 1995, p. 510, note 6, citing figures from the VIIth Corps Report 'Operation DESERT STORM: A Fire Support Perspective.'
40 *United States Army Weapons Systems*, 1995, 'Multiple Launch Rocket System (MLRS)', 'Extended Range Multiple Launch Rocket System (ER-MLRS)', 'Army Tactical Missile System (Army TACMS)'.

41 Gordon and Trainor 1995, pp. 407–408, 390–93. The M1s reportedly needed to be topped off 'every eight or nine hours'.
42 *United States Army Weapons Systems*, 1995, 'Abrams Tank'.
43 ibid., 'Bradley Fighting Vehicle'; 'TOW Weapons System'.
44 Gordon and Trainor, p. 457. To this day controversy persists over the number of Iraqi casualties, with some giving figures as high as 100 000+ military and 30 000 civilian deaths and others giving much lower estimates.
45 ibid., pp. 64–65, 305–308, 346, 353–54, 361–68; Army News Service, *Army Link News*, 'Chemical Corps, MPs Head to Hood for Advanced Warfighter Exercise', 16 September 1997, online version.
46 Joseph, Dr S. 1997. For several years the Pentagon denied that there was any truth to complaints from Gulf War veterans about after-effects from the war. Outside researchers helped prompt an official recognition that the episode at Khamisiya was significant.
47 Gordon and Trainor 1995, Chapter 11 'The Great Scud Hunt', pp. 227–48.
48 *United States Army Weapons Systems*, 1995, 'Patriot', 'Theater High Altitude Area Defence/Ground-Based Radar (THAAD/GBR)'; Cohen 1997a, The Secretary's Message, p. 7.
49 *United States Army Weapons Systems*, 1995, 'National Missile Defense (NMD)'; Cohen 1997a, The Secretary's Message, pp. 7–8, online version.
50 Allard 1995, pp. 13–18.
51 ibid., pp. 18–20.
52 ibid., pp. 30–31; US Army Special Operations Command, *SINE PARI Without Equal: The Story of Army Special Operations*, Directorate of History and Museums, 1995, p. 13.
53 ibid.
54 'History of the 10th Mountain Division', 1997, p. 5.
55 Allard 1995, pp. 19–20.
56 ibid., pp. 63, 90.
57 Cohen 1997, p. 197.
58 'Special Operations Command' (SOCOM), 1997, Department of Defense, *Fact File*; 'An Army Special Operations Forces Primer', 1997, US Army Special Operations Command, 8 August, online version.
59 Cohen 1997, pp. 193–94.
60 ibid., p. 197; 1998b, pp. 51–56; '1st Special Forces Group (Airborne) History', 1997.
61 Cohen 1997, p. 197.
62 ibid.
63 'Navy SEALs: Overview, Training', 1997.
64 Cohen 1997, p. 197; *SOF Vision 2020*, 1998.
65 ibid.; Air Force News Service,1995, 'Air Force Special Operations Command'; 1995d, 'MC-130E/H *Combat Talon I/II*'; 1996d, 'MC-

130P *Combat Shadow*'; 1995f, 'MH–53J *Pave Low IIIE*'; 1995e, 'MH–60G *Pave Hawk*'; 1995c, 'AC–130H *Spectre*'.
66 Cohen 1997, p. 197; Howard and Nelson 1996, pp. 18–27; 'Guiding US Military into a New Era: Clinton Picks Shelton to Head Joint Chiefs', *Seattle Post-Intelligencer*, 18 July 1997.

CHAPTER 9

1 Cohen 1998, p. 2., emphasis added.
2 'US Economic Relations with East Asia and the Pacific', 1997, pp. 1–3.
3 Cohen 1998, p. 12; Cohen 1998, p. 5.
4 'Kurt Campbell Interview on Asia-Pacific Security', 1998, p. 2.
5 *A National Security Strategy for a New Century* 1997, p. 23.
6 'DOD News Briefing: Defense Guidelines Review', 1997, p. 1.
7 'Completion of the Review of the Guidelines for US–Japan Defense Cooperation' 1997.
8 'The Guidelines for US–Japan Defense Cooperation' 1997, Section V.
9 'US and Japan Agree to Bolster Military Ties for Regional Crises,' *New York Times*, 24 September 1997; Cohen 1998b, p. 2.
10 Cohen 1998, p. 3.
11 ibid., p. 4.
12 Cohen 1998b, p. 3.
13 ibid., p. 4; 'Agreement Between the Department of Defense of the United States of America and the Ministry of National Defense of the People's Republic of China on Establishing a Consultation Mechanism to Strengthen Military Maritime Safety', 19 January 1998, Beijing; 'Cohen Hails Achievements in China Visit', *Washington Post*, 20 January 1998; 'Cohen Warns China on Iran Threat' *New York Times*, 19 January 1998.
14 'A Korean Leader for These Times', *Los Angeles Times*, 23 December 1997.
15 'New South Korean President Banking on Democracy', *Seattle Post-Intelligencer*, 13 January 1998.
16 Cohen 1997b, Section VII, p. 1.
17 ibid.
18 *Strategic Assessment 1997: Flashpoints and Force Structure*, pp. 264–86.
19 'Weak Procurement Outlook Belies Potential Growth Areas', *Aviation Week and Space Technology*, 15 December 1997, pp. 66–67.
20 *Transforming Defense: National Security in the 21st Century* 1997, p. ii.
21 ibid., p. iii.
22 ibid., pp. 1–7, 21.
23 Cohen 1997b, p. 3.
24 'Department of Defense Budget for FY 1999', 1998, p. 1.

25 Cohen 1997b, p. 4; 'NDP Chairman Sees Little Change in Defense Strategy in Near Term', *Defense Daily*, 16 January, 1998, p. 1.
26 Cohen 1997a, Secretary's Message, p. 7.
27 ibid., Section VII, pp. 10–11.
28 'Joint Strike Fighter News Briefing', 16 November 1996; 'Department of Defense Budget for FY 1999', 2 February 1998; 'Joint Strike Fighter Fighting Superiority', 1997, the Boeing Company.
29 'Navy Fact File: Amphibious Transport Dock-LPD', 1998; 'LPD–17— The Navy's Next Generation Amphib', 1997, pp. 33–12 to 39–19.
30 Krulak 1997d, pp. 6–7.
31 *Transforming Defense: National Security in the 21st Century* 1997, p. 34; Cohen 1997b, Section VII, p. 2.
32 *Proliferation: Threat and Response*, 1997, Section I, pp. 1–12.
33 Kaminsky 1997, pp. 1–11; Cohen 1997b, Secretary's Message, p. 7, Section VII, pp. 3–4, 14.
34 *Proliferation: Threat and Response* 1997, Section II, p. 12.
35 Cohen 1997a, Section VII, p. 16.
36 *Proliferation: Threat and Response* 1997, Section II, pp. 27–32.
37 'US Plan Shows New Work on Designs for Nuclear Arms', *New York Times*, 18 August 1997.
38 *Proliferation: Threat and Response* 1997, Section II, pp. 31–32.
39 The only publicly available information about Delta Force comes from those few occasions when its operations received after-the-event media coverage, such as the failed 1979 attempt to rescue US hostages in Tehran, various operations during the 1991 Gulf War, and the costly raid in downtown Somalia in 1994. Cf., for example, Gordon and Trainor 1995, pp. 242–46 for a description of the role of Delta Force in hunting Iraqi Scuds and the extraordinary series about the Somalia raid entitled 'Blackhawk Down' in the *Philadelphia Enquirer* in January–February 1998.
40 Cohen 1997a, Section VII, p. 17.
41 *Proliferation: Threat and Response* 1997, Section II, pp. 32–35.
42 Cohen 1997a, Section III, p. 16; Section VII, p. 8.
43 ibid., Section VII, p. 7; Podlesny 1998, pp. 50–53; Van Riper 1997, p. A–1.
44 *A Strategic Framework for the Asian-Pacific Rim*,1990, p. 16; *Strategic Assessment 1997: Flashpoints and Force Structure*, p. 106.
45 'Backer of US Base Wins in Okinawa', *Seattle Post-Intelligencer*, 9 February 1998; 'Okinawa Governor Opposes Plans for US Heliport', *Los Angeles Times*, 7 February 1998; 'Japan Blasts Okinawa Refusal of US Heliport', Reuters, 6 February 1998; 'Okinawa Town Defiantly Rejects a New US Base', *New York Times*, 22 December 1997.
46 'Greater China', *Financial Times*, 16 January 1998, p. 13; 'DOD News Briefing and Press Conference on US–Philippines Visiting Forces Agreement', 1998.

Bibliography

BOOKS AND BOOK CHAPTERS

Acheson, Dean, 1971, *The Korean War*, W. W. Norton & Company, New York

Allard, K., 1995, *Somalia Operations: Lessons Learned*, National Defense University Press, Ft. McNair, Washington DC

Allen, Thomas B. & Norman Polmar, 1995, *Code-Name Down-Fall: The Secret Plan to Invade Japan—and Why Truman Dropped the Bomb*, Simon & Schuster, New York

Alperovitz, Gar, 1995, *The Decision to Use the Atomic Bomb and the Architecture of an American Myth*, Harper Collins, London

Arkin, William M. and Richard W. Fieldhouse, 1985, *Nuclear Battlefields: Global Links in the Arms Race*, Ballinger Publishing, Cambridge, Massachusetts

Arkin, William M., Robert S. Norris and Joshua Handler, 1998, *Taking Stock: Worldwide Nuclear Deployments 1998*, Natural Resources Defense Council, Inc., Washington DC

Ball, Desmond, 1995, *Signals Intelligence (SIGINT) in South Korea*, Strategic and Defence Studies Centre, Research School of Pacific and Asian Studies, The Australian National University, Canberra

Ball, Desmond and Jeffrey Richelson eds., 1986, *Strategic Nuclear Targeting*, Cornell University Press, Ithaca, New York

Berger, Carl ed., 1977, *The United States Air Force in Southeast Asia 1961–1973*, Office of Air Force History, Washington DC

Blair, Bruce G. 1995, *Global Zero Alert for Nuclear Forces*, Brookings Institution, Washington DC

Converse, Elliott, 1984, *United States Plans for a Postwar Overseas Base System, 1942–1948*, PhD dissertation, Department of History, Princeton University Press, Princeton, New Jersey

Cossa, Ralph, 1997, 'Nuclear Forces in the Far East: Status and Implications for Proliferation', in *Peace and Security in Northeast Asia: The Nuclear Issue and the North Korean Peninsula*, Young

Whan Kihl and Peter Hayes eds, M.E. Sharpe, Armonk, New York, pp. 359–80

Dingman, Roger, 1980, 'American Policy and Strategy in East Asia 1898–1950: The Creation of a Commitment', in *The American Military and the Far East*, ed. Joe C. Dixon, US Government Printing Office, Washington DC, pp. 20–45

Donovan, Robert, 1982, *The Tumultuous Years*, Norton, New York

Dower, John W., 1986, *War without Mercy: Race and Power in the Pacific War*, Pantheon Books, New York

Eden, Lynn and Steven E. Miller eds, 1989, *Nuclear Arguments: Understanding the Strategic Nuclear Arms and Arms Control Debates*, Cornell University Press, Ithaca, New York

Flint, Roy R., 1980, 'The United States Army on the Pacific Frontier, 1899–1929', in *The American Military and the Far East*, ed. Joe C. Dixon, US Government Printing Office, Washington DC, pp. 139–59

Friedman, Donald, 1968, *The Road from Isolationism: The Campaign of the American Committee for Non-Participation in Japanese Aggression 1938–1941*, Harvard University Press, Cambridge, Massachusetts

Friedman, Norman, 1991, *The Naval Institute Guide to World Naval Weapons Systems 1991/2*, Naval Institute Press, Annapolis, Maryland

—— 1994, *The Naval Institute Guide to World Naval Weapons Systems 1994 Update*, Naval Institute Press, Annapolis, Maryland

Gates, John M., 1980, 'The Pacification of the Philippines' in *The American Military and the Far East*, ed. Joe C. Dixon, US Government Printing Office, Washington DC, pp. 79–91

Gordon Michael R. & General Bernard E. Trainor, 1995 *The Generals' War*, Little, Brown & Company, Boston

Gottfried, Kurt & Bruce G. Blair, 1988, *Crisis Stability and Nuclear War*, Oxford University Press, New York

Graebner, Norman A., 1980, 'The United States and East Asia, 1945–1960: The Evolution of a Commitment', in *The American Military and the Far East*, ed. Joe C. Dixon, US Government Printing Office, Washington DC, pp. 46–64

Hagan, Kenneth J., 1973, *American Gunboat Diplomacy and the Old Navy 1877–1889*, Greenwood, Westport, Connecticut

Halperin, Morton, 1966, *The 1958 Taiwan Straits Crisis*, Rand, Santa Monica

Hayes, Peter et al., 1986, *American Lake: Nuclear Peril in the Pacific*, Viking Penguin, New York

Hayes Peter and Young Whan Kihl eds, 1997, *Peace and Security in Northeast Asia*, M. E. Sharpe, Armonk, New York

Hersh, Seymour M., 1987, *'The Target Is Destroyed': What Really Happened to Flight 007 and What America Knew About It*, Vintage Books, New York

IISS, 1996, *The Military Balance 1996/97*, Oxford University Press, London
Karnow, Stanley, 1991, *Vietnam: A History*, revised and updated edition, Penguin, New York
Kaufman, Robert Gordon, 1990, *Arms Control During the Pre-Nuclear Era: The United States and Naval Limitation Between the Two World Wars*, Columbia University Press, New York
Kerr, Pauline, 1991, *Eyeball to Eyeball: US & Soviet Naval & Air Operations in the North Pacific 1981–1990*, Peace Research Centre, Australian National University, Canberra
Kissinger, Henry, 1979, *The White House Years*, Little, Brown and Company, Boston
Kristensen, Hans, 1998, *Nuclear Futures: Proliferation of Weapons of Mass Destruction and US Nuclear Strategy*, The British American Security Information Council, London
Lavalle, Lt. Col. Jack ed., 1980 *Air War Vietnam*, Bobbs-Merrill, New York
Leckie, Robert, 1962, *Conflict: The History of the Korean War 1950–1953*, Avon, New York
Lockwood, Dunbar, 1997, 'The Status of US, Russian, and Chinese Nuclear Forces in Northeast Asia', in *Peace and Security in Northeast Asia: The Nuclear Issue and the North Korean Peninsula*, Young Whan Kihl and Peter Hayes eds, M. E. Sharpe, Armonk, New York, pp. 318–58
McNamara, Robert, 1996, 'Next Steps in Arms Control: How Far, How Fast?', in *Next Steps in Arms Control and Non-Proliferation: Final Report of the US–Japan Study Group on Arms Control and Proliferation After the Cold War*, eds William Clark, Jr and Ryukichi Imai, Carnegie Endowment/Brookings Institution Press, Washington, DC, pp. 111–16
Mack, Andrew & Paul Keal eds, 1988, *Security & Arms Control in the North Pacific*, Allen & Unwin, Sydney
Maclear, Michael, 1981, *The Ten Thousand Day War: Vietnam 1945–1975*, St Martin's New York
Meconis, Charles A. & Michael D. Wallace, 1990, 'Naval Rivalry and Command Survivability', in *Superpower Maritime Strategy in the Pacific*, eds Frank C. Langdon & Douglas A. Ross, Routledge, London, pp. 131–53
Montaperto, Ronald, 1995, 'Asia Pacific', ed. Patrick Clawson, in *Strategic Assessment 1995: US Security Challenges in Transition*, Institute for National Strategic Studies, National Defense University, Washington DC, pp. 17–30
Morimoto, Satoshi, 1996, 'US Nuclear Strategy: Adapting to the New World Disorder', in *Next Steps in Arms Control and Non-Proliferation: Final Report of the US–Japan Study Group on Arms Control and Proliferation After the Cold War*, eds William

Clark, Jr. and Ryukichi Imai, Carnegie Endowment/Brookings Institution Press, Washington, DC, pp. 127–35

Morison, Samuel Eliot, 1963, *The Two-Ocean War: A Short History of the United States Navy in the Second World War*, Little, Brown & Company, Boston

Owens, Admiral William A., 1995, *High Seas: The Naval Passage to an Uncharted World*, Naval Institute Press, Annapolis, Maryland

Payne, Robert, 1951, *The Marshall Story*, Prentice Hall, New York

Posen, Barry, 1991, *Inadvertent Escalation: Conventional War and Nuclear Risks*, Cornell University Press, Ithaca, New York

Sakitt, Mark, 1988, *Submarine Warfare in the Arctic: Option or Illusion?*, Center for International Security and Arms Control, Stanford University, Stanford, California

Schlight, John, 1980, 'The Impact of the Orient on Airpower', in *The American Military and the Far East*, ed. Joe C. Dixon, US Government Printing Office, Washington DC, pp. 160–71

Schratz, Paul R., 1980, 'The Orient and US Naval Strategy', in *The American Military and the Far East*, ed. Joe C. Dixon, US Government Printing Office, Washington DC, pp. 127–38

Segal, Gerald, 1997, 'Nuclear Forces in Northeast Asia', in *Peace and Security in Northeast Asia: The Nuclear Issue and the North Korean Peninsula*, Young Whan Kihl and Peter Hayes eds, M. E. Sharpe, Armonk, New York, pp. 305–17

Sharpe, Richard, 1994, *Jane's Fighting Ships 1994–95*, Jane's Information Group, Surrey, United Kingdom

Sheehan, Neil et al., 1971, *The Pentagon Papers as Reported by the New York Times*, Bantam, New York

Simmons, Edwin H., 1980, 'Commentary: Marines in East Asia', in *The American Military and the Far East*, ed. Joe C. Dixon, US Government Printing Office, Washington DC, pp. 172–76

Smallwood, William L., 1993, *Warthog: Flying the A–10 in the Gulf War*, Brassey's US, Washington DC

Smurthwaite, David, 1995, *The Pacific War Atlas 1941–1945*, Facts on File, New York.

Solomon, Richard H. and Masataka Kosaka, 1986, *The Soviet Far East Military Buildup: Nuclear Dilemmas and Asian Security*, Auburn House, Dover Massachusetts

Spector, Ronald, 1980, 'The First Vietnamization: US Advisors in Vietnam, 1956–1960', in *The American Military and the Far East*, ed. Joe C. Dixon, US Government Printing Office, Washington DC, pp. 109–15

——1985, *Eagle Against the Sun: The American War with Japan*, Free Press, New York

Stefanick, Tom, 1987, *Strategic Antisubmarine Warfare and Naval Strategy*, Lexington Books, Lexington, Massachusetts

Sunderman, Major James F., USAF ed., 1962, *World War II in the Air: The Pacific*, Watts, New York

Trask, David F., 1981, *The War with Spain in 1898*, Macmillan, New York

Tritten, James John, 1992, *Our New National Security Strategy: America Promises to Come Back*, Praeger, Westport, Connecticut

Watts, Barry D., 1996, *Clausewitzian Friction and Future War*, McNair Paper 52, October, Institute for National Strategic Studies, National Defense University, Washington DC

Weinberger, Caspar and Peter Schweizer, 1996, *The Next War*, Regnery, New York

Wiley, Peter B., 1990, *Yankees in the Land of the Gods: Commodore Perry and the Opening of Japan*, Viking, New York

JOURNAL ARTICLES AND REPORTS

'Air Force Deploys "New" Earth-Penetrating Warhead', 1997, *Arms Control Today*, vol. 27, no. 1, March, p. 29

Arkin, William M., 1995, 'A Tale of Two Franks' *Bulletin of the Atomic Scientists*, March/April

Ball, Desmond, 1985, 'Nuclear War at Sea' *International Security*, vol. 10, no. 3, (Winter 1985/1986) pp. 103-31

——1993, 'Arms and Affluence: Military Acquisitions in the Asia-Pacific Region' *International Security*, vol. 18, no. 3, (Winter 1993/1994), pp. 78–112

Bathrick, Mark L., 1997, 'Digital F–14s Get the Picture—Fast' *US Naval Institute Proceedings*, vol. 123, no. 10, October, pp. 74–76

Brinkerhoff, J., 1997, 'The Brigade-Based New Army' *Parameters: the US Army War College Quarterly*, (Autumn), pp. 60–72

——1996, 'The Army National Guard and Conservation of Combat Power' *Parameters: the US Army War College Quarterly* (Autumn), pp. 4–16.

Brookings Institution, 1997, 'Global Nuclear Stockpiles, 1945–1996', Washington DC

Broughton, Buzz and Jay Burdon, 1998, 'The (R)evolution of Mine Countermeasures' *US Naval Institute Proceedings*, vol. 124, no. 5, May, pp. 55–58

Bunn, George, 1996, 'Expanding Nuclear Options: Is the US Negating Its Non-Use Pledges? *Arms Control Today*, vol. 26, no. 4 (May/June)

Burton, J., 1993, 'Pushing Them Out the Back Door' *US Naval Institute Proceedings*, vol. 119, no. 4 (June), pp. 37–42

Butler, Gen. George Lee, 1994, '"Reengineering" Nuclear War Planning' *Strategic Review*, Summer 1994

CISSM, 1991, 'Reversing the Arms Race' *CISSM Commentaries*, no. 4, November, Center for International Security Studies at Maryland

'The Carriers: Why the Aircraft Carrier; Carriers—Powerhouse of the

Fleet', 1997, US Navy Office of Information, Washington, DC, online version

Conneta, Carl and Charles Knight, 1997 'Post–Cold War US Military Expenditure in the Context of World Spending Trends', Project on Defense Alternatives Briefing Memo 10, Commonwealth Institute, Cambridge, Massachusetts, January

Conoley, Col. Ellis K., 1997, 'Global Command and Control System (GCCS) Status Briefing at the Software Technology Conference (STC)', Salt Lake City, Utah, 29 April

Cushman, John H., 1993, 'Maneuver ... From the Sea' US Naval Institute Proceedings, vol. 119, no. 4 (April)

Department of the Navy, 1992, 'Power from the Sea', unpublished draft, 27 August

Estes, General Howell M. III, 1997, 'Sustaining the Strategic Space Advantage' Defence Issues, vol. 12, no. 15

'F/A-18E/F Super Hornet ... Leading Naval Aviation into the 21st Century', 1997, Navy Office of Public Information, Washington DC

'Factfile: Fifty Years of Nuclear Testing', 1995, Arms Control Today, vol. 27, no. 6, July/August, pp. 33–35

Fogelman, Gen. Ronald R., 1996, 'Preparing for the 21st Century', 21 November, Office of the Chief of Staff of the Air Force, online version

Forces/Capabilities Handbook Volume I: Organizations, 1993, US Army War College, Department of Military Strategy, Planning and Operations, Carlisle Barracks, Pennsylvania

Gaffney, Frank J., Jr, 1997, 'Sellout at Helsinki?', Washington Times, 25 March

Hattendorf, John B., 'Evolution of the Maritime Strategy 1977–1987' Naval War College Review, vol. XLI, no. 3 (summer 1988), pp. 7–19.

Horner, Gen. Charles A. (Retired), 1997, 'What We Should have Learned in Desert Storm, But Didn't', US Air Force Link online article, 5 May

House Committee on Foreign Affairs, 1994, The War Powers Resolution—Relevant Documents, Reports, Correspondence, 103d Congress 2nd session, US Government Printing Office, Washington DC

Howard, R. and Nelson, M., 1996, 'Army Special Operations and the "Pacific Century"' Special Warfare, vol. 9, no. 1, January, pp. 18–27

Johnson, Captain Robert F., US Navy (Retired), 1996, 'Carriers Are Forward Presence' US Naval Institute Proceedings, vol. 122, no. 8 (August), pp. 37–39

'Joint STARS: Opening the Door to the Future', 1996, Air Force Electronic Systems Center, Public Affairs Office, Hanscom Air Force Base, Massachusetts

Kennedy, Floyd Jr., 1997, 'US Naval Aircraft and Weapon Developments' US Naval Institute Proceedings, vol. 123, no. 5 (May), pp. 122–30

Kristensen, Hans M. and Joshua Handler, 1995, Changing Targets: Nuclear

Doctrine from the Cold War to the Third World, revised edition, 1 March, Greenpeace USA, Washington DC

Krulak, Gen. Charles C., 1997, 'Operational Maneuver From the Sea: Building a Marine Corps for the 21st Century' *National Security Studies Quarterly*, Spring, online version

——1997b, 'Operational Maneuver From the Sea' *US Naval Institute Proceedings*, vol. 123, no. 1, January, pp. 26–31.

——1997c, 'OMFTS Article' *Military Review*, February, online version

——1998, 'MPF 2010 and Beyond', 30 December, printed in *Inside the Navy*, 12 January 1998, pp. 6–7

'Kurt Campbell Interview on Asia-Pacific Security', 1998, *US Foreign Policy Agenda*, online journal of the US Information Agency, January

Lockwood, Dunbar, 1994, 'The Status of US, Russian and Chinese Forces in Northeast Asia' *Arms Control Today*, vol. 24, no. 9 (November), pp. 21–24

——1994b, 'New Nuclear Posture Review Shows Little Change in Policies' *Arms Control Today*, vol. 24, no. 9 (November)

'LPD–17—The Navy's Next Generation Amphib' *Naval Forces*, vol. XVIII, no. V, 1997, Special Supplement, pp. 33–12 to 39–19

Lorber, General John G., 1996, 'The Importance of the US as a Credible Component in Asia-Pacific Security', Address to the Third Asia-Pacific Defense Conference, Singapore, 6 February

——1996a, 'PACAF: Air Power for Peace' *Asia-Pacific Defense Forum*, vol. 21, no. 2, summer, pp. 16–25

——1996b, 'Protecting the Pacific: An Interview with the Pacific Air Forces Commander' *Airman*, vol. 12, no. 5, May, online version

Myers, Lt. Col. Gene US Air Force (Retired), 1996, 'Bomber Debates' *US Naval Institute Proceedings*, vol. 122, no. 8, August, pp. 34–36

Navy Carrier Battlegroups: The Structure and Affordability of the Future Force, 1993, US General Accounting Office Report (GAO/NSIAD-93-74), Washington, DC

Nellis AFB, 1997, 'Overview of Nellis Air Force Base'; 'Air Warfare Center'; 'Red Flag'; 'Green flag 97–3', online articles

Novichkov, Nicolay and Paul Mann, 1997, 'Decay Eats at Vitals of Russian Air Force' *Aviation Week & Space Technology*, 17 March

Podlesny, Robert E., 1998, 'MOUT: The Show Stopper' *US Naval Institute Proceedings*, vol. 124, no. 2 (February), pp. 50–53

'Power from the Sea', 27 August 1992, unpublished draft

'Report of the Canberra Commission on the Elimination of Nuclear Weapons', *Arms Control Today*, 1996, vol. 26, no. 6, August, pp. 35–37

'Retired Generals Re-Ignite Debate Over Abolition of Nuclear Weapons', 1996, *Arms Control Today*, vol. 26, no. 9, November/December, p. 14

Rumbaugh, L. et al., 1951, *Tactical Employment of Atomic Weapons*, Operations Research Group, Johns Hopkins University, Baltimore, Maryland, March 1; available at Library, Army War College, Carlisle Barracks, Pennsylvania

Schwartz, Stephen I., 1996, 'US and Overseas Bases and Facilities with a Significant and/or Historical US Nuclear Weapons Mission', 17 December, The Brookings Institution, Washington DC

Stephens, Alan, 1997, 'Weapon of First Choice: Strike Aircraft in the Asia-Pacific Region' *Asia-Pacific Defense Reporter 1997 Annual Reference Edition*, vol. XXXIII, nos. 1–2, pp. 26–27.

Strategic Air Command, 1982, *The Development of Strategic Air Command 1946–1981*, Office of the Historian, Omaha, Nebraska, July

Strategic Assessment 1997: Flashpoints and Force Structure, Institute for National Strategic Studies, National Defense University, Washington DC

Swartz, Peter M. and Jan S. Breemer, with James J. Tritten, 'The Maritime Strategy Debates: A Guide to the Renaissance of US Naval Strategic Thought in the 1980s', 30 September 1989, revised edition, Naval Postgraduate School, Monterey, California

Swartz, Peter M., 1996, 'Forward . . . from the start: The operational record of the US Navy', Center for Naval Analyses, Alexandria, Virginia, Draft, 14 August

Truver, Scott C., 1997, 'Tomorrow's Fleet' *US Naval Institute Proceedings*, vol. 123, no. 9 (September), pp. 90–96.

US Air Force UAV Battlelab, 1997, 'Endurance UAVs', Eglin Air Force Base, Florida, online version

US Army Special Operations Command 1995, *SINE PARI Without Equal: The Story of Army Special Operations*, Directorate of History and Museums, online version

Van Riper, Paul K., 1997, 'A Concept for Future Military Operations on Urbanized Terrain' *Marine Corps Gazette*, October

Watkins, Admiral James D., 1986, 'The Maritime Strategy' *US Naval Institute Proceedings*, vol. 112, no. 1 (January), Supplement.

NEWSPAPER, NEWS SERVICE AND MAGAZINE ARTICLES

'Airborne US A-Arms To Stay in South Korea' *Washington Post*, 12 October 1991

'Air Force Admits It's Running Out of Spare Parts', CNN, 7 August, 1997.

'Air Force General Calls for End to Atomic Arms' *Boston Globe*, 16 July 1994

Air Force News Service 1991, 'Airpower in Operation Desert Storm' USAF Fact Sheet 91–03 Special Edition

——1992, 'F–16 *Fighting Falcon*' USAF Fact Sheet 92–60

——1992a, 'F–15 *Eagle*' USAF Fact Sheet 92–61

——1994, 'GBU–15' USAF Fact Sheet 94–03

——1995, 'Air Force Special Operations Command' USAF Fact Sheet 95–8

—— 1995a, 'Pacific Air Forces' USAF Fact Sheet 95–16
—— 1995b, 'Organization of the United States Air Force' USAF Fact Sheet 95–17
—— 1995c, 'AC–130H *Spectre*' USAF Fact Sheet 95–25
—— 1995d, 'MC–130E/H *Combat Talon I/II*' USAF Fact Sheet 95–26
—— 1995e, 'MH–60G *Pave Hawk*' USAF Fact Sheet 95–28
—— 1995f, 'MH–53J *Pave Low IIIE*' USAF Fact Sheet 95–30
—— 1996a, 'F–117A *Nighthawk*' USAF Fact Sheet 96–04
—— 1996b, 'B–52 *Stratofortress*' USAF Fact Sheet 96–11
—— 1996c, 'E–3 *Sentry* (AWACS)' USAF Fact Sheet 96–13
—— 1996d, 'MC–130P *Combat Shadow*' USAF Fact Sheet 96–14
—— 1996e, 'U–2R/U–2S' USAF Fact Sheet 96–21
—— 1996f, 'A–10/OA–10 *Thunderbolt II*' USAF Fact Sheet, April
—— 1997a, 'B1-B *Lancer*' USAF Fact Sheet, February
—— 1997b, 'Stealth Bomber Makes Asian Debut' USAF Fact Sheet, February
—— 1997c, 'Air Education and Training Command' USAF Fact Sheet, April
'Air Force Unveils Predator UAV', Air Force News Agency, 31 January 1997
'A Korean Leader for These Times' *Los Angeles Times*, 23 December 1997
'B–2 Reaches Initial Operational Capability', 1997, Office of the Assistant Secretary of Defense (Public Affairs), Washington DC, 1 April
'Backer of US Base Wins in Okinawa' *Seattle Post-Intelligencer*, 9 February 1998
Boeing Company, 1996, 'F–22 Air Dominance Fighter', Seattle, Washington, 5 November
—— 1997a, 'E–3 AWACS in Service Worldwide', Seattle, Washington, 12 May.
—— 1997b, '767 AWACS', Seattle, Washington, 13 May
'Boeing wins orders worth $3 billion: S. Korea, Kuwait buying military aircraft' *Seattle Post-Intelligencer*, 4 September 1997
'Chemical Corps, MPs Head to Hood for Advanced Warfighter Exercise' *Army Link News*, 16 September 1997, online article
'China Imports Reach New High' *Seattle Post-Intelligencer*, 20 February 1997
'Clinton Directive Changes Strategy on Nuclear Arms' *Washington Post*, 7 December 1997, p. A01
'Cohen Hails Achievements in China Visit' *Washington Post*, 20 January 1998
'Cohen Warns China on Iran Threat' *New York Times*, 19 January 1998
'Denuclearization Drive May Imperil East Asian Security' *Defense News* 6–12 January 1997
'DOD News Briefing: Defense Guidelines Review', 1997, Office of the Assistant Secretary of Defense (Public Affairs), Washington DC, 19 September

'DOD News Briefing and Press Conference on US–Philippines Visiting Forces Agreement', 14 January 1998, Office of the Assistant Secretary of Defense (Public Affairs), Washington DC

'F–117 Pilot Logs 1000 Hours', Air Force News Agency, 2 November 1996

'Gen. Moorman Flies Rivet Joint', Air Force News Agency, 5 February 1997

'Greater China' *Financial Times*, 16 January 1998

'It's Raining on US Air Force Parade', Reuters, 18 September 1997

'Japan Blasts Okinawa Refusal of US Heliport', Reuters, 6 February 1998

'Japan Takes Delivery of First Boeing 767 AWACS', *Jane's Defence Weekly*, 18 March 1998

'Joint STARS Returns from First Deployment', Air Force News Agency, 30 January 1997

'Joint Strike Fighter News Briefing', Office of the Assistant Secretary of Defense (Public Affairs), 16 November 1996

'Mildenhall Units Reach Flying Milestone', Air Force News Service, 17 October 1996

'Moscow Builds Bunkers Against Nuclear Attack' *Washington Times*, 1 April 1997

'Move Grows to Ban All Nuclear Weapons — For All Time' *Boston Globe*, 25 December 1997

'Naval Nuclear Cuts' *Navy Times*, 14 October 1991

'Navy Intercepts Ballistic Missile; Accelerated TBMD Program', 24 January 1997, Navy News Desk, Washington DC, online version

'Navy Phasing Out Nuclear Rockets for Close Combat' *New York Times*, 30 April 1989

'NDP Chairman Sees Little Change in Defense Strategy in Near Term' *Defence Daily*, 16 January 1998

'New South Korean President Banking on Democracy' *Seattle Post-Intelligencer*, 13 January 1998

'News Release: Secretary Cohen Appoints National Defense Panel', Office of the Assistant Secretary of Defense (Public Affairs), Washington DC, Ref. No. 057–97, 6 February 1997

'No A-arms in S. Korea, Roh Says' *Washington Post*, 19 December 1991

'Off Taiwan, US Sailors Are Unworried' *New York Times*, 19 March 1996

'Okinawa Governor Opposes Plans for US Heliport' *Los Angeles Times*, 7 February 1998

'Okinawa Town Defiantly Rejects a New US Base' *New York Times*, 22 December 1997

'One on One with General Howell Estes—Commander in Chief US Space Command' *Defense News*, 6 May 1997

'Pacific Air Forces' *Airman*, January 1997, vol. 12, no. 1, online version

'Pilots Stressed—Air Force Cutting Down Their Flights' *Seattle Post-Intelligencer*, 20 August 1997

'Pilot with Most F-16 Flying Hours Honored', Air Force News Service, 10 December 1996

'Press Briefing', White House, Office of the Press Secretary, 11 April 1996
'RC–135 Flies 1000th Mission in SWA', Air Force News Service, 22 February 1997
'Reappraisal Led to New China Policy' *The Washington Post*, 22 June 1998
'Regional Security through Air Power Diplomacy' *The Straits Times*, 1 May 1997, online version
'Report of the Canberra Commission on the Elimination of Nuclear Weapons' *Arms Control Today*, August 1996
'Retired Generals Re-Ignite Debate Over Abolition of Nuclear Weapons' *Arms Control Today*, November/December 1996
'Seoul Says It Now Has No Nuclear Arms' *New York Times*, 19 December 1991
'STRATCOM Offers to Play Role in Counterproliferation Target Planning' *Inside the Pentagon*, 15 December 1994
'STRATCOM sees new role in WMD targeting' *Jane's Defence Weekly*, 14 January 1995
'UK, Russia Agree to End Targeting' *Jane's Defence Weekly*, 26 February 1994
'USAF Air Power Move into Qatar is "Routine"', *Jane's Defence Weekly*, 12 February 1997
'US Already Redirected Its Missiles from China' *Seattle Post-Intelligencer*, 2 July 1998
'US and Japan Agree to Bolster Military Ties for Regional Crises' *New York Times*, 24 September 1997
'US and Russians Agree to Put Off Arms Deadline Until 2007' *New York Times*, 27 September 1997
'US, China Nearly Came to Blows in '96' *The Washington Post*, 21 June 1998
'US Is Considering Aiming Its Missiles Away From Russia' *New York Times*, 6 December 1993
'US Naval Chief Rejects Idea of Asian Arms Race' Reuters, 2 May 1995.
'US Navy Exercise to Assess Firepower of Carriers' *Defense News*, 24 February–2 March 1997
'US Navy Lost H-Bomb Off Okinawa in 1965' *Mainichi Daily News*, 9 May 1989.
'US Nuclear Weapons Plan Under Fire' *Los Angeles Times*, 19 February 1997
'US Tells Russians It Is Ready to Negotiate Deeper Cuts in Nuclear Weapons' *New York Times*, 9 March 1997
'Weak Procurement Outlook Belies Potential Growth Areas' *Aviation Week and Space Technology*, 15 December 1997, pp. 66–67

OFFICIAL DOCUMENTS

'1st Special Forces Group (Airborne) History', 1997, US Army Special Operations Command, online version 30 April

'1992 Joint Military Net Assessment', August 1992, US Joint Chiefs of Staff, Washington DC

1997 Posture Statement: The Navy-Marine Corps Team, Enduring Impact...From the Sea, 1997, Department of the Navy, Washington, DC, online version

'2nd Infantry Division: Mission & Training, History', 1997, 2nd Infantry Division Office of Public Affairs, online version, 17 July

'25th Light Infantry Division', 1997, US Army Pacific, Public Affairs Office, online version, 2 August

The 600 Ship Navy and the Maritime Strategy: Hearings Before the Seapower and Strategic Materials Subcommittee of the House Armed Services Committee, 1986, Washington DC, US Government Printing Office

'About GCCS', 1997, Defence Information Services Agency online article at spider.osfl.disa.mil

'Agreement Between the Department of Defense of the United States of America and the Ministry of National Defence of the People's Republic of China on Establishing a Consultation Mechanism to Strengthen Military Maritime Safety', 19 January 1998, Beijing

'A Handout on US Army Organization for Combat', 1995, US Naval War College, NWC 3009 WR–6/SO–9, pp. 1–8

Air Force Issues Book 1997, Department of the Air Force, Washington DC, online version

'An Army Special Operations Forces Primer', 1997, US Army Special Operations Command, 8 August, online version

A National Security Strategy of Engagement and Enlargement, 1994, White House, Washington DC

A National Security Strategy of Engagement and Enlargement, 1995, White House, Washington DC

A National Security Strategy for a New Century, 1997, White House, Washington DC

'Arctic Warrior Brigade', 1997, US Army Alaska Office of Public Affairs, online version, 19 September

'Army Mission and Vision', 1997, Department of the Army, Washington DC, online version

Army Vision 2010, 1997, Department of the Army, the Pentagon, Washington DC

Aspin, Les, 1993, *Report on the Bottom-Up Review*, Department of Defense, Washington DC

——1994, *Report of the Secretary of Defense to the President and the Congress*, US Government Printing Office, Washington DC

A Strategic Framework for the Asian Pacific Rim: Looking Toward the 21st Century, April 1990, Department of Defense, Washington DC
A Strategic Framework for the Asian Pacific Rim: Report to Congress 1992, Department of Defense, Washington DC
'Background Briefing by a Senior Administration Official', 1997, White House, Office of the Press Secretary, Helsinki, Finland, 21 March
'Carrier Air Wings and Squadrons', 1997, Office of Public Affairs, Naval Air Force, US Pacific Fleet, Hawaii, online version
Certain Victory: The US Army in the Gulf War, 1993, Office of the Chief of Staff United States Army, Washington DC
Challenges to Naval Expeditionary Warfare, 1997, Office of Naval Intelligence, Washington DC
Cheney, Dick, 1990, 'Testimony before the Senate Committee on Appropriations', Defense Subcommittee, 12 June
——1992, *Report of the Secretary of Defense to the President and the Congress*, US Government Printing Office, Washington DC
Cohen, William S., 1997, *Annual Report of the Secretary of Defense to the President and the Congress*, US Government Printing Office, Washington DC, April
——1997a, *The Quadrennial Defense Review*, Office of the Secretary of Defense, Washington DC, online version
——1997b, 'Response to the National Defense Panel Report', Office of the Secretary of Defense, Washington DC, 15 December
——1998, 'Continuity, Change and Commitment: America's Asia-Pacific Security Strategy', Remarks Prepared for Delivery at the Institute of Defense and Strategy Studies, Singapore, 15 January, Office of the Assistant Secretary of Defense (Public Affairs), Washington DC
——1998a, 'Remarks Prepared for Delivery to the Academy of Military Sciences, Beijing, China, 19 January
——1998b, *Annual Report of the Secretary of Defense to the President and the Congress*, US Government Printing Office, Washington DC, February
'Command Brief CincPacFlt Plans and Policy', 1997, Office of the Commander in Chief, US Pacific Fleet, slides, online version
'Completion of the Review of the Guidelines for US–Japan Defense Cooperation', 1997, Office of the Assistant Secretary of Defense (Public Affairs) Press Release, New York, NY, 23 September
'Defense Nuclear Weapons School' 1997, Defense Special Weapons Agency, Public Affairs Office, Alexandria, Virginia, 26 February
'Department of Defense Budget for FY 1999', 1998, News Release, Office of the Assistant Secretary of Defense (Public Affairs), 2 February
'Doctrine for Joint Nuclear Operations', 1993, Joint Pub 3-12, US Joint Chiefs of Staff, Washington DC, 29 April
'DOD News Briefing and Press Conference on US–Philippines Visiting Forces Agreement', 1998, Office of the Assistant Secretary of Defense (Public Affairs), Washington DC, 14 January

'Fact Sheet: Joint Statement on Parameters on Future Reductions in Nuclear Forces', 1997, White House, Office of the Press Secretary, Helsinki, Finland

'Forward ... From the Sea' 1994, Department of the Navy, Washington DC

'From the Sea: Preparing the Naval Service for the 21st Century', 1992, Department of the Navy, Washington DC, 29 September

'Global Engagement: A Vision for the 21st Century Air Force', 21 November 1996, Department of the Air Force, Washington DC, online version.

Goldwater-Nichols Department of Defence Reorganization Act, US Congress, US Code, Title 10, 1986

Hearings on Crisis in the Persian Gulf Region: US Policy Options and Implications, 1990, US Senate Committee on Armed Services, 101st Congress, 2nd Session, p. 701

'History of the 10th Mountain Division', 1997, 10th Mountain Division, Office of Public Affairs, Ft. Drum, New York, online version

'International Defense Commitments in the US Pacific Command', 1996, USCINCPAC Public Affairs Office, Hickam AFB, Hawaii, April

'Investigation Report: Formal Investigation into the Circumstances Surrounding the Downing of Iran Air Flight 655 on 3 July 1988', 1988, Department of Defense, Washington DC, 28 July

'Joint STARS: Opening the Door to the Future', 1996, Air Force Electronic Systems Public Affairs Office, Hanscom Air Force Base, Massachusetts

Joint Vision 2010, 1996, Office of the Chairman of the Joint Chiefs of Staff, Washington DC

Joseph, Dr S., 1997, 'Treatment, Tracing Origin Top DOD Gulf Illness Concerns' *Defence Issues*, vol. 12, no. 6, Prepared remarks of the Assistant Secretary of Defense for Health Affairs to the Military Personnel Subcommittee, House National Security Committee, 11 February, online version

Kaminsky, Paul G., 'DOD's Ballistic Missile Defense Programs' *Defense Issues*, vol. 12, no. 14, 1997, pp. 1–11, online version, Prepared Statement to the Military Research and Development subcommittee, House National Security Committee, 6 March

Keaney, Thomas A. & Eliot A. Cohen, 1993, *Gulf War Air Power Survey: Summary Report*, US Government Printing Office, Washington DC

'National Defense Panel: Assessment of the May 1997 Quadrennial Defense Review', Department of Defense, online version, 20 May 1997

National Military Strategy of the United States of America: A Strategy of Flexible and Selective Engagement, 1995, Office of the Chairman of the Joint Chiefs of Staff, Washington DC

National Military Strategy of the United States of America: Shape,

Respond, Prepare Now: A Military Strategy for a New Era, 1997, Office of the Chairman of the Joint Chiefs of Staff, Washington DC

'Navy Fact File', 1997, an online encyclopedia produced by the Public Affairs Offices, Naval Systems Commands, Washington DC, Internet address: http://www.chinfo.navy.mil/navpalib/factfile

'Navy Fact File: Aircraft Carriers—CV, CVN', 1997, Public Affairs Office, Naval Sea Systems Command, Washington DC, online version

'Navy Organization: Mission of the Navy; The Operating Forces; The Shore Establishment', 1997, Navy Office of Information, Washington DC, online version

'Navy SEALs: Overview, Training', 1997, US Naval Special Warfare Command Public Affairs Office, Coronado, California, online version, 5 August

'News Briefing on the Quadrennial Defense Review', 1996, Department of Defense

'Nighthawks over Iraq: A Chronology of the F-117A Stealth Fighter in Operations Desert Shield and Desert Storm', 1991, Special Study 37 FW/HO-91-1, Office of History 37th Fighter Wing, Twelfth Air Force, Tactical Air Command

Nuclear Posture Review, 1994, Department of Defense Briefing Slides, 22 September, the Pentagon, Washington DC

On Orbit: United States Space Command, 1997, US Space Command Office of Public Affairs, Peterson Air Force Base, Colorado, online version

'Opening Statement of Secretary of Energy Designate Federico Pena to the Committee on Armed Services', 5 February, 1997, US Senate, online version.

'Overall Effects of Atomic Bomb on Warfare and Military Organization', 1945, JCS 1477/1, 30 October, Washington DC

'Overview of National Security Structure', 1997, US Joint Chiefs of Staff, JCSLink online article, 5 May

PACOM Digest, 1996, Office of Public Affairs, US Pacific Command, Hawaii, April

'President Bush's Nuclear Weapons Initiative', 2 July 1992, White House, Office of the Press Secretary, Washington DC

'Presidential Initiative on Nuclear Arms', 27 September 1991, White House, Office of the Press Secretary, Washington DC

'Press Availability by President Clinton and President Jiang' Office of the Press Secretary, Beijing, 27 June 1998

'Press Briefing' 11 April 1996, Office of the Press Secretary, White House, Washington DC

'Press Conference with Secretary of Defense William J. Perry, General Shalikashvili, Chairman, JCS, Deputy Secretary of Defense John Deutch, Mr Kenneth H. Bacon', 1994, News Release 546-94, Office of the Assistant Secretary of Defense for Public Affairs, Washington DC, 22 September

'Prohibition on Research and Development of Low-Yield Nuclear Weapons', FY 1994, US Congress, House 1993 Defense Authorization bill, Section 3136, *Congressional Record*, 10 November

Proliferation: Threat and Response 1997, Department of Defense, Washington DC, November, online version

Reed, Thomas C. and Michael O. Wheeler, 1992, 'The Role of Nuclear Weapons in the New World Order', Statement before the Senate Armed Services Committee, 23 January

'Special Action Committee on Okinawa Final Report', 1996, by Minister for Foreign Affairs Ikeda, Minister of State for Defence Kyuma, Secretary of Defense Perry, and Ambassador Mondale, 2 December

'Special Operations Command' (SOCOM), 1997, Department of Defense, *Fact File*, August, online version

'START I Memorandum of Understanding', 1 July 1997

'Statement by the President on Advancing US Relations with Russia and the Other New Independent States', 23 April 1993, White House, Office of the Press Secretary, Washington DC

'Statement of Admiral Joseph W. Prueher, US Navy, Commander in Chief, United States Pacific Command, Before the Committee on National Security, United States House of Representatives, 4 March 1998

'Statement of Secretary Cyrus Vance' 1978, US State Department Bulletin, August

'Statement of Secretary Warren Christopher' 1995, US State Department, 5 April

'Status of the Navy', 17 November 1997, Navy Office of Information, Washington DC, online version

'Status of the US Pacific Fleet as of July 24, 1998', Pacific Fleet Public Affairs Office, Hawaii

Submarine Challenges, 1997, Office of Naval Intelligence, Washington DC

'The Air Force and National Security: Global Reach—Global Power', June 1990, Department of the Air Force, Washington DC

'The Guidelines for US–Japan Defense Cooperation', 1997, Security Consultative Committee, New York, NY, 23 September

The Constitution of the United States of America: Literal Print, 1996, US Senate, US Government Printing Office, Washington DC

'The Joint Chiefs of Staff (JCS)', 1997, US Joint Chiefs of Staff, JCSLink online article, 16 May

'The Navy Operational Concept', 1997, Department of the Navy, Washington DC

'The Unified Combatant Commands', 1997, Department of Defense, DefenseLink online article, May

'Third Fleet: Mission and Capability, Area of Responsibility, Assets, Operations, Carrier Battle Group, Amphibious Ready Group', 1997, Third Fleet Public Affairs, San Diego, online version

Transforming Defence: National Security in the 21st Century, 1997,

Report of the National Defense Panel, December, Arlington, Virginia, online version.
'United States Air Force in Europe', 1997, US Air Force in Europe Public Affairs Office, Ramstein Air Base, Germany, online version
'United States Army Pacific: America's Army in the Pacific', 1997, US Army Pacific Public Affairs Office, online version, 2 August
United States Army Weapons Systems, 1995, Department of the Army, online version.
United States Security Strategy for the East Asia-Pacific Region, 1995, Department of Defense, Office of International Security Affairs, the Pentagon, Washington DC
'United States Strategic Command: The Forces', 1997, US Strategic Command Public Affairs, Offutt Air Force Base, Nebraska, February, online version
'US Army Japan and 9th Theater Army Area Command', 1997, US Army Japan, Office of the Chief of Public Affairs, online version, 30 July
'US Army Major Commands (MACOM) Online', 1997, Department of the Army, online version
'US Atlantic Fleet Fact Sheet', 1997, US Atlantic Fleet Public Affairs Office, Norfolk, Virginia, online version
'USCINCPAC at a Glance', 1996, USCINCPAC Public Affairs Information Office, Hickam AFB, Hawaii, March
USCINCPAC Command History 1991, Volume I
'US Economic Relations with East Asia and the Pacific' 1997, Fact Sheet, Bureau of East Asian and Pacific Affairs, US Department of State, Washington DC, 6 November
'USFK Mission Statement, United Nations Command History, Combined Forces Command History, USFK History', 1997, US Forces in Korea Office of Public Affairs, South Korea, online version, 31 July
US Marine Forces Pacific Command Brief, 1998, Force Public Affairs, US Marine Corps, online version.
'US Pacific Command 50th Anniversary', 1997, Headquarters, USPACOM, USPACOM Public Affairs Office, Hawaii
'US Policy on Spratly Islands and South China Sea', 10 May 1995, Daily Press Briefing, US State Department, Office of the Spokesman, Washington DC
'US Requirements for Post-War Air Bases', 1943, US Joint Chiefs of Staff, Joint Strategic Survey Committee, JCS 570, Modern Military Branch, US National Archives, Washington DC
'US Seventh Fleet: Facts, Composition, Forward Deployed Units, Forward Presence', 1997, Seventh Fleet Public Affairs, Yokosuka, Japan
Watkins, James D. 'The Maritime Strategy', 1986, Office of the Chief of Naval Operations, Washington DC
Weinberger, Caspar, 1982, *Annual Report to the Congress for FY 1983*, US Government Printing Office, Washington DC
West, T. D. Jr & General Dennis J. Reimer, 1997, 'A Statement on the

Posture of the United States Army Fiscal Year 1998', presented to the Committees and Subcommittees of the United States Senate and the House of Representatives, 105th Congress, First Session, February, online version

Worldwide Challenges to Naval Strike Warfare, 1997, Office of Naval Intelligence, Washington DC

Index

Because this book is about the Armed Forces of the US, not all references to the Department of Defense, Pacific Command, Air Force, Army, Navy and Marine Corps have been indexed.

I Corps, 192–3
I Marine Expeditionary Force, 86, 140, 245
2nd Infantry Division, 85, 96, 194, 232–3, 247, 255, 271
III Marine Expeditionary Force, 92–3, 140, 245, 254
5th Air Force, 90–1, 167
6th Light Infantry Division, 84, 195–6, 248–9, 255, 271
7th Air Force, 95–6, 167
7th Fleet, *see* Seventh Fleet
25th Light Infantry Division, 85, 88, 195–6, 248–9, 255, 271
100,000 forward deployed US forces, vi, 1, 6, 35–6, 41, 44, 53, 98, 213–14, 237

access agreements, 53, 234
Aegis Combat System, 133, 148–9, 154, 226–7
Agreed Framework, 51
aircraft carrier, 13–14, 21–2, 34, 41, 53, 85, 87, 91, 129, 132–4, 138, 142–4, 163–4, 238, 242–4, 253–4, 266
Air Expeditionary Force, 163–4
Air Force, US: capability and limitations, 169–82; force structure, 165–6; Gulf War combat, 171–82 *passim*; Korean War combat, 21, 166; mission and organization, 157–9; nuclear role and forces, 99–121 *passim*; presence in Asia–Pacific, 166–9, 254–5; strategic vision, 159–65;

strength, total, 158; Vietnam War combat, 23–5 *passim*, 166; World War II role in Pacific, 14, 166; *see also* Pacific Air Forces, Space Command, Strategic Command
air lift, 60, 85, 91, 140, 142, 151, 165–6, 182, 196–7, 249
air-to-air combat, 144–5, 174–6
Alaska, US bases and forces, 82–4
American Samoa, 47
amphibious capability, US, 131–2, 150–2, 224–5; *see also* Inchon, Naval Expeditionary Force
amphibious ready group, 53, 92, 129, 132, 137, 238, 244, 253
Andersen Air Force Base, 89, 167, 179–80, 255
ANZUS treaty, 22, 47
APEC, 43–4
ARF, 44, 47–8, 56, 215
Army, US: capability and limitations, 196–211; force structure, 190–3; Gulf War combat, 196–204 *passim*; Korean War combat, 19–21; mission and organization, 184–6; presence in Asia–Pacific, 193–6, 255; Somalia combat, 204–7; strategic vision, 186–90; strength, total, 185; Vietnam War combat, 23–5; World War II role in Pacific, 14; *see also* US Army Pacific Command, Eighth Army, 2nd Infantry Division,

25th Light Infantry Division, 6th Light Infantry Division
Army Vision 2010, 186–90, 246
ASEAN, 33, 44, 46–9, 56, 213, 215
Asia–Pacific strategy, 30–6, 45–53, 56, 212–14, 232
Asiatic Fleet, US, 10
Aspin, Les, 38, 205, 259, 262–3, 266
asymmetric threats, 201–22, 225, 229–30
atomic bomb, 14, 16
Atsugi Naval Air Facility, 32, 91
Australia, vi, 22, 26, 45–7, 53, 76–7, 96–7, 116, 156, 166, 168, 214, 231
AWACS aircraft, 94, 146, 168, 170–1, 269

ballistic missiles, v, 36, 39, 42–4, 52, 99–101, 103–4, 106, 108, 110–13, 115, 119, 121, 134, 149, 173, 202, 226–7, 239, 243, 252, 262, 264; see also ICBM, Scud, SLBM, Theater Ballistic Missiles
Bangor Naval Submarine Base, 85, 111, 252–3
Bering Sea, 135
Blue Ridge, USS, 137
bombers, US: A–10, 84; B–1, 100–11, 179; B–2 stealth, 100–11, 145, 179–80; B–17, 14, 178; B–29, 14, 18; B–52, 25, 100–11, 178–9; F–117 stealth, 145, 176–9
Bosnia, 38, 146–7, 171–2, 187, 206
Bottom-up Review, 38–42, 129–32, 193
Brunei, 47, 50, 156
budget, defense, 2–3, 34, 38, 43, 133, 191, 217, 219, 221, 239, 274
Burma, 13, 45
Burke class destroyers, 148
Bush, President George, 3, 29, 33, 37–8, 40–1, 44, 66, 101–3, 112, 132, 253, 262
Butler, General Lee, 104, 116

C^4, see command, control, communications and computers
Cambodia, 24, 49, 166, 211
Camp Butler, 92
Camp Casey, 96
Camp Henry, 94
Camp Hialeah, 94
Camp H.M. Smith, 75–6, 240
Camp Humphreys, 96
Camp Pendleton, 86, 140, 245
Camp Red Cloud, 96
Camp Zama, 91, 195, 248
carrier, see aircraft carrier
carrier air wing, 91, 142, 148, 238, 266
carrier battle group, 28, 34, 40–1, 53, 62, 84, 91, 129–30, 132, 136–7, 145, 156, 163, 238, 244, 253, 266
Carter, President Jimmy, 3, 26, 28
casualties, US: concern over, 166, 204, 206; Gulf War, 201; Korean War, 25; Somalia, 206; Vietnam War, 25, 166; World War II in the Pacific, 13
Cheney, Dick, 103, 262
Chiang Kai-shek 12, 22
Chief of Naval Operations, 123, 150, 156
China, v, 6–13, 16–22, 26, 36, 44–50, 52, 74, 99, 105–6, 108–10, 116–17, 120–1, 149, 156, 177, 215–17, 220, 226, 236, 238, 250, 259, 263, 273–4
Chinhae naval base, 94
CIA, 67
CINCPAC, 75–7, 80, 135, 141, 168–9, 193, 240–7 *passim*, 261; cooperative engagement strategy, 168; headquarters 75, 88; see also US Pacific Command
Clinton, President Bill, 37–8, 42–4, 47–8, 60, 106, 109–10, 117, 119, 132, 206, 256, 263, 265, 273
Cobra Gold exercise, 168
Cohen, William, 63, 212–13, 215–26, 221, 260, 265–6, 268–70, 272–4
command, control, communications, computers (C^4): global (GCCS), 79–81, 164; national, 65–74; nuclear, 104–13; Pacific Command, 74–9; space systems, 161–2, 170–2, 230
Commander-in-Chief (CINC), US armed forces, 65–7

computers, *see* command, control, communications, computers
Congress, US, 2, 65–6, 69, 103, 122, 184
Constitution, US, 65, 67
Continental US, (CONUS), 34, 160, 225
Cooperative Engagement strategy, 168–246
Cope Thunder exercise, 84, 168
Cope Tiger exercise, 168
Coronado Naval Base, 87, 207, 209
Coronado, USS, 135
cruise missile, 103, 112–13, 117–18, 144, 146, 179, 239

defense budget, 2–3, 34, 38, 43, 133, 191, 217, 219, 221, 239, 274
Defense Department, 69–70
Defense Secretary, 66–9; *see also* Aspin, Cheney, Cohen, Perry, Weinberger
Delta Force, 229, 274
Deng Xiaoping, 48
Department of Defense, 69–70
Diego Garcia, 97, 140
DMZ, Korea, 20, 96, 194, 233, 247, 255
DOD, *see* Department of Defense
DPRK, *see* North Korea

E–2C aircraft, 145–6
E–3 aircraft, *see* AWACS
EA–6B aircraft, 146
EASI, 30–3
EASI II, 34–6
East Asia Strategic Initiative, *see* EASI
Eielson Air Force Base, 82, 168
Eighth Army, 96, 185, 193, 255
Eisenhower, President Dwight, 21
electronic warfare, 145–6, 170–2
Elmendorf Air Force Base, 76, 84, 167, 171, 241, 254
Everett Naval Station, 84–5

fighter pilots, 144, 174–5
fighters, US: A–10 *Warthog*, 84, 152, 167, 180; AV–8 *Harrier*, 92; F/A–18 *Hornet*, 86, 91–2, 140, 144, 152, 167, 174; F–117 Stealth, 145, 176–9; F–14 *Tomcat*, 91, 143–4; F–15 *Eagle*, 84, 94, 167–8, 173–6; F–16 *Falcon*, 84, 90, 96, 167–8, 180; F–22 *Raptor*, 176, 218, 223; Joint Strike Fighter (JSF), 223–4
Fighter Wing, 34, 40, 62, 84, 90, 95
Fiji, 76–7
Fleet Marine Force Pacific, 124–5, 245
Fogelman, General, 180, 268
Formosa, 7, 10, 19; *see also* Taiwan
Fort Irwin, 86
Fort Lewis, 85, 193–4, 196, 209, 247, 249
Fort Shafter, 88, 193, 196, 248–9, 255
Fort Wainwright, 84, 195, 248, 255
forward deployed forces, US, 1, 6, 22, 31–2, 34–6, 41, 44, 53, 89–98, 137, 141, 167–8, 193–6, 208–11, 213–14, 237, 240–9, 252–5
Forward. . .from the Sea, 129–30
French Polynesia, 76
From the Sea, 127–9
Futenma Marine Corps Air Station, 92, 233
Futuna, 76

GCCS, 79–81
Global Engagement, 159–65, 245
Global Reach, 159
Goldwater/Nichols Act, 71–2, 261
Gorbachev, President, 28, 101, 120, 253
GPS, 147, 179, 181
Guam, 9, 11, 26, 35, 47, 76–7, 89–90, 103, 137, 140–1, 167, 209, 233, 236, 245–6, 253–5, 270
Gulf War, 52, 145, 147, 152–3, 170, 174, 176–82, 196–204 *passim*
Gulf War Air Power Survey, 174

Halsey, Admiral 'Bull', 14
Hawaii: US bases and forces, 87–8; *see also* Pearl Harbor
Hawkeye aircraft, *see* E–2C
head up display, 174
helicopters: Air Force, 210; *Apache*, 198; Army, 198–9; *Blackhawk*,

199; Marines, 151–3; Navy, 149–50, 154–5
Hickam Air Force Base, 88, 159, 255
Hiroshima, 14, 16
Holloman Air Force Base, 177; see also F-117 stealth fighter
Hong Kong, 46
Hoover, President Herbert, 12
Horner, General Charles, 110, 180

ICBM, v, 41, 100, 104, 110–13, 115, 203, 239
IMET, 53
Inchon landing, 20, 132, 153
Independence, USS, 143
India, 7, 13, 47, 117, 187
Indonesia, 47–9, 97, 156
information warfare, 58, 73, 164–5, 190, 208, 230
integrated air defense system, 146, 223
intelligence: air systems, 145–6, 164, 170–3; ground systems, 229–30; human 207–10, 229; sea systems, 148, 153–4; space systems, 161–2, 170–2, 230
Iraq, 34, 38, 42, 52, 66, 128, 147, 152, 170, 174, 177, 179, 181, 197–204, 223, 274
Iwakuni Marine Corps Air Station, 32, 91, 254

Japan, v, 7–8, 10–19, 22, 26–7, 31–5, 41, 44–7, 50–1, 53, 75, 77, 90–2, 98, 103, 137, 140–2, 150, 156, 166–8, 171, 184, 193, 195, 203, 210, 214–16, 231–3, 236–8, 241, 244–5, 247–8, 253–5, 271, 273–4; strategic partnership with US, 31–5, 41, 44–7, 50–2, 53, 214–16; US bases and forces in, 75, 90–4, 140, 195, 231–3, 241–5, 254, 271
Jiang Zemin, 109, 263
Johnson, Admiral Jay, 156
Johnson, President Lyndon, 2, 23–4
Joint Chiefs of Staff, 15–17, 19–20, 29, 34, 37, 53, 63, 71–2, 105; see also National Military Strategy, US
Joint Strike Fighter (JSF), 223–4

Joint Vision 2010, 2, 72–4
joint warfighting, 58, 72–4, 128

Kadena Air Base, 93–4, 167, 171, 210, 254
Kaneohe/Hawaii Marine Base, 88, 141, 244–5
KEDO, 51
Kennedy, President John F., 3, 23
Kim Dae-Jung, 216
Kim Il-Sung, 49
Kirtland Air Force Base, 104
Kitty Hawk, USS, cover, 191
Korea, 1, 4, 8, 16, 19–22, 25, 27–9, 32–5, 44, 46–7, 49, 51, 56, 75, 77, 80, 128, 141, 156, 159, 166, 174, 184, 193–4, 203, 210–11, 215–17, 222, 232–3, 237, 241, 244–5, 247–8, 250, 273; see also North Korea, South Korea
Krulak, General Charles, 132, 225
Kuwait, 33, 38, 66, 152–3, 179, 181, 196, 198–9, 203, 269
Kunsan Air Base, 95–6, 102, 167, 254

Laos, 23–4, 47, 166
Lemoore Naval Air Station, 86
Lorber, General John, 268
Los Angeles class submarines, 154
LPD-17, 225

MacArthur, General Douglas, 14, 18, 20
McChord Air Force Base, 85, 194, 247
McKinley, President William, 10
McNamara, Robert, 116, 264
Madagascar, 74
MAGTF, 138–41
Mahan, Admiral Alfred, 8
major regional conflict (MRC), v, 38, 58
major theater war (MTW), v, 61
Malaysia, 47, 50, 97, 156, 168, 206
Maldives, 76–7
Manchuria, 10, 12
Mao Zedong, 22
Marianas, 11, 47, 76–7, 90
Marianas US Naval Forces, 90

MARFORPAC, *see* Marine Forces Pacific
Marine Air-Ground Task Forces (MAGTF), 138–41
Marine Corps, US: capability and limitations, 150–3; force structure, 138–41; Gulf War combat, 152–3, 198; Korean War combat, 19–21; mission and organization, 122–6; presence in Asia–Pacific, 122, 140–2, 253–4; strategic vision, 126–32; strength, total, 126; Vietnam War combat, 23–5; World War II role in Pacific, 13–14; *see also* Marine Forces Pacific, III Marine Expeditionary Force, I Marine Expeditionary Force
Marine Expeditionary Brigade (MEB), 140–1
Marine Expeditionary Force (MEF), 139–40; *see also* I Marine Expeditionary Force, III Marine Expeditionary Force
Marine Expeditionary Unit (MEU), 140–1
Marine Forces Pacific, 141–2, 244–5, 254, 266; bases, 83–93 *passim*, 244–5; strength, 141–2, 244–5
Maritime Strategy, US: Cold War version, 27–8, 126–7; current, 126–32
Marshall, General George, 15
Marshall Islands, 11, 47, 76–7, 87
MEB, *see* Marine Expeditionary Brigade
MEF, *see* Marine Expeditionary Force
MEU, *see* Marine Expeditionary Unit
MFN, 45
Micronesia, 16, 47, 76–7, 87
mine countermeasures (MCM), 149–50
mines, naval, 149–50
Miramar Marine Corps Air Station, 86–7
Misawa Air Base, 32, 90, 167, 254
Missile Technology Control Regime (MTCR), 52

Mongolia, 74
MRC, v, 38–42, 61
MTW, v, 61
Myanmar, 45, 47
MX missile, 100

Nagasaki, 14, 16
National Command Authorities (NCA), US, 65–9
National Defense Panel (NDP) 63, 220–2
National Military Strategy, (NMS) US: 1992 version, 33–4; 1995 version, 54–60; 1997 version, 63–4, 191
National Security Council, 3, 21, 67–9
National Security Strategy, US, 33–4, 42–5, 60–1, 213–14; 1991 version, 33–4; 1994 version, 42; 1995 version, 42–5; 1997 version, 60–1, 213–14
Nauru, 76
Naval Expeditionary Forces, 127–8, 147–8
Navy, US: capability and limitations, 142–55; force structure, 132–4; Gulf War combat, 145–7, 149; Korean War combat, 19–22, 131–2; mission and organization, 122–6; nuclear role and forces, 100–15 *passim*; presence in Asia–Pacific, 122, 134–8, 253–4; strategic vision, 126–32; strength, total, 124, 133; Vietnam War combat, 23–5; World War II role in Pacific, 13–17; *see also* Pacific Fleet, Seventh Fleet, Third Fleet
Navy Operational Concept (NOC), 130–1
Nellis Air Force Base, 168, 175
New Caledonia, 76
New Zealand, 22, 26, 28, 47–8, 76–7, 168
Nimitz, Admiral Chester, 14
Nimitz class carriers, 142–3
Nimitz, USS, 156
Niue, 76
Nixon, President Richard, 3, 24, 26, 66

North Island Naval Air Station, 87
North Korea, 20–2, 31, 34–6, 38, 42, 44–6, 48–9, 51, 53, 74, 94, 108, 110, 120–1, 193, 216, 222, 226, 231, 232; Agreed Framework with, 51; KEDO, 51; nuclear weapons program, 36, 44, 51, 121, 226; threat posed by, 31, 34–6, 38, 42, 44–6, 49, 222
North Vietnam, 23–5, 237
Nuclear Posture Review, 55, 106–15
nuclear weapons, US, 99–121; bases and forces, 100, 110; command and control, 111–13; non-strategic nuclear forces, 101–3, 112–13; removal from Asia–Pacific, 101–3, 112; role in deterrence, 107, 119; World War II use against Japan, 14, 16–17; *see also* US Strategic Command, *Nuclear Posture Review*
Nurrungar Facility, 96–7

Okinawa, 7, 16, 19, 32, 34, 92–4, 103, 140–1, 193, 195, 209–10, 233, 245, 247–8, 254, 261–2, 274; Futenma controversy, 233, 274; US bases and forces, 32, 34, 92–4, 140–1, 209–10, 233, 245, 254, 261, 274; World War II battle, 16
OMFTS concept, 131–2, 224
Osan Air Base, 96, 167, 172, 210, 254
OSD, *see* Secretary of Defense
Osprey aircraft, 151–2, 224–5
Owens, Admiral William, 73, 261

P–3 aircraft, 84, 90, 155
PACAF, *see* Pacific Air Forces
PACFLT, *see* Pacific Fleet
Pacific Air Forces, 75, 77, 159, 166–9, 245–6, 254–5, 268; bases, 82–97 *passim*, 167, 245–6, 254–5; exercises, 168; strength, 167, 245–6, 254–5
Pacific Command, *see* US Pacific Command
Pacific Fleet, 10, 13, 18, 28, 75, 77, 83–95 *passim*, 124–5, 134–8, 155, 241–4, 266; bases, 83–95 *passim*,

243–4; CARAT program, 155; organization, 136; RIMPAC exercise, 156; strength, 134–5
PACOM, *see* US Pacific Command
Pakistan, 22, 117, 187, 206, 220
Palau, 47, 76–7, 87
Panmunjon, 20
Papua New Guinea, 48
Pearl Harbor Naval Station, 11, 13–14, 87–8, 113, 124, 135, 209, 236
Perry, Commodore Matthew, 67, 236
Perry, William, 108, 263–4
Persian Gulf War, *see* Gulf War, Iraq, Kuwait
PGM, 177–81, 222–3, 228–9; *see also* smart bombs
Philippines, 8–14, 16, 19, 22, 31–3, 35, 41, 45–7, 49–50, 53, 97, 156, 159, 166, 184, 211, 214, 234, 236–8
Plan ORANGE, 11
Powell, General Colin, 34
PRC, *see* China
prepositioning forces, US: afloat, 90, 97, 140–2, 197–8, 225, 245, 254; ashore, 198
proliferation, *see* ballistic missiles, theater ballistic missiles, weapons of mass destruction
Proliferation: Threat and Response, 1997, 274
Prueher, Admiral Joseph, 261
Puget Sound Naval Shipyard, 85
Pyongyang, 21, 110

Quadrennial Defense Review (QDR), 2, 60–4, 118–19, 132, 150, 176, 213, 217, 219–22, 230, 238, 260

Reagan, President Ronald, 26, 117, 119, 120
Reed Panel, 104, 262
Reimer, General Douglas, 186
Republic of Korea (ROK), *see* South Korea
revolution in military affairs, *see* RMA
RIMPAC exercise, 156
RMA, 4, 62, 217–22

Roh Tae Woo, 192
ROK, *see* South Korea
Roosevelt, President Franklin D., 12, 15–16
Roosevelt, President Theodore, 8, 10
Russia, 8, 27, 29, 34–5, 48–50, 99–101, 103, 105, 107–10, 116–20, 153, 163, 169, 226, 244, 263

San Diego Naval Station, 86, 113, 135, 243
Sasebo naval base, 92, 137, 141, 244, 253
satellites, 161–2, 170, 179, 181, 230
Schwarzkopf, General Norman, 152, 197
Scud missiles, 36, 39, 52, 103, 161, 170, 181, 202–3, 274
SEALs, 209–10
sea lanes of communication, 50, 213, 222
sealift, 60, 134–5, 140, 142, 197–8
SEATO, 22
Seawolf class submarines, 153–4
Secretary of Defense, Office of, 66–9
Seventh Fleet, 19, 22, 36, 41, 53, 135, 137–8, 156, 244, 253–4, 266; bases, 83–95 *passim*, 244, 253; strength, 137–8, 253–4
Shalikashvili, General John, 54
Shelton, General Henry, 211
shipping lanes, 50
Singapore, 35, 46–8, 76–7, 97, 156, 168–9, 180, 234
SIOP, 104–5, 108–9, *see also* US Strategic Command
situation awareness, 174–5
SLBM, v–vi, 100, 111–12, 119, 239, 252
SLOC, *see* sea lanes of communication
smart bombs, 25, 177–81, 222–3
Somalia, 128, 196, 204–6, 231, 274
South China Sea, 7, 36, 50, 222
South Korea, 4–5, 26–7, 31–2, 35–6, 38, 41, 45, 53, 56, 75, 94–6, 98, 102, 131, 142, 153, 166–8, 172, 184, 193–4, 200, 214, 216, 231–2, 236, 238, 245–7, 254–5, 262, 269, 272; strategic partnership with US, 31–2, 35–6, 38, 41, 45, 53, 56; US bases and forces in, 80, 85, 94–6, 193–4, 232–3, 241, 247, 255, 271
South Vietnam, 23–5, 237
Soviet Union (USSR), 18–21, 26–8, 30–1, 33, 36, 38, 42, 47, 99–103, 105, 107–8, 113, 115, 126–7, 133, 153–4, 159, 173, 196, 200, 226, 236, 249
Space Command, US, 161–2, 268
space operations, 161–2, 170, 179, 181, 230
Special Operations Command, US, 207–11
Special Operations Forces, US: bases and forces, 207–11; Delta Force, 229, 274; Green Berets, 209; Gulf War combat, 202, 274; mission and organization, 207–8; presence in Asia–Pacific, 209–11; Rangers, 204–7, 209; SEALs, 209–10
Spratly Islands, 36, 50, 260
Spruance class destroyers, 154
Sri Lanka, 76
stealth weapons: B-2 bomber, 100, 111, 179–80; F-117 fighter, 145, 176–9; *see also* submarines
STRATCOM, *see* US Strategic Command
Strategic Framework for the Asian Pacific Rim, *see* EASI II
submarines, US: nuclear attack (SSN), 87–8, 112–13, 134, 137–8, 153–4; nuclear ballistic missile (SSBN), vi, 85, 111, 134
Syngman Rhee, 19

THAAD, 203, 227
Thailand, 22, 45–7, 76–7, 97, 156, 166, 168, 211, 214
theater ballistic missiles (TBM), 149, 202, 226–7, 250; *see also* Scud missiles
theater missile defense (TMD), 5, 52, 149, 202–3, 226–7, 250
Third Fleet, 135–7, 243–4, 266; bases, 83–8 *passim*, 243–4; strength, 137, 243–4, 266
Ticonderoga class cruisers, 148

Tokelau, 76
Tomahawk cruise missile, 112–13, 146–8, 239, 242, 253, 264, 267
Tonga, 76
Torii Station Army Base, 94, 209
Truman, President Harry, 16, 19–21
Tuvalu, 76

U-2 aircraft, 172, 254
Unified Combatant Commands, 69–71
United States East Asia Strategic Initiative, see EASI
United States Security Strategy for the East Asia–Pacific Region, 45–53
urban warfare, 231
US Army Pacific Command (USARPAC), 75, 77, 185, 194–6, 241, 248–9, 255, 271; bases, 83–94 *passim*, 195–6, 248–9, 255; strength, 195–6, 248–9, 255
US Forces Japan (USFJ), 75, 90–4, 195, 241, 271
US Forces Korea Command (USFK), 80, 94–6, 185, 193, 241, 271
US Marine Corps (USMC), *see* Marine Corps, US
US Navy (USN), *see* Navy, US
US Pacific Command (USPACOM): area of responsibility, 74–5, 78; bases, 82–98, 242–9, 253–5; command relationships within, 76–7; forces, 75, 242–9, 253–5; future of, 231–4; mission and strategy, 242; role in chain of command, 69, 71, 74; service components, 75; strength, total, 75, 241
USSPACECOM, 161–2, 268
US Special Operations Command (USSOCOM): assigned forces and bases, 208–10; capabilities, 208–10; mission, 207–8; service components, 207; strength of assigned forces, total, 207
US Strategic Command (USSTRATCOM): assigned forces and bases, 111, 239, 252–3, 262–3; command and control 111–12; mission and organization, 104, 111; role in Asia–Pacific planning, 113, 264; role in chain of command, 104, 111; service components, 104; SIOP developments, 104–5, 108–9

Vietcong, 23
Vietminh, 76
Vietnam, 23–5, 28, 45, 47–8, 50, 57, 76, 97, 122, 166, 178, 184, 198–9, 209, 230, 234, 237, 242
Vietnam War, 22–6
Vincennes, USS, 149

Wallis, 76
Watkins, Admiral James, 73, 265
weapons of mass destruction (WMD), 5, 39, 42, 58, 61, 99–121 *passim*, 208, 222, 225–30; biological, 39, 61, 120, 202, 226; chemical, 39, 61, 120, 202, 226; defenses against, 149, 201–3, 208, 225–30; nuclear, 39, 61, 106, 119, 208, 225–30; proliferation, 36, 42, 44, 51, 121, 208, 225–30
Weinberger, Caspar, 115, 258, 264
Western Pacific (WESTPAC), US bases in, 89–98; *see also* forward deployed forces
Western Samoa, 76
Westmoreland, General William, 23–4
Whidbey Island: class ships, 151; Naval Air Station, 151
WMD, *see* weapons of mass destruction

Yalu River, 20
Yeltsin, Boris, 106, 117
Yokosuka naval base, 91, 103, 137, 148, 244, 253
Yokota Air Base, 32, 75, 90–1, 167, 254
Yongsan Garrison, 80, 96